PUTIN'S NEW ORDER IN THE MIDDLE EAST

TALAL NIZAMEDDIN

Putin's New Order in the Middle East

HURST & COMPANY, LONDON

First published in the United Kingdom in paperback in 2013 by
C. Hurst & Co. (Publishers) Ltd.,
41 Great Russell Street, London, WC1B 3PL

Printed in India

Distributed in the United States, Canada and Latin America by
Oxford University Press, 198 Madison Avenue, New York, NY 10016,
United States of America.

A Cataloguing-in-Publication data record for this book
is available from the British Library.

ISBN: 9781849042598

www.hurstpublishers.com

This book is printed on paper from registered sustainable
and managed sources.

CONTENTS

BOOK SUMMARY

Vladimir Putin has almost by stealth transformed himself into an historic Russian figure. Putin's undeniable political dominance was reflected in his return to presidential control after the elections of March 2012, having placed an obedient Dmitry Medvedev for four years in a stop-gap presidency. From 1999 Putin's growing power transposed itself into foreign affairs. Nowhere did Russia's reemergence on the world stage have more impact than the turbulent Middle East. Russia's new role and identity had its roots in the late Yeltsin era, but the Putin era witnessed the emergence of an assertive Russia that by 2013 subtly deflated the balloon of US power by cleverly manipulating developments in the Middle East including Iraq, Lebanon, the Palestinian-Israeli conflict, the Syrian revolution and other regional issues. Twenty years earlier Russia was a very different place. Like a weak and hesitant foal a new Russia was taking its first fragile steps after birth in a world full of dangers. This book charts this remarkable conversion in Middle East policy with an identifiable turning point in 2005–06 that mirrored Putin's authoritarian deviation. The jury is still out on whether Putin's increasingly pugnacious Middle East policies can be reconciled with Russia's long-term interests to implement meaningful economic reforms to institute democratic freedoms and the rule of law.

ACKNOWLEDGEMENTS

The writing of this book was a long, tortuous process but certain people in my life remained constant and inspirational.

I would like to dedicate this book to my mother Ghania, who passed away while this work was being completed. How I wish she was here with me now.

Also to my three children: Lola, Rafi, Timi. Just the thought of them fills my heart with joy and love.

1

INTRODUCTION

The era of President Vladimir Putin presented an image of a traditionally forceful Russia in an age of uncertainty characterised by unfamiliar non-state dangers. From the first days of his rapid rise to power in 1999 and following his presidential election victory in 2012 Putin was, and remained, an enigma. The elusive feature of the Putin era also typified Russian policy in the Middle East, most controversially highlighted in Moscow's disconcerted reaction to the Arab Spring, and most specifically its staunch support for the isolated and widely condemned Syrian regime led by President Bashar Asad.

This book will attempt to cast some light on Russian foreign policy in the Middle East during the Putin era by highlighting dominant and outstanding features and noting aspects of continuity and change. In doing so a subtle sub-theme is introduced that charts the interplay between traditional realist state-to-state relations and the growing impact of supranational and non-state actors. In the early phase of Putin's rule international terrorism posed an immediate danger for Russia, as it did for the United States. The audacious aerial attacks on the Twin Towers of the World Trade Center in New York and the Pentagon in Washington DC on 11 September 2001 uncovered a vast network of terrorist cells that had been festering during the 1990s. Based in Afghanistan, these groups were inspired by Wahhabi and Salafi Islamic ideas that emerged from Saudi Arabia and Egypt to fight Soviet occupation in the 1980s. Cells from these movements fought post-Soviet Russian forces alongside Chechen rebels in the breakaway republic of Chechnya.

Early in the 1990s some of these Jihadi cells attempted to hijack the war of independence from Yugoslavia that was being fought by Bosnian Muslims. Following the 11 September attacks many of these cells were identified by the global media as Al-Qaeda under the leadership of Osama Bin Laden and Ayman Al-Zawahiri, implying a unified hierarchical structure. Eventually it became clear that this terrorist danger was instead more of a loose collection of destructive extremists, sometimes claiming allegiance to Al-Qaeda while at other times the connection was rather dubious. Indeed, following the US invasion of Iraq in 2003 some of these groups were being tacitly encouraged by the intelligence organs of states such as Iran and Syria, which were seeking to assert their influence in the Middle East and undermine the US presence in the region. Other powerful militant Islamic groups such as Palestinian Hamas, Lebanese Hezbollah and the Iraqi Mehdi Army were largely candid about their activities and their connections to Syria and Iran.[1]

Member nationalities of more obscure Jihadi cells with links to Afghanistan varied: Pakistanis, Saudis, Syrians, Egyptians, Iraqis, Jordanians and Palestinians were typical but by no means exclusive nationals belonging to such groups. What was evident and beyond doubt was the fluidity of these cells and their ability to move around, buy weapons, carry out their actions and often disappear while leaving minimal trace. Groups such as Hamas and Hezbollah focused their activities to a specific struggle and geographic location, often becoming a state within a state, while Al-Qaeda and other cells operated surreptitiously, without a hint of where, when and how they would strike.

International crime in all its forms and guises, including money laundering, the drug trade and human trafficking, often intertwined with worldwide militant activities and revealed the way operations and tactics became global and more complex to the extent that no single state was capable of dealing with such threats alone. The need for new investigative and combat techniques was widely recognised, but more importantly there were growing calls for different approaches and levels of international cooperation that challenged existing classic legal notions of sovereignty. Environmental degradation and its international economic dimension created another difficult test to traditional inter-state relations. As the pleas to save our planet intensified the state appeared somewhat smaller and less significant in light of the existentialist challenges to humanity that lay ahead. The global financial crisis in 2009 provided a harsh confirmation that we live in an interdependent world. The power of the popular revolutions that exploded in Tunisia in 2010 and then spread to Egypt, Libya, Syria and other countries in the Middle East shook what were considered long-lasting and stable regimes to the core. Significantly, the speed of events seemed to also take Moscow, Washington, London, Paris and other decision-making centres by surprise.

Understanding Russian behaviour during this period of turmoil revealed much about the Putin era in light of the decline of US power and influence. In this atmosphere of emerging global threats Putin's Russia became more introspective, increasingly nationalistic and more suspicious of outsiders. There were frequent reports of violent attacks by Russians against foreigners in Moscow, St Petersburg and other parts of the country. This xenophobia was directed against immigrant Chinese in the far east of the country, Muslims, blacks and even Europeans in major Russian cities. In 2006 and 2007 there were hostile media attacks on Estonians and the British in particular that culminated in violent reprisals against diplomats from each of those countries in Russia.

It is less generally noted that the Boris Yeltsin era in the 1990s laid the foundations for the hostile mentality that became prevalent under Putin. Yeltsin's longest serving adviser from his inner circle was Sergei Shakhrei, who brought with him 'the peculiar psychology of a survivor from a besieged fortress…and cultural intolerance', having been raised in Rostov, a city with a pugnacious Cossack history.[2] The sudden appearance of the theatrical right-wing populist Vladimir Zhirinovsky, espousing his vision of restoring the Russian Empire, would not have been possible without the tacit approval of the Kremlin during Yeltsin's presidency. It did not go amiss that in the June 1991 presidential elections Zhirinovsky's 'campaign lasted only twenty days but he still got six million votes, or 8 per cent'.[3]

Putin's Russia had nonetheless come to be regarded as very different in style and substance to the leadership of his predecessor Yeltsin, a feature Putin deliberately sought to emphasise. Yeltsin's desire and efforts to integrate Russia into the Western community of nations was portrayed, often unfairly, as a form of capitulation by his political opponents. Putin's message to his people and to the world was that Russia had the confidence, strength and resources to stand on its own feet and defy the

West to protect its interests. The intensifying hostility from Moscow reached such an extent that in the 17 July 2007 edition of The Guardian in Britain the front page headline read: 'Cold War Diplomacy is Back as UK Expels Spies.' The sub-heading was no less dramatic: 'Moscow warns of "the most serious consequences" for UK-Russia relations.' The dispute was over a murder case in Britain of the Russian-born Alexander Litvinenko but the setting exposed a much deeper and broader sense of distance between Moscow and other Western capitals.

In this context Russia's cultivation of relations with states such as Iran and Syria were interpreted as signalling a new era of confrontation. Putin's overtures to Iran, despite its controversial nuclear programme, and Syria, with its belligerent regional agenda that included support for militant groups considered as terrorists by most Western countries, led to strong doubts that Russia and the West could cooperate to face the challenges of the modern era. Instead there were deep suspicions that Russia was exploiting the fluidity in the international system and the role of militant non-state actors to promote the interests of the political elite in Moscow. The deliberate stalling of investigations and analyses of cross-border political assassinations such as the murder of the Lebanese politician Rafiq Hariri in 2005 and Alexander Litvinenko in London in 2007 provided striking examples of Moscow's cynical approach, according to critics. However, it was Russia's stubborn resistance at the UN Security Council in 2012 that prevented action that could have ended the bloodshed in Syria which best highlighted the new ruthlessness under Putin.

Putin wanted to be known as the man who restored law and order to Russia, with law being a minor element in the equation unless it was Putin's law. The West had shown that it was ready to tolerate a degree of authoritarianism if that was the price for order. Putin would have noted the West's tolerance of Islam Karimov, the President of Uzbekistan who ruled his country since the Soviet disintegration and won an average of 90 per cent of votes in the highly dubious elections during his reign. Karimov was ruthless in eliminating opposition and in 2005 soldiers opened fire on protesters, killing and injuring hundreds in the process. Yet Karimov was considered by Washington and other Western capitals as an ally in the fight against terrorism. This was the Karimov who once said 'if you have noticed, Wahhabis have a characteristic feature—they have beards, untidy beards' and such people 'must be shot in the head'.[4]

A dominant view emerged in Russia, as in the Middle East, that the West ultimately respected political power and not human rights. This attitude partially explained Moscow's efforts under Putin to deflect international pressure away from Syria and Iran, both of which were considered as valuable regional partners. The establishment of an international order based on a balance of powers was the major driving motive of Putin's foreign policy despite all the rhetoric in Moscow of endorsing international law and cooperation. Syria and Iran had become important tools in this strategy that was primarily focused on limiting US power. According to critics, Russia under Putin was a deliberately destructive player in the Middle East by manipulating the untraditional but potentially dangerous post-Cold War order to strengthen its own standing in the world. In its drive to enhance its status in the Middle East, Moscow in the first decade of the twenty-first century stood accused of passing on nuclear technology (Iran); illicit sales of advanced conventional weapons (Iran, Syria, Hezbollah); hindering UN Resolutions on the Security Council; political cover and support for terrorist organisations (Hamas, Hezbollah); and blocking peaceful democratic development (Syria, Lebanon and indirectly Iraq).

Russia's power play helped to transform the region's political and geostrategic landscape from a decade earlier in the 1990s. An immediate consequence of Russian diplomatic and military support for Iran and Syria was that they emerged as dominant players in the region. Syrian and Iranian proxies Hezbollah, Hamas and others also become more potent and therefore Moscow was culpable in undermining the sovereignty of Lebanon, the security of Israel and generally damaging the standing of Western governments in the Middle East. The rise of Iran, with Russian backing, also increased the sense of danger felt by the Arab Gulf monarchies. The Russian leadership vehemently rejected all of these accusations, arguing strongly that it had in fact tried to play a positive role in all these areas. But Putin and the Russian Foreign Ministry did not deny that Moscow was not obliged to tow the line defined by Washington and reserved the right to act independently in the Middle East, as in any other region in the world, in pursuit of its national interests.

Post-Soviet Russian foreign policy undertook a revision of its outlook during the Yeltsin presidency, evolving organically to the uncompromising latter Putin era. Yeltsin and his first Russian foreign minister, Andrei Kozyrev, started out with great hopes for Russia as a partner for global peace alongside the Europeans and the United States. In 1996 Kozyrev was removed from office after years of harsh vilification as the Russian political elite became embarrassed at the sometimes naïve policies of the late 1980s and early 1990s. The authoritarian, militaristic and typically anti-Western forces in the Middle East correspondingly looked at that liberal interlude of Russian foreign policy with disdain and enthusiastically welcomed the return of the Cold War bear they had been accustomed to in the past. Comparisons between post-Soviet and Soviet foreign policy during the Cold War era that implied continuity were often misleading though. Russia under both Yeltsin and Putin was politically, economically and culturally more pluralistic than before 1991 as policies became prone to competing interest groups.

One of Putin's important contributions after Yeltsin was to emphasise the economic dimension to foreign policy in terms of advancing Russian national interests. The oil and gas sectors had transformed Russia into a major world actor and there was an accompanying realisation that this new role demanded a sense of responsibility and maturity that elevated expectations by the international community. The new financial, oil and gas lobbies in Russia each competed for control of the state apparatus and the direction of its policies. Putin's political standing and domestic reputation were also influenced by the demands of the ailing military-industrial complex that employed tens of thousands of people and was a source of national pride for many decades. Selling weapons to clients to prevent the sector from collapsing became a factor of consideration equal in weight to the geo-strategic chess game with global rivals and to some extent guided decision-making.

Despite the image of the strongman, Putin was therefore often a follower of internal pressures and external trends, which made Russian behaviour in the world all the more fragile. As president, one of Putin's main goals was to establish a policy in the Middle East that enhanced domestic stability and yet projected greater influence in the world. It was therefore not contradictory that Moscow would court Iran, Saudi Arabia, Syria, Turkey and Israel in equal measure during his two presidential terms. This was a far cry from the world of enemies and comrades that characterised the Soviet era.

This book will analyse internal aspects of foreign policy-making in the context of Russian political, cultural and economic revival. It will then examine cases of key countries in the Middle East that are of particular importance and relevance to Russian foreign policy. The following chapter provides a historic background, noting the impact of the Cold War on nation-building among the Middle East countries and the challenge of competing ideologies, including Communism. Chapters 3, 4 and 5 focus specifically on the internal Russian context, starting from the turmoil and stabilisation of the Yeltsin era to the slowly evolving characteristics of Putinism. The remaining chapters focus on relations between Russia and the countries of the Middle East, which for the sake of this study extends to Iran in the east and Turkey in its north, the Levant and Saudi Arabia to the south. Moscow's outlook views Turkey, Iran, the Gulf and the Levant as distinct geo-strategic areas where political issues deeply overlap. North Africa, including Egypt, is excluded from this work. One of the reasons for this is a self-imposed limit to the study is recognition of the geo-strategic specifics of North African politics.

The US-led invasion and occupation of Iraq, non-Arab Turkey and Iran bordering the post-Soviet space, the on-going Palestinian-Israeli conflict, Lebanon's bid for independence from Syrian control, the opportunity of new relations with the traditionally pro-Western but influential monarchies of Saudi Arabia and Jordan, the transforming Middle East and the popular uprisings posed major challenges for Russian foreign policy under Putin. Each of these areas had its own unique dynamics, yet all were also tightly interrelated and the security implications of each impacted the others.

Moscow claimed to offer solutions and cooperation that could finally bring hope of stability and peace to this troubled part of the world but its critics argued otherwise. One perspective maintained that Putin cut the United States down to size in the Middle East and avenged the years of humiliation in which Russia was treated haughtily in the era of US President Bill Clinton. The riddle remains whether this payback defined the full extent of Russian goals or whether in light of its growing authoritarianism and an ever more timid Washington the horizons of Moscow's political and military ambitions extended beyond the naked eye of the contemporary international affairs specialist.

2

THE COLD WAR AND THE DEMISE OF MIDDLE EAST NATION-STATES

Few parts of the world were as negatively and directly impacted by the US-Soviet Cold War as the Middle East. The newly independent states in the region during the 1940s and 1950s were fragile and remained so for the following decades. With the obvious exceptions of Turkey and Iran, until the 1970s the peoples of the region were offered the choice between the revolutionary ideologies of either Communism or Pan-Arabism. Loyalty to one's nation-state was presented by the self-proclaimed progressives as being pro-Western and an alien neo-imperialist, neo-capitalist import, conveniently ignoring the fact that both Communism and Pan-Arabism in the Nasserite model were also modern creations without historic roots in the region. For decades, violent and passionate political conflicts driven by the competing ideologies within the countries of the Middle East, and between them, as well as the sequence of Arab-Israeli wars combined to stoke raging fires and silence rational debate. This climate suited the establishment of repressive regimes throughout the region with an attitude typified by Egyptian President Gamal Abdul Nasser, the undisputed leader of modern Pan-Arabism, who famously declared that 'no voice is tolerated that is louder than the voice of the battle' (against the West and Israel).

In the Middle East, reference to the Sykes-Picot Agreement was predictably recalled when Arab nationalists and radical Muslim activists offered an explanation for the root causes of the violence and social backwardness of the region. According to such groups the agreement was the first blow of many misfortunes that befell the region throughout the twentieth and early twenty-first century. Signed in 1916, the agreement between Britain and France was a response to the rapidly disintegrating Ottoman Empire. The Anglo-French collusion took place a year before the overthrow of Tsar Nicholas II in Russia that resulted in the Bolshevik takeover. In a telling precursor of things to come Lenin deliberately publicised the then still secret Sykes-Picot Agreement because it contradicted promises made by the British to the Arabs and generally showed the Western powers to be slyly conspiring to divide up the region without consulting the local peoples. This was the first strike by revolutionary Moscow in its foreign policy to foment anti-Western revolt in the region.

Despite the rejectionist Arab rhetoric the Sykes-Picot Agreement arguably did not automatically have to lead to the supposed calamities thereafter and there were positive features. One of its principal aims was to establish lines of separation for port and railway facilities as well as establishing trade zones for British and French interests. But for Lebanese nationalists, as well as many Jordanian, Iraqi, Syrian and Palestinian nationalists, the Sykes-Picot Agreement outlined legal borders for their nation-states that had been previously merged for the convenience of Ottoman administration. For secular nationalists the agreement also protected religious minorities in the Middle East, of which there were many, from a large but unrestrained and undefined Islamic zone. The agreement did not succumb to the myth of Pan-Arabism, born out of the Arab revolt against the Turks in the early twentieth century, since it could have effectively created major friction between the urbanised citizens of Levantine cities, historically Canaanite, such as Haifa, Beirut, Tripoli and Aleppo and the tribal Arab people living south of the Syrian desert.

Nonetheless, Pan-Arab nationalists and later on Islamist activists continued to consider the Sykes-Picot Agreement as the fruit of colonial arrogance and indisputable proof of Western motives to divide up the region for their own benefit rather than the welfare of the local peoples. Indeed, the second paragraph of the Agreement unabashedly stated that: 'In the blue area France, and in the red area Great Britain, shall be allowed to establish such direct or indirect administration or control as they desire and as they may think fit to arrange with the Arab state or confederation of Arab states.'[1] The colours indicated areas on a map that had been marked out by the two governments, Britain and France, as if the object was a board game rather than a geographic region characterised by thousands of years of history, cultures and communities.

In retrospect, the Sykes-Picot Agreement was signed in a bygone era by two players who by the 1940s had lost their influence and status in the Middle East. The demise of Britain and France was paralleled by the rise of the Soviet Union as a new global power after the Second World War caught in an ideological confrontation with the West, led by the United States. The Cold War, beginning in the late 1940s, became a dominant feature under Soviet leaders Nikita Khrushchev and Leonid Brezhnev. In the Middle East the Soviet Union sought to manipulate political divisions and social turmoil in order to strengthen its position vis-à-vis the United States. Soviet ambitions were aided by a tendency among the Middle East's intellectual elite to blame their failings on Western interference. The unequivocal failure of the Middle East peoples to take their fate into their own hands, to get themselves organised, to produce effective governments and fair societies made it all too strenuous to blame themselves, so blame was cast on others. Western media sources and some academics alluded that this was symptomatic of Middle Eastern peoples, like most developing world people, who blamed everything on imperialism and Western neo-colonialism.

An even more extreme version of this view suggested that the peoples of the Middle East were culturally inferior and lacking any sense of values or decency. Such views were not expressed only in smoky apartments by shady neo-Nazi groups in Europe, but had become transmitted through the popular Western press by well-known figures of the establishment. A prime example of this was the controversy raised by Robert Kilroy-Silk, a popular BBC TV presenter and former Labour MP, who wrote an article in the right-wing British newspaper *The Sunday Express*[2] on 4 January 2004 suggesting that Arabs and Muslims have given the world nothing but suicide bombers and woman oppressors. Many in Britain, including those working in the media, were quick to criticise the daytime TV host. *The Guardian* correspondent Derek Brown, however, picked up on the important revelation raised by this controversy: 'The Arab people have been traduced enough in the Western world and—let's be honest—the Western media.'[3]

The most stunning aspect of this controversy however was that there was controversy at all. Many others clamoured to defend Kilroy-Silk's remarks, leading one frustrated commentator, Marina Hyde, to note that if there was any doubt one need only 'replace the word Arab with Jew to see the offence'.[4] The author's clever little pointer in this remark effectively revealed that while the West was extremely sensitive to Jewish feelings, it had become conveniently thick-skinned when it referred to Arab and Islamic concerns. This relatively minor episode highlighted a wide gap of understanding that remained gaping between Britain and the West in general on one side and the Arab and Islamic world on the other almost a century after the Sykes-Picot Agreement.

The European legacy did not end before leaving behind one final contribution that has since left the region in perpetual turmoil. Nazi German and European atrocities against members of their Jewish communities were so horrific it became obvious at the end of the Second World War that a permanent solution had to be found that would give Jews a safe homeland. Understandably, many if not most Jews objected to continue living in German, Austrian, Polish and other European neighbourhoods near people who had in one way or another contributed to the extermination of their people. Despite the post-1945 European effort to display shame and horror at what they had subjected their Jewish communities to, Jews, wisely, were not going to sit around waiting for the next Hitler to come along. It was in this context that the creation of a Jewish state became unavoidable in the late-1940s.

After the creation of modern Israel, all modern Middle East states found themselves in tragically hopeless situations that were not helped by superpower interference. Palestine ceased to exist and was, in the eyes of Arab and Islamist activists, forcibly converted to a Jewish state called Israel in 1948. The bitter struggle between the Palestinians and the Israelis broadened to include other states in the region which in turn invited the Cold War to the Middle East. As a result of the Arab-Israeli wars Lebanon became a victim of civil and sectarian strife and to unrelenting Syrian attempts at asserting its hegemony. Syria, Iraq and other states in the region were ruled by ruthless and corrupt Stalinist regimes, stifling social justice, freedom and economic development. It is no wonder that many people in the region began to form an illusion of an ideal world prior to the Sykes-Picot dissections and free from imperialist intrigues.

Israel was portrayed as a vestige of the old Western imperialism in the modern era under US protection and states such as Egypt and Syria looked to Soviet support in their bid to drive out the Jews from the

Middle East. The Soviet Union readily obliged to join an alliance of forces that was hostile to the West despite the ideological differences between socialism and its contemporary Pan-Arab nationalism. The justification used by both parties in the alliance was that this was a struggle against Western imperialism, and from the 1940s the Middle East became a key battleground in the Cold War where Moscow could depend on a deep reservoir of resentment directed at both Americans and Europeans to serve its goals.

Stalin, the Cold War and the Middle East

Britain and France were abruptly pushed aside in the 1950s by the two new emergent superpowers: the United States and the Soviet Union. The buoyant citizens of the new independent states in the Middle East relished the exit of Britain and France as a new beginning but found themselves as part of one of the two camps in the Cold War struggle. The initialisation of the Cold War was associated with the Iron Curtain splitting Europe in two and with the division of Germany. In fact, the first area of post-War open diplomatic hostility, between the United States and Britain on one side and Soviet Union on the other, was in the Middle East. Iran was historically under the spotlight of longstanding strategic rivalry between Russia and Britain. Britain took advantage of relative Soviet weakness and isolation in the interwar years to establish valuable petroleum contracts that gave the declining imperial power major concessions in Iran.

The Anglo-Russian-Iranian Treaty signed on 29 January 1942 divided Iran into two zones of influence because of perceived fears that the regime was displaying sympathy towards Nazi Germany during the Second World War. While Soviet troops occupied the north of the country the British were stationed in the south to ensure the safe supply of energy, arms and other goods. Significantly, both powers were required to leave the country six months after the termination of the war.

After the Second World War the Soviet Union became much more assertive as Stalin sought to take full advantage of his country's new weight on the international stage and redress the prewar retreat. At the end of the war communist separatists in the Azerbaijan region of Iran initiated a revolt, which was supported by the Soviet Republic of Azerbaijan across the border. Soviet troops stationed in northern Iran prevented the Persian armed forces from putting down the revolt and the government in Tehran was subsequently handed a list of demands by Moscow, 'which included indefinite retention of Soviet troops in northern Iran, recognition of the autonomy of Azerbaijan, and the formation of a Russian-Iranian joint stock company to develop the petroleum resources of the northern provinces'.[5]

The 2 March 1946 deadline for Soviet withdrawal from Iran was ignored by Moscow, leading Washington and London to initiate a diplomatic offensive that also warned of a military intervention. Stalin's intimidating blustering was exposed and he duly ordered the withdrawal of Soviet troops out of Iran. Firm backing by Britain and the United States enabled the Tehran regime to reclaim the upper hand by annulling existing agreements with the Soviet Union. Moreover, proposed agreements between the two countries were no longer viable because Stalin's actions had nourished existing suspicions in Tehran about Soviet intentions. In fact, as a consequence of this episode Iran became firmly entrenched in the Western camp for another three decades. From a Western standpoint, the Persian regime was an important and loyal ally and any internal dissent was looked upon with disdain, especially as one of the largest opposition groups in the country, with genuine popular support, was the communist Tudeh party.

In tandem with the tussle over Iran Moscow had also been applying pressure on neighbouring Turkey, beginning with a demand made on 7 June 1945 by Soviet Foreign Minister Vyacheslav Molotov from the Turkish government for: 'The cession of territory in the Caucasus annexed by Russia in 1878 and reacquired by Turkey after the First World War, the revision of the Montreux Convention of 1936 governing the Turkish Straits so as to establish joint Russian-Turkish jurisdiction over this vital waterway, and the leasing of Soviet bases on its shores to ensure its defence.'[6] This strategic wish list reflected a centuries-old ambition by the Russians to gain access to the Mediterranean Sea at the expense of Turkey. Historically, Britain had supported the Ottomans and its successor the Turkish Republic to halt Russian southwestward expansion, but after the Second World War only the United States was able to effectively play that role. Put succinctly by one historian, 'To Washington, as to London during the era when the "eastern question" had preoccupied the architects of British foreign policy, Russian control of the Straits would entail domination of the eastern Mediterranean.'[7]

The extent of the geo-strategic ambitions of Soviet leader Joseph Stalin remains a contentious issue for historians. Stalin was rather dismissive of the Middle East in general and showed little interest in countries to the south of Turkey, strengthening the argument that Soviet behaviour in Iran and Turkey, as in Europe, was defensive rather than ideological. In parallel to the strong demanding language directed at Turkey, Stalin had no qualms about abandoning the communists in neighbouring Greece, whose doomed uprising was supported by Yugoslavia's Marshall Tito. In light of this, Stalin's behaviour after the Second World War was seemingly prompted by a desire to uphold and fulfil earlier agreements with Britain and the United States concerning spheres of influence in Europe to strengthen Moscow's aim of creating secure buffer zones around the Soviet border. Stalin was locked in the geo-strategic mentality of the pre-war era but in the cases of Iran and Turkey, as in Eastern Europe, he utilised the ideological card to attempt to fulfil his political goals. In Persia Soviet troops provided cover for a manufactured uprising by the northern Azeri people, portrayed by Moscow's propaganda machine as a populist national struggle. The same propaganda tools described the Turkish leadership as willing puppets of Western imperialist expansion threatening Soviet security to justify Moscow's demands for joint control of the Straits.

The opportunistic Stalin sought to extend this buffer zone in Eastern Europe to the southwestern borders of the Soviet Union with the hope that Moscow's restraint with regard to Greek, Italian and other West European communist movements would be rewarded with British and US consent without too much of a fuss over Iran and Turkey. Soviet propaganda manipulated genuine Turkish hostility towards it springing from Ankara's ostensible neutrality during the war that belied a general sympathy among Turkish officers, as was also the case among Persia's senior military ranks, for the Germans. The Turkish media and politicians immediately after the Second World War inflamed fears that the Soviet Union would forcibly seize territory won by the Ottomans in previous battles under the guise of reuniting Turkish Armenian territory with its Soviet counterpart. Fears were stoked that Moscow would demand the repatriation of Christians and Armenians forcibly exiled during and after the First World War. Stalin's ingrained suspicions that both the Persian and Turkish military and political leaderships viewed the Soviet Union with hostility and traditionally admired Prussian militarisation, having considered Germany a useful ally in blocking not only Russian but also British expansion in the Middle East, motivated his intimidation tactics after the war but in both cases the outcome of Moscow's actions on its southwesterly borders was counterproductive.

Stalin's behaviour in Iran and Turkey after the Second World War was a consequence of the greater role given to the International Department (ID) of the Central Committee (CC) of the Communist Party of the Soviet Union (CPSU). The ID provided ideological support and direction to communist and other leftist resistance groups in Europe against the Nazis and after the war coordinated with these allies, particularly in Eastern Europe, to bolster their position in the governments of the countries they were active in. This enhanced status allowed the ID CC chair, Mikhail Suslov, to complain in the summer of 1946 about 'the limited scope of information [it receives] about the political situation in foreign countries', and the lack of 'access to materials of the Ministry of Foreign Affairs'.[8] This was accompanied by a request for the ID to receive more insight regarding 'decisions of the CC of the CPSU on Soviet foreign policy concerning distinct countries and distinct international problems'.[9]

This request by the ID CC in the summer of 1946 signalled a turning point in Soviet foreign policy. Before the Second World War the Soviet Union was effectively in isolation, partially self-imposed, as Stalin tightened his grip on power. In ideological terms the state was subservient to the CPSU in diplomatic matters but the Foreign Ministry faithfully implemented the guiding thrust of the Soviet dictator and this allowed it to acquire a degree of autonomy. After the war the Soviet Union emerged as the dominant military power in Europe. Soviet standing was enhanced by communist partisans who had fought German occupation in most of Europe as part of national resistance fronts. This emergent Soviet power with continental reach was balanced by a powerful United States which had displayed to the world its atomic bomb capability in Japan. Stalin correctly concluded in 1946 that a direct confrontation with the US military and its allies was counterproductive and chose to focus instead on asserting firm Soviet rule in the so-called buffer states of Eastern Europe while exploiting the relationship with proxies in other countries.

The rise of Suslov in the CC during that period and his personal influence in the ID was more than simple coincidence as it highlighted a rejuvenated ideological foundation in Soviet foreign policy. The Soviet foreign minister at the time was the experienced Vyacheslav Molotov, a loyal and experienced diplomatic official under Stalin. Symbolically and practically, the increased role of the ruling party's CC suggested that foreign policy had become more than a technical diplomatic instrument of the Kremlin; it had become an extension of Communist Party power beyond the borders of the Soviet Union. The 'socialism in one country' slogan of the 1930s was eclipsed by a more ambitious internationalism after the Second World War when Stalin sensed an altered power structure in the international system.

Suslov was a ruthless henchman during the purges of the 1930s but it was his role during the war that defined his future in the Soviet state. Appointed first secretary to Stavropol Krai in 1939 and promoted to full member of the CC in 1941, Suslov became a pivotal political administrator in the northern Caucasus region, particularly in light of the rapid German advance and occupation of the area. Efficiently but mercilessly, Suslov was responsible for organising partisan and resistance forces against the Germans and endeavoured to erase or remove people deemed unreliable or insufficiently loyal in the war effort. Thus it was Suslov who was chiefly responsible for the mass deportation of Chechen and other Muslims in the northern Caucasus during the Second World War and who oversaw the ideological purification of the Communist Party apparatus in the region.

The expulsion of Chechens and other Muslims under Suslov's supervision during the Second World War revealed a deep-rooted suspicion and sense of insecurity felt among Moscow's leaders concerning the fragility of the Caucasus in terms of its ethnic make-up and the loyalty of the people there. Implicitly this anxiety was caused by concerns that the region was a soft underbelly open to exploitation by the enemies of the Soviet Union. Suslov's effectiveness in the Caucasus impressed Stalin and he was later called upon to crush Lithuanian dissention following the German retreat from the Baltic state, and his reward came in 1947 when he was promoted to CC secretary. This launched Suslov's career as a major behind-the-scenes power broker in the Soviet Union for the following thirty-five years, acquiring the reputation as the chief Party ideologue. In the late 1940s it was Suslov who castigated Marshal Tito's rebellion, ultimately distancing Yugoslavia from the Soviet Union. Suslov was also among the small but powerful group of men in Moscow who sanctioned the Soviet invasion of Afghanistan in 1979.

The CPSU's CC ID played a driving role in Soviet foreign policy after Stalin's death, especially as it was allocated the responsibility of overseeing relations with communists and Soviet allies in states that were not governed by communist parties. Suslov's experiences during the war and his rise in the Communist Party apparatus complemented an increasingly ideological and confrontational foreign policy that began well before Nikita Khrushchev became the unrivalled leader of the Soviet Union. One assessment noted that: 'Although Suslov did not occupy any formal post within the ID, he exercised broad influence over foreign policy for nearly 35 years in his capacity as a Central Committee Secretary (1947–1982) and Politburo member (1952–1953, 1955–1982).'[10] Boris Ponomarev, the influential Soviet foreign policy architect, led the ID under Suslov's patronage from 1955, enjoying prominence during the internationalist and radicalised foreign policy of the Khrushchev era.

The ideological shift reflected in the emergent role of the ID of the CC and the rising profile of Suslov undermined the portrayal of the Soviet posturing towards Iran and Turkey in the late 1940s as being purely pragmatic and defensive. In the Persian case the bid by Stalin to keep Soviet troops in the northern part of the country admittedly took advantage of an Anglo-Soviet understanding that allowed Moscow to maintain military influence there. Stalin had only agreed to withdraw Soviet troops from Persia after a compromise forcing Tehran to accept communists into the government before the withdrawal of its troops in May 1946. Within a year after the Soviet military exit the communists were ejected from the Tehran government but, as in Eastern Europe, the episode reflected Moscow's utilisation of communist allies to extend Soviet influence.

In the case of Turkey, fulfilment of Moscow's demands in 1946 would have expanded Soviet influence into the eastern Mediterranean as well as the Balkans. US President Harry Truman, correctly assessing the implications of Moscow's ambitions, ordered a naval force to patrol the eastern Mediterranean in the late summer of 1946 as a response to Soviet intimidation of Turkey and rejected any compromise over the Straits issue. Facing such a firm response from Washington, Moscow toned down diplomatic hostility and at least temporarily put demands regarding the Straits on hold. The Turkish episode exposed Soviet intentions because unlike in Eastern Europe and Persia, where a Soviet presence existed as a consequence of the war, Moscow was making demands for influence in new areas. The Anatolian provinces of Kars and Ardahan were under Russian control before the First World War but the Dardanelles and Bosphorus Straits were a longtime Imperial Russian ambition that had been thwarted by Western powers. The combination of the revival of strategic territorial ambitions and the promotion of an ideological internationalist element to foreign policy under Stalin became a major feature of the Cold War in the following decades and heightened Western fears and perceptions about Soviet intentions.

Beyond Turkey, in the Middle East the Soviet Union was vocal in its support for independence movements in Syria and called for British withdrawal from Egypt, thus promoting itself as the patron of anti-imperialist forces and popular revolutionary struggles. In this context the immediate Soviet recognition of Israel and providing indirect military support during its first war with its Arab neighbours in the late 1940s was partially based on an assessment that the Jewish state was guided by leftist cooperative ideals and propelled by revolutionary fervour that coincided with Moscow's newly found internationalism under Stalin. It was not long before Stalin's attitude towards Israel would change.

Following the Berlin blockade and the symbolic recognition of the Iron Curtain in Europe a state of stalemate was recognised by the Soviet Union and its Western counterparts on the continent, particularly as the cloud of mutual nuclear annihilation began to loom. Towards the end of the Stalin era Western countries genuinely feared Soviet intentions beyond Europe and specifically the Middle East. As a result the West sought to block Soviet expansion by forming the Middle East Command comprising the United States, Britain, France and Turkey. US Secretary of State John Foster Dulles hoped to create an anti-Soviet alliance in the Middle East but he was frustrated by Arab unwillingness to participate due to the Palestinian-Israeli conflict, noting after a trip to the Middle East in June 1953 that only 'the northern tier [Iran, Iraq and Turkey] of nations shows awareness of the [Soviet] danger'.[11]

Ideology and conflict under Khrushchev

Stalin's expanding support for communists outside the Soviet Union was not simply due to a wholehearted endeavour to spread Marxist doctrine, as the tensions with Yugoslavia and China suggested, but was rather driven by a desire to install subservient and obedient allies in strategic areas around the Soviet borders. Under Khrushchev Stalin's foreign policy approach was modified in two key ways: first, Moscow's outlook would become global and expand beyond the Eurasian mass in the confrontation against the capitalist West; second, flexibility was introduced that encouraged non-communist but anti-Western allies. Khrushchev also honed the style of foreign policy as he cleverly manipulated the trend of decolonisation to place developing countries at the heart of what was described as the historic battle between imperialist-capitalist oppressors and freedom-seeking national liberation movements. This approach, during a time of rapid progress in space travel, military prowess and technological advances, converted the image of the Soviet Union from a somewhat introverted continental power to a confident world superpower. The language of national liberation and social justice was an additional propaganda instrument to portray the Soviet Union as a progressive and civilised model as opposed to the belligerent and exploitative United States and its Western allies.

The Middle East offered fertile feeding ground for Khrushchev to practise what was being preached. The creation of the state of Israel and the dislodging of the Palestinians, continued British interference in Egypt and the Gulf states, animosity between poor uneducated masses led by middle-class intellectuals and opulent Western-backed monarchies linked to centuries of colonial domination were all arrows in the Soviet bow. Moscow's intention of raising its global profile in the Middle East was more than matched by local pleas for Soviet support by movements seeking to reshape the regional landscape.

The military regime in Egypt led by Gamal Abdel Nasser, after it had overthrown the monarchy in 1952, soon began making overtures towards Moscow. Colonel Abdel Nasser was the leader of a group of so-called Free Officers, a term they coined because Nasser's rank was the highest an ordinary indigenous Egyptian could reach in the military. Higher ranks were reserved to the local aristocracy that was made up essentially of ethnic Caucasians and Albanians. The success of the officers was partly due to the military defeat inflicted on Egypt by Israel upon its creation and partly a revolt against non-Egyptian domination. The takeover was more of a coup than a revolution but was nonetheless hailed by Nasser and his supporters as a victory for the simple people of Egypt in the struggle against occupation. In fact, due to the long history of foreign conquests Nasser was portrayed by his admirers as the first ruler of true Egyptian heritage since the last of the Pharaoh dynasties.

In June 1954 Nasser introduced the Soviet ambassador in Cairo, Danil Solod, to Lieutenant Colonel Gamal Salem, who as a member of the Revolutionary Council was tasked with all major industrial and economic projects. According to minutes of the meeting recorded by Solod, while talks touched upon the possibility of major projects 'such as the construction of a dam in the upper Nile…Salem explained that he wanted to meet me rather than our commercial attaché, so that the discussion would not revolve solely on economic issues but on political ones as well'.[12] In a second meeting on 21 June of the same year Nasser elaborated by complaining about the poor standard of weapons supplied by the British to Egypt and that the United States was placing unacceptable conditions attached to proposed aid.

Solod's minutes implied surprise that Egypt under Nasser was asking the Soviet Union for military aid. According to the Ambassador's notes when Nasser asked: 'What was the Soviet government's position on selling arms to Egypt. I said I knew very little about this matter…Nasser explained that Egypt did not approach the Soviet government directly because it was apprehensive that it might receive a negative response.'[13] This exchange illustrated that in mid-1954 Moscow had not broadened out its foreign policy strategy and had not yet fully grasped the available potential in the Middle East. At the same time Egypt was also still uncertain about Soviet willingness to get involved in the region.

In part the mutual hesitation was due to a lingering twilight period of uncertainty regarding succession following Stalin's death. Khrushchev had yet to consolidate his position in 1954 and Nasser was in a similarly vulnerable position, facing strong pressure from Washington to join the anti-Soviet bloc known as the Middle East Command (later known as the Middle East Defense Organization). The Nasserite coup rode on a wave of anti-Western and anti-Israeli rhetoric and for Nasser to suddenly place Egypt in a Western-led alliance could have destroyed his standing among his military colleagues in the governing Revolutionary Command Council and turn popular and intellectual leftist support in the country against him. Moreover, Nasser had his own ambitions of regional leadership and this would have been severely curtailed had he placed himself in the service of Western powers in their confrontation with the Soviet Union.

Egyptian reticence was central to the collapse of the idea of creating a Middle East Defense Organization based on the NATO model to counter the Soviet threat. In response, Washington and Britain created the Baghdad Pact, signed on 24 February 1955, which included new regional powers including Turkey, Iraq, Iran and Pakistan as major Islamic states excluding Egypt. The Baghdad Pact created a powerful rim across the Soviet Union's southwestern border from the Black Sea to Central Asia. Iraq was a historic rival to Egypt, and its Western backing and centrality was intended to create an alternative pole to Egypt in the Arab world.

The convergence of Egyptian and Soviet insecurities opened the way for the $250-million Czechoslovak-Egyptian arms deal in September 1955. Nasser had eyed Czechoslovakia as a military provider for Egypt because it was a major arms exporter to poorer countries. Indeed, the Egyptian leadership was aware that it was Czechoslovakian arms that helped tilt the balance in the first Arab-Israeli war in 1948 in the latter's favour. The deal set the stage for a two-decade long winding path of violence between Egypt and Israel that was a recurring feature of global Cold War superpower rivalry. The 1955 arms deal supplied Egypt with 100 MiG-15 fighters, forty-five Il-28 jet bombers and 150 T-34 tanks to significantly boost Nasser's standing in his own country and also regionally. Simultaneously, Nasser also cultivated relations with radical officers who had seized power in Syria in 1949, in order to create a regional balance to Iraq and its Baghdad Pact allies.

The Suez Crisis in October 1956 further strengthened Nasser's position and pulled the Soviet Union directly into the heart of Middle East politics. The confident Nasser, to further enhance his standing at home and regionally, announced the nationalisation of the Suez Canal. Although the Egyptian leader offered shareholders compensation and promised adherence to the 1888 Constantinople Convention on the freedom of navigation, London and Paris conspired with Israel and executed a military attack on Egypt called Operation Musketeer to place the canal zone under French and British control. Israel and its allies in the operation had also hoped the action would humiliate Nasser and limit his regional influence and popularity. Instead, despite Egypt's military inability to defend itself, the conspiracy was a terrible diplomatic and public relations blunder for the aggressors and proved to be a short-sighted calculation. Both the United States and the Soviet Union demanded that Britain and France withdraw from the Sinai canal zone and Nasser emerged as a hero in the eyes of his people and many in the developing world for having stood up to the old imperialist powers.

The outcome of the Suez Crisis allowed Nasser to effectively utilise the Egyptian media with powerful anti-Israeli and anti-Western propaganda and to promote the notion of a Pan-Arab superstate spanning the Gulf to Morocco under his leadership. The downtrodden masses across the region were charmed by his pledge to liberate Palestine from the occupying Jews and to regain pride after centuries of inferiority to Europe and the West. Seeing the rising star of Nasser in Egypt, Khrushchev was quick to manoeuvre himself to his side in order to promote the Soviet Union as a supporter of developing world liberators. In the late 1950s the prospect of Nasser uniting and leading the region became a significant possibility and Washington found itself being outmanoeuvred in the Middle East.

The language emanating from Moscow against Israel echoed the belligerent calls that were heard in Cairo after the Suez affair, with Khrushchev describing Israel as 'a country without any great importance in the world, whose only task is to play the role of provocateur before an aggression. If the Israelis did not feel that they had the support of the Great Powers, they would be sitting quietly like little boys.'[14] The anti-Israeli rhetoric by the Soviet leadership strengthened Moscow's standing in the Middle East and, as the Suez Crisis had undermined Baghdad Pact signatories, Washington looked increasingly to Israel as its most reliable ally, which turned Arab countries and peoples further against the United States and towards the Soviet Union as their superpower patron.

During this period Moscow also provided Syria with economic and technical assistance following an agreement signed on 29 October 1957 estimated to be worth US $579 million. One year later in 1958 Syria used its Nasserite allies in Lebanon to attempt to topple the democratic government in Lebanon. It was only a plea by the Christian Maronite president, Camille Sham'oun, for US military assistance that prevented Lebanon from falling under the Egyptian-Syrian sphere but the country became fragmented and weakened, with pro-Pan Arab and pro-Soviet elements remaining strong until the outbreak of civil war in the 1970s. Also in 1958 the Iraqi monarch was violently deposed and a year later the new military regime there withdrew the country from the Baghdad Pact, obviously terminating the value of the agreement.

By the end of the Khrushchev era the Soviet Union appeared to have immensely improved its position in the world in general and the Middle East in particular. All three centres of Arab power, Baghdad, Cairo and

Damascus, were ruled by anti-Western, military regimes, with strong ties with Moscow. Khrushchev was determined to promote the Soviet Union as a power that stood on an equal footing with the United States and his new friends were apparently confirmation of foreign policy successes. Yet the huge military and economic investment the Soviet Union had placed in the Middle East under Khrushchev to maintain these friendships became a source of discomfort for and criticism from his opponents. Not only had the Soviet Union become entangled in complicated local disputes but Khrushchev had made substantial military and economic commitments with political leaders in the Middle East who were anti-communist, unreliable and, as the Brezhnev leadership would discover, largely disloyal. The military coups supported in Moscow proved to be artificial and failed to create strong, pluralistic nation-states. While Soviet military and political support helped sustain them, their domestic weakness and hollow projection of power ironically made them vulnerable to US enticements to switch sides during the Cold War.

Disillusionment and failure

The Soviet leadership after Khrushchev was eventually dominated by Leonid Brezhnev after an interim of a collective leadership. Brezhnev's style of leadership differed from the dynamic Khrushchev era by emphasising stability and consolidation among the Communist Party elite. Conservatism prevailed, in both deeds and words, and the progressive radicalism in internal politics and external affairs of the previous era was eschewed. The idealism and ideological fervour of the Khrushchev era had eventually all but disappeared under Brezhnev and cynicism among Soviet citizens quickly spread. Strong criticisms of Israel were influenced by more prevalent anti-Semitism, especially as it came under the guise of anti-Zionism. Moscow equated Zionism with racism and even fascism, yet there were other factors under Brezhnev related to the domestic politics of the time that influenced Soviet policy towards the Middle East and particularly Israel. Dissident movements rapidly emerged in all parts of the country, often reflecting the hostility of many of the national groups of the Soviet Union, which in turn created underlying friction between nationalities, and particularly against Jews.

While the general association between the Brezhnev era and stagnation is commonplace, the seeds of Soviet failure in the Middle East could largely be attributed to the role Khrushchev played during the superpower rivalry in his time as leader. Soviet support had helped build strong military regimes in the Middle East but it had prevented the development of meaningful state structures and institutions in those countries after they acquired independence after the Second World War. The toning down of ideology in foreign policy in the Brezhnev era, particularly during phases of *détente* that characterised US-Soviet relations, undermines interpretations that there was 'no change in Soviet policies' towards the Middle East after the removal of Khrushchev in October 1964.[15] There was continuity in the 'peaceful coexistence' doctrine espoused by Khrushchev that reaffirmed the assurance to the West that direct conflict was not inevitable. But in the Middle East, Moscow had become more restrained in its support for the militaristic regimes there, particularly after 1967. This was partly because by then Brezhnev and Prime Minister Kosygin had politically asserted themselves following the jostling for leadership after Khrushchev's forced removal. A more important reason that caused change was the experience of the Six Day War in 1967 that nearly led the superpowers into direct confrontation and highlighted how little control Moscow had over their unstable allies.

Under Brezhnev there was less enthusiasm for supporting a movement or regime simply because it presented itself as a struggle for national liberation or as being anti-Western. The Soviet Union was increasingly embarrassed that in Egypt, Iraq and Syria communist parties and their members were being purged and persecuted by ostensibly friendly regimes. Moreover, rather than relying simply on gaining international public and moral sympathy the Brezhnev leadership began looking for more concrete returns, either in the economic sphere or particularly in terms of establishing military and naval bases that would enhance Soviet global reach.

The Communist Party had since the end of the Stalin era established a guiding mechanism for foreign relations through the ID of the CC. Initially, with the demise of Cominform, the ID was meant to coordinate relations with all external communist parties. In 1957 Khrushchev formed the Department for Liaison with Communist and Workers' Parties to handle relations with communist governments in Eastern bloc countries, leaving the ID, headed by Boris Ponomarev, with the task of guiding relations with developing world communist and national liberation movements. The ID was therefore a useful element for Khrushchev in his policy of backing 'anti-imperialist' movements or countries with a 'socialist orientation' in the developing world.

With the backing of the powerful and ideological Suslov, Ponomarev and the ID continued to be influential after Khrushchev. However, Brezhnev's pragmatic foreign minister, Andrei Gromyko, did not always share the same global view with Ponomarev and his patron Suslov. Until the end of the Brezhnev era: 'The ID was consistently the most vigorous bureaucratic advocate of a forceful Soviet presence in the Third World, a theme espoused with particular vehemence by Ponomarev and his top deputy, Rostislav Ul'yanovsky.'[16] In contrast, Gromyko and the Foreign Ministry approached foreign relations in the context of broader East-West considerations and direct US-Soviet issues. As Brezhnev and Gromyko pursued efforts to ease tensions with Washington in light of slowing down the arms race, improving relations with China and broader economic considerations, friction emerged with radical anti-US elements in the Middle East. According to one observation 'Gromyko disliked Ponomarev' who 'for his part, was tenacious in sticking to his ideological principles, knowing that he could ultimately rely on Suslov's authority to overcome most bureaucratic obstacles'.[17]

The Ponomarev-Gromyko discord was a reflection of the institutional differences between the CPSU and state but it was the intensification of the Arab-Israeli conflict between 1967 and 1973 that significantly undermined Party ideologists in foreign policy making. This was paralleled by the rising prestige and influence of Gromyko during the 1970s even though the ID, as part of the CPSU, was formally the guiding light in all decision-making aspects of the state. Brezhnev aspired to portray the Soviet Union as a responsible superpower to distinguish himself from the idealistic rhetoric of the Khrushchev era. The Cuban missile crisis in 1963 was ultimately instrumental in Khrushchev's downfall for its adventurism and his association with reckless Middle East leaders and movements in the Middle East that drew the Soviet Union into the conflicts with others in distant lands.

The military humiliation of Nasser in the 1967 war widened the gulf of mistrust between the Egyptian leader and the leadership in Moscow. Syrian and Egyptian propaganda in particular was vitriolic about the level of Soviet assistance and blamed low-standard weaponry for their military failures. Soviet leaders were offended at these allegations, with Brezhnev telling Arab emissaries immediately after the 1967 war: 'We feel deeply hurt when we hear Israeli officers say that our tanks and aircraft that you abandoned are the best kinds of weapons.'[18]

The heavy defeat for the Soviet Union's principal allies, Egypt and Syria, at the hands of Israeli military forces damaged Moscow's standing and soon after the war Soviet military aid was drastically increased to levels higher than before 1967 as it included advanced air defence systems through a Surface to Air Missiles (SAM-3) network fortified by 150 new MiG21s and up to 20,000 technicians.[19] Yet this rush of support was not due to the ascendancy of the ideological wing of the party or a will to defeat Israel but rather in order to restore some pride to Soviet standing in the Middle East and, more importantly, to reestablish a balance in the region following Israel's overwhelming domination. This balance was deemed necessary as part of a global bi-polar equilibrium in the world system that placed the two superpowers on equal footing in broader bilateral negotiations.

After 1967, while rearming its allies, Moscow actively promoted hosting a peace process under the patronage of the two superpowers. Cynics of Brezhnev's approach to the Middle East suggested that the Soviet Union was directly benefiting from a no-war-no-peace scenario that kept the region purposely on the brink. One author described Soviet policy at that time with the oxymoron 'collaborative competition'.[20] In essence, while Moscow competed with Washington intensely in regions such as the Middle East it simultaneously sought collaboration on a security level to ensure that the conflict did not escalate to an uncontrollable level that would threaten global peace and on a political level to create a situation whereby the United States and the Soviet Union were equal partners in the management of regional and international conflicts.

The easing of Soviet-US tensions in the 1970s gave Brezhnev hope that his approach was succeeding, particularly as Moscow briefly received some encouragement over its policies in the Middle East. An article in *Time Magazine* in September 1970 opened with the following optimistic outlook: 'The most hopeful factor in the Middle East crisis is the attitude of the two superpowers that stand behind the antagonists' adding that 'in unmistakable words and diplomatic signals, the US and the Soviet Union told their respective allies that it was time to stop stalling and get on with negotiations.'[21] Israel's absolute rejection under then Prime Minister Golda Meir of a Soviet role ultimately stifled Brezhnev's ambitions because of Israeli calculations that Moscow had an interest in strengthening the hand of Egypt and Syria in peace negotiations. Israel was also unwilling to recognise Yasser Arafat's Palestine Liberation Organization (PLO) as a legitimate counterpart in any process as Moscow had insisted.

Despite Israeli obstacles the biggest dent in Soviet aspirations in the Middle East was caused by its two key partners, Egypt and Syria. Anwar Sadat of Egypt and Hafez Asad in Syria both coincidently assumed power in 1970 and the two leaders were quick to show their eagerness to establish relations with the United States. The experience of the 1967 War and the ongoing war of attrition by PLO guerrillas on Israel's borders taught the two men that Washington would not allow Israel to be defeated militarily and more crucially they recognised that the Soviet Union was not willing to go to war with the United States in support of the Arab cause. Sadat in particular increasingly grew to consider peace with Israel as a serious option for several reasons. Primarily, peace would silence his radical Nasserite rivals at home by eliminating the belligerent political atmosphere and secondly it would facilitate large-scale economic aid from the United States to help him improve the living standards of his rapidly growing but impoverished population. Sadat aspired to lead the Arab world into a new phase of relations with Israel that would extract the region from perpetual conflict. The prospect of wars with no end in sight was not deemed in Egypt's interest according to Sadat and his supporters.

A prevailing perception during the early 1970s was that US power was diminishing, largely because of the Vietnam War and a world economic slowdown. Meanwhile, the Soviet Union was considered a growing military force with a stable regime. Yet Sadat was among a few at that time who had the foresight to calculate that in the long run Soviet backing would not be as favourable as that which the United States had to offer. The pragmatic Asad in Syria also sought to open links with the US administration in the early 1970s to strengthen his position domestically but also to pave the way for fulfilling his regional ambitions, including control over Lebanon. The two leaders evidently held a sustained faith in American power and disdain for the Soviet Union.

Relations between the Soviet Union and Egypt deteriorated drastically in 1972. In a tense meeting between Sadat and Brezhnev in April that year, the Egyptian president complained that the 'United States controls everything. [...] It manoeuvres in the region—politically and militarily—as it pleases.' Brezhnev's displeased response was that Sadat 'has spoken much and has given the impression that the Americans are all heroes'.[22] During the meeting Brezhnev sharply reminded his counterpart of the billions of rubles of debt that Cairo had accumulated over the years. Soon after, on 7 July 1972, Sadat stunned the Soviet leadership by demanding the immediate withdrawal of the 15,000 technical advisers, with only ten days' notice to evacuate. Twenty years of political, military and economic investments in Egypt gave back nothing to the Soviet Union.

To compensate for the loss of Egypt Moscow upgraded its relations with oil-rich Iraq, which was able to pay in hard currency for the weapons it purchased from the Soviet Union. Iraq in the 1970s was led by Saddam Hussein, an ambitious and ruthless political figure who sought to usurp Egypt's regional dominance. There were no ideological factors behind the growing relations between Iraq and the Soviet Union, as Saddam Hussein had brutally repressed communist compatriots. Moreover, Hussein did not display any ideological rejection of capitalism and sought to build good relations with some West European countries such as France to bolster his regional power. Soviet-Iraqi relations were based only on convenience and re-adjusted towards an increasingly pragmatic outlook in a changing world.

As détente faltered in the late 1970s Moscow resumed behaving on the basis of a confrontational and hostile world. Brezhnev's pragmatism, as much else in the political life of that era, was never wholehearted. After Egypt signed a peace agreement with Israel in 1978 the Middle East became divided into two opposing camps with Syria leading a group of countries alongside the PLO under the banner of the Front for Steadfastness and Confrontation. These were countries that opposed peace with Israel and believed that the only means of retrieving occupied territories was through violence. Fearing that neutrality jeopardised the Soviet position in the Middle East, Moscow moved quickly to support the coalition of self-styled anti-imperialist and anti-Zionist forces that also included Libya. This not only worsened Soviet-Israeli relations but also placed Moscow in opposition to moderate Arab states, including Egypt and Jordan, in a bitterly fragmented region. Moreover, the Soviet Union's support for hardline Syria resumed, after the latter's overtures to the United States cooled in light of the outbreak of the civil war in Lebanon. Damascus was pivotal in inciting radical Palestinian factions to defeat Christian pro-Western forces in Lebanon, although Syria ostensibly entered the country for the benefit of the Christians. The Soviet Union became embroiled in the dark labyrinth of inter-Arab rivalries as a result of the divided camps and the complex Lebanese conflict.

To compound the flaws of the regional policies of the Brezhnev era the Soviet Union had come to be associated with some of the most horrific and dramatic international terrorist acts of the time that were committed around the world by radical Palestinian-, Syrian- and Libyan-backed militants. Consequently Moscow's image was badly tarnished and its claim to endorse a peace process in the Middle East floundered as a result of its direct and indirect support for radical militant states and proxies. Soviet behaviour in the Middle East revealed that the leadership was unwilling and unable to move beyond *détente*, which reached its peak in 1975, towards genuine integration in the world system and openness to the West. Increasing political authoritarianism, repression of dissidents and a stagnating economy made the Soviet leadership more focused on political control and on preserving the superpower image. A powerful Israel and the loss of Egypt, which joined Jordan and Saudi Arabia as key US allies, placed Moscow on the side of unstable and belligerent regimes in the Middle East, even though they did not share any ideological links with communism. Moscow had very little real control over any of the countries belonging to the Front of Steadfastness and Confrontation but it entered a marriage of convenience with them simply to maintain rivalry to US influence in the Middle East.

The skewed vision of the world and sense of insecurity that permeated among the Soviet leadership in the late 1970s culminated in the decision to invade Afghanistan in December 1979. Suslov, Stalin's henchman who had applauded the intimidation of Turkey at the end of the Second World War, was among those present in the informal meeting with Brezhnev that led to the poorly considered decision. Among the consequences of the occupation of Afghanistan was that it antagonised much of the Muslim world and created a militant Islamic reaction. The Afghan war ended up gravely damaging Soviet military and political prestige and placed an unsustainable burden on the economy that ultimately threatened the integrity of the Soviet Union with its own Muslim population to consider. Soviet policy in the Middle East during the Brezhnev era had failed conclusively in terms of enhancing Soviet geo-strategic and economic interests, causing Moscow's standing in the world to become irrecoverably damaged by the 1980s. Moreover, Moscow's actions were arguably major contributors to spreading extremism, violence and poverty in the region.

The demise of Soviet foreign policy

The death of Brezhnev in November 1982 did not drastically impact foreign policy thinking immediately as key members of the old guard such as Ponomarev and Gromyko remained influential. However, subtle changes were beginning to take shape with the death of Suslov in January 1982 and the appointment of Yuri Andropov to the post of general secretary after Brezhnev's death. A faction within the ruling elite led by Andropov and with KGB endorsement pointed to serious social and economic flaws in the Soviet Union. Widespread corruption resulted in centrifugal processes and threatened Moscow's control over decision-making. Initial attempts to tackle these challenges were cosmetic, blaming alcoholism and an anti-work culture. Andropov's efforts to introduce a more serious approach to reform were stalled by conservatives in the system and he died before significant changes were implemented. His main legacy was to promote young and enthusiastic reformers to the central decision-making process, the most notable being Mikhail Gorbachev who became leader of the Party in 1985 after a brief reactionary interlude with Konstantin Chernenko at the helm.

The Middle East in 1985 was in turmoil. The Lebanese war since 1976 led to the fragmentation of the state as a result of separate Palestinian and Syrian aspirations to dominate the country. Israel simultaneously invaded the country in 1982 and occupied its southern half including Beirut, attracting the interest of the superpowers. To further complicate matters the Shi'a Islamic Revolution in Iran in 1979, led by Ayatollah Ruhollah Khomeini, invigorated Lebanese Shi'is and led to the formation of Hezbollah, a radical group that was both anti-Western and anti-Soviet. The Iranians were also at war with Iraq and the new regime threatened the rest of the Arab Gulf countries. Meanwhile, the bitter Palestinian-Israeli conflict remained unresolved without a sign of a peaceful settlement. The rise of militant Islamic movements, born out of the Soviet occupation in Afghanistan and in Shi'a Iran, created another dimension that posed a challenge to the Soviet Union and eventually to the rest of the world. Decades of manipulation of Middle East issues by the two superpowers resulted in the emergence of popular movements that eschewed both the Communist and Western models. The erupting Islamist movements were inheritors of the ideological vacuum in the Middle East. These developments occurred within the context of an aggressive administration in Washington under President Ronald Reagan and a hawkish right-wing government in Britain led by Margaret Thatcher during the 1980s.

Gorbachev's political inheritance was therefore a stagnant Soviet Union, a hostile West and a dangerous Middle East, with the occupation of Afghanistan draining Soviet resources and deflating military morale. Further still, it had incurred the wrath of Arab and Muslim public opinion. Although in the mid-1980s Syria was the closest to Moscow among the Middle East states, the Soviet leadership had become aware that there was no reliable partner in the region. Meanwhile, relations with Israel were rotting in a sour atmosphere of mutual hostility. From the latter part of the Brezhnev era an organised movement of Soviet Jews with support from fellow Jews in the West and Israel were asking for permission to emigrate. While a small number was allowed to leave in the late 1970s and early 1980s permission tended to be arbitrary and was used as a bargaining chip by Moscow in negotiations with the West. Thus, the new term Refusnik entered the lexicon of Soviet and Cold War politics to describe the tens of thousands of Soviet Jews that had their request to leave the Soviet Union rejected. The Reagan administration was supported by a rising and dynamic Christian Right movement in partnership with influential Zionist lobbies in the United States and the Jewish Refusnik problem further heightened tensions in relations between Moscow and Washington.

One of Gorbachev's first major actions as Soviet leader was to appoint his long-time political friend, Eduard Shevardnadze, as foreign minister to replace the ageing Gromyko to send a strong signal that he prioritised foreign policy and relations with the West in particular. This was to be only the first step towards change in line with foreign policy reforms as Shevardnadze systematically removed key figures from the Ministry of Foreign Affairs and injected new blood to promote change in thinking. In a few years, 'between 1986 and 1989 all nine deputy ministers and three out of four senior officials in the Foreign Ministry were replaced',[23] to dislodge the deeply entrenched old guard of the Gromyko era. On the ideological front, a significant appointment was that of Evgenii Primakov as director of the World Institute of Economy and International Relations in 1985. Primakov became a leading proponent of reform in foreign policy, criticising the invasion of Afghanistan and 'as early as 1987 he appeared in *Pravda* to condemn the idea of exporting revolution, creating a sensation for Western observers'.[24] In 1989 Primakov became an influential foreign policy advisor to Gorbachev at a time when Shevardnadze was facing intense criticisms from Gorbachev's political rivals.

Officially, the Foreign Ministry was guided by the Communist Party in the Soviet system and so Gorbachev faced the difficult challenge of reforming the ID in order to fundamentally change foreign policy thinking. In 1986 Gorbachev succeeded in replacing the long-serving Ponomarev with Anatolii Dobrynin, who had served as ambassador to the United States. Although Dobrynin was a seasoned bureaucrat in the Soviet system and was by no means a radical reformer he was considered as a suitable compromise when compared to his predecessor, whose career began during the Stalin era and whose die-hard communist views were best revealed in his support for the 1991 August coup that aimed to topple Gorbachev. Dobrynin proceeded to make his own personnel changes in the ID and appointed three new deputies in his first two years in office. Changes in both the Foreign Ministry and the ID were not limited to the highest levels as both Shevardnadze and Dobrynin pressed for a rapid turnover at the lower bureaucratic levels, including the heads of various sections and departments. The diplomatic corps was also not spared, and 'in just the first two years Gorbachev was in power, Soviet ambassadors were replaced in 60 per cent (seventy-four of 124) of the countries maintaining full diplomatic relations with the Soviet Union'.[25] The diplomatic corps answered to the Foreign Ministry in the Soviet Union, as was the international norm, but the ID and the CPSU as well as the KGB played a significant role in the screening of diplomats. This Soviet tradition was preserved with Dobrynin apparently playing a key role in the replacement and appointment of new ambassadors around the world as well as other personnel designations in the Foreign Ministry.[26]

Superficially, sustaining such influence for the CPSU ID in foreign policy contradicted Gorbachev's New Thinking and promises of reform. However, as a long-serving and well-connected diplomat, Dobrynin was deemed useful to bolster Shevardnadze, who was a novice in the foreign policy realm. In light of the personnel turnover: 'The more forceful presence that Shevardnadze displayed in 1987 and 1988 confirmed that the partial eclipse of the Foreign Ministry in 1986 was merely a transitory phenomenon, not a lasting trend. By 1989 the ministry had gained a dominant role in almost all areas of foreign policy.'[27]

Alongside the bureaucratic readjustments, Gorbachev transformed Soviet foreign policy and its approach to international relations. Ignoring the war-ravaged Middle East and security dangers arising from there, Gorbachev's focus was to establish a thaw with the West by pleading for a reprieve in the nuclear arms race. Gorbachev's first speech as Communist Party general secretary at the 27th Congress in 1986 was unique by a Soviet leader 'since...1952 not to express itself explicitly to the problems of the Third World'.[28] In part this reflected the disillusionment among the new foreign policy elite with their traditional so-called friends in the developing world. One Gorbachev adviser had complained that Soviet 'allies were primarily underdeveloped countries in the Third World whose interests were purely mercenary'.[29]

Placing heavy emphasis on good relations with the West required fundamental changes to Soviet behaviour in many regional conflicts. In the Middle East Gorbachev sought primarily to improve relations with Israel because it was an obvious conduit to better relations with the West. Thus Moscow eased the emigration of Refusniks and placed pressure on the PLO and Syria to transform their belligerent stance vis-à-vis Israel. The Soviet Union at that time significantly diminished arms sales to Syria, arguing in part that this was because of an accumulating debt owed to Moscow, but it also sent the message to Damascus that it would not endorse anything but a peaceful solution to the Arab-Israeli conflict. Moscow unambiguously and firmly relayed to the Syrian leader, Hafez Asad, and Yasser Arafat, as leader of the PLO, that it completely condemned terrorism as a political tactic.

The image that Gorbachev wished to portray to the West as a democratic, reforming and progressive leader did not accommodate well with Moscow's traditional allies. Although Gorbachev's efforts risked losing a Soviet foothold in the Middle East the strategy was deemed necessary for his new overall foreign policy offensive to succeed. One of the most positive outcomes of the new Soviet approach was that in 1988 the PLO renounced terrorism and Arafat expressed his willingness to recognise the state of Israel in the context of a peace agreement that incorporated the founding of a Palestinian state. The Palestinian concession to Israeli demands was the first step towards the Israeli-Palestinian agreement signed in Washington in September 1993. This positive trend in Palestinian-Israeli relations was arguably evidence that Moscow's negative role of supporting and encouraging radicalism for decades during the Cold War had prolonged the Middle East conflict and probably hindered rather than helped the Palestinian cause.

Full diplomatic relations between the Soviet Union and Israel were established in 1991. For Gorbachev and his reforming supporters Soviet foreign policy had corrected some of the erroneous policies that had existed since the start of the Cold War. In their view it was unnatural that a major world power such as the Soviet Union did not have diplomatic ties and contact with key Middle East states such as Israel. The establishment of relations with Israel opened the door for Moscow to join Washington as a co-sponsor of the Middle East Peace Conference, held in Madrid on 30 October 1991.

Gorbachev also reached out to old foes in the region other than Israel. The Soviet leader healed damaged ties with Egypt, improved relations with Jordan and, most challengingly, he reached out to Saudi Arabia, which had been instrumental in supporting the Afghan Mujaheddin against Soviet occupation. It was Saudi money and militant Wahhabi ideology that had been transported in the 1980s to Afghanistan that effectively defeated the Red Army occupiers. Historically, Soviet propaganda described Saudi Arabia as a backward, dark, religious entity ruled by a desert tribe of Western puppets. In turn, Saudi society rejected the atheistic Soviet society as evil. With Gorbachev's New Thinking a new opportunity arose to open a new chapter in relations that offered benefits to both parties. Several years of tentative approaches and the complete Soviet withdrawal from Afghanistan allowed diplomatic ties to be established between the two countries in September 1990. Soon after, Gorbachev was rewarded 'in the form of a Saudi loan of almost $4 billion'.[30]

Gorbachev's benign neutrality in the face of the US-led military liberation of Kuwait from Iraq in 1991 proved to be his most forceful statement on Soviet policy in the Middle East. Despite the longstanding political and economic ties between Moscow and Baghdad, Gorbachev tacitly supported international action that reversed the illegal occupation of another UN member-state. Iraqi leader Saddam Hussein had wrongly calculated that the Cold War scenario that typically prevented direct Western intervention in the Middle East because of the Soviet counterbalance still prevailed. Gorbachev's New Thinking, however, had ended the Cold War, and blatant acts of hostile actions and international violations became difficult to justify. Cynics could point out that Gorbachev's respect for international law and his encouragement of moderate and civilised international behaviour was less due to his benevolent goodwill and more as a result of the reality that the Soviet Union was rapidly fragmenting and was in no position to defy the United States. Yet the reality of the Soviet demise did not necessarily determine the behaviour of political leaders in Moscow, which could have become more violent and belligerent and Gorbachev deserves credit in this regard. New Thinking was a confession that Soviet foreign policy had done little to promote national interests and international stability.

Soviet leaders periodically took the Cold War to the brink, starting with Stalin's behaviour in the cases of Turkey and Iran, through to Khrushchev in the 1960s and culminating with the invasion of Afghanistan in 1979. Quite often this was done from a position of weakness, indicating a reckless approach, although pragmatism always prevailed to avoid escalation to a direct confrontation with the United States. Gorbachev's approach spared the international community the manipulation of regional conflicts through proxies to barter with the West. In the end though, four decades of the Cold War took its toll on the Middle East by assisting the rise of militarism, extremism and repression, which prevented the building of stable democratic states. Gorbachev was ultimately swept aside by the forces of change he set in motion and by the end of 1991 the Soviet state ceased to exist but the Middle East regimes it had consolidated for so long continued to linger.

3

YELTSIN AND THE DECADE OF TRANSITION

The Russian Federation was immediately recognised as a legitimate sovereign country by the United Nations as successor to the Soviet Union and preserved its seat at the UN Security Council as a permanent member. The new pro-Western political leadership in Moscow was welcomed into the arms of the international community but it inherited mangled state structures that did not provide the mechanisms to effectively govern the land and the people. The Soviet Union was a rigid, centralised, authoritarian state and the borders of the republics and other autonomous regions within it were largely artificial in the minds of the Kremlin rulers. Historically, populations were purposefully shifted around either forcefully or through incentives that further undermined existing national boundaries. The centrifugal tendencies that emerged during the Brezhnev era quickly spun out of control under Gorbachev. State institutions throughout the Soviet Union, including those at the republic level, had been systematically overshadowed by the Communist Party and the KGB. Consequently, the Soviet system was not immediately replaced by well-defined alternative state structures after 1991 but by self-serving political, economic and security cliques often connected to criminal organisations.

Soviet foreign policy was tightly controlled and dictated by the Moscow leadership until the end of the Cold War. Gorbachev attempted to downplay ideological differences between the Soviet Union and the West by focusing on the rather idealistic and vague shared goal of saving humanity from a potential nuclear disaster, as outlined in his speech to the United Nations in 1988. This approach was in part an attempted cover-up for the lingering power of the Communist Party and foreign policy was in reality designed for the Soviet Union or a very similar geographic entity, and not an independent democratic Russia. With the fragmentation of the Soviet Union, Moscow's Cold War foreign policy became increasingly irrelevant and unfocused.

In many respects the foreign policy domain required emphasis on the birth of a new Russia, rather than a post-Soviet Russia, despite the pedantic nature of the difference. Boris Yeltsin, Russia's first democratically elected president, was compelled to design a foreign policy for a smaller country (though still the largest in the world) with altered geographic boundaries and a smaller population with new irredentist challenges. A completely new security and geo-strategic outlook became necessary for a country that redefined itself as being a democratic member of the Western family and an integral part of the global market economy. Disengagement from regional conflicts began under Gorbachev but under Yeltsin Moscow was forced to gradually come to terms with new neighbours with a potential for dangerous military entanglements, particularly on its long southern front.

The early Yeltsin era

Yeltsin's immediate objective after the dissolution of the Soviet Union was to build strong relations with the United States because the Russian president wanted international support for domestic consolidation of his own fragile political position. The strategy was also based on global realities resulting from Russia's military and economic limitations. The Moscow leadership's policies towards the Middle East were largely influenced by Russia's view of itself in the early 1990s. Despite the rapid political, economic and military deterioration of the Soviet Union under Gorbachev there was still general surprise that the once powerful Cold War giant would disintegrate quite so drastically and easily. One indicator of this collapse was explicitly revealed in the nation's arms exports as 'Russia's share in global trade dropped to 7.5 per cent in 1992 (US $2.6 billion). For comparison, in 1988 the Soviet Union exported US $27.4 billion worth of weapons, which was equal to 35.6 per cent of the world market.'[1]

Russians, especially the nation's youth, viewed the Soviet experience negatively and opened up with great appetite to Western ideas, values and popular culture after many years of restrictions and the dull monotone that prevailed. There was an undercurrent of a sense among the youthful democrats that the Soviet past was linked to Russia's Eastern heritage, which was stereotyped as one characterised by authoritarianism, despotism, intolerance, secrecy and an unhealthy obsession with power. Andrei Kozyrev, Russia's first foreign minister, characterised the spirit of the times in his attitude and world outlook. Kozyrev's task was made easier because Gorbachev and his reforming foreign minister, Eduard Shevardnadze, had already began the process of correcting the one-sidedness of Soviet foreign policy in the late 1980s, which included the re-establishment of diplomatic ties with Israel as well as improving relations with moderate Arab states such as Jordan, Egypt and Saudi Arabia. Tacit Soviet support for the US-led military coalition that reversed the Iraqi occupation of Kuwait between August 1990 and February 1991 paved the way for better relations with many former Soviet foes.

Moscow's non-intervention in a variety of Middle East conflicts that began under Gorbachev was pursued more systematically and purposefully in the early 1990s under Yeltsin. Kozyrev's active non-intervention was most evident in the Palestinian-Israeli dispute despite Russia inheriting the official role of co-sponsor of the Middle East peace process. Following the ceremonial initiation in Madrid during the last months of the Soviet era the serious negotiations involving the Israeli, Syrian, Lebanese, Palestinian and Jordanian delegations took place in the State Department building in Washington DC. Kozyrev's enthusiasm for good relations with the United States and the support granted to him by President Yeltsin during the 1992 to1993 period were sufficient to convince the Arab delegations that they could not count on Moscow's support as in Soviet times. Consequently, Russian retreat from the Middle East during the early Yeltsin years was a considerable factor that allowed for the 1994 peace agreement between Jordan and Israel and the partial agreement between Palestinian leader Yasser Arafat and Israeli Prime Minister Yitzhak Rabin that was signed on the White House lawn in September 1993. Only Syria's President Asad, who managed to convince the Clinton administration and other Western governments that his role in stabilising Lebanon was too valuable to risk, enjoyed the luxury of procrastination. Syria's dominant role in Lebanon, with tacit approval by the Clinton administration, actually prevented Beirut from reaching a settlement with Israel and, more troubling for the West in the long term, allowed the militant pro-Iranian group Hezbollah to expand its base and power.

Criticisms of the Russian president by his political opponents for his perceived subservience to the West became intensely vocal in the summer of 1993 and, as a response, on 21 September Yeltsin dissolved the parliament, a move that created a constitutional crisis and an open revolt by the mainly communist opposition in alliance with nationalist hardliners. Yeltsin ordered the military to mobilise tanks and heavy weaponry to confront the rebellion, which was crushed by mid-October. The doomed Russian parliament that confronted Yeltsin in 1993 had been elected in 1991, when the Soviet Union's political system remained overshadowed by the Communist Party and its constitutional privilege. Despite forcing the opposition into submission on the streets of Moscow, Yeltsin faced a setback due to the unfavourable results of the first post-Soviet parliamentary elections, which took place on 12 December, 1993. Yeltsin's preferred parliamentary candidate, Egor Gaidar, leading the Russia's Choice bloc, performed badly while the opposition communists and extreme nationalists led by newcomer Vladimir Zhirinovsky emerged as the largest groupings.[2]

Russia's fractious domestic politics permeated the realm of foreign policy debate at that time. The supporters of Gaidar and Kozyrev were broadly labelled as Atlanticists, while the opposition outlook was generally referred to as Eurasianist. The Atlanticists saw Russia's fate as being tied with the West, while the Eurasianists believed that Moscow should focus on geo-strategic factors by prioritising regions directly bordering the Russian Federation. This approach was based on the notion that Russia was a great power in Europe and Asia. The labels attributed to the opposing factions were vague and rather simplified the complexities of the foreign policy debate. During the 1990s these two main views developed more nuanced strands within them, which fragmented the two-block division. There were some, for example, who prioritised good relations with the West but simultaneously understood the importance of traditional geo-strategic approaches to foreign policy. Likewise, there were Eurasianists who recognised that there were limits to Russian provocations against the West. Additionally, a group emerged that was neither Eurasianist nor Atlanticist but simply held an ideologically intransigent view that the West and its values were incompatible with the Russian heritage and that conflict between them was inevitable. This was a view espoused by the so-called Red-Brown alliance, comprising hardcore remnants of the CPSU and neo-fascist groups.

The December 1993 elections allowed for a wide spectrum of political parties to compete, in theory at least, on an equal footing to promote their distinct vision of Russia and its place in the world. This reflected an outburst of political pluralism that had long been missed. More significantly, on the same day as the 1993 parliamentary elections, 12 December, Yeltsin triumphed in a referendum for a new federal constitution that substantially strengthened presidential powers. Thus Russia's modern political system, dissected completely from the Soviet era, can be more accurately traced back to mid-December 1993. The strengthening of the powers of the Russian president and the creation of a multiparty parliamentary system representing diverse political views and interests had a considerable impact on Russian foreign policy and the decision-making process thereafter. Until the end of 1993 the relationship between the major state institutions, including the presidency and the parliament, were opaque and this undermined Yeltsin's and Kozyrev's early efforts join the Western family. After 1993 there was greater domestic and international certainty that the Kremlin formally represented important Russian interest groups including the overall outlook of the state's bureaucratic structure and political system.

Moreover, 1992 and 1993 were an anomaly in the sense that foreign policy was made without the existence of a stable foreign policy infrastructure. The Foreign Ministry itself required a top-down revision in those years, as it experienced a rapid rate of defections by its long-serving Soviet diplomats who were tied to the old Communist Party ruling elite as well as by capable and forward-looking Soviet diplomats who happened to be not Russian but citizens of one of the other new fourteen post-Soviet republics, each with its own newly established foreign ministry. Many diplomats, considered among the best educated in Soviet society, also resigned because they were attracted to the lucrative private sector after 1991, when state sector employees remained woefully underpaid, so that the number of Foreign Ministry staff shrank by a quarter by the middle of 1993 'to around 3,000, of whom 60 per cent were described as diplomats'.[3]

Considering that Russia's new post-Soviet neighbours were all sovereign independent states, mostly belonging to a loose post-Soviet structure called the Commonwealth of Independent States, Russia's diplomatic outlook required a complete overhaul in its world outlook. For Moscow, the abroad had become much nearer. In bordering countries such as Ukraine and Kazakhstan there were sizeable Russian communities. If Russian foreign policy was designed to defend the rights and security of the Russian state and its territories, what about the 25 million Russian nationals living in surrounding states? 'What about their interests?' Yeltsin asked.[4]

Re-orienting Russian interests

After the parliamentary elections of December 1993 the advocates of unrestrained free market economics and proponents of unquestioning faith in US intentions experienced growing marginalisation in the successive Russian governments and parliaments under Yeltsin. The dominant prime minister in the mid-1990s was Viktor Chernomyrdin, a pragmatic politician with links to the country's energy sector. The Chernomyrdin government, formed in 1994, followed a policy of reforms geared towards a freer market economy but there was more emphasis on the value of 'state intervention in the market, support for industrial production' and a generally more state-oriented organisation of Russia's social, agricultural and industrial sectors.[5] Kozyrev survived as foreign minister but his tone had changed considerably by 1994 to reflect a more sceptical approach to relations with the West. The publication in November 1993 of the Russian Military Doctrine revealed a resumption of great power aspirations promoted by the powerful defence lobby. Within Russia's political administration the defence and security sectors emerged to challenge Kozyrev for leadership in foreign policy making. The Military Doctrine's first stated aim was to 'strengthen Russia's military-political positions in different regions of the world' by promoting military-technical cooperation with other countries,[6] to counteract the previous policies of disengagement.

The winds of change in Moscow's international outlook also breached the Kremlin walls. Partnership with the West, according to Yeltsin in 1994, did not mean 'attempts to dominate or to foist on us their own actions which run counter to Russia's interests. It [domination] is unacceptable to Russia.'[7] Such comments were in part a reaction to internal political factors but Yeltsin was also concerned about Washington's unilateral actions in various regions of the world. The proposition of NATO expansion, Western encouragement of the dissolution of Yugoslavia and the uncompromising attitude towards Serbia, considered a natural ally of fellow Orthodox Russia, all led to negative assessments of US motives and behaviour among the country's national security elite.

Russia's sense of unease, bordering on paranoia, was not helped by the eruption of conflicts and hostilities within some of the former Soviet republics. A civil war in Tajikistan threatened the infiltration of extremist Islam into Central Asia and a spillover from the Afghanistan war was feared. Tense relations with Ukraine, Georgia and the Baltic states all increased Moscow's insecurities. However, the most dangerous development was the bid by the Chechens to break away from the Russian Federation. This not only threatened the unity of the Federation, posing an immediate challenge to the authority of Moscow, but also opened up the Caucasus to infiltration and domination by traditional rivals there including Turkey as well as NATO and the United States. A military operation to quell the Chechen rebellion was deemed necessary as demands for political autonomy from other non-Russian minorities, typically Muslims, began to be heard across the Russian Federation. Yeltsin's reaction was to order a full military operation in 1994 but Russian forces met stiff resistance from Chechen fighters, further undermining the credibility of Russia's standing in the world and its capacity to defend not only its international interests but also its own territorial integrity.

In 1995 Yeltsin distanced himself further from the liberal free-market clique that was dominant until 1993. This was predictable considering that former Prime Minister Gaidar's Russia's Choice party that year won only a third of the votes it won in 1993, which even then had been a disappointment. Kozyrev's influence on foreign policy became minor, with Yeltsin keeping him in that post merely to avoid sending a wrong signal to the West as an assurance that he did not succumb to the communist and ultra-nationalist hardliners. The tide of nationalist forces became too strong for Yeltsin to resist and strong leadership of the country's foreign policy, reflecting the views of the dominant political elite, needed to be imposed. This was accomplished with the appointment of Evgenii Primakov on 9 January 1996 as foreign minister, finally replacing the ineffectual Kozyrev. The appointment accompanied the prevailing sentiment among Russia's political leadership that foreign policy had to be more assertive because recent experience had shown that the

United States and the West did not listen or take into account the views and concerns of an apparently compliant partner.

A Russian strategy emerges

Russia's post-Soviet global disengagements led to a sense of encirclement with NATO expanding in the West and potentially hostile Islamic states scattered along the southern rim, a fear that was aggravated with the eruption of the Chechen rebellion in 1994. China's rapid military and economic growth posed a direct challenge to Russia in the Far East. By the mid-1990s Moscow's expectations of political and economic support from the West began to recede and public opinion turned against President Yeltsin's foreign policy, discrediting his key pro-Western foreign minister, Andrei Kozyrev, and deputy prime minister, Egor Gaidar, for not sufficiently defending the country's national interests against a demanding Western agenda. Russian opinion expressed a sense of hurt pride that Washington was behaving as a victorious adversary seeking to maximise its position by extending its global power and extinguishing the revival of its international competitors.

The appointment of Evgenii Primakov in January 1996 as foreign minister was a turning point in Russian foreign policy. In effect, it marked the systematic implementation of realism to foreign policy thinking. Primakov was a sophisticated diplomat with years of service in the web of Soviet bureaucracy. He was also considered an intellectual with a respected academic background and he spoke Arabic as well as Georgian fluently. At the same time Primakov was well-connected to the Soviet and post-Soviet security services. Indeed, it was during his time as the head of Russia's Foreign Intelligence Service in the early 1990s that he began crafting the post-Soviet world view that was adopted and implemented later in the same decade. Primakov did not accept the inevitability of US dominance in the world system, yet at the same time he was not an irrational anti-Western nationalist or diehard communist who believed that it was in Russia's interest to adopt a belligerent pose vis-à-vis Washington. The consensual nature of his thinking was evident in 1996 when 'all factions in the State Duma approved the appointment of [...] Primakov as Foreign Minister'.[8] Another biographical account pointed out that: 'Primakov was welcomed on all sides as a respite from political polarisation and uncertainty.'[9] Helped by this consensus Primakov was successful in restoring foreign policy administration to the Foreign Ministry and brought a much desired sense of centralisation of policy-making in Russia's relations with other countries.

Primakov's political ascendancy confirmed the widespread view that Russia would play a more dominant role in world affairs and that this change was intertwined with internal political and administrative transformations. One example was in the revitalisation of the arms exports sector, which had suffered a dramatic collapse immediately after the Soviet era because of 'the radical shift from ideologically based trade to cash-on-delivery'.[10] By the time Primakov was appointed prime minister in 1998, 'Russia's military output had dropped more than 80 per cent compared with 1991, and more than 2 million jobs had been eliminated.'[11] Primakov's government sought to unify the fragmented components of the Russian arms sector by appointing Iurii Masliukov, former chair of the Soviet Military-Industrial Commission and of the Soviet State Planning Commission as first deputy prime minister. According to one author, 'After several years of neglect Russia's military-industrial complex finally had a man in the cabinet.'[12] While the move could have been perceived as a victory for the military-industrial complex by imposing a representative in a senior position in the government, it was also considered as a means of restoring order to the fragmented military sector and integrating it with the political establishment. This was significant for reviving an arms sector with ambition to become a valuable source for national exports during a period of economic decline.

At the heart of Primakov's thinking was that two unchanging features should characterise Russian foreign policy: first that pragmatism, rather than an ideological commitment, should dictate policy-making; second, that Russia's international position could and should be strengthened in the world by forming and nurturing strategic alliances with other poles, or regional powers, such as China, India, both accounting for three-fourths of Russia's arms exports and Iran, which was considered a highly attractive potential market. This multi-polar approach was favoured by a school of thought that considered Russia as an essentially Eurasian power although strictly speaking Primakov did not fall under the umbrella of this thinking because of its contradictions with his realist approach. Primakov's political ascendancy reveals that there was no schism between the Putin and the Yeltsin eras in the foreign policy domain. Despite the departure of Primakov from the formal foreign policy structure under Putin, his influence continued. Indeed, Putin's popularity in Russia was partially due to the adoption and continuation of these policies through Primakov protégés in the Russian Foreign Ministry. Primakov also served as an informal adviser to Putin on foreign affairs matters.

In substance the Yeltsin presidency in its final years initiated the direction that Putin would follow and Primakov's successor as foreign minister in 1998 until 2004, Igor Ivanov, maintained this path. The appointment of Ivanov as foreign minister in 1998 was paralleled by Primakov's promotion to the post of prime minister. Ivanov, known for his opposition to NATO expansion and for his criticisms of US policies in the Balkans and in Iraq, confidently announced in 2002 that: 'There is now every reason to assert that the formative period of Russian foreign policy is essentially complete. The primary principles guiding the course of Russia's foreign policy, grounded in a clear understanding of the country's national interests, have been fully worked out.'[13]

Quite to the contrary, in 1996 Russia's view of itself was difficult to present in a positive light. Aside from a host of serious social and economic problems, including widespread corruption, the prevalence of criminal gangs and a criminal culture permeating the economy and the political class, widespread developing world-type poverty that became the norm outside of Moscow and St. Petersburg, a declining population and a general sense of fragmentation at the federal and state levels, a severe blow struck the nation's self-confidence after the defeat of the Russian armed forces against a small group of Chechen fighters fighting for national independence. Naturally, the Chechen war soured relations between Moscow and the wider Muslim world and potentially with the rest of Asia.

Yeltsin's pro-Western approach enjoyed relative success in ensuring that the Clinton administration supported Moscow against the Chechen's bid for self-determination and Washington turned a blind eye to the widespread reports of human rights violations that became common practice by Russian security and military units operating in the breakaway republic. The Europeans followed Clinton's lead by calculating that a unified Russia under Yeltsin was better than the devils of a fragmented Russia or a hostile and aggressive ultra-nationalist or communist leadership on their doorstep. The war turned out to be a huge embarrassment for the Kremlin and there was a sympathetic Western public opinion during the mid-1990s for what appeared to be a legitimate struggle of the underdog against an oppressive giant. One author and traveller in the Caucasus region, who made a point of asserting the significance of his Jewish background, opined that the Chechen struggle 'has taken so many ugly, bloody, and cruel turns as to exasperate even the most devoted friends of the Chechen cause. Nevertheless, the astonishing courage and audacity that this small nation displayed, and the improbable, unprecedented victory they scored in 1996, have left me in awe time and again.'[14] To compound the bitter Chechen experience US insistence on the expansion of NATO played an important role in creating a more suspicious mentality among ordinary Russians and the political leadership. Public opinion and policy makers feared encirclement and isolation so that 'in Moscow's eyes, the United States was dismantling the basis of Russia's global role'.[15]

It was in this setting that Moscow's political elite viewed the Middle East as an area of opportunity to regain a stronger standing in the world due to the deep and broad rejection of US policies in the region. Primakov's appointment was not simply a tactical compromise with the hostile parliament but was part of a new mindset that Russia could not ignore nearby geo-strategic interests. Kremlin leaders became convinced that the retreat from various strategic regions, notably the Middle East among others, was interpreted by the West as a sign of weakness rather than a genuine bid by Moscow to re-structure international relations and integrate Russia into the Western politico-economic sphere. This was part of the evolving consideration that relations with the Middle East and Asia in general were vital for Russia's immediate security concerns. Thus Primakov 'brought drastic changes in Moscow's foreign policy [...] The main manifestation of the change was the process of rapprochement between Russia and the Arab world, India and Iran.'[16] This thinking, influenced by Primakov, found its base in the Russian Foreign Intelligence Service (Sluzhba Vnesnei Razvedki, SVR), which he headed under Yeltsin in the early 1990s. The appointment of Primakov's close confidant, Vyacheslav Trubnikov, as his successor to head of the SVR preserved continuity in one of Russia's key foreign policy domains.

Western political and media specialist circles generally reacted negatively to the path Russian foreign policy was pursuing upon Primakov's appointment. The British daily *The Guardian* summed up the general mood in the headline 'Russia selects troublemaker.'[17] In retrospect Primakov's troublesome nature was attributed to him as a result of his rejection of US unilateralism in international affairs that emerged in the Clinton era and his insistence that the UN and other world poles provide a meaningful counterbalance. The harsh accusations in the Western media ignored the fact that Primakov's outlook was formed in the atmosphere of the Khrushchev thaw, joining the Communist Party at the age of thirty in 1959. Under Gorbachev he was a leading intellectual voice in support of New Thinking and his ties with reformists continued under Yeltsin. When Yeltsin was forced to find a new prime minister in 1998 'it was [the reformist Yabloko leader Grigorii] Yavlinskii who made the first publicised mention of Primakov for the post'.[18] Regardless of this, in some Western circles Primakov's centrist position was enough to brand him as a hostile element, and neglected the reality that the Russian political elite was ripe for a transformed foreign policy in 1996 after years of living in the shadow of the United States.

This revised Russian approach after 1996 coincided with significant regional developments. The most prominent of these were Israel's annulment of the Oslo Peace Agreement following the assassination of Prime Minister Yitzhak Rabin in November 1995 and Washington's intensifying pressure on Iraq based on allegations that President Saddam Hussein had resumed an illegal weapons of mass destruction programme. Moscow used the darkening clouds of conflicts that gathered over the Middle East during the second term of the Clinton presidency to show that the remaining self-proclaimed mighty superpower, the United States of America, was in reality impotent when it came to resolving the complex issues of the region. As a result, Russian foreign policy under Primakov promoted the idea that its cooperation, pooled with the support of the European Union and other major world powers, would be a valuable factor in helping the United States overcome the myriad Middle East challenges, if it was serious about doing so.

The United States was not particularly welcoming of Russia's growing enthusiasm for upgrading its international influence. Consequently, Moscow and Washington drifted further apart after 1996 especially as the Russian political elite had felt slighted that the $24 billion aid-package promised by the West turned out to be a mirage. Former Soviet Foreign Minister Eduard Shevardnadze's conclusion in late 1995 was that: 'Having spent a lot of money on ending the Cold War, the West did not invest in support of democracy and freedom.'[19] The reformers and liberals in Russia's political domain felt particularly undermined and disappointed by Washington's lack of support for their cause.

In the larger context of East-West relations there were factors directly related to the Middle East that led Moscow to redirect its foreign policy approach in the region. Iran and Turkey were significant geographic, cultural and political poles on Russia's south-western front. The vision of a grand Turkestan, with its implication of uniting the countries of Central Asia and the Caucasus with Turkey through ethnicity and language across Russia's southern border, was considered as a realistic possibility in some quarters in Moscow. More potent was the Islamic challenge posed by the militant and radical Shi'a form in Iran and puritanical Wahhabism rooted in Pakistan and Afghanistan. Policy makers during the Yeltsin presidency were forced to consider the possibility that the behaviour of the republics in Central Asia and the Caucasus would be determined by 'links with the Muslim countries of the Middle East and Asia', dragging Moscow directly into the chaotic and dangerous Middle East arena.[20]

There were sceptical voices countering that the Muslims of Central Asia and the Caucasus had a long tradition of secularism and a tolerant brand of Islam influenced by peaceful Sufi sects. In the Caucasus, for example, where anti-Russian sentiments were historically most strong, Islam, one author noted: 'Is relatively new, just two or three centuries old, and in any event, it is highly idiosyncratic, a far cry from what Westerners name, and sometimes misname, "Islamic Fundamentalism".'[21] Yet it became increasingly difficult to convince Russian public opinion and policy makers with such reassuring statements as the early nationalist tone of the Chechen rebellion mutated into a brazenly militant Islamic movement symbolised by Shamil Basaev and his comrades, with their years of experience fighting as Jihadis in Afghanistan against the Soviet Union. The Russian anti-Wahhabi hysteria drowned out sincere and credible arguments, while Moscow purposefully exaggerated such fears for domestic and international audiences in order to hide unsavoury actions by the Russian military in the Caucasus. This did not preclude the genuine uncertainty in Moscow at the time, even among its most well-informed intelligence sources about how deeply or how quickly radical Islam would spread along Russia's southern borders.

The challenge for Primakov and the Yeltsin leadership in the second half of the 1990s was balancing between stifling the rise of political

Islam on its doorstep while promoting friendly relations with major Islamic states in the Middle East such as Iran and Saudi Arabia. Moscow attempted to present itself as the friend of the Muslims and Arabs by increasing diplomatic support for the Palestinians and raising more forceful vocal criticisms of the Clinton administration's uncompromising approach towards Iraq. US unwillingness to criticise Israeli Prime Minister Benjamin Netanyahu for his unilateral termination of the Oslo Peace Agreement and the intensive drive by his government to build and expand Jewish settlements in the West Bank as well as Washington's refusal to ease sanctions on Iraq despite a rapidly deteriorating humanitarian crisis during the late 1990s were sources of strong anger among Arabs and Muslims. Primakov's experience and sound understanding of the Middle East allowed Russia to promote itself as the natural alternative to US policies in the region by lending a sympathetic ear to Arabs and Muslims. The approach also conveniently enabled Russia to muffle the sound of its critics in the Muslim world concerning Chechnya and to neutralise any possible hostile actions. In the longer term it was the beginning of Russia's reestablishment of an active role in the Middle East.

Reforming the reforms

Russia's quest to find a meaningful role for itself in the world in the late 1990s was a far cry from the country that was in turmoil during the early part of the decade. This was to a degree linked to the desire for political stabilisation as a necessary precursor to steadying the erratic and fragile national economy. One observer compared the decimation of the Russian economy in the 1990s to Soviet losses during the Second World War, using figures that showed a 43.3 per cent decline in GDP between 1991 and 1998 and a 56 per cent decline in industrial production.[22] In 1992 alone the real earnings of Russians fell by 46 per cent.[23] This economic factor set the scene for the stormy political setting that culminated in the violent clashes between the presidency and the parliament in 1993.

Russian political thinking during the second part of the Yeltsin era and beyond was determined by a firm belief that the weak, obsequiously pro-Western Russia of the early 1990s practising experimental economic reforms was an episode to be forgotten and avoided at almost any expense. The strengthening of the Russian state was aided by Yeltsin's victory over his political rivals with the adoption of the new constitution in late 1993 that helped establish a strong presidency and paved the way for a more unified political structure centred in the Kremlin. Yeltsin, however, did not control the centrifugal tendencies that were driven by the emerging powerful regional and financial elites, partly due to a lack of commitment on his part to do so as he attempted to consolidate his advantage over his rivals.

Yeltsin's critics and admirers agreed that the dilemmas facing Russia's first post-Soviet president were near impossible to resolve due to the complexities and scale of the challenges he faced. When Yeltsin was first sworn in as president of Russia on 10 July 1991 his supporters were anti-Soviet radicals seeking to eliminate all remnants of the system Gorbachev was attempting to merely reform. The vision was an idealistic one that was propelled by a Western-minded intelligentsia and the youth who wanted a liberal, free market, consumer culture in a modern Russia that merged easily with other European and North American models. But Yeltsin quickly realised that the Soviet bureaucracy was deeply entrenched and sustaining his presidency required support from at least some elements of the former Soviet nomenklatura. Having abandoned the Soviet system for Yeltsin, it was many of 'those groups in the Soviet elite that had amassed wealth through corruption and abuse of power in the institutions of the state and the Party'.[24] During Yeltsin's first term, influential members of the state apparatus took up the mantle of rapid economic reforms, supporting crash privatisations of key state-owned sectors and with it initially accepted Moscow's compliance with Western expectations. As the Russian leader became increasingly reliant on military-security personnel in his political confrontation with the Communist Party and other rivals he distanced himself from the idealistic Westernisers and drifted towards increasingly authoritarian methods in domestic policy, which in turn alienated Russia from the West. After 1993 figures such as Defence Minister Pavel Grachev and Federal Counter Intelligence Service Chairman Sergei Stepashin became instrumental in their support for Yeltsin, while Aleksandr Korzhakov, who was promoted to head the President's security guards, played an influential role in national security matters until 1996.

Fearing over-reliance on the nomenklatura as well as heads of the military and security apparatus, Yeltsin had hoped, as a counterbalance, his shock therapy in the early 1990s would 'create a privileged class of committed supporters ... at the expense of the majority of Russians and also of the state treasury'.[25] This group was popularly known as the oligarchs, a super wealthy elite group of men, who were arguably responsible for keeping Yeltsin in power in Russia through their control of the media and the bankrolling of political campaigns. Men such as Boris Berezovsky, Rem Vyakhirev, Vladimir Potanin and Vladimir Gusinsky were embodiments of the new rich whose influence in political affairs far outweighed ministers and party leaders in Russia. They found a useful ally, and arguably protective godfather, in the reformer but classic behind-the-scenes state bureaucracy operator Anatolii Chubais in the power struggle with the old nomenklatura and security apparatus. Yeltsin complicated the political landscape further by ceding more power to local governors in Russia as well as Federal level presidents and leaders to ensure popular support during key elections and also to provide him with loyal support against the other power blocs. Yeltsin therefore became in the late 1990s the fulcrum between the nomenklatura members who had forsaken the old Soviet system for a new Russia, the military-security network, the oligarchs, and the local governors and rulers of the Federation. These groupings successfully weakened the old nomenklatura represented by the Communist Party which enjoyed public support from those with nostalgia for the Soviet system.

The often fierce and sometimes violent power game between the competing forces trampled on and virtually eliminated the idealistic Western-minded intelligentsia that was prominent in Russian politics until 1993. Broadly labelled as Atlanticists, a more accurate definition of this outlook is pro-Western radicals who opposed the conservative Russian nationalist viewpoint that was often simplistically labelled Eurasianist. The pro-Westerners were divided in their foreign policy perspectives between radical idealists and pragmatists who suggested that integration with the West should be done gradually while preserving core and distinct Russian interests. Both Western-oriented wings were vehemently opposed by the extreme nationalists, with their illusions of restoring Russian greatness by focusing on rebuilding military strength, recapturing what were considered lost territories and emphasising the superiority of Russian culture over others in the former Soviet space and beyond. Vladimir Zhirinovsky emerged as the best recognised exponent of this view, which, while eccentric, could not be ignored because of the electoral success of his Liberal Democratic Party of Russia. Zhirinovsky's views enjoyed significant sympathy in the national media and held more popular appeal than the pro-Western radicals for most of the 1990s. An article in a Moscow newspaper in 1995 characterised the mood of the time by mocking the pro-Western radical approach for the capitulation and expectation that Russia would 'obediently follow the United States'. It particularly aimed its venom at Kozyrev, as foreign minister and ideological figurehead associated with the pro-Western radicals, for promoting the 'idea of a strategic partnership that assumed a subordinate role for Moscow in matters of world politics'.[26]

Between the opposite poles of radical pro-Westerners and extreme nationalists two main pragmatic strands emerged in Russian foreign policy thinking from 1993: the pragmatic pro-Western approach that was largely associated with the new class of entrepreneurs and which was the general policy of the Russian government between 1993 and 1996; and the pragmatic nationalists which found sympathy in a disparate range of groups including the military and security elites, the Russian nomenklatura, as well as the opposition Communist Party. The pragmatic pro-Western policy in response continued to prioritise cooperation with the West but with caution, recognising that differences were inevitable over areas of vital Russian interests but maintaining that it was possible to resolve them by consolidating mutual trust and understanding. Unlike the radical pro-Westerners, the approach reflected the subtle shift of emphasis from ideological partnership to practical cooperation. The pragmatic nationalists saw no useful reason why Russia needed to prioritise good relations with the West, which was viewed by them as being intrinsically hostile. Russia's immediate interests in the opinion of the pragmatic nationalists should be the only priority and wherever this conflicted with Western objectives settlements should be reached on the basis of equal standing. At the heart of this approach was an insistence on emphasising Russia's great power status and a refusal to acknowledge decline in its military, political and economic capabilities. Although tactically pragmatic, this group shared many of the same great power and expansionist ideals as the extreme nationalists, such as restoration of the Soviet Union, at least in a geographic sense.

Between these two competing perspectives, with their pragmatic and extreme strands, a centrist position was introduced with Primakov's appointment in 1996. Because this approach openly distanced itself from any pro-Western strand that had dominated Russian foreign policy since 1991, and also due to its emphasis on national interests and pragmatism, it was widely assumed in the West that Yeltsin's opponents in parliament had successfully imposed the pragmatic or even radical nationalist approach in the Foreign Ministry. The appointment of Primakov was thus often interpreted as a victory for the communists in parliament and a retreat by Yeltsin and his pro-Western allies of the early 1990s. In fact, Primakov's centrist position, while apparently appeasing the communists and their allies by adopting some of the nationalist language, subtly differed from the pragmatic nationalist approach because of its raw realism. Primakov's appointment after Kozyrev's dismissal was not a concession or compromise but an attempt to place a neutral candidate who had no apparent political affiliations.

Primakov was a career bureaucrat whose service was to the state rather than any party. Since the stormy clashes of 1993 the Russian Foreign Ministry had endured persistent targeted attacks due to Kozyrev's unpopularity. Primakov's appointment deflected criticisms and helped rebuild a Foreign Ministry apparatus that did not represent only one facet of the country's political spectrum. The traditional role of foreign ministries in Britain, Germany or France of being generally disentangled from the political squabbles in pursuit of a general national strategy became the models to emulate after 1996, so that core strategic goals remained constant regardless of the parliamentary party in power. Primakov's understanding was that a strong and sound national foreign policy was not sustainable if it antagonised the national popular view of the world and self-identity. At that time this led to the mistaken perception of communist influence on foreign policy. In reality Primakov's centrist realism was anathema to an ideological foreign policy.

During Kozyrev's last two years as foreign minister a growing fear emerged, fuelled by Yeltsin's political opponents and an excited media, over an arc of instability which stretched from Central Asia (particularly Tajikistan), through the northern parts of the Middle East and the Caucasus, to the Balkans. This arc of instability nullified enthusiasm for an energetic approach to building bridges with the West and made more urgent the need to focus on conflicts spanning Russia's immediate borders. Considering the predominantly Muslim population in this arc, in addition to the war in Chechnya, the Muslim factor rapidly climbed Russia's foreign policy agenda. Kozyrev's neglect of the Near Abroad and a simultaneous chauvinistic, patronising and neo-imperialist approach to relations with the Islamic world and Russia's bordering states by his adversaries made the need for a balanced, objective and experienced leader of the Federation's foreign policy more urgent by 1996. The background and experience of Primakov in Middle East affairs, contrasting sharply with his predecessor, provided a further illumination on the changed world-view in Moscow in the late Yeltsin era based on a perception that Moscow had naively overlooked its immediate interests and, more worryingly, its short-term threats to homeland security and stability. One newspaper comment in 1996 noted that 'The geo-political significance of the Muslim East demands not only the consideration of people as a resource, and of the extensive territory, but in the strategic location of the region, with trade-economic opportunities powered in the spiritual-historic potential of the Islamic Community.'[27]

The transformation of Russian foreign policy was also partially a result of the changes within the dynamics of internal struggles between the enterprising and largely independent rising financial elite on one side, and the vast state bureaucracy and political class on the other. This feature of the country's politics became openly publicised in the international media under President Vladimir Putin when he either forced into exile or imprisoned leading members of the oligarchs who challenged the Kremlin's authority. According to one particularly pertinent and long-sighted analysis: '...the state-centralising and institution-building needs of the Kremlin, as well as the imperative to provide for a sustainable revenue base, will diverge from the interests of the plutocratic clans more and more.'[28] The shift in the political balance in Russia among the power groups in the late 1990s impacted the foreign policy outlook that lead at least one assessment to conclude following Kozyrev's departure that: 'Russia's relationship with the great powers and the West is now a function of Russia's relations with the new post-Soviet states—not the other way around.'[29] Over time, particularly in light of the significance of Turkey and Iran, the Middle East acquired similar value on Russia's priority list.

The rise of Primakov represented the reasserting of authority by the state apparatus in which the security services became an important component. To describe this transformation of Russian foreign policy as moving from a pro-Western to an anti-Western approach is too simplistic. There existed in Russia under Yeltsin pragmatic and ideological factions within each wing. The policy that emerged was a centrist one that took elements of both approaches but was not a straightforward amalgam of the two. In fact, the centrist approach that later characterised foreign policy in the Putin era was an independent strand in its own right with a broad and comprehensive strategic vision of the world based on the idea of a strong Russian state with an organic and effective bureaucracy. While this generalised vision appeared close to that of the radical and pragmatic nationalists, aspiring to the reestablishment of Russia's control over former Soviet states, the centrists eliminated such language from Russian foreign policy from 1996. This neutral and detached state foreign policy was largely successful in silencing critics from both sides of the political spectrum and found broad support for its common-sense approach that was devoid of ambitious or inflammatory rhetoric.

Having removed foreign policy making from Russia's fractious political debates, Primakov began promoting the necessity and obvious logic of building close relations with neighbouring China, a rapidly growing world military and economic power. Bilateral relations brought together the world's largest population with the largest country on earth. The two countries 'are permanent members of the United Nations Security Council. Obviously, the significance of Sino-Soviet relations extends far beyond the interests of the two nations. It also affects the stability of Asia and the world at large'.[30] Unlike the superficial view of Russia as a Eurasian power allied with China against the West the centrists considered close relations with China as only one part of a global puzzle aiming to revive a multi-polar international system. Under Primakov's guidance Russia began developing multi-track and multi-directional relations on the international level, which created the possibility of nourishing and building alliances with Asian powers such as China and India while simultaneously preserving cooperative relations with Europe and the United States. To further boost this approach, while the United States augmented its list of enemies through its unilateral actions in the 1990s and after, Russia promoted itself as the natural bridge between East and West with the purpose of facilitating the resolution of international conflicts. This role emerged most evidently in the Middle East in the mid-1990s in contrast to Washington's tense relations with Iran and Iraq and its one sidedness in the Israeli-Palestinian conflict.

The effectiveness of Russian foreign policy under Primakov had its roots in Yeltsin's stifling of the 1993 rebellion because the installation of a presidential political system enabled the Kremlin to centralise the grand foreign policy strategy and disperse roles to formal state foreign policy institutions. The mechanism for this process was put in place through the constitutional establishment of a National Security Council headed by the president in which military, diplomatic, foreign intelligence and international economic tracks became coordinated in order to eliminate the apparent chaos of 1992 and 1993 in Russia's relations with the rest of the world. The National Security Advisor to the president provided an alternative voice and emphasis in the world to that of the foreign minister when a situation demanded subtle diplomacy. The 1993 Constitution stated clearly that the president 'directs the foreign policy of the Russian Federation'[31] and with this indisputable clarification it became possible for the Foreign Ministry to promote strong ties with China or Iran while the head of the National Security Council released statements highlighting the desire for better relations with the United States.

Yeltsin's centralisation of power in the Kremlin and the drift to authoritarianism in the second half of the 1990s was not completely frowned upon in the West because the fear of complete Russian disintegration was judged as a more dangerous alternative. Local wars spanning Central Asia, the Caucasus and the Balkans threatened international security. The weak leadership in Moscow in the early 1990s had allowed the smuggling of weapons around the world, and, most perniciously, materials that could help smaller or weaker states build weapons of mass destruction. Alongside this it was noted that a soft leadership in Moscow could have led to a takeover of power by either a belligerent and inexperienced military clique or radical anti-Western extremists with ambitions to forcefully restore the territories of the Russian Empire or former Soviet Union. Western tolerance of Yeltsin's abandonment of the early pro-Western zealousness and political and economic reforms by the second half of the 1990s entailed an understanding and sympathy for Moscow's efforts to restore some international prestige by healing the wounded pride Russia had suffered in the late Gorbachev and early Yeltsin eras.

While in the late 1980s and early 1990s the themes were crash capitalism and rapid market reforms, in the late 1990s terms such as authoritarian modernisation became widely heard, not just in Russia but also among Western elites. In Washington, the Clinton administration increasingly touted the idea that market reforms, as implemented in the early 1990s, could not succeed without a strong guiding state. Within Russia the beneficiaries of the hurried privatisations and state sell-offs, the new rich, themselves were keen to protect what they had gained and feared that disintegrating state unity and lawlessness would eventually threaten their acquired wealth. This allowed a consensus to emerge among the decision-making elites that post-Soviet Russia should reconfigure itself towards political authoritarianism functioning hand in hand with the free market, arguing that democracy was counterproductive for Russia's long-term development.

The Chinese model became a formula to admire among Russians and some Western political circles because of the emphasis on stability on both the national and international levels. This craving for stability by leading Western governments at the expense of democratisation was not widely approved of among liberal Russian opposition figures such as the Yabloko party, as well as European and US human rights groups. Washington's failure to recognise the distinction between radical economic reformers and democrats enabled the Russian nomenklatura and ruling political elite, having established connections with some of the oligarchs, to impose authoritarian government while conveniently promoting market liberalisation without accountability. Commenting on this partnership Boris Berezovsky, Russia's infamous oligarch who ruthlessly manipulated the media to favour Yeltsin's re-election in 1996, declared on more than one occasion that 'we are all children of [Anatoly] Chubais',[32] Russia's privatisation tsar who successfully operated from within the state bureaucracy.

The end of an era

Critics of Yeltsin argued that his legacy created a Russia that was not too dissimilar to the Brezhnev era when the state had become a 'chief joint venture run by the Mafia and corrupt Soviet bureaucrats'.[33] The challenges of leading a territorially huge, multinational, nuclear power out of a complex global Cold War and through fierce internal political divisions were great and required near miraculous efforts to overcome them. Yeltsin's sympathisers pointed out that extraordinary times required an extraordinary man who was able to deal with such difficult choices, which included making concessions on economic reforms and political freedoms. In foreign policy terms, Yeltsin succeeded in keeping Russia a moderate and rational player on the international stage despite the fierce internal conflicts. A change in direction from the idealistic early years was inevitable because of national and international realities. The reasons for the transformation were neatly summarised by a commentator who noted that, 'the collapse of the Soviet Union created early hopes that American-Russian relations would be warm and broad-based. These hopes have been dashed by exaggerated expectations, a lack of political will, and recurring Cold War-based tensions.'[34]

The Yeltsin era was undoubtedly controversial and created a wide gulf between sympathisers and critics. Supporters of Yeltsin claimed that the Russia he left behind at the end of the 1990s, despite the wild vacillations, was a better and more stable one than the Russia he inherited at the beginning of the decade. Critics of Yeltsin portray an image of a cynical and devious politician who manipulated idealistic democrats and masses of ordinary citizens yearning to escape from the tyranny of the Soviet Union and hoping for a better standard of living to attain more personal power. Upon securing the presidency and consolidating personal power he abandoned his democratic supporters for allies in the old Soviet bureaucracy he previously served. In the process his family and close allies created a super-wealthy clique that stripped the country of its most valuable assets. There were doubts in some quarters that Yeltsin had any understanding of democratic reforms at all, despite the flowery language he utilised. One analyst even considered Gorbachev, the last Soviet leader, 'as more democratic because he encouraged power through parliament. Gorbachev clipped the power of the security apparatus while Yeltsin helped it grow under his reign.'[35] Yeltsin destroyed parliamentary life and slowly eroded opposition to the Kremlin.

Final judgement on Yeltsin's political achievements may never be harmonised but there is at least a clearer assessment in terms of Russia's foreign policy development during the Yeltsin era. It is evident, for example, that the radically pro-Western approach in 1992 was a deviation from the national norm at the time because its proponents in Russia were so few in number and their influence was barely felt after 1993. Western governments and the media erroneously presumed that all those who were anti-Soviet were naturally pro-Western, and neglectfully concluded that popular Russian nationalism, including the desire to forfeit domination over the other Soviet republics, brought them closer to Western values. Arguably, many, if not most, Russian nationalists who were anti-Soviet were also instinctively suspicious of the West. In a study examining Russian attitudes to the United States from Stalin to Putin, the author concluded that, 'the pro-Americanism of Yeltsin's supporters was based on specific material reasons. They expected that a massive programme of economic assistance, similar to the Marshall Plan, would be provided to a new democratic Russia.'[36] This did not mean there was a deep-rooted sense of affinity with the Western world but rather a relationship based on expectations. As the reality of international affairs re-established itself in Russia and emphasis returned to interests rather than hopes, Moscow's foreign policy naturally readjusted to focus on foreign policy issues that either posed threats or offered lucrative rewards. It was in this context that relations with the Middle East became increasingly relevant in Russia's foreign policy planning.

By the end of 1995 any form of pro-Western orientation in Russian foreign policy had become unsustainable, yet Yeltsin and the Russian political elite were unwilling, largely out of genuine conviction, to adopt a strategically hostile anti-Western approach because it was considered damaging not only to Russian interests but to the integrity and existence of the country itself. Primakov offered the most viable alternative of a centrist pragmatic and realist approach that was detached from ideological divisions within Russian politics and his appointment as foreign minister in 1996 and promotion to prime minister in 1998 set the stage for a new type of foreign policy that was passed on to Yeltsin's successor, Vladimir Putin. The impact of this transformation in Russia had important consequences for the Middle East, while the abandonment of a pro-Western stance for a pragmatic approach opened a window of opportunity for a measure of defiance against the United States, having endured Washington's unilateralist policies in the region for a decade. Such defiance, as in the Middle East, nonetheless remained measured and calculated to preserve the goal of always keeping the door open for a mutually beneficial resolution in collaboration with the United States.

The emergence of an independent Russian foreign policy from 1996 paralleled general disillusionment and failure in the Clinton administration's Middle East policies. The Palestinian-Israeli peace process was stalled while Israel was ruled by a hardline Likud government led by Benjamin Netanyahu that sought to: humiliate Palestinian leader Yasser Arafat; resume rapid settlement of disputed territories; and extinguish the possibility of any final settlement negotiations relating to the key issues of the status of Jerusalem, the fate of Palestinian refugees and recognition of a contiguous Palestinian state. The humiliation of Arafat by Israel and the discrediting of the Oslo Peace Accord strengthened Hamas and other extremist Palestinian groups who carried out brutal suicide attacks against innocent civilians, further undermining the possibility of success in the peace process. Clinton's crowning moment when he stood on the White House lawn alongside Arafat and Rabin in September 1993 was but a distant memory by Yeltsin's last year in office when hopes of a lasting Middle East peace lay in ruins.

Clinton's failures in the Middle East were compounded by Washington's Iraq policy. The US image in the Arab world, already not positive due to a lack of pressure being exerted on Israel to honour the Oslo Peace Accord, was made to appear worse by the hard-hitting sanctions on Iraq that caused the deaths of hundreds of thousands of ordinary Iraqis due to hunger or lack of medicine without having any real negative impact on its ruler Saddam Hussein. In fact, the Iraqi president became ever more defiant and capitalised on sporadic military strikes by the United States on Iraq, exploiting the deaths of ordinary civilians and destruction of infrastructure to solidify accusations against Washington of bias against Arabs and Muslims, and its collusion with Israel. Neither taking decisive military action on a major scale nor being able to retreat in the face of Saddam Hussein's bravado, Clinton became entangled in a vicious quagmire that caused widespread suffering among millions of Iraqis and contributed to the deterioration of the US image in the world.

Other ill-thought US policies in the Middle East were also significant in influencing regional developments. Washington's focus on weakening Iraq raised fears in other Arab Gulf states, including Saudi Arabia, that it would allow Iran the opportunity to expand its regional influence. There were existing signs of this in Lebanon, where the Iranian-backed Hezbollah imposed itself as a powerful military and political force. Utilising its own television station, Al-Manar, Hezbollah projected its message of resistance against Israel and the United States to the whole of the Arab and Muslim world with great effect. The rise of Hezbollah in the 1990s contributed to the erosion of the role and effectiveness of the Lebanese state and added instability and the danger of violence between the various factions within Lebanon.

The Clinton administration's tacit approval of Syrian hegemony in Lebanon and its naïve assumption that this would aid the prospect of a Syrian-Israeli peace agreement was largely blamed for creating this volatile situation in the country and its results were largely counterproductive. Eventually Lebanon became a secure base for anti-Western forces and gave Iran an important foothold and considerable reach in the Middle East, undermining stability in the whole region. The illusion of civil peace in Lebanon did not deceive the Israelis, who withdrew from southern Lebanon in May 2000 following Ehud Barak's election as prime minister a year earlier and in fulfilment of the pledge he made upon taking up office. Hezbollah claimed the Israeli withdrawal as a moral as well as military victory, which in turn enhanced the position of their patrons Syria and Iran both in Lebanon and the region. The apparent Israeli retreat was also considered as another US setback in the region and enhanced the status of Hezbollah, Hamas, Syria and Iran by the end of the Yeltsin era.

Squandered opportunities by a short-sighted Clinton administration that failed to foresee the sources of danger and in light of deteriorating Palestinian-Israeli relations and a confused strategy over Iraq arguably allowed Cold War-era Middle East conflicts to re-emerge out of control by opening a back door for Moscow to re-establish itself in the region. This snowballing US slide in the Middle East increased the sense of urgency in Washington for decisiveness and made the option of unilateral military action unavoidable. Yet ironically one influential Russian foreign policy adviser reflected in 2007 that 'the United States squandered its chance' in the 1990s as the 'only global superpower' as it 'increasingly substituted international law with the law of force, legitimate decisions of the UN Security Council with directives of the US National Security Council, and prerogatives of the OSCE with NATO actions'.[37] Washington's failing was not in the use of force but in using it without a strategic vision of how and where it should be used.

The NATO bombing of Serbia in the spring of 1999, during Yeltsin's last year as president, allowed Kosovo independence from Belgrade and yet it also created almost a quarter of million Serb refugees. Most disturbingly for Moscow, the experience revealed a risk that NATO aspired to replace the UN and other traditional consensual means of peacekeeping. To compound Moscow's fears Hungary, the Czech Republic and Poland joined NATO in 1999 after they were originally asked to join in 1997. These events were in parallel to a collision course between the United States and Iraq over the role of UN weapons inspectors.

Washington's unravelling policy in the Middle East by the late 1990s was a significant development that was well read by Moscow in light of the considerable challenges it faced at the time, confronting an ambitious NATO and the emergence of hostile forces in many former Soviet Republics. The pro-Western factions in Russian politics evaporated and their cause was not helped by a virtually bankrupt Russian state due to the financial crisis of 1998, set off by external factors such as the Asian crisis. Corruption, weak banking systems and bad loans, low raw materials prices and ineffective tax collection systems all pointed to an urgent need to revise the whole process of interaction between the government and the economic system. Yeltsin's deteriorating health added further to the sense of a crisis of governance as tens of thousands of state employees did not receive salaries and hundreds of thousands of needy civilians were denied pensions and other state benefits as a result of mismanagement and corruption.

Primakov's appointment in September 1998 as prime minister signalled the beginning of the end for the financial elite who believed they could act independently of the state, and as in the case of Berezovsky and a number of oligarchs, overtly override official authority. Indeed, Berezovsky, who also had Israeli citizenship, was among the first targets of Primakov. Aside from his impact on foreign affairs 'the most intriguing feature of Primakov's rule was the tense manoeuvring between his government, the President and the oligarchs'.[38] His government began to initiate legal investigations into the transactions of Berezovsky and other new rich Russians, who became targets of popular and widespread resentment. Despite Primakov's strong ties with the state bureaucracy and the Duma Yeltsin fired him when the investigation's tentacles became too close for comfort for the president's own family. But this could not erase the dominant new mood in Russia which demanded a strong state to control corruption linked with rampant capitalism and install order to control crime and abuse.

Wounded national pride led to accelerated calls during Yeltsin's last two years for a Russia that was able to stand up for itself internationally and protect its interests in the face of perceived Western encroachment and a growing Islamic menace from its south. It was in this context that Russia and the world witnessed the meteoric rise of Vladimir Putin, first as prime minister in August 1999 and within a few months as acting president appointed by Yeltsin in December 1999. From the outset Putin portrayed an image of decisiveness, reacting without compromise to resurging rebellions in Chechnya and Dagestan, where militant Wahhabi Islam had hijacked the national resistance and seemed to be spreading in the Caucasus, even threatening the security of major cities in the Russian Federation. Putin's KGB past and connections with the post-Soviet security agencies added to his reputation as a law and order figure but at the same time his rise from within the Yeltsin camp and association with notable oligarchs suggested that he would guarantee that Russian capitalism was not going to be reversed by communists and extreme nationalists in the Duma.

Unlike Primakov, his main rival for the presidency in 1999, Putin was young and gave the image of being dynamic and somewhat detached from the old order. In the foreign policy domain both men offered the most moderate positions vis-à-vis the West compared to the options available in the Russian parliament and the prevailing introverted mood in the country. The emphasis was on pragmatism that demanded constructive working relations with the West but both men also stressed the need for Russia to reassert itself and its interests more forcefully in an unstable world. In typically dramatic fashion Yeltsin stepped down from the helm on the last day of 1999, paving the way for a new leader and a new era in Russian politics.

4

FROM SEEPING TERRORISM TO CREEPING AUTHORITARIANISM

Vladimir Putin was able to make good use of his youthful looks and sudden appearance onto the centre of Russia's political stage to win confidence in the West that he did not belong to the viscerally anti-Western old Soviet clique. His backing by Yeltsin for the presidency further bolstered Putin's position internationally and created the impression that the pragmatic pro-Western camp in Moscow had been able to retain control of Russian politics and decision-making. Putin's early emphasis on restoring order in Russia and prioritising security in the Commonwealth of Independent States (CIS) turned out to be a sweetener for the West and particularly the United States because it suggested disinterest in building global influence and an unwillingness to interfere in regions such as the Middle East. Putin presented himself as the president of cautious economic reforms under the umbrella of law and order, which in light of the turbulent Yeltsin years was welcomed among many Russians and Westerners alike.

Putin had very little experience of the world outside of Europe and during the early years of his presidency he considered, as the Primakov Doctrine suggested in the 1990s, the CIS states as an external affairs area in need of Moscow's special attention. Primakov's leadership of the Foreign Intelligence Service influenced the Foreign Policy Concept of the Russian Federation that was first adopted by Yeltsin in April 1993 and it highlighted terrorism, particularly the form linked with Islamic fanaticism, as one of the most prominent foreseeable threats facing Russia. Putin was able to successfully manage the transition in 2000 from acting president to a popularly elected president in a matter of months by promoting himself as an uncompromising strongman in the face of the threat of Islamic terrorism that had rooted itself in the northern Caucasus.

Igor Ivanov, foreign minister under Yeltsin, was retained under Putin to project continuity and stability in Russia's international outlook. At the same time Putin introduced new elements to Russian foreign policy by highlighting the importance of international economic relations, which in time would emerge as a substantial foreign policy augmentation and alteration to Primakov's world view because it would drive Russia towards greater global integration. Putin was eager to cultivate the image of friend to Western leaderships by capitalising on his links with the Yeltsin entourage but he also sought to show his domestic audience, Russian public opinion, that he did not suffer from an inferiority complex vis-à-vis the West. The tarnished experiences of Gorbachev and to a large extent the early Yeltsin period had shown that it was far more important to be a strong and respected leader at home than a popular statesman in the West. The show of proud refrain towards the West was not discouraged by Washington because Russia's friendship and expectations had become burdensome. Leaders in the United States and Europe were happy to see Putin and Russia cutting the cord of dependency.

The priority for Putin was to begin building authority for himself and the Russian state under the declared pretext of dictatorship of the law, and it was this limitless quest that would characterise the rest of the Putin era. In an overview of the era, Richard Sakwa justifiably concluded that: 'Throughout his presidency Putin appealed to the principles of stability, consolidation and the reassertion of the prerogatives of the state.'[1] The drive for authority resulted in authoritarianism as the emphasis on order and security led to more power to the country's official security branches and the military. Initially, neither Russian nor international public opinion protested much as Chechen insurgents, often linked with international Islamic terrorism, were dealt a severe blow to their efforts to extend their influence into the northern Caucasus.

Taking good advantage of initial Western support, the Kremlin began to impress its authority across Russia's borders and even beyond the CIS, leading to a growing international concern about the true intentions of

Russian foreign policy. During Putin's second term as president, particularly in the years 2005, 2006 and 2007, Russian policies in the Middle East peaked in terms of defiance against the United States. Yet there was enough vindication for Putin and the Russian elite that some quarters in the West, as it was stereotypically alleged about many Russians, valued authority more than genuine popularity. As a minor but telling example Putin was named Person of the Year for 2007 by the US *Time* magazine at the end of December that year, only a matter of weeks after a highly dubious Russian general parliamentary elections contest and days after he practically appointed his presidential successor Dmitry Medvedev. Despite widespread concern about the state of democracy and civil liberties in Russia, *Time* argued that Putin had performed an 'extraordinary feat of leadership' during his two terms in power.[2]

The Putin era displayed a discernible adaptation in foreign policy leading to a marked contrast between his first term (2000–2004) and his second term (2004–2008) and thereafter. Ivanov stressed in 2002 the goal of 'forming a belt of good-neighbourliness along the perimeter of Russia's borders and helping to extinguish the existing seats of tension and conflicts and prevent the emergence of potential ones in regions adjacent to the Russian Federation'[3] as the central feature of wider foreign policy strategy. Ivanov simultaneously emphasised good relations with the United States as being 'an important tool in responding to the new threats and challenges the world faces'.[4] In light of the 11 September 2001 terrorist attacks on the World Trade Center in New York the implication was that Moscow and Washington were destined to coordinate and cooperate in the face of Islamic terrorism that ominously surfaced along Russia's southern borders.

However, there was a noticeable deviation in language and attitude as the Putin presidency evolved after his first term. The steep rise in oil-income and the growing power of the Russian state fuelled ever higher international ambitions and a more defiant posture. In May 2006 Putin warned against a wolf-like United States. This 'wolf knows whom to eat. He eats without listening and he is clearly not going to listen to anyone.'[5] A partial explanation for this shift lay in Putin's assessment that the US administration under Bush behaved unilaterally to the point of arrogance, as typified by the character of the confrontational defense secretary Donald Rumsfeld. To some extent, Putin's unabashed support of the besieged Syrian regime until 2013 was motivated by a desire for retribution for perceived US arrogance and unilateralism.

The Muslims within

Power was transferred to Putin in late 1999 during a period of widespread and bitter resentment among many Russians. There was resentment against the oligarchs, portrayed as parasites responsible for impoverishing ordinary citizens. There was re-emerging anti-Semitism linked to the disproportionately high number of Jewish oligarchs, but generally it was part of a general social trend to blame a minority group, and the Jews were historically a favourite choice in Russia, for the country's economic misfortunes and political problems. Most intense under Yeltsin though was the pervasive and deep resentment among Russians of Caucasians in general and Muslims specifically.

Crime in many cities, including Moscow, had become a common feature in Russian life during the 1990s and street crime was typically blamed on Caucasians. Chechens were stereotyped as violent gangsters or wheeler-dealers who tainted the idealistic portrayal of the pure and ordered Slavic, Christian way of life. The humbling of Russian troops in Chechnya in the military campaign between 1994 and 1996 added to the general dislike of Chechens and Muslims, and consolidated the perception of the Caucasus region as a dangerous black hole of conflict and disorder that threatened to spread into other parts of the country. One Western study of Caucasian culture highlighted this antipathy in the words of a local Cossack Ataman soon after the first Chechen war under Yeltsin: 'Chechens have always just been bandits. If we had been called on to do the job, then we would have annihilated them all, left nothing but ashes. Next time the Chechens won't be so lucky.'[6] Racist attacks on Chechens and Muslims in Moscow and other cities became more frequent and were often characterised by brutal violence. In July 2007 Imam Ravil Gainutdin, the chairman of the Council of Muftis of Russia, appealed to President Putin and the political leadership: 'Why should we, Muslims, non-Russians, be afraid of sending our children out to schools, universities?' and expressed fears that 'the sparks of worsening relations and people killing each other may erupt into a blazing inferno'.[7] The typical visceral fears were exploited to create an atmosphere through the mass media and in social gatherings of a terrified urgency to protect women and property from the black people, as Russians call them, flowing out of the south of the former empire.

A convenient correlation occurred in August 1999 with the appointment of Putin as prime minister when militant Islamist rebels in Chechnya attacked neighbouring Dagestan that same month and a series of residential apartment bombings rocked Moscow and other cities the following September, creating a sense of panic in Russia and beyond. Putin's response was tough, launching a new major military campaign in the northern Caucasus and clamping down on the activities of Chechens and other Russian Muslims in Russian cities. Putin's resolute handling of the crisis was further illustrated positively in contrast to Yeltsin's then ailing health and apparent political paralysis. In many respects therefore 'the second Chechen war was more than a ticket to win the presidential elections in March 2000. Russia never looked [as] weak as it did in August 1999; for Putin, Russia's rebirth was to start in Chechnya.'[8]

Appointed acting president by Yeltsin at the end of December 1999, Putin quickly utilised the media to focus on his direct handling of the military and security operations, which included a visit to Chechnya to boost the morale of Russian soldiers. Despite the widespread accusations of human rights abuses committed by the Russian military and the anti-Muslim fervour, Russian public opinion appeared to support the uncompromising stance adopted by Putin. Western governments also generally chose to ignore major human rights violations and the harassment of Chechens and Russian Muslims because Putin successfully justified that he was waging a war against terrorism to protect Russian citizens and to prevent chaos in the Caucasus.

The Chechen cause was not helped by the emergence of a new brand of guerrillas influenced by the Taliban in Afghanistan and the Wahhabi sect in Saudi Arabia. These fighters represented a violent so-called Takfiri and intolerant form of Islam. Those not adhering to their form of Islam, including other Muslims, were considered heretics and executing them was religiously sanctified. Since the late 1990s and throughout the Putin period these groups, broadly referred to as Wahhabis in Russia, were responsible for a series of brutal terrorist operations including mass kidnappings, beheadings and spates of hostage-taking. Among the most notorious leaders of this movement was Shamil Basaev, whose ability to evade Russian forces became legendary. Basaev and his comrades converted the Chechen cause from a national liberation struggle into a wider Islamic jihad, something that was not acceptable to Russians and the West alike.

The Kremlin was able to shape public perceptions of the conflict by utilising the Chechen violence to exaggerate the Islamic terror threat within Russia. Alexei Malashenko, a professor at the Moscow State Institute of International Relations of the Ministry of Foreign Affairs of the Russian Federation, alluded to the alarmist approach that was manipulated by the Putin leadership with some effect. According to Malashenko, for example, a 'vast' Wahhabi network existed throughout Russia from 'Kaliningrad to Vladivostok and from Murmansk to Orenburg. Manifestations of Wahhabism have been noted in Tatarstan, Bashkiria, Mordvinia, in the Samara oblast, and in Kurgansk, Orenburg, Penza, Perm, Ulianovsk, Cheliabinsk and Tiumen oblasts; not to mention southern Russia from Rostov and Volgograd to the republics in the northern Caucasus.'[9] Yet according to one Western commentator, Wahhabism 'has become, as it were, a generic term that covers all kinds of "extremist Muslim activity" in particular insofar as they are linked to the war in Chechnya'.[10]

The usage of the term Wahhabi indicated that the threat is a foreign one seeping into Russia. Contrary to the interpretation expressed by Malashenko, other perspectives suggested that the Islamic factor was far more complex in Russia than that of booming Wahhabism. Idiosyncratic or esoteric Sufism was much more traditionally ingrained in the Caucasus and among other Russian and Central Asian Muslims than the Wahhabi form based in Saudi Arabia, Pakistan and Afghanistan. Russian Federation Muslims belonged to a large collection of ethnic groups, sometimes hostile to one another and usually alien to each other in terms of culture, language and history. Moreover, Moscow's attitude to Muslim militants in the former Soviet zone was not always consistent, considering its support for the Muslim Abkhaz rebels in their effort to break away from Georgia. This suggested a degree of expediency in Russia's policies in terms of magnifying the threat posed by non-state Islamic militants when it was useful for Moscow to do so while supporting other such groups when it served Russian interests.

Violent resistance to the Russians in the Caucasus, often extreme and brutal, had been a feature of the region since the late eighteenth century and was not necessarily a result of a sudden Wahhabi upsurge as Kremlin officials implied for much of the Putin era. The purported linkage between rampant Wahhabism and violence in the Caucasus as claimed by Malashenko was largely convenient for the Russian political leadership because it underplayed the degree and intensity of the conflict in the past and enabled it to promote relations between the ethnic and religious constituencies of the old Russian Empire and the new Federation as being historically natural and harmonious. This approach contradicted a reality of a bitter history of violence and bloody reprisals. The perpetrators of such violence were as often Russian as they were Chechen. The words of the nineteenth-century Russian military hero General Aleksey Yermolov, upon his appointment as commander-in-chief of the Russian forces in the Caucasus, reflected the Russian attitude when he stated that: 'Moderation in the eyes of the Asiatics is a sign of weakness, and out of pure humanity I am inexorably severe.'[11] To further underline the historical patterns, a recollection of the uprising by Imam Shamil in the 1840s revealed that the war inflicted heavy casualties on the Russians and the nationalist struggle was then also strongly dependent on religious fervour to motivate fighters before there was any notion of Wahhabi infiltration. Imam Shamil was usually portrayed as a nationalist hero but as Imam he was also a religious figure and he later adopted the title of the commander of the believers, underlining the argument that it was not unusual for nationalist struggles to adopt a religious dimension to motivate its soldiers.

The ongoing conflict in Chechnya under Yeltsin and Putin was therefore a part of a history of rebellion beginning with Imperial Russia, continuing into the Soviet era, until Stalin's mass deportations and murders led to a period of temporary pacification before resurfacing with the fragmentation of the Soviet Union. While the infiltration of foreign fighters or Jihadis with Wahhabi influence into the Caucasus was to increase under Yeltsin and then Putin, claims by Malashenko that by 2006 most or all men in some Muslim republics such as Dagestan belonged to radical Islamic groups, or Jama'a, were excessive.[12] Yet such sweeping claims were not confined to members of Russia's intellectual and political elite. In the West some scholars too claimed as late as 2007 that despite Putin's best efforts to assert state control Moscow was facing a 'radical re-Islamisation of some of Russia's Muslims and the formation of a geographically expanding, ethnically diverse, and flexibly organised terrorist Islamist network across Russia'.[13]

This menacing scenario was widely refuted by Malashenko and others who acknowledged that 'an entire mythology' has been manufactured around the Muslim threat, 'created by forces within the state—above all, politicians and the security services… [to] inflate the powers of the adversary, and by doing so accentuate their own strength and political significance'.[14] In many respects Putin's rise during his early years as president were partly characterised by this myth-making. The Yeltsin era oligarch Boris Berezovsky and others offered the conspiracy theory, without providing much evidence, that the apartment bombings and the second Chechen war in 1999 were contrived by the security services close to Putin in order to promote him to the presidency and re-install authoritarian rule in Russia. Such scenarios were too far-fetched for many, yet manipulation of Russia's proclaimed war against terrorism was likely designed for domestic political purposes and also to create the impression of shared values and interests with the West. The latter was evident and emphatically highlighted during Putin's US visit in November 2001, two months after the 11 September attacks in New York carried out by the terrorist Islamic network Al-Qaeda. Yet despite the media fever and the political propaganda accompanying Putin's early rise, Malashenko concluded after some consideration that 'there is no threat of any kind of an Islamic revolution in the Russian Federation'.[15]

Forming a Russian Order

In the build-up to the parliamentary elections of 2007 President Putin's personal and political authority in Russia had reached a level not witnessed since the era of Soviet leader Leonid Brezhnev in the 1970s. Brezhnev's Soviet successors either ruled too briefly due to old age or, as in the case of Gorbachev, adopted a bold reform programme which led to major opposition from within the Communist Party and from more radical nationalist and democratic anti-communist groupings. While Yeltsin was a towering figure at the centre of Russian politics throughout the 1990s his authority was always challenged by a parliamentary coalition led by the communists and other opposition groups ranging from radical liberal democrats to extreme nationalists.

The parliamentary party of power under Putin, *Edinaia Rossiya*, implying in its name an indivisible Russia and hereafter referred to as Unity, won over 64 per cent of the votes and 315 out of a total of 450 seats in the December 2007 Duma elections. The once powerful Communist Party was reduced to a mere 11.5 per cent of votes, winning only fifty-seven seats compared with 157 seats and almost 35 per cent of votes after the 1995 elections, when it was far ahead of its nearest rivals. For the first time since the end of the Soviet era Russia's president enjoyed dominance of the legislative branch of the state, and with Unity's allies controlled the two-thirds necessary to make major constitutional amendments. While debate was vigorous over the fairness and legality of the election process, as well as the true measure of Putin's popularity, there was little doubt that the Kremlin and the presidency had taken almost full control of Russia's political life in the two terms since Putin was appointed acting president in late 1999. Putin had also managed to impose strict censorship and control of the media, reintroduced state management of large industrial and agricultural sectors, and placed the broad national economy in the shadow of the Kremlin and the omnipotent state bureaucracy.

Perhaps a superficial yet telling indication of the transition Russia's political system had undergone since the early 1990s can be found in the name of the parliamentary parties of power. The Yeltsin-endorsed party in the early 1990s was called Russia's Choice, with the second word suggesting plurality to consolidate the aspiration of democracy. This pro-Egor Gaidar and pro-Western party did poorly in the 1993 elections and the pro-Kremlin party in the 1995 elections became Our Home is Russia, which was a pragmatic grouping around Prime Minister Viktor Chernomyrdin. The name clearly suggested a stress on nationalism, rather than choice, subsequently implying a more introverted perspective. By 1999, in the build up to the handover of power to Putin the party of power was then called Unity, or roughly translated, A One (as in unified or indivisible) Russia—*Edinaia Rossiya*. This provided a sharp contrast in its political message to the first party of power, Russia's Choice. In many respects the unity theme came to be representative of the whole of the Putin era, with little tolerance for dissenting voices and criticisms. The Russia of Putin was a Russia in a world full of hostile forces, sometimes real but more often exaggerated or carefully manufactured to justify the urgent need to unify around a strong leader for the protection of the fatherland and its people. Speaking about the United States in 2006, in light of growing difference over a range of issues, Putin's message to his people was clear: 'Their house is their fortress—good for them. But that means that we also must make our house strong and reliable…The stronger our military is, the less temptation there will be to exert such pressure on us.'[16] This political climate after 2000 impacted delicate political balances in the international system and was most dramatically visible in the Middle East.

The evolving contrast from the early 1990s under Yeltsin to the Putin era, however, did not contradict the reality of a smooth transition and handover between the two presidents. Considering the apparently fractured political groupings and parties during the Yeltsin era, the relative ease for Putin in assuming the presidency and consolidating his position was largely due to a consensus that emerged in the final years of Yeltsin's rule over Russia's role in the world and where national priorities should lie. This was well reflected in the 1999 parliamentary elections results, which created six major blocs with a span of ideological positions and foreign policy outlooks, as shown in the table below:[17]

Union of Right Forces	29 total seats	Reformist/radical pro-Western
Yabloko	20 total seats	Reformist pro-Western
Unity (pro-Putin)	73 total seats	Centrist/pragmatic Western-leaning
Fatherland-All Russia	67 total seats	Centrist/pragmatic pro-Multipolar world
Communists/allies	114 total seats	Leftist/pragmatic anti-Western
Liberal Democratic Party	17 total seats	Ultra nationalist/radical anti-Western

The total seats captured by the parties and blocs with a clear pro-Western outlook was very small in relation to the other major parties, confirming the perception that Russian public opinion, whether because of deep cultural traditions or because of political design, did not feel positive towards the West and harboured suspicions about its intentions. The blatantly anti-Western parties and blocs, including the Communist Party and the Liberal Democratic Party of Vladimir Zhirinovsky did very well, with the communists and their ideologically associated allies accumulating the largest number of seats. Nonetheless, the pragmatic centrists of the pro-Putin Unity bloc and the Primakov-led Fatherland-All Russia bloc, despite being election rivals in 1999, emerged as the dominant forces of the Russian parliament that would initiate the eventual decline of Communist Party influence in the nation's legislature. The centrists adopted a traditionally nationalist tone, highlighting the desire for Russia to restore respect and influence on the world stage, and stole the Communist Party thunder by stressing that this could only be achieved by restoring order at home by stifling the cowboy capitalism of the 1990s.

Putin was therefore a product and natural continuation of the late Yeltsin era, and not in spite of it. While the emphasis on raising Russia's international economic profile was closely associated with his era, 'Putin's second foreign policy priority has been to continue Yeltsin's attention to Russia's nearest neighbours.'[18] Although his rapid rise to power was largely unexpected and unpredicted, 'Putin did not come out of a vacuum, for in many ways he is an extension of the dynamic that propelled Evgenii Primakov to the post of foreign minister in 1996, and then to prime minister in 1998.'[19] His main rival for the presidential elections in 2000, Primakov eventually stood aside because Putin was favoured in the West, which mistakenly assumed that he was more pro-Western. Putin also had the edge over his rivals within Russia because as an incumbent he was able to utilise the privileges of the state and authority, and he used those in an efficient manner in light of the terrorist attacks in Russian cities leading up to the elections. Putin was also originally better favoured by the business community and the oligarchs because Primakov was associated with an anti-corruption drive during his term as prime minister in 1998, which came close to implicating the Kremlin elite and the Yeltsin family itself. Upon his election as president with 54 per cent of the votes in March 2000, Putin's first decree was to ensure for Yeltsin 'immunity from prosecution and [he] could not be arrested, searched, interrogated, or subjected to administrative penalty'.[20] A clear message was sent through this act that there would be no engineered reprisals against the former president and all those who remained loyal to the Kremlin and, in the interest of stability, Putin would turn over a new leaf and ignore previous financial irregularities.

As an interesting illustration of Putin's style during the first term of his presidency, Primakov was soon co-opted into the system and was appointed as the head of the Russian Chamber of Commerce and Industry. Meanwhile, the supposedly pro-Western privatisation godfather Chubais was given charge of the important national electricity grid, ensuring that he too was not excluded, despite the fierce opposition he traditionally stirred among communists and their allies. Chubais had shown himself to be an astute political player under Yeltsin and he made the transition easily into the Putin era by recognising that loyalty to the state apparatus was necessary for political survival and this took priority over reform agendas and naïve Westernisation. Putin was well connected to the security elite of Russia and was familiar with its state network but at the same time, like Chubais, he enjoyed the confidence of many within the new business elite that arose in the 1990s, enabling him to co-opt many of the components of power in the new Russia. The inclusive spirit of the Putin era, however, would over time show a ruthless streak in the way it dealt with those who refused co-option into the system. Unity, as the party of power and the catchword of Putin's regime, was not an option but a reality that was imposed with gradually tightening authoritarianism. Thus the political cohesiveness of the Putin era was to a large extent a combination of the centrist nationalist pragmatism that evolved in the late Yeltsin era and growing intolerance of diversity and variety in thinking and policy.

The Putin presidency was in many respects a dictatorship of the political centre-ground formed by a diverse combination of forces with shared concerns about the potential success of radical democratic forces or ideological conservatives such as the communists. The ruling coalition, although disparate, feverishly sought to consolidate the state's power and the geographic survival of the Russian Federation to preserve its shared financial and security interests. Among Putin's supporters were the former exponents of rapid economic liberalisation and privatisation who made their wealth in the 1990s but wanted an effective state that imposed law and order to allow them to keep and safely enjoy what they had acquired. Putin's sympathisers argued that despite his tough statements on foreign policy 'his real goal is to deepen Russia's interdependence with Western economies and attain a greater level of cooperation with the West'.[21] This financial elite often faced competition for influence from the *siloviki* (a name given to those whose power derives from the state security apparatus) and they would have an important bearing on Russian foreign policy as would the military-industrial complex personnel because of their generally hostile outlook towards the West. Another important component of the Putin-led political clique was the group representing the gas sector, which some argued was 'the most powerful lobby, largely because it [with oil sector] accounted for more than three-fourths of Russia's annual budget revenue'.[22] The financial and gas lobbies both generally preferred a more Western-friendly foreign policy because an isolationist Russia undermined their business opportunities. The military-industrial lobby, along with LUKOIL and Tatneft representing the oil sector placed Asia as a greater priority for Russian foreign policy.

In the late 1990s the financial lobby lost its pre-eminent position of influence and the military-industrial complex regained a strong foothold in the Kremlin. Although Yeltsin began relying on military-industrial lobbyists for support from the mid-1990s, it was the Primakov-led government in 1998 that re-established and formalised their role as an important lobby in Russian affairs. The military-industrial complex in alliance with the Foreign Intelligence Service was a strong proponent of reasserting Russia's role on the international stage and weapons exports were considered as a key component in this regard. Putin 'consolidated Russia's arms sales agencies into Rosoboronexport in an effort to gain greater control over a major source of foreign exchange'.[23] Putin expressed a will to revive the defence industry, which under Yeltsin: 'Was one of the sectors of the Russian economy most seriously affected by the economic crisis…in 1997–98 the level of military production was less than 10 per cent of that reached in 1991.'[24]

Countries such as Iran and Syria offered lucrative opportunities for military sales because of restrictions that prevented them from purchasing weapons from Western countries. Military production plants were major employers in far-flung regions of Russia. The Federal Security Service elite repeated warnings 'about the possibility of social unrest resulting from further degradation of the military industrial-complex'.[25] The challenge of balancing the rivalry between the military-industrial sector and the oil and gas lobbies as well as to a lesser extent the financial lobby, each forming an important pillar in the national economy, was efficiently managed and exploited by Putin and was considered as among his greatest achievements of leadership. The Russian security services, from where Putin emerged, had successfully penetrated all these sectors and thus became the real powerbroker in Russian political affairs and policy making. Putin admirers among Western academics such as Timothy Colton and Michael McFaul readily admitted that in attaining power 'The Unity bloc and Vladimir Putin had formidable political arsenals and wielded their weapons in cutthroat, if not undemocratic, fashion.'[26]

Upon assuming power Putin immediately highlighted that central to his agenda were the values of *derzhavnost* (great-powerness) and *gosudarstvennichestvo* (state-centredness) and he reflected that in Russia 'a strong state is not an anomaly. It is not something one should try to combat…The public wants to see the re-establishment of the guiding and regulating role of the state, to such a degree that this is necessary, on the basis of the country's traditions and taking into account the contemporary situation.'[27] In the early 1990s these were attitudes and terms associated with the Soviet era and, to a large extent, Imperial Russia. Putin's main achievement was in embodying these values and applying them to a post-Soviet Russia that remained in theory at least a democratic country. In practice Putinism signified the interchangeability between a strong state in Russia and a strong Russia in the world, and asserted that such values were a natural part of Russian society and culture. It stopped short of the messianic nationalism of Russia of the nineteenth century as it was instead mainly rooted in nationalist pragmatism. Such nationalist pragmatism nonetheless demanded a high degree of international respect and threatened retaliation against those who dared to insult national pride.

The modern nationalism of Russia did not always display self-discipline and possessed an extreme and violent side to it that was reflected in the surge of racist attacks against ethnic non-Slavs, particularly Muslims. The victims were not only street traders or those on the lower socio-economic scale but also university students including one reported instance of a student who was savagely attacked and killed in his dormitory room as he slept. In one study a senior Dagestani official noted that as a result of racist attacks 'many young Dagestanis now go to Islamic religious schools in Pakistan, where graduates are expected to acquire basic skills not only in holy scriptures but in martial arts and machine-gun operation as well. So it's no longer Russia that young people look up to.'[28] Despite the difficulty in justifying the motives and the accuracy of such assertions it is nonetheless possible to argue that the radicalisation of Russia's Muslims, particularly in the Caucasus, was aided by the sometimes intolerant Russian nationalism of the post-Soviet era.

The insensitive streak of this new *derzhavnost* and Russian nationalism was also to create a barrier with the West. Putin's growing authoritarianism and intolerance among the Kremlin leadership was blamed for the harassment and sometimes murder of political opponents and free thinkers. The assassination of the brave journalist Anna Politkovskaia in 2006 was widely reported in the Western media, which pointed out that this was 'the thirteenth Russian journalist to be killed in a contract-style killing since President Vladimir Putin came to power in 2000'.[29] Such episodes played a part in changing Western public opinion towards

Russia in the context of Moscow's hostility towards NATO expansion and the establishment of an independent Kosovo. As winter set in that year Russia cut off energy supplies to Europe as a political muscle-flexing exercise in a dispute over prices but the outcome was that the Putin era endured a European-Russian chill in relations that was last felt before Gorbachev came to power twenty years earlier.

Relations with the United States became equally problematic, with Secretary of State Condoleezza Rice openly stating in 2005 that Washington was disappointed with Putin's path and that this feeling was due to negative 'democratic developments in Russia...[and also] developments in the whole of Europe and all of the neighbors of Russia'.[30] The complaint was echoed by the US defense secretary, Donald Rumsfeld, who accused Russia of being 'unhelpful—using energy resources as a political weapon, for example, and its resistance to positive political change in neighboring countries'.[31] Such criticisms only seemed to strengthen Putin among most Russians by creating the impression that he was a strong nationalist standing up to the West and defending his country's interests. Putin responded to his critics in Washington with equal vigour, accusing the United States of seeking to create a 'world in which there is one master, one sovereign...the unipolar model is not only unacceptable but also impossible in today's world'.[32]

The few remaining critics of Putin's belligerent policies and de-democratisation inside Russia were the liberalisers and democrats, including members of Yavlinsky's Yabloko Party. But Yavlinsky was also disappointed with the West, arguing that in their relations with Russia: 'It is impossible to escape the feeling that Western Europeans and the Americans were eager to exchange their strategic Cold War perspective for one focused narrowly on trade and commerce...the West chose to pursue only a tactical relationship with Russia's post-Soviet bureaucracy.'[33] Yavlinsky's disappointment was marked by clear strands of cynicism towards the moral index of 'Western leaders' for failing 'to engage with the Russian people in a spirit of full cooperation, and at the same time openly to condemn the new Russian state's human rights violations. The West overlooked authoritarian tendencies as long as Russia's problems were not exported.'[34]

Such disappointment and cynicism towards the West was shared by Alexei Arbatov, one of the few pro-democracy figures with influence in the foreign policy sphere under both Yeltsin and Putin. First elected to the Russian State Duma in 1993 he became deputy chairman of the Duma Defence Committee and continued to be an active participant in the security and foreign policy debate throughout the Putin era. His fears about the way relations between Russia and the West were unfolding under Putin led him to ask in February 2007, 'Is a New Cold War Imminent?'[35] Arbatov's answer to his question was that because the ideological gap that existed before 1990 had disappeared, a similar Cold War was unlikely but he feared the rise of what he termed a 'cold wave' due to a more confident Russia strengthened by economic stability that allowed it to 'increase by 300 per cent (since 2001) the funding of national defence, and suppress mass armed resistance in the North Caucasus'.[36] It was a telling indicator of the shift in Russian thinking under Putin that the Yabloko Deputy in the Russian Parliament would state: 'The idea that Moscow—voluntarily or not—follows in the footsteps of US policy, while its interests and opinions are ignored, has become unacceptable to all political parties and government agencies in Russia. Meanwhile, a majority of American politicians—and almost as many European—view the 1990s model of Russia-West relations as natural and the correct variation.'[37] Yet by the time of Putin's re-election for his third presidential term in 2012 criticisms resurfaced that he had taken Russia's intransigent stance too far in light of Moscow's failure to support the Syrian revolution against the Asad regime, which complicated relations with important regional players including Turkey and Saudi Arabia as well as other positions that antagonised Britain and France in particular.

A decade earlier a different image of Putin prevailed. Due to his experience in East Germany and having worked in the St Petersburg Mayoral office under the reformer Anatolii Sobchak, Putin was viewed during the first two years of his presidency as being Western-inclined. As deputy mayor in St Petersburg, Putin was responsible for encouraging international investment to revive the city and this further bolstered the perception that he understood the Western business mentality. Putin's pre-presidential political experience did indeed solidify his opinion that Russia's economic weakness was a crippling handicap for national security and development that could only be remedied with Western cooperation within the framework of modernising the country. Putin never displayed any romantic notions of the Western world, nor did he ever present a view of Russia as a natural partner of the United States. A fairer depiction was that 'for Putin, the West is not an ideal—it is a vehicle for Russia's development'.[38]

Paradoxically, the creeping authoritarianism in Russia was initially tolerated in the West because it was believed that this would safeguard against a hostile, communist-led assault on domestic economic reforms and a Western-friendly foreign policy. The communist threat was indeed effectively tamed under Putin but doubts became widespread in the West about Russia's threatening behaviour in the world, as well as its stalled internal reforms. The West's complaints were late considering that early warning signs were raised with one Russian commentator lamenting that 'the greatest threat to reform now comes from the inflated, corrupted and uncontrollable bureaucracy'.[39] This was a telling indication of the linkage between Russia's internal politics and its external behaviour as the Putin era depended increasingly on oil and gas exports as well as a return to state-managed weapons exports.

While oil and gas exports at least provided revenues to the state, the military-industrial complex was initially a negative burden, employing some 2 million people scattered across Russia's regions and relying on arms sales to keep afloat. Despite Putin's emphasis on economic development there was little diversification in the national industry that could have led to meaningful job creation and wealth generation. Moreover, the telescopic economic approach bound Moscow to certain modes of behaviour in its international affairs because of its heavy dependency on limited sectors. Without fully recognising the negative consequences of his remarks, the correlation between Russia's relations with the world and its internal political developments was directly stated by Putin's first foreign minister, Igor Ivanov. In what with hindsight appears to be an accurate summary of the direction in the dynamics between internal politics and foreign policy, Ivanov noted in 2002 that in Putin's view 'foreign policy is both an indicator and a determining factor for the condition of internal state affairs'.[40]

National values and the world

The debate over national identity and values is as complex in Russia, if not more so, as anywhere else in the world. A stereotype of Russians exists, in the same way the English, Americans and French are stereotyped, but in the Russian case the experience of the Soviet era adds another layer of confusion because Soviet identity was officially placed above national identity. After the Soviet Union, fifteen republics, of which Russia was one, became independent states, with freedom to pursue their own national and cultural tracks. Russia itself was a Federation containing many religions, nationalities and ethnic groups. The Chechen conflict highlighted the many fiercely independent cultures and identities that existed in the Caucasus, which generally resisted Russian hegemony. Beyond the diverse national identities Russians were also divided in terms of their civilisational identity. Typically, this was about whether Russia was European, Eurasian, Asiatic or a distinct civilisation with its own unique message and role in the world. Certainly, the new Russia after 1991 had a distinct identity, despite the obvious historic links, from Imperial Russia and Soviet Russia.

Contemporary Russia's political elite was united in principle by a determination to preserve the geographic integrity of the Russian Federation. The basis of this stance was not motivated by ethnic or religious bonds because Moscow was willing to respect the independence of Ukraine and Belarus as well as other predominantly Christian Soviet republics, while it was intolerant of secessionist ambitions of non-Slavic Muslim republics in the Federation. The foundation of identity in post-Soviet Russia was essentially a political one based on the geographic borders that were inherited from the Soviet era, defined by the reality of the time. It was this same political pragmatism that led Moscow to recognise the borders and sovereignty of the neighbouring republics despite the presence of large Russian communities in many of them. The borders of modern Russia contained within them a highly diverse mixture of peoples and the political elite faced the difficult task of forming a set of common values to define the national character. After the failure of Russia's Choice it was not surprising that the parliamentary parties of power in the 1990s and 2000s, were called Our Home is Russia initially and later Unity to reflect the fear of national, cultural and political fragmentation.

A study published in 2004 found that in Russia social and political values widely differed as a result of geographic distance and ethnicity as well as between the city and the country. While such findings were predictable in a country as vast and as diverse as Russia, the study found that the biggest gap in values was recorded in the age category, which 'seemed to be the most important variable explaining differences in moral values'.[41] In the early 1990s, Yeltsin strongly defended many of his political appointments, including Egor Gaidar, on the basis of their youthfulness because he believed them to be free of the shackles of years of Soviet propaganda and Soviet thinking. Many members of the new business elite were also relatively young, with figures such as Roman Abramovich and Mikhail Khodorkovsky becoming billionaires in their early thirties. Chubais and other influential political figures in the Yeltsin era were also youthful, thus it was also not unexpected that Yeltsin would designate a relatively young unknown figure at the time. Putin was in his late forties, as his presidential successor. Putin symbolised the important role young Russians played in defining their future national character.

Segments from all the opposing forces and values in post-Soviet Russian society, in all its regions, whether young or old, Eastern or Western, Christian or Muslim, National or Imperial, were to some extent united behind Yeltsin from 1990, despite all his critics, because he symbolised a democratic Russia. Only democracy provided the adequate assurance to most of Russia's disparate groups that the state and country they inhabited would protect their rights and allow them to express their views without risk of persecution. Russia under Putin contrasted with this in that democracy no longer became the most important ideal and goal. The yearning for a strong state and a strong Russia appeared as a result of the disillusionment that arose with the broken promises of democracy during the last years of the Yeltsin presidency. To some extent democracy in Russia developed an association with social and political disorder and international weakness in light of the experiences of the Yeltsin era. One Russian commentator summarised this outcome at the beginning of Putin's second term in office by noting that while 'some people are concerned by the present government's departure from democratic ideals…Both politicians and experts actively discuss the "uniqueness" of Russia, which many believe cannot follow any other path of development but its own.'[42] The revived pro-democracy forces, largely centred in Moscow and St. Petersburg, after almost a decade of Putin's domination have arguably found it difficult to get more mainstream support because of lingering negative associations of democracy.

The shifting emphasis from democracy to the uniqueness of Russia entailed a rejection of universalism and a degree of suspicion of what were perceived to be imported ideas. This change in values had a fundamental impact on the way Russia viewed the world. Significantly, it clashed with Western, and particularly American, tendencies to override the sanctity of national sovereignty and to internationalise domestic human rights or democratic violations. This was often evident in the Middle East where Washington's efforts between 2002 and 2006 to promote democracies in Iraq, Lebanon, Syria and among the Palestinians were treated with disdain in Russia. US pressure on Syria and Iran to conform to international requirements by means of tough UN Resolutions on a variety of issues from 2001, including restricting their interference in Lebanon, were constantly stalled by Russia under Putin, which served to undermine Washington's position in the Middle East as a whole. Russia's reaction to the Arab Spring and its behaviour from 2011 best epitomised its abhorrence of such change with almost hysterical vocal rejection of Western support for anti-regime movements in Libya, Egypt and most controversially Syria, where Moscow supplied the Asad government with weapons to suppress the popular revolt.

The anti-universalism that prevailed during the Putin era developed traits of anti-Americanism. In the view of Russian intellectual and deputy director of the Institute of International Security Studies at the Russian Academy of Sciences, Alexei Bogaturov, 'Confidence in their own superiority is probably the dominant attribute of the American.'[43] The inference of American arrogance was obvious and he clarified further by complaining that, 'American patriotism has yet another side—a genuine, sometimes blind and frightening, conviction that the US has a calling to "set an example to the world" and to "help" it adopt their notions of good and evil.'[44] Such opinions were widespread among the Russian elite and were interestingly not dissimilar from common stereotypes of Americans held by many of the Middle East's political and cultural elites.

Immense American global power after the Cold War was understandably intimidating, sometimes even unsettling some of its European allies, but Russian hostility during the Putin era was a reaction caused by a sense that the Russian political leadership was being directly challenged by the values espoused in Washington. This defensive posture in Moscow was reflected brashly in Bogaturov's comments regarding US attitudes to democracy: 'It is hard for Americans to understand why other countries show a reluctance to replicate on their soils the practices and institutions that have proven effective in the US. Their almost morbid desire to "democratize" other peoples against their wishes (as is the case with Iraq and Afghanistan) is a strong characteristic of the US vision of the world.'[45] This prevailing fear that the United States was driven by a mission to change the world to fit its own image increasingly influenced Putin's language in his political speeches, openly protesting in early 2007 that 'the United States, has overstepped its national borders in every way…It results in the fact that no one feels safe. I want to emphasise this—no one feels safe!'[46]

The Kremlin-led assault on US arrogance did not allot much relevance to its own rampant xenophobia in post-Soviet Russia. One poll as early as 1994 'showed that 80 per cent of [Russian] respondents feared the Chechens and hated them. Only a fraction of them had ever actually spoken to a live Chechen.'[47] From 2000, Russia's security apparatus had skilfully used material enticements and intimidation to ensure the subservience of the official Muslim clergy in the Federation so that they 'no less than Orthodox prelates go out of their way to underscore their loyalty toward the central Russian state'.[48] Anti-Americanism in Russia did not necessarily lead to sympathy with the East and Muslims but was typical of the classic Pan-Slav view of the nineteenth century. Fyodor Dostoyevsky, an icon of Pan-Slavism had famously written that 'Constantinople is Orthodox, and everything Orthodox is Russian.'[49] The anti-Ottoman, anti-Muslim undercurrent in this sentence was stark and expressed a widespread perception in Russia at the time. This similar xenophobic undercurrent was present during the Putin era.

The transformation of the national and consequently international outlook under Putin was associated with the war against Islamic terrorism in Russia, yet Moscow still offered political support to the Palestinian Islamic militant group Hamas and the Lebanese-based Hezbollah. Both groups were considered by much of the Western world as terrorist organisations and Putin's overtures openly defied the United States. Ironically, Putin was favoured by the West in 1999 and 2000 over Primakov because the latter was considered more anti-Western but Putin's policies reflected a subtle veering away from Primakov's pragmatic world view to an ideologically hostile position. Primakov had emphasised multi-polarity as a substitute for US or unipolar hegemony which required the cooperation and harmonisation of many poles, including Europe, China and India as well as Russia and the United States. This was a vision of a multi-directional foreign policy in which Russia would be strengthened by its location as a natural geo-strategic bridge among the poles, and specifically between Asia and the West. Therefore, according to Primakov, excellent relations with Europe were necessary for the revival of Russia's international role, as was continued coordination and cooperation with the United States. Primakov's ultra-pragmatism did not place or require the same emphasis on a Russian national ideology in its foreign policy as became the case under Putin because it undermined a realist approach to international political issues.

Putin's slow but sure foreign policy drift eventually created a distance not only with the United States but also with the European Union, which was seen as an important potential ally by Primakov, as it was by the pro-democracy opponents of Putin. With the fading of dissident voices in Russia under Putin there were few who openly questioned Moscow's reorientation in national values and consequently international outlook. Criticisms were mostly heard by those residing outside the country by figures such as Arkady Moshes, who was the director of the Russia-EU Institute of International Relations at the Finnish Institute. Moshes complained that: 'Some people tend to conclude that integration into Europe will strip Russia of its influence in the immediate region, not to mention around the world, and turn it into a second-rate power even on the continental scale.'[50] In an obvious reference to Putin's policies, he warned that Russia's growing isolationism from 'Europe is not accompanied by a build-up of its own influence, contrary to the logic of those who support its independence from institutional restrictions. Russia is losing its positions in the former Soviet republics and will most likely see a further loss of its international power.' Moshes encouraged Moscow's leadership to 'reject its position as an external player toward the EU and attempt to influence the system from the inside the way leading European powers do'.[51]

The problem for Russia, as Moshes pointed out, was that Moscow would have to adhere to the economic, political and social standards expected by the EU, which the Kremlin and the ruling elite considered to be another form of intrusive universalism that was no more desirable than the US version. Moscow's defensiveness led to a changed European attitude towards Russia creating genuine fears about a new authoritarian and militaristic regime with unknown ambitions. Should Russia continue to be 'an alien body for the Europeans—a Nigeria or Algeria, for example, in the Siberian style—it is natural to expect that Europe will resort to an egoistic policy toward it', warned Moshes, that is 'aimed only at winning access to Russia's sources of natural wealth and transit routes, as well as stripping it of natural competitive advantages. Simultaneously, the Europeans will seal themselves off from the associated risks of cooperating with Moscow.'[52] Comparing Russia to Nigeria, Algeria or any other fairly large authoritarian developing world state, however sensationalist, was deliberately stated to illuminate Russia's own insecurities about its values and to underline the perceived gulf between Europe and Russia.

Strong geographic bonds and shared history between Russia and the rest of Europe did not prevent some Europeans from highlighting the differences in values and culture between them. One Western academic study, for example, had found that while in Germany only 10 per cent of people thought it desirable to have a strong leader the figure in Russia was 52 per cent. A higher than average 60 per cent of Russians thought it was not their personal responsibility but the responsibility of the state to make their 'neighbourhood beautiful and prosperous'.[53] The implication that the Russian personality preferred to be led rather than assume self-responsibility was obvious enough. Such observations implied that Russians could not be trusted enough with full freedom and needed a strong regime to put order in their lives.

This lack of faith transcended beyond the social and cultural and into the political. Senior Western figures such as Strobe Talbott who served as ambassador at large and special adviser to the secretary of state for the new independent states of the former Soviet Union in the US Department of State from 1993 to 2001 and Sir Roderic Lyne who was British ambassador in Moscow between 2000 and 2004 reflected such concerns in their assessment of Russia's post-Soviet transition. They noted that during Yeltsin's first years as president, 'The worst nightmare of Western governments was that Russia might fall apart, leaving a vast and important area of the world in a state of disorder and economic collapse, without secure control of her arsenal of weapons of mass destruction.'[54] The authors, who were joined in these views by former Japanese ambassador to Moscow Koji Watanabe, were candid about these fears and more crucially about what Western leaders had hoped for in light of this insecurity about Russia. Washington, London, Tokyo and other Western political capitals ultimately 'wanted Russia not to be weak but to be strong, orderly and prosperous—in their own interests, and for very obvious reasons'.[55] There seemed to be a convergence therefore between what realist Western policy makers wanted and what Russian's themselves began to establish in the time of Putin. But who would determine the features of the true Russia considering there were so many views on the subject? In this context order became the safest remaining option and inevitably its meaning became closely intertwined with political power and strength.

In a similar vein the Putin era did not encourage a meaningful debate on Russian identity in the post-Soviet era that allowed for greater democratisation but reverted into conservative and traditional views. Putin, however, succeeded in solving the short-term goal of strengthening the state and bringing a degree of order to the nation's political life by deliberately undermining a diversity of perspectives. Russians under Putin had largely come to an agreement, if the national media was to be believed, about the two fundamental values of love for Putin as the image of a strong leader and love for Russia as a strong state.

The stability and relative successes of the Putin presidency, particularly during his second term, were partially due to good fortune because high energy prices, reaching record levels, allowed for a degree of prosperity among a larger number of Russians better than ever before. During Putin's first term in office 'the average Russian saw a 26 per cent annual growth in income, whereas the average Chinese saw only a 10 per cent rise'.[56] The revenues from energy exports also allowed the government to invest in large-scale re-militarisation to consolidate the perception of Russia as a great power and in turn enhance Putin's prestige as a great world leader. Putin placed the economy high on the list of both domestic and international politics and preserved much of what was established under Yeltsin, who 'linked controls on international weapons transfers to Russian commercial interests' in his first State of the Union address.[57] For all the criticisms against Putin for stifling democracy and discarding human rights there were strong arguments in support of his leadership because the political and economic stability that was achieved created solid foundations for a modern, evolving and developing state that could democratise as the nation became more comfortable in its own skin.

The Putin era ensured that the communists were marginalised and consumerism became ingrained in a new generation of Russians, serving as a powerful propeller of social and political individualism. There was, as an example, a new vibrant pop culture among young Russians that typically encouraged freedom of expression and individualistic ideals.

There was immense national pride at Russia winning the Eurovision Song Contest in 2008 by the contestant Dima Bilan even though in Britain and other Western states this was considered a rather dubious honour. Authoritarian rule allowed for stability which gave Russia the time it so urgently needed to construct a mature, balanced and more objective evaluation of its values in light of its disorientating Soviet experience. These were at least the arguments that Putin's supporters would have endorsed and espoused and they found strong sympathy in some Western quarters.

Regardless of the debate and the validity of arguments, the changes in Russia had a negative impact on international affairs. In the Middle East, as elsewhere, the Russian experience under Putin indirectly strengthened authoritarian regimes by showing that rapid democratisation was a guaranteed road to chaos if it directly challenged the existing status quo in seeking more freedom. This was a particular blow to US stated plans under President George W. Bush to spread democracy in the Middle East. Western idealism had in the aftermath of the Cold War expected authoritarian and tyrannical regimes which were propped up by the competing superpowers to tumble. Expectations in the 1990s of a democratic domino effect spanning the Middle East and the former Soviet space failed to materialise and Putin's Russia showed, to the contrary, that authoritarianism was reversing the Western democratic tide. Russia became more authoritarian by the end of Putin's second presidential term, as did most of its former Soviet neighbours aside from the Baltic Republics and to some extent Ukraine. In the Middle East Moscow increasingly gravitated towards authoritarian soul-mates such as Syria and Iran. A more serious criticism was that the Putin leadership gave these regimes the impetus to survive and become stronger, undermining reform and peace in the region as a whole.

The weakness in the arguments of Putin's supporters was the positivist assumption that stability and time would lead to a better and more democratic political system, whereas the trend revealed that the authoritarianism required for stability only created impetus for more authoritarianism and political and social restrictions. This trend led to a more confrontational Russian foreign policy in the Middle East as well as in other regions, including Europe, which further heightened Moscow's sense of international encirclement in a downward cycle of suspicion and paranoia. In 2008 Putin's policies left his successor President Dmitry Medvedev in an awkward international position. Medvedev's first term as president was noted for the overbearing influence of Putin, then serving as prime minister, on major military and foreign policy decisions. Putinism had successfully ensured that President Medvedev was merely an instrument of its system and set of values. Surely enough Putin returned to the Russian presidency in 2012 as the chief bulwark against the tide of democratic reform and change in Russia and this was transposed in the nation's policy towards the Middle East.

A Great Power foreign policy?

In light of the evolution of Russia's political order under Putin into a vertical system and the steady attempts to construct a unifying national identity, the foreign policy sphere was consequently unable to immunise itself against being directly impacted by the transformation. As the values of Putin's Russia became more systematically fused into society and the pressure to conform became more intense a strong hand was deemed necessary to maintain order and loyalty to the state among Russia's diverse ethnic and religious peoples. The challenge of a significant Muslim population in the context of the anti-Russian rebellion in the Caucasus required special consideration and Russian foreign policy makers could not ignore the six predominantly Muslim former Soviet republics located over its southern borders, although Kazakhstan blocked land access to the four other Central Asian Republics. The very early telescopic vision of Russia joining the Western family because it considered it as the source of its natural cultural heritage while cutting all its ties with the East, including the Muslim world and the Middle East, had become irrelevant.

The pragmatic pro-Western mood evident since 1993 was replaced by Primakov's neither East nor West approach that viewed the international system as being based on geo-strategic multi-polar alliances. Russia's geographic location, its size and its composition were ideal for bridge-building between the Eastern Chinese and Indian poles and the Western European pole, as well as the United States pole. This was a positive image of the world but in the realism of international politics where competition and rivalry were inevitable Russia's location also placed it in a position of great influence because it could manipulate the balance of powers, depending on which pole it chose to move closer to. As the

United States was by far the most powerful state, which, acting unilaterally, went against Russia's interests, it was natural for Moscow to consider China as an important partner to balance the international system. Taking into account the expansion of NATO, which placed Europe as an integral ally of the US, Primakov promoted the possibility of expanding the Russian-Chinese counter-balance to include significant poles such as India and, most controversially, Iran because of its essential geo-strategic location, bearing in mind its proximity to the Caucasus, Central Asia and the energy-rich seas of the Caspian and the Persian Gulf. Iran also possessed significant regional political influence because of its alliance with Syria and its support for militant Palestinian groups. Iran also provided material backing to Arab Shi'is in Lebanon, Iraq and Yemen.

This global outlook inherited by Putin was the framework to build on in the following decade but with the progression that took place in Russia's political culture and system this approach was modified with a change in emphasis in two key ways. First, on an international level, the previous emphasis on a pragmatic, multi-polar system in which Russia was virtually a neutral component that manoeuvred to ensure that unilateralism did not dominate or that other poles did not form blocs against it was modified with a greater emphasis on a foreign policy that demanded respect and consideration for Russia, along with its Russianness, and its rightful role and place in the world. In 2012 President Putin led a Russia that shifted from the pragmatic nationalist centrist position a decade earlier to a pragmatic but ideologically anti-Western Russia.

Domestically, while in the 1990s Primakov's approach sought to extract the foreign policy domain from the fierce debate and political struggle between the communists and ultra-nationalists on the one side and the pro-Western radical democrats on the other, hence the non-ideological flavour to the Primakov Doctrine, Putin gradually oversaw a tightening grip by the Kremlin on foreign policy with a more prominent Russian ideological undertone. In a sense, while foreign policy throughout the 1990s was considered more fractious and unclear in its motives and organisation it was also arguably closer to a foreign policy-making process of a democratic country, where different interest groups and forces competed, often openly, for influence.

Putin promoted the idea of a foreign policy of a great Russian power and state in his image, or at least of the political system he nurtured that had its seeds in the Yeltsin era. This was possible because of support since the 1990s among most Russians, 75 per cent according to one study, for some form of state ideology to be adopted.[58] *Derzhavnost* ('great-power-ness') and *gosudarstvennichestvo* ('statecentred-ness') were the central pillars of this new state ideology with an emphasis on Russian greatness and uniqueness. A word of caution is necessary at this point when thrusting forward public opinion surveys as a tool to justify the actions of the Putin leadership: both Russian and Western observations tended to not question adequately the reasons for such favourable responses to Putin's leadership, which could be positive purely because of a lingering fear by those questioned of undermining the authority of the state and its leader. People want to please those in authority and say what they think their leaders would like to hear. But these same people could change their responses if leaders change or their policies begin to display flaws. Putin's overall popularity, for example, clearly diminished in 2012, highlighting a palpable change in public attitudes.

Russian supporters of Putin persevered in their insistence that democracy was preserved under his leadership and that he merely pursued a policy that reflected the national will, rejecting any suggestion of a creeping authoritarianism. Putin's greatest achievement was simply to replace the chaos of the Yeltsin years with order, which ordinary Russians craved for, and a more rational assessment of Russia's place in the world. In a frank assessment Putin stated that: 'We are well aware of how the world has changed and we have a realistic sense of our own opportunities and potential.'[59] This view was shared by some Western politicians and academics who also rejected the notion of creeping authoritarianism in Russia and instead adopted the term 'managed democracy' to describe the political system under Putin.

In simple terms, this meant that while Putinism stretched all the given notions of democracy to the absolute limits, including highly questionable results for parliamentary elections at the end of 2011 and presidential elections in 2012, they were nonetheless still within acceptable boundaries. So while critics of Putin such as Garry Kasparov, the chess legend, were allowed to criticise the President in street protests such oppositionists had to be willing to accept intimidation and harassment by the political elite and efforts by the security services to silence them. This facetious proposition merely highlighted that the debate about whether Russia was undergoing authoritarian modernisation or a managed democracy process under Putin was reminiscent of the Byzantine arguments about the gender of angels, especially as authoritarianism was a description that encompassed a wide range of regimes. In the Middle East, for example, Egypt, Jordan and Syria were all considered authoritarian despite ritualised parliamentary elections and theoretical multi-party political life; yet among that range of countries monarchist Jordan was far more liberal than the rigid Syrian authoritarianism with Mubarak's Egypt lying somewhere in between. Ultimately all three Middle East states, like Russia, did not meet Western standards of democracy, human rights and liberal freedoms, making the term managed democracy rather obsolete.

The transformation in style and substance of Russian politics over the decades was reflected in foreign policy through Moscow's desire under Putin to make a show of Russia's military strength and diplomatic leverage in the international order. Part of this show was intended for the domestic audience, to boost the credibility of the Kremlin and the Russian state, but to some extent it was also a reaction based on the revision of the way the world was viewed. Up until the mid-1990s Moscow 'overestimated the impact of international law, as well as the authority and benevolence of those international organizations, such as the IMF, the G-7…and even NATO'.[60] Putin and his associates shared a different mindset that was convinced that Russia was in a world characterised by fierce competition. Among those credited with the rise of Unity and Putin was Sergei Shoigu, who was appointed as a member of Russia's Security Council in 1993 and remained an influential figure in the Russian ruling security and political network. He did not mince words when he stated: 'We have no reason to frighten the whole world, but we should force them to take us into account. Then they will take notice of us and speak with us as equals.'[61] Soon after Putin's re-election as President in 2012 Shoigu was appointed as minister of defence, perhaps the most difficult and sensitive ministry to manage in the Russian government. Shoigu, like Primakov and Chubais, has revealed incredible powers of political survival. All enjoyed influence as Kremlin insiders under Yeltsin and later on under presidents Putin and Medvedev. Such perseverance not only serves as an indicator of continuity but also of the rather narrow circle of decision making in three decades of Russian policy making.

Putin's political style has been unique and largely effective, often countering tough statements with conciliatory remarks. Putin focused on the need for consolidation, normality and political management rather than revolutions, transformations and radical actions. As an indicator of his character Putin told his people in a nationwide TV interview on his fiftieth birthday: 'I would like to remind you that I am a lawyer and I think that one's actions should be based on law, and not revolutionary expediency.'[62] Yet as the Kremlin tightened its grip on political power, Russian cabinet ministers in the government were presented as conformist technocrats rather than politicians. In the televised segments of cabinet meetings ministers stood obediently as Putin entered the room to take his seat at the head of the table, and the general presentation was more of a professional meeting by a board of directors reporting to the company chief executive, rather than an exchange of views to tackle pressing political matters and state strategy.

An important distinction between Putin's foreign policy and his predecessors was the greater centrality economic interests were allocated in the foreign policy domain, often overriding traditional political relations with countries. The instrumentalist approach to the process of government was extended to the foreign policy domain, with Putin frequently pointing out 'that Russia's foreign policy should serve the country's economic interests'.[63] This innocuous claim subtly suggested a steely intent to broaden the sphere of Russian influence to wherever the country's economic interests demanded. In the oil and gas sectors, for example, this meant more intrusive activity not only in the former Soviet republics but also in the Middle East and Europe. Military sales and supplies were also given high priority under Putin as part of the national economic revival although such transactions, with China and the Middle East in particular, were naturally to have a damaging impact on Russia's relations with the West. Russia's delivery of sophisticated arms to Syria was a good example where there was a direct consequence on Moscow's international reputation and standing.

The identifiable features of Russian politics under Putin gave the impression that Moscow was an emerging threat but cautious pragmatism typically prevailed. Russia did not shift from a radical pro-Western position in 1992 to a radical anti-Western position by the end of the Putin era. Under Putin Russia was transformed from the pragmatic pro-Western position of the mid-1990s to a pragmatic but difficult and sometimes uncooperative position with generous servings of measured anti-Western rhetoric. Yet it remained at its core pragmatic, meaning that the elite continued to understand the wisdom of avoiding a full-scale military, political and economic confrontation with the West. Nonetheless, while Shoigu spoke of forcing the West to treat Russia equally, Putin said the same thing but in more reserved language: 'Russia should be treated as a "normal" great power.'[64]

The fear persisted that Putin, much as was his public style, was a man whose softly spoken manner disguised a ruthless and ambitious mentality. The rhetoric by Putin, Shoigu and others in the Russian elite betrays a deep sense of hostility and resentment towards the West as well as notions of grandeur. The West was arguably weak in facing up to Putin, and Moscow's reaction to a more forceful Western position was never tested. As prime minister in 2008, soon after completing his presidential term, Putin's brazen belligerence was exposed by ordering a military invasion of Georgia, taking the world by surprise. Despite Western mediation efforts Putin's stubborn and militaristic mindset shone through to confirm the self-assured buoyancy he had in his and Russia's power. It was just one example of the West letting Putin get his way.

5

A COHESIVE FOREIGN POLICY FOR A DISORDERED WORLD

When Putin became president in May 2000 Russia faced an international climate filled with emerging dangers and lingering traditional threats. The Putin years were marked by fears of encirclement based on classic geo-strategic concerns stemming from the ascending Chinese powerhouse in the East, rivalry between nuclear-armed India and Pakistan to the south, and, to the west, Moscow watched with unease the prospect of further NATO expansion. The NATO encroachment was made more threatening by the US determination 'to install an anti-ballistic missile (ABM) system in Eastern Europe that Moscow consider[ed] both unnecessary and provocative'.[1] Through Russia's eyes the old enemy the United States appeared to be driven by a refreshed zeal to unilaterally extend its influence without limits, leading to genuine uncertainty in Moscow about Washington's true global ambitions. Over the course of the decade Putin's leadership was best characterised by a relentless effort to create a strong and cohesive state as a prerequisite for defending national interests in the world and this approach was widely supported among his compatriots and beyond.

Putin's first term as president encountered a new global challenge resulting from the US-declared global war on terrorism. Russia and the United States had during the Clinton-Yeltsin era identified an expanding network of Islamic terrorism rooted in Afghanistan but the attacks on the World Trade Center buildings in New York and the Pentagon in

Washington DC on 11 September 2001 took the world by surprise and radically changed the international scene. The attackers were associated with an extremist brand of Sunni Islam that consisted of active cells around the world, posing an equal danger to the security of countries both in the East and the West. Russia, the United States and other countries in the world were victims of audacious yet murderous attacks and in most cases the perpetrators were usually an international mixture of people united by a shared hatred for Western values and a goal to rid what they considered to be Muslim-inhabited territories of non-Islamic occupiers.

From Russia's viewpoint the international instability from 2001 and internal rebellion in the Caucasus meant that Moscow's unstable security zones in the former Soviet Union among neighbouring countries became areas of particular concern in light of what was then controversially termed the clash of civilisations. Central Asia, the Caucasus and neighbours to the West such as Ukraine and Estonia represented different types of challenges for Russia, ranging from hostile regimes to fervent Russo-phobia, particularly in light of the large Russian populations living in surrounding countries. The Putin leadership had legitimate reason to feel at the time that Russia's world seemed to be falling apart around them.

Putin's political ascent and enhanced authority owed substantial credit to his strong rhetoric and firm action in confronting Russia's already existing terrorist threat that was based in the Caucasus and primarily inflamed by the Chechen insurgency. Yet the events of 11 September 2001 created a convenient convergence of objectives between the United States and Russia that aided Putin's political rise. According to one analysis at the time 'Putin, of course, has good reason to show solidarity with Washington—at least for now. Russia's president is keen to link America's new battle against terrorism with his own country's campaign against rebels in Chechnya.'[2] This cooperation was not risk-free and potentially antagonised the hundreds of millions of Muslims living in or around Russia. Moreover, Washington's view of the world and its international behaviour became more belligerent and uncompromising, particularly in the Middle East, in response to the 11 September attacks, eventually posing a difficult dilemma for Russian foreign policy under Putin. Did the situation resulting in 11 September 2001 mean that Moscow was resigned to follow Washington's lead in the Middle

East and towards Muslims? If so, what were the costs to Russian interests? What were the risks to its national security?

Putin, Bush and Islamic terror

Putin's election as Russian president in spring 2000 was followed later in that same year by the election of George W. Bush, inaugurated in January 2001 as the forty-third US president. The two presidents in Moscow and Washington DC, the former Cold War capitals, led their respective countries in a parallel time-span but with the benefit of hindsight it eventually became obvious that Russia under Putin did not adopt a similar view of the nature of Islamic terrorism as well as regarding other threats to global security that were highlighted by the United States. Raising the priority status of international Islamic terrorism on Russia's foreign policy agenda was made temporarily unavoidable only because the Chechen conflict had become a magnate for non-Chechen Islamic militants to enter the Russian Federation, which undermined national security. Russia also feared that such movements would spread from Afghanistan into Tajikistan and other parts of Central Asia, yet on the whole Moscow believed that combating these groups would remain a localised affair.

During the Cold War era there were transparently identifiable local non-state actors fighting for national or ideological causes, such as the Palestine Liberation Organisation. The modern global challenge of Islamic terrorism was more complex, with its membership being scattered around the world. Operationally, the effectiveness of these groups was made easier by rapidly developing technologies such as satellite communications and the internet. The United States unified the scattered network of terrorist cells under the heading of Al-Qaeda, which in 2001 was based in Taliban-ruled Afghanistan. After the US-led invasion of Afghanistan in late 2001 and the toppling of the Taliban, Al-Qaeda members became dispersed, mostly settling in Pakistan, Iraq, Syria, Yemen and Iran. Initially, Washington placed Al-Qaeda as the greatest single threat to US national security only to amalgamate this danger, offering dubious evidence, with Iraq in 2002 and 2003 to justify the military occupation of the country and the toppling of the regime there.

During the first term of the Bush presidency, Washington's policy espoused fighting militant Islam and regimes linked with terrorism in any part of the world, even when it did not directly threaten the territory of the United States, because of moral, strategic and economic implications: morally, because the ideology challenged universal human values and the development of democracies and tolerant societies; strategically because such movements threatened to topple Western allies in Muslim countries; and economically because Islamic extremism posed a direct danger to international energy supplies in vital regions and the worldwide free movement of trade.

Beyond the ideological differences the initial support and sympathy Russia offered to the United States following the 11 September 2001 attacks gave way to intensifying rivalry that was most prominent in the Middle East because of a distinct divergence of views between Washington and Moscow towards the militant forms of Shi'a and Wahhabi Islam. Putin and Bush largely agreed on the unacceptability of the latter but Moscow conveniently minimised the Iranian-led Shi'a threat to the Middle East region and beyond. During Putin's first term the differences between Washington and Moscow were less pronounced until the toppling of the Saddam Hussein regime in 2003, when Iran emerged as a dominant regional power that effectively undermined the standing of the United States in the Middle East. The contrast in perspectives between Russia and the United States towards Iran and the wider militant Shi'a threat that developed during the Putin era revealed a deep-seated mutual mistrust between the two countries.

Putin and Bush were in many ways very different characters in their public image. The Russian president was reserved, calm and somewhat detached while his US counterpart was emotional and impulsive. Although not originally from Texas, Bush adopted the stereotypical Texan attribute of wearing his heart on his sleeve and his 'you are either with us or against us' remark made in the context of the US-declared war against international terrorism in 2001 became a trademark stamp of his presidency that was indicative of his foreign policy style and approach. This was most apparent during his first term in office but diminished towards the end of his leadership as US credibility in the Middle East became severely tested. In contrast, one of the most striking features of Russian foreign policy under Putin was its consistency and pragmatism throughout his presidency, despite the diverse range of threats facing the country. The framework and much of the language of this foreign policy was inherited from the late Yeltsin era under the direction of Primakov but as Putin's grip on power tightened his personal influence on the style and conduct of foreign policy became increasingly distinguishable.

Despite the characteristic differences, Putin shared with Bush the same ruthlessness in their early years in power in their handling of the threats to their respective countries posed by Islamic terrorism, although each president acted in a different setting. The challenge of Islamic terrorism, sometimes erroneously portrayed as a transnational phenomenon that emerged in the post-Cold War era, was in fact first violently encountered by Washington in the wake of the 1979 Islamic Revolution in Iran that was led by Ayatollah Ruhollah Khomeini. The radical Islamic ideology in Iran challenged neighbouring Arab Gulf and predominantly Sunni countries that were rich in oil and gas reserves. Among the defining features of the revolutionary regime in Tehran was the feverish anti-Americanism at the core of its ideology. The Reagan administration during the 1980s was especially disturbed by Iranian backing for regional militant groups, including Hezbollah, based in Lebanon, which conducted a spree of hostage-taking, suicide bombings and other attacks against Western interests, including the 1983 coordinated suicide bombings that killed over 300 US and French servicemen.

Accusations against Hezbollah for its role in Lebanese and international terrorism were confirmed, according to its critics, following the mysterious assassination in Damascus, Syria, of Imad Mughniyeh in February 2008. Renowned for his central role in organising many kidnappings and bombings for three decades from the 1980s, the Hezbollah leadership openly mourned him, after years of purposeful ambiguity about his relationship with the group, as one of its most treasured sons and the party's secretary-general Hassan Nasrallah, in eulogising his death, revealed that he had been one of Hezbollah's most senior military commanders since its founding in 1982.[3]

Hezbollah's claim that its only goal was to end Israeli occupation in Lebanon and denials that it harboured greater regional ambitions were undermined when the group forcefully occupied Beirut and the surrounding mountain areas in May 2008 to alter the political balance in the country in its favour. The incident strengthened suspicions that it was a proxy group acting at Iran's behest during growing tensions between Tehran and the United States over the former's nuclear programme. A further blow to Hezbollah's reputation and claims was struck following confirmation by Nasrallah in 2012 in a live television speech on the party's channel that Hezbollah fighters were actively fighting in Syria against rebels. In early 2013 media reports suggested that some 5,000 Hezbollah fighters were deployed in Syria to fight on behalf of the crumbling Asad regime.[4]

It was highly significant, therefore, that from the onset Russia's foreign policy under Putin era aligned with the radical Shi'a Islam in Iran, which was a primary sponsor of militant anti-Western groups, including Hezbollah. Moscow also coordinated with Syria, a close ally of Iran and arms supplier to Hezbollah, in order to impede Western support for the 2005 Cedar Revolution in Lebanon. Because Moscow did not have the military and economic means or influence to directly challenge the United States its strategy was to often act as hidden saboteur by adopting a range of tactics such as blocking UN Security Council Resolutions or backing regimes that were energetically seeking to undermine the United States in the region by diplomatic efforts or through arms sales. Russia's task was made easier by the hasty US build-up to the war against Iraq in 2003 and the ineffective and negligent administration of the country during the military occupation after the toppling of the Saddam Hussein regime.

In parallel to the radical and militant Shi'a Islam promoted by the Iranian regime thousands of members of radical and militant Islamic movements from many Arab and Muslim countries had converged in Afghanistan in the 1980s, with Saudi funding and tacit US encouragement, to defeat the Soviet army which invaded the country at the end of 1979. These Jihadis, as they came to be known, were trained in guerrilla warfare and their experience of the rugged Afghani terrain against a well-armed opponent created efficient, battle-hardened and determined fighters united by a mission to evict the infidel communist presence from a Muslim country. Their eventual success forced the Soviet withdrawal from Afghanistan under Gorbachev, signifying an admission of defeat by the mighty Red Army, which gave these fighters great confidence to set wider aims and to expand their ambitions. In alliance with the Afghani Taliban movement the global Jihadis took control of most of Afghanistan during the 1990s. One of the lasting consequences of the Afghan war was that it solidified the bond of Sunni Muslim guerrillas from different nationalities fighting for the same cause and thus created a coordinated military network. As a result Muslims from geographic zones spanning from Algeria in the Maghreb to Pakistan and reaching Indonesia in the East coordinated within the framework of a global combative Islamic ideology. This network, inspired by an ascetic form of Islam rooted in Saudi Arabia, began to expand its activities beyond Afghanistan in 1989, after the Soviet withdrawal, unsuccessfully attempting with local allies to topple the military regime in Algeria in the early 1990s. Soon after, Jihadi cells actively sought but failed to infiltrate the Muslim Bosnian fighters in the Balkans following the disintegration of Yugoslavia. There were also targeted attacks against US interests in and around the Arabian Peninsula that were attributed to cells from this network throughout the 1990s.

The Afghani-graduate guerrillas contrasted with the political and military activities of long existing groups such as the Muslim Brotherhood of Egypt or Hamas in the Palestinian territories during the 1980s, with both latter cases largely focusing on their specific national struggles. Egypt's Muslim Brotherhood enjoyed significant popular support and influence for decades as well as official recognition. The pervasive presence of the Muslim Brotherhood in Egyptian politics was further underlined after the election victory of Mohammad Mursi as president in 2012 to replace the deposed Hosni Mubarak. Mursi was the Muslim Brotherhood candidate and the group also simultaneously dominated parliament to consolidate powerful sway in Egyptian politics.

When President Anwar Sadat signed the Camp David Peace Treaty with Israel in 1978, radical and violent splinter groups detached from the mainstream Muslim Brotherhood. A militant faction of the Brotherhood was accused of carrying out the assassination of Sadat in October 1981. The combination of the Egyptian-Israeli Peace Treaty and the Soviet invasion of Afghanistan in the late 1970s created a sense of passive helplessness towards external non-Islamic powers over the wider Muslim world. This mood facilitated the rise and evolution of radical Islamic movements, both Sunni and Shi'a, which sought to uproot the existing status quo in the region and consequently replaced radical secular movements, including leftist revolutionary groups that had been the dominant opposition since the 1950s.

The eruption of the Chechen War in the early 1990s proved to be a powerful magnate that attracted Jihadis who were veterans of the Afghan war. Originally the struggle for Chechen independence, led by army General Djokar Dudaev, was nationalist in character and was part of a tradition of war and rebellion dating back to Tsarist Russia. By the time Putin was elected president the war was characterised by the Kremlin and the media in Russia as part of a wider Muslim menace that was popularly referred to by Russians as Wahhabi terrorism. A Russian commentary explained that, typically, 'Wahhabi is the term used in Russia for all supporters of radical Islam.'[5] This definition was flawed because of a classic Russian tendency to view the world through its own cultural and traditionalist telescope. In fact, there were many forms of radical Islam that were not Wahhabi. Among Sunnis, for example, there were Salafi groups that were sometimes revolutionary and militant but distinct from Wahhabism. Another feature was that not all Salafi groups were necessarily militant, but rather believed that the ideal way of life was attainable by peacefully and precisely emulating the life of the Prophet Muhammad by segregating themselves from the modern material world. The Russian explanation also failed to consider the Western viewpoint shared by many moderate Muslims that the radical Shi'a groups sponsored by the revolutionary regime in Iran harboured similar hostility to non-Muslim ways and potentially posed an equal challenge to international stability as radical Sunni militant movements.

The global Sunni network that was based in Afghanistan and known as Al-Qaeda in the United States and other Western countries was under the ideological leadership of the Egyptian cleric Ayman Al-Zawahiri and the wealthy Saudi citizen of Yemeni origin, Osama Bin Laden. The two men became household names in the United States after televised pictures of the planes flying into and destroying the two World Trade Center towers became deeply imprinted images in American minds at the start of the millennium after the 11 September 2001 attacks. The shock that the financial capital of the world's remaining superpower was such a vulnerable target had a strong impact on public opinion by consolidating the belief in the West that the main threat to the international system was no longer classic inter-state rivalry but the transnational terrorist menace. The US reaction to the attacks was swift in mobilising a large multinational military operation in Afghanistan in October 2001 which replaced the Taliban regime with a new US-friendly government in Kabul in 2002.

The war declared by President Bush against Islamic terrorism and Al-Qaeda was well received in Moscow, particularly as it offered moral and practical justifications for its own war in Chechnya. The events of

11 September 2001 halted the pattern of decline in bilateral relations that was set at the end of the Yeltsin era and 'US-Russian relations seemed to take a decisive turn for the better again…Optimism emerged that Russia had decided that it truly belonged in the West.'[6] However, Bush's declaration of a global war on terror in his State of the Union speech on 29 January 2002 revealed much wider US ambitions and marked the initiation of a new aggressive foreign policy, described as the Bush Doctrine, which labelled Iran, Iraq and North Korea as part of an axis of evil. The Bush Doctrine implied that pre-emptive attacks on sovereign states were excusable if deemed necessary to protect national security and international order. This marked a shift away from the trend of US policy during his father's presidency, George H. Bush, when it was 'undergoing a post-cold war transformation' that made 'collective goals on a multilateral basis…a cornerstone of US foreign policy'.[7]

In Moscow, Putin had cynically exploited the behaviour of Chechen rebels and used the September 2001 attacks to stoke up traditional Russian Islamophobia in order to extract Western favour and enhance his own position as a nationalistic leader. The Kremlin's manipulation of public opinion was easy to do in light of prevalent Russian hostility towards Muslims in the Yeltsin and Putin eras. As a minor indication of this mood, leaders of the largely Muslim Republic of Tatarstan within the Russian Federation were driven to complain to the Russian Ministry of Education in an official memo about 'numerous aspects of the textbook literature…connected to old clichés and interpretations [which] revolve around a failure to adequately address the multiethnic and multicultural foundations of Russian civilisations'.[8] Putin's calculated reaction to Islamic terrorism came despite concerns that a shift 'toward authoritarian nationalism based on Russian Orthodoxy or ethnicity would deepen conflict with Russia's own substantial Muslim minority and with the rapidly growing Muslim populations in Central Asia'.[9] This outward convergence of values with the Bush administration was too eagerly accepted in the West and neglected to adequately evaluate Moscow's true motives for its stance.

Over the course of time the reality of a large Muslim population within the Russian Federation, combined with a revised foreign policy, led to a more cautious approach by Putin during his second term. Evolving Russian strategy required courting the Islamic Republic of Iran and Palestinian Hamas without undermining the obvious advantages of promoting trade with wealthy Arab states such as Saudi Arabia and this resulted in a new approach by Moscow towards Muslim countries by the end of Putin's first term. A positive outcome of this new approach was when Russia was granted, with Saudi backing, observer status at the Organization of the Islamic Conference in 2007. During the Conference in Senegal on 13 March 2008 the participating Russian foreign minister, Sergei Lavrov, conveyed Putin's message that 'deeper relations of friendship and cooperation with the Islamic world are Russia's strategic course. That is why we note with pleasure that ...our constructive cooperation with the Muslim world acquired a new dynamic.'[10] The message was a culmination of a revised course of Russian foreign policy from 2003.

US-Russian divergence

Bush's declared war against Islamist terrorism was intended to be, in principle at least, a rallying call for enlightened liberal democratic societies to defend themselves and their future existence from an onslaught by violent, repressive ideologies hiding behind a mask of religious interpretation. Bush's State of the Union address to the nation in 2002 tested the existing consensus when it was used as a pretext to attack and occupy Iraq, marking the start of a deepening rift in relations between Russia and the United States in the Middle East. The address to the nation in 2002 outlined the framework for the so-called Bush Doctrine, which introduced a reasoning that would allow for pre-emptive strikes against a state on the basis of the assessment of risk it presented to other states. More controversially, the intent of a state to harm the United States was considered a sufficient danger to national security despite uncertainty about its actual ability to implement plans. Bush justified occupation and regime change in a country that was considered as posing a danger to the United States.

The US-led military operation against Iraq was based on claims by the Washington administration, without providing solid evidence, that the Saddam Hussein regime was at an advanced stage of a nuclear programme and that the Iraqi leader was secretly stockpiling weapons of mass destruction, which if transferred to terrorist groups such as Al-Qaeda threatened national security and the international system as a whole. The occupation of Iraq in 2003 greatly enhanced, at least initially, the US geo-strategic position in the Middle East and beyond, which in the context of controlling the world's energy supplies had a global dimension and seen in the context of NATO expansion would potentially leave Russia surrounded by a hostile arc spanning from the Baltic Sea to Afghanistan and Pakistan. Moscow, while sympathetic when it came to Washington's reaction to the terrorist attacks in New York and Washington in September 2001, felt directly threatened by the invasion of Iraq and US policies in the Middle East and Europe thereafter.

One Russian politician and academic lamented that in light of 'the horrible shock that the American nation experienced on September 11 [...and] Following the legitimate and successful operation in Afghanistan, the United States—under a far-fetched pretext and without a UN Security Council sanction—invaded Iraq, seeking to "reformat" the entire Greater Middle East to suit its own economic, military and political interests.'[11] This regional reformatting was driven by a revived US idealism which promoted greater democratisation in the Middle East and the bringing down of stale Cold War regimes.

The Russian view was that the Bush Doctrine was a US ploy to expand its global reach and entrench its unrivalled global superpower status, using the war on terror as a pretext. The Bush Doctrine directly challenged Russia's Foreign Policy Concept, approved by Putin in 2000, and its 'rejection of new approaches and principles that belittled the role of the sovereign state'.[12] The new thinking in Washington, espoused fervently by influential neo-conservative decision-makers led by Vice President Dick Cheney and Secretary of Defense Donald Rumsfeld, defied the traditional norms of international politics and was considered particularly radical by the Putin leadership, which viewed 'foreign policy in predominantly geopolitical terms'.[13]

Moscow was deeply uneasy about Washington's unilateral eagerness to change the rules of the international game in the guise of democratisation and liberalisation. Putin was vehement that 'the implementation of those principles in any country must fit the conditions that are distinctive for that country'.[14] The emphasis and urgency placed on democratisation and the imposition of values such as human rights, individual liberty and economic liberalism was interpreted as a direct challenge by the political leadership in the Kremlin. Deputy Foreign Minister of the Russian Federation Alexander Saltanov warned in one interview that Washington's approach created more conflict and instability in the world due to the imposition of cultural hegemony. Saltanov pointed to a conference bringing world religious leaders to Russia, organised by Patriarch

Alexis II in July 2006, where Putin 'made a memorable speech at the opening ceremony' that focused on 'who is trying to stir up the so-called clash of civilisations. President Putin stressed the dangers of such moves [and instead promoted better] understanding between different civilisations, cultures, countries.'[15]

The character and features of international relations were, according to the Putin mind-set, very much tied to the nature of the political system as defined by distinct cultural values that determined prevailing attitudes towards the role of the state. In an interesting study by Gulnara Khasanova on the development of school textbooks in the Yeltsin and Putin eras, a common thread she found was 'the revival of the ideas of a single and indivisible Russia, great power status, imperial stereotypes and messianism...[as] dominant ideas in most textbooks'.[16] While Putin's policies preached understanding between cultures and nations it did not find an open, dynamic and fluid interaction between peoples, economies and ideas in the international system as particularly appealing. Moscow preferred discernible boundaries between systems and nations and considered each state in the world as a pyramid-like structure with international relations utilising diplomacy as the primary form of interaction between the political summits.

Russia's political, security and military elite never fully detached themselves from the Cold War era when the Soviet Union was a global player rivalling the United States in key regions of the world, including the Middle East. The US invasion of Iraq in 2003 was a major landmark that further reinvigorated proponents of a Soviet mentality under Putin. During the Cold War the limit of US power was Soviet power, as was the reverse. Many of the constraints faced by Washington were dismantled during the 1990s and the United States did not hesitate to press home its advantage as the sole remaining superpower after the Cold War, in Moscow's view, culminating in the invasion and occupation of Iraq.

Negative perceptions by Russia's post-Soviet elite towards the United States had their seeds sown during the Clinton administration and well before the Bush Doctrine. This disillusionment in Russia with the United States was not limited to ultra-nationalists and die-hard communists but permeated liberal and moderate circles, who complained that the US 'presumptuously challenged the new global system and embarked on a path of unilateral and arbitrary use of force'.[17] Washington's unilateralism in the world was doomed to failure, according to one

Russian analysis and its author suggested that as a result of US behaviour since the 1990s, 'An unprecedented growth of anti-American sentiments began throughout the world, along with a new wave of international terrorism and the proliferation of nuclear and missile weapons.'[18] The eye-catching aspect of this remark was the implication that international terrorism and the proliferation of weapons of mass destruction was a consequence of US unilateralism, contradicting Washington's justification for pre-emptive strikes and unilateral actions on the basis of the urgency required to deal with the global terrorist threat.

From Washington's perspective it was disappointment with Russia that led to the deterioration in bilateral relations. In light of Western fears about weapons proliferation and Moscow's lack of funds and organisational know-how in managing the potentially catastrophic risks US President George H Bush created the Cooperative Threat Reduction Program to provide support for Russia in controlling the vast Soviet nuclear arsenal it inherited. The United States also endorsed Russia's ownership of nuclear missile sites based in other former Soviet republics including the Ukraine and Kazakhstan despite suspicions that 'some of those with access to nuclear materials might engage in theft for economic gain due to their desperate financial situation' and a general dissatisfaction with the maximisation of the material support provided. Washington maintained that this was evidence of its genuine conviction regarding shared interests between Russia and the United States.[19] As a further sign of goodwill, Washington and its Western allies proactively endorsed the integrity of the Russian Federation in the 1990s, most notably by having 'refused to recognise Chechen independence' throughout the conflict.[20]

Yet Moscow continued to haggle, in the eyes of Washington's elite, over its willingness to downgrade its nuclear capacity and the number of missiles aimed towards Europe and the United States. There was no cause for optimism, as far as US leaders were concerned, in light of the unwillingness of the Russian Duma to ratify the Strategic Arms Reductions Treaty (START) II Treaty until 2000 even though the treaty was signed in 1993 and ratified by the US Senate in 1996. START I was important because of its focus on reducing first strike capabilities that was considered as a key component in easing mutual suspicions and promoting trust between the two countries. Russia withdrew from the Treaty in 2002 in protest over a range of US actions, including in the

Middle East but mainly in response to the announcement of a US missile defence system plans for Europe. The Strategic Offensive Reductions Treaty signed in Moscow in May 2002 was a significant alternative in the context of placing a cap on offensive nuclear weapons but the Putin leadership remained unconvinced however as to why the United States was so eagerly pursuing NATO expansion into Eastern Europe and why it sought to widen its missile capabilities in a way that left Russia strategically vulnerable. On 20 August 2008 a bilateral agreement for a US defence system to be established in Poland was signed between Warsaw and Washington after years of negotiations. The Russian elite at the time considered the agreement to be a hostile act, with General Anatoly Nogovitsyn warning that 'Poland, by deploying [the system] is exposing itself to a strike—100%.'[21]

From Washington's perspective the end of the Cold War left a void that needed to be filled by a new world order. The United Nations was criticised by Presidents Bill Clinton and George W. Bush in line with longstanding US disapproval of the world body for being prone to administrative mismanagement and corruption as well as the Security Council's failure to act decisively to tackle urgent issues due to abuse of the right of veto and political rivalry among the five permanent members. Because the United States considered itself as the leader of the free world and a beacon of democracy Washington's political leadership assumed moral responsibility to take the initiative in global security issues. The misconceived notion that this approach was initiated by Bush and the neo-conservatives after 2001 had failed to take into account US behaviour during the Clinton era, which shared the same conviction that US global leadership was necessary not only for protecting national security but also to maintain the stability of the international system and defending human rights simply because no other country or body existed that could do so. In fact, President Clinton at various stages under his leadership initiated a long list of military campaigns in the Balkans, Somalia, Haiti, Iraq and Sudan, in which forceful US actions took for granted that the rest of the world would follow its lead. The suspicion lingered in Moscow that the end of the Cold War was being treated as a US victory in which post-Soviet Russia was in a position of weakness.

An influential lobby of policy makers emerged in the United States in the 1990s, well before George W Bush was elected president, to counter the idealistic approach aiming to invest in the democratic forces of Russia by arguing that efforts to influence Russian internal affairs would be futile. This school of thought, referred to as the 'power balancers' argued 'that American leaders had to take advantage of Russian weakness to lock into place a balance of power in favor of the United States'.[22] This contrasted with the approach that 'Washington should make democracy promotion a bigger part of its assistance programs to Russia'[23] by emphasising security cooperation, economic reforms and trade agreements. The Bush administration vociferously promoted democratising the Middle East and the former Soviet states but distanced itself from interference in internal Russian affairs by turning a blind eye to the military campaigns in the Caucasus and general counter-democratic measures initiated by the Kremlin. Predictably, this aspect of Bush's policy was appreciated by the Putin leadership.

The emerging friction in relations between Russia and the United States during the 1990s was mainly aggravated by unilateral US actions and, rather ironically, as a result of Washington's desire for a strong leadership in Moscow. This was a response to fears that stemmed from the Gorbachev experience of a weak Western-friendly leader unable to lead his country with authority and so 'the authoritarian modernisation doctrine was offered to the team of Boris Yeltsin'.[24] Early evidence for this, according to one analysis, was Western support for Yeltsin's bombing of the Russian parliament in 1993 to stifle the mini-revolt led by communists and extreme nationalists. Simultaneously, Yeltsin marginalised and abandoned the liberal Westernisers, his original supporters, and asserted greater media control.

On the whole, the authoritarian modernisation model did not fully succeed under Yeltsin because of the uncontrollable mushrooming of corruption and general mismanagement so that: 'The Russian state surrendered its monopoly on the use of force on its own territory (not only to organised and disorganised crime but also increasingly to legally established private armies of big businesses).'[25] Putin's immediate aim therefore was to assure his people and the West that he was determined to strengthen the Russian state and to restore social, economic and political order. To do this successfully the post-Yeltsin leadership believed that it would be necessary to restore international prestige and influence. In this context the Middle East provided an excellent opportunity to challenge the United States because of the multitude of complex disputes there, which offered opportunities to re-enter the world stage with greater impact.

The controversy surrounding the invasion of Iraq and subsequent failures after 2003 conveniently allowed Putin to play the role of the sensible moderate. During the launch of the US-led military action against Iraq in March 2003 polls showed that '59 per cent of Russians believed that the United States was not a country friendly to Russia'.[26] The Kremlin, the Duma, academics and the media in Russia were united in severe attacks on the use by the Bush administration of 'false information to justify the invasion of Iraq, the flagrant violations of human rights under the occupation regime in Iraq... the biased trials over Iraqi leaders and their barbarous executions, obviously approved by Washington (in defiance of protests from Europe)—all these scandalous facts have besmirched the moral image of the United States.'[27] This provided plenty of ammunition to attack US policy, in tandem with partners in the Middle East and Europe, from the premise of defending international law and human rights.

The US invasion of Iraq also conveniently gifted Moscow the opportunity for sweet revenge after years of humiliating acquiescence on the sidelines of world affairs. The general lack of protest by Moscow against US behaviour around the world until the war in Iraq was largely because there was little importance attached to many of the regions where Washington was active and because of the unavoidable reality of Russian weakness and its inability to defy the United States at that time. It was only in the Balkans, due to the priority accorded to defending Serbia during Yeltsin's latter years, that Moscow openly criticised Washington's actions on the international stage.

The war against Iraq allowed Russians and many in Europe to become more vociferous in arguing that the unifying effect of the war against Al-Qaeda in Afghanistan was being erased by the controversial and divisive act of toppling the Saddam Hussein regime and installing a US-friendly counterpart in its place, particularly as it was done under the seemingly false pretext that Iraq was hiding weapons of mass destruction and concealing its potential for nuclear capability. Visceral anti-American sentiments and suspicions consequently became openly expressed in Russia as they were in Europe and the Middle East. This was well expressed by a senior Russian political scientist at the Russian Academy of Sciences who complained that: 'Americans do not think that the spread of their controls to Bosnia and Kosovo in the 1990s, and then again to Iraq and Afghanistan in the 2000s, is synonymous with expansionism. However, this is not the way that peoples in Russia, Germany, Japan, or China, for example, view it.'[28]

US-Russian relations worsened further as a consequence of the Orange Revolution, a popular pro-democracy uprising, in Ukraine in late 2004 and other so-called coloured revolutions surrounding Russia. Moscow faced the scenario that American expansionism had reached the countries of the former Soviet Union. In light of this, Russia placed greater emphasis on the sanctity of sovereignty and the need to respect different cultures and, implicitly, all types of political systems. Deputy Foreign Minister Saltanov, expressing a Russian perspective that was in harmony with the mainstream in Europe, suggested that for the war on terrorism to succeed 'I think rather that, first of all, we must preserve the identities of the different cultures, but at the same time we must come together more.'[29] This reflected the basic concept that was prevalent among the critics of the Bush administration and its universal approach to moral political values, arguing instead that the international order required acceptance and tolerance among very diverse political systems and cultures. In light of this Moscow re-discovered its shared history and value of good-neighbourliness with the Muslim world, with Russian Foreign Minister Lavrov pointing out in 2007 that: 'Having lived for centuries at a junction of civilisations, multinational and multi-confessional Russia has made a conscious choice in favour of unifying politics' declaring 'We will not allow ourselves to be put at loggerheads with the Muslim world.'[30] This attitude contrasted considerably with that of the the early Putin era, which was marked by a powerful undercurrent of Islamophobia.

Moscow's motives

There were three main analytical approaches to the US-Russian interplay in light of the war on terrorism and developments in the Middle East during the Putin presidency. Among them are longstanding discussions about whether Russian foreign policy was reactive or if it was driven by a powerful impetus to impose national and strategic demands on the external world. Adopting the first approach placed a greater portion of the blame on US behaviour to explain Russia's hardening of its own international outlook under Putin as a means of self-defence. Russia's encirclement and Moscow's feeling of impotence that emerged in the 1990s was caused by NATO expansion into Eastern Europe as well as US assertiveness in the Balkan conflicts following the break-up of Yugoslavia. This contrasted sharply with arguments that overriding domestic and national factors act as determinants of foreign policy, explicitly implying a correlation between the state of democracy in Russia and the struggle with deep expansionist aspirations since Tsarist times.

The debate over 'what drives Russian policy in the Middle East?' and beyond, according to another perspective, was that it was 'nothing in particular'.[31] Moscow's foreign policy was here presented as a meandering entity in a changing world. The implication of this approach was that, as in domestic politics, Putin's apparent international success had been accidental. US failures in the Middle East and the tarnishing of its reputation were down to Washington's own series of mistakes and poor calculations. The desire in Russia and for Putin to project the image of power and strength at home merely coincided with events in the Middle East. At its core, according to this view, Russia did not have fundamental principles or objectives directed against the West other than maximising economic and political opportunities that became available.

A more forgiving view of Putin's sense of purpose suggested that while Moscow initially did not intend to challenge Washington in the Middle East and originally did not develop a clear strategy to do so, US behaviour in the region allowed Russia to exploit developments in its favour to construct a policy that allowed it a distinct and prominent role. The international criticisms of unilateral US military actions and the lack of evidence regarding suspicions over Iraq's nuclear capabilities provided by Washington following the occupation all enhanced Russia's reputation as a reasonable and moderate member of the international community acting at the time in accordance with many European countries including France and Germany.

Opponents of proactive US intervention in the Middle East eagerly offered Russia new avenues to re-enter the region as an important diplomatic actor and arms provider. Iran and Syria were particularly keen to encourage Russia to play a balancing role in the Middle East to defend themselves against potential future attacks instigated by the United States and its principal regional ally Israel. Washington's threat to topple the regimes in Damascus and Tehran during Bush's first term led to a natural reaction of sympathy towards them in Moscow. Russia fervently rejected the concept of violating another state's sovereignty and defended the right of each country to be shielded from outside interference because upholding the principle also applied to its own ability to act independently in the global community. The concept of the sovereignty of the state also provided legal protection against outside interference in internal matters. It was widely acknowledged that 'under Putin, 'sovereignty' has become the code word for the demand that the West accept Russia's right to make its independent choice of political and economic institutions.'[32]

The third and arguably more feasible approach portrays Russia as an expansionist, hostile and calculating actor in the Middle East. Its ability to either directly or indirectly benefit from US mistakes in the Middle East and the war on terror would not have been possible without an original intention to exploit such weaknesses. Washington's warming to Ukraine, Georgia and other neighbouring former Soviet republics with a hostile attitude to Russia led the Russian leadership to look for an outlet that would serve as a bargaining chip with the Bush administration and create limitations to Washington's global ambitions. The Middle East, or rather Bush's stated idealistic goals of transforming and democratising the region as a continuation of the war on terror after 2002, conveniently provided such an outlet for Russia to confront the United States. The application of a more assertive foreign policy under Putin was made possible by the emerging influence of Russia in the global energy sector. Gas and oil production and exports at record high prices were the cornerstone of economic success under Putin, particular during his second term. The gas and oil sector required securing land routes for pipelines and sea access for shipping and this further helped define Russia's geostrategic view of the world and its behaviour. There was thus a direct link between Russia's international behaviour and its domestic political and economic interests, represented by the ever more powerful Putin.

An obvious criticism of the third approach would point out that Russia and Putin initially supported the US war against Al-Qaeda and the invasion of Afghanistan to oust the Taliban. Russia also did not attempt to prevent the toppling of long-time associate Saddam Hussein. Furthermore, critics of the hostile-Russia approach highlighted Putin's efforts for improved relations with Israel and his emphasis on building relations with Saudi Arabia and other Middle East states with moderate regional policies that historically clashed with Soviet policies in the region. These valid arguments in fact are consistent with the hostile-Russia perspective if understood in light of a policy typical of Putin's character: thoroughly pragmatic and cautious but nonetheless obsessed with power. A central aspect of these characteristics ensured that Putin did not challenge the United States directly but Moscow's keenness to expand its influence in the Middle East was achieved, unlike the United States, by promoting good relations with opposing sides such as the Israelis and Palestinians or the Iranians and Saudis.

Under Putin trade and economic relations were arguably placed higher up on the foreign policy agenda than it had ever been placed since the Bolshevik Revolution. Putin's global ambitions were restrained by an ultra-sensitive concern for protecting domestic economic interests, with the emergence of the oil and gas sectors and the military complex as major pillars that influenced Russian foreign policy. Traditionally, foreign policy had a geostrategic and diplomatic dimension to counter security dangers and to project a great power image. This continued to be true under Putin but international trade was seen not only as a new and important means of enhancing Russia's international status but was to some extent an end in itself. This had the effect of minimising the attractiveness of direct military confrontation with the West. A characteristic of the Kremlin's mentality under Putin was that in the conduct of politics, whether domestic or external, wealth and power complemented each other and neither was attainable without the other.

Oil and gas became fundamentally important economic weapons used by the Kremlin to project and exert domestic and international political power and influence. In turn Moscow found it necessary to project more power and influence to secure the full value of oil and gas, in terms of prices and payments due, and their safe supply routes to vital markets. This excessive interdependence between power and energy had its drawbacks. According to the influential Alexei Arbatov: 'The main problem with Putin's "managed democracy" and "executive vertical" is that the country's present economic wellbeing and political stability rest on a very fragile and short-lived foundation' because it was based on 'unprecedented global energy prices'.[33] Contrary to the view of the Kremlin elite, the interdependent dynamic of wealth and military-security power upholding the authority of the state were counterproductive and Arbatov warned that 'democracy is incompatible with an economic model that is dependent on the export of raw materials. This model has always been the basis of authoritarian-bureaucratic political systems.'[34] Among the implications of this analysis was that Russian policies were guided by motives of a narrow financial clique with short-term self-interests.

Moscow's eager defence of the principle of national sovereignty and the extolling of the values of diverse cultures ultimately safeguarded Russia's ruling clique from reformist ideas blowing in the international system that were promoted by the Bush presidency. Challenging the validity of this somewhat cynical view of Moscow's leadership did not negate the fact that the Putin clique benefited immensely from simmering tensions in the Gulf. Both US-Iranian hostilities and instability in Iraq resulted in high energy prices which vastly multiplied Russia's foreign revenues and allowed the ruling elite around Putin to consolidate its power in Russia. Paradoxically, the stabilisation of Russia's economy and the relative prosperity that was achieved in the Putin era was precisely what the United States had been encouraging. An economically fragile Russia undermined a stable international order because fears existed that it would result in unmanageable territorial and political fragmentation. Potential secessionist wars along the wider Eurasian landmass would disrupt important energy supplies and create new arenas for terrorist networks to consolidate themselves and expand. Such chaos caused by a weakened Russia also heightened the risk of facilitating the smuggling of drugs, weapons and nuclear-related materials to further destabilise the international system.

The Putin era allowed Russia to develop greater capabilities to assert itself, enabling it with confidence to vigorously pursue its own set of interests that diverged from those of the West. Moscow intimidated neighbours in Eastern Europe and played a more energetic role in the Middle East to discredit bold plans by the Bush administration to transform the region. On a broader level Moscow strived to build economic and political relations with important Asian players, including China, India and, specifically in the Middle East, Iran, Syria, Israel and Saudi Arabia. By doing so Russia presented a conservative alternative to the adventurous US model during Bush's first term and, significantly, democratisation, regime change and increased liberalisation were not desirable for the major Asian players.

Bush's idealist foreign policy during his first term was, for the Asian powers, a storm of anti-state globalisation with the powerful US economy at the centre of its vortex. Russian trade relations came without moral lectures on human rights and democratisation as attached preconditions. Russian foreign policy under Putin was therefore motivated by a quest to promote Moscow as, if not the leader, then at least at the centre of a coalition of countries that counterbalance US ambitions to transform the post-Cold War world system in its favour. Relative success in this regard strengthened Putin's stature as a national and international leader and re-established Russia's position as a world power.

The Middle East battleground

The divergence in views between the United States and Russia on the international stage coincided with an intensifying regional struggle in the post-Saddam Hussein Middle East, with Iran and Syria making a bid for regional supremacy. The Shi'a in Iraq governed after 2003 through their representatives in the government in Baghdad or on the ground through Iranian-backed militias. The non-Arab Kurds in northern Iraq were also successful in gaining significant autonomy that was of particular concern to neighbouring Turkey. The losers in this new arrangement were the Sunni Iraqis and the minority Christians, who felt that they had become politically marginalised and feared for their personal safety. The political and military balance in the Middle East was also transformed so that Iran and its allies in Iraq, Syria and Lebanon through Hezbollah became the most powerful actors in the region while the United States found itself stuck in a thorny and lengthy military entanglement.

Almost immediately after Saddam Hussein was toppled Iranian and Syrian coordination undermined the US military presence in Iraq by supporting Shi'a and Sunni insurgents as evidence emerged that Al-Qaeda, the original target of the US-declared war on terror, converged in Iraq thanks to Syrian facilitation. Al-Qaeda terrorists in Iraq were responsible for some of the most grotesque violence imaginable, killing not only American soldiers but also bombing innocent civilians in market places, mosques and other centres of gathering. Ironically though, events in Iraq arguably consolidated and confirmed Bush's accusations that international terrorist networks were made more potent and effective through the support and endorsement they received from rogue yet legally sovereign states. Whereas Russia and most European states believed the war on terrorism was specifically a war against Al-Qaeda and Wahhabi extremism, Bush and his supporters viewed it as a broader struggle against tyrannical regimes supporting terrorist non-state actors as a political end in international relations.

With the Saddam Hussein regime defeated Syria and Iran were considered by the United States as the remaining elements of the axis of tyrannical regimes that had expansionist regional ambitions. This was an aspect that Russia's leadership refused to acknowledge. Moscow instead argued, with sympathy from much of the European political and intellectual elite at the time, that Bush's declared war on terrorism was in disarray because Washington had lost focus by attacking Iraq and targeting other UN-member states rather than concentrating on Islamic extremism associated with Al-Qaeda. Russian defiance of US policies in the Middle East increased in boldness as a result of the invasion of Iraq, which was vividly illustrated by the surprise invitation by Putin to the Hamas leadership to visit Moscow in 2006 following their success in Palestinian legislative elections. Considering the US-Israeli view of Hamas as a militant Islamic terrorist group, Putin's welcoming gesture was an unambiguous statement that his perception of terrorism differed from that widely held among Washington's political elite. Moscow's increasingly sympathetic stance towards Lebanon's Hezbollah, another group considered by the United States as a terrorist organization and bearing in mind the history of kidnappings and murders of American citizens by the Shi'a organization—gave the sense that Russia was rubbing more salt into the US wound.

Russia's relationship with Hezbollah, prioritised because of Iranian and Syrian sponsorship of the militant party, was made more complex by the militant organisation's direct support for radical Palestinian groups in Israel and the Occupied Territories. Hassan Nasrallah, Hezbollah's leader, had stated in an interview in 2006 to a leading Lebanese daily that while the Palestinians 'have fighters and expertise…What they need is financial, political and media support. And we do not deny that we help them on those fronts.'[35] US accusations concerning Hezbollah's regional motives fitted well with warnings by some of the most prominent Middle East leaders that a Shi'a crescent was being formed that spanned from Iran, through Iraq and Syria to Lebanon on the Mediterranean. A warning of this scenario was first presented by King Abdullah of Jordan and he was later followed by President Hosni Mubarak of Egypt, who was forced to step down in 2011, and Lebanese Druze leader Walid Jumblatt, who transmitted his concerns directly to the Saudis in the spring of 2006 as the political situation in the region deteriorated. By 2009, Iranian support for rebels in the war in Yemen indicated that Tehran's tentacles of influence reached well beyond the Levant.

A US Congress report in 2006 took note of the significant landmark that Russia had emerged as the largest arms supplier to the developing world, overtaking the United States. Among the most lucrative deals for Moscow was a $700 million agreement 'to supply Iran with surface-to-air missile defence systems which American military planners fear could prove a serious obstacle if Washington ever decided to bomb Tehran over its nuclear plans'.[36] The timing of the report and its contents indicated a growing sense in Washington that Putin's Russia was evidently providing an umbrella to those in the Middle East considered as posing the greatest security risk to US interests. Russian arms sales from 2006 thereafter followed an upward trend, reaching $10 billion in annual sales in 2010 and $12 billion in 2012, with Putin proudly noting that annual sales exceeded expectations for the year by $500 million.[37] This record-breaking figure for arms sales in 2012 coincided with sharp criticisms levelled against Moscow for its continued supply of weapons to the Syrian regime which was accused of committing horrific atrocities against its own people.

Russia remained defiant, maintaining that its drive to increase its share of the world's arms market was normal, in keeping with similar ambitions being pursued by the United States, Britain, France and other major powers. Responding to the US Congress report in 2006 that linked Russia's arms export industry to international terrorists, Moscow released a list of terrorist groups which included Al-Qaeda but failed to list Hezbollah despite Washington's obvious hostility towards it. Yuri Sapunov, head of anti-terrorism at Russia's Federal Security Service, explained that this was because the group did not have links to 'organisations regarded as terrorists by the international community'.[38] This response intended to show that Moscow did not adopt Washington's view of the world or its definition of good and bad international actors.

Hezbollah's raid on Israel that instigated the fighting in July and August 2006 dominated the G8 Summit held in St. Petersburg on

15–17 July. The meeting was originally expected to be a forum used by the West to put pressure on Russia to agree to a strongly worded joint statement directed against Iran's plans to speed up its nuclear programme but the war side-tracked the issue and gave Russia the initiative by demanding an immediate ceasefire, which Israel and the United States initially rejected. Putin remained unbending until the end of the summit despite his knowledge of Washington's desire for action to limit Iran, stating that 'it is too early to speak about sanctions against Iran'.[39] The Russian media made much of the gulf in perspectives on the issue, noting that statements by the leaders during the meeting 'hardly inspired hope that any unambiguous statements could be hammered out' leaving Putin 'in the minority'.[40]

The Summit in 2006, hosting the world's largest economies, provided Putin with an opportunity to offer the West the hand of compromise and accommodation. Instead, Putin placed lower priority on Russia as an integral family member of the largest Western economies than he did on defending geo-strategic interests in the Middle East. Russia's stance strengthened Hezbollah's position against Israel during the 2006 war by forcing the United Nations to adopt Resolution 1701. The Resolution implied that Israel and Hezbollah stood on an equal footing and, more significantly, the ceasefire allowed the Iranian-backed group to claim victory by confronting the celebrated Israeli army.

Israel's failure to limit Hezbollah's influence in Lebanon allowed the Iranian-backed party to emerge stronger after the 2006 war. Meanwhile, Hamas consolidated itself in Gaza and survived a major Israeli military offensive in early 2009 at the expense of the moderate Palestinian leader Mahmoud Abbas. The election of President Barack Obama in the United States reflected a sense of failure in foreign policy. Among Obama's early pledges was to replace the 'reset' button in relations with Russia following years of diverging ambitions. US forces in Iraq and Afghanistan, where Taliban fighters were once more on the offensive, sought a hasty retreat to avoid humiliation under President Obama. Washington began openly reaching out to Syria in 2009 despite the implication of the leadership in Damascus in a series of political assassinations and other terrorist acts in Lebanon and its support for violent militant groups responsible for killing US soldiers in Iraq. Iranian influence in Iraq continued to grow while President Mahmoud Ahmadinejad, controversially re-elected in June 2009, refused to compromise with regard to transparent international inspections of Iran's nuclear programme.

Putin's second term therefore can be characterised by an assertive, if not sometimes belligerent, foreign policy at a time the United States, highlighted by the election of Obama, responded with a strategic retreat from a range of international and regional challenges. A symbolic consequence of this turnaround took place in 2010, with Syrian hegemony in Lebanon largely restored, when the Western-supported Prime Minister Saad Hariri found himself being forced to drink from the poisoned chalice by visiting Syria to meet President Asad, who was widely accused of ordering his father's assassination in 2005.

Consequences of Russia's policies

The euphoria of Washington's bid to strengthen and promote democracy in the region became a distant memory by the time of Barack Obama's election to the presidency in 2008. Syria and Iran continued to support and directly manipulate Hamas, Hezbollah and a number of powerful militant organisations in Iraq, including the Shi'a Mehdi Army as well as former Ba'athists, which all unsettled the establishment of stable, tolerant and democratic societies in the Middle East. For most of the Putin era Russia not only stonewalled US-led military action against the Syrians and Iranians but also undermined firm UN-led diplomatic measures that could have presented a more unified international stance by the world powers. In doing so, Moscow carries substantial responsibility for undermining peace and stability in the Middle East, particularly in Lebanon, Syria, and among the Palestinians and left the region hanging in a fragile balance. Moreover, as epitomised by Russia's support for the Syrian regime against a popular uprising, Moscow has stalled and delayed democratic reform in the region. In fairness the United States shared a portion of the blame, largely due to an increasingly confused and rudderless policy in the Middle East and failure to properly understand and appropriately respond to Russia's bold agenda.

In Moscow's zero-sum world of international relations US setbacks were Russian gains. In the early 1990s Russia was depicted as taking orders from the United States on the world stage. A decade after Yeltsin relinquished the presidency Russia had become once more a major world actor with the capacity to influence events in the Middle East.

Putin found much sympathy in Europe where the political elite was not welcoming of the Bush Doctrine. Relations with Germany were given a particularly high status in the Kremlin. Such sentiments were reciprocated, leading Alexander Rahr, from the German Council for Foreign Relations and specialist on Russia, to remark in 2004 that 'Germany's Federal Chancellor Gerhard Schröder believes that relations between his country and Russia are now much better than at any time in the past 100 years. His rapport with President Vladimir Putin reveals greater friendliness, even mutual trust, in comparison with his relations with US President George W. Bush.'[41] These relations developed because, alongside shared economic interests, 'Germany, Russia and France put up mild opposition to the US-led war in Iraq in 2003, thus opening, albeit cautiously, a new chapter in postwar European history.'[42]

The vision of post-Soviet Russia as a senior partner in a Eurasian balance to the United States, as espoused by Primakov during the 1990s was evidently being realised by Putin. Moscow was satisfied that, due to the war on terrorism reaching a cul-de-sac and the Afghanistan and Iraq occupations exacting a high cost in terms of the reputation of US military forces and the American economy, Washington's international influence was faltering. Russia nurtured other regional alliances including the Shanghai Cooperation Organization in Asia, which included China as a powerful partner. In April 2007, during a forum in Qatar, Russia lobbied for a gas-exporting association akin to OPEC with Iran being among a group of anti-Western states that supported the cause, indicating Russia's new sense of self-confidence and its perceived role as an alternative to the West. A commentary noted that: 'Russia stands at the forefront of this initiative by dint of its disproportionate strength … in terms of gas reserves, field technology, export potential, control of key export routes, and presence on lucrative markets.'[43] During the presidential interim when Putin was prime minister, Moscow energetically marketed the rising role of BRIC, an association of rising economies comprising Brazil, Russia, India and China, as a counterbalance and potential challenger to US hegemony. Putin was visibly happier playing the role of the resolute Russian leader defending national interests at the forefront of predominantly anti-Western alliances rather than as a Westernised liberal reformer.

Despite Washington's failures and Moscow's international successes under Putin, there were strong alternative arguments suggesting that

Russian foreign policy under Putin was on the whole self-destructive and in the long run potentially dangerous. Putin's chosen path has arguably left Russia more internationally isolated than it had ever been since the fall of the Soviet Union. Moscow's behaviour became a source of concern for many European states when Russia began cutting off gas supplies to Eastern Europe. NATO expansion into Eastern Europe became a reality during the Putin era. Relations between Russia and Britain were particularly strained due to the politically motivated assassinations in Russia and abroad that placed the Kremlin as the prime suspect. Putin's relative military success of subduing the Chechen insurgency and the attainment of stability in the northern Caucasus was tentative and the situation remained precarious. Moreover, simmering military tensions with neighbouring Georgia, in light of a pattern of Russian bullying tactics used against other recalcitrant post-Soviet neighbours, had resulted in a full-scale war during Medvedev's first year as president.

Beyond Europe, Moscow's bid to align the poles of China and India was never a realistic goal as both Asian powers were not willing to undermine their relations with the West. Moreover, China's rapid military expansion and development continued to pose a long-term threat to Russia. In the Middle East, Putin's flirtations with the Iran-Syria-Hezbollah nexus and the radical Shi'a wave in the region had not allowed Moscow greater leverage in a constructive sense. As was the case during the Soviet era, states such as Syria and Iran were using Russia's support and partnership to ultimately haggle with the United States. This was confirmed following the election of Barack Obama as president of the United States and the overtures the leaders in Damascus and Tehran made to the post-Bush administration in 2009. Aside from its links with disruptive states in the Middle East, Russia also further tarnished its international image by associating with major sponsors of world terrorism and violently repressive authoritarian regimes as in the case of Syria. Moscow's unwavering support for Syria and Iran undermined Russian relations with Sunni Muslim populations spanning from Indonesia to Morocco.

As early as 2001, Russian foreign policy experts were warned that 'practically unnoticed, Moscow is once again making a bid for international dominance' and 'expanded its sphere of influence beyond its "near abroad" and into the Gulf and Levant'.[44] In the early 1990s there were genuine hopes that Russia would develop into a normal European power, to borrow foreign minister Kozyrev's description, in tune with Western economies and political and social values. Within a decade such aspirations had become far-fetched. Successive US administrations instead pursued a realist approach in which little attention was given to the nature of Russia's political system and the apparent drift towards authoritarianism. This approach was of great benefit to Putin, enabling him to assert his power and restructure the political system in his favour by means that included silencing the media. Obama, for example, was conspicuously timid in his response to the harsh treatment of Russian dissidents, dubious elections and rough suppression of protests in Russia in 2011 and 2012. This lame approach by Washington had allowed Moscow to violently and often brutally crush the Chechen resistance. Washington's approach did not consider that the domestic nature of a political system impacts the character of foreign policy.

After the Cold War there was a growing view in Washington that aside from terrorism the greatest nation-state threat to US, and ultimately Western values and interests, came from the Far East. Russia's decline during the chaotic years of the 1990s further confirmed China's rise as the main competitor to the United States. Putin's consolidation of power was therefore greeted by the anti-China lobby in Washington because Russia was then considered to be a useful potential ally and important balance in Asia against Chinese political aspirations. Russia's ranking as a menace to American national security fell further because of Islamic extremism and its supposed threat to US values and interests. Bush's war on terrorism and specifically the quarrel with the Muslim world that it created enabled Putin to enhance his international standing, particularly in the Western family. The Bush Doctrine portrayed a divided world and 'at least until the American war against Iraq that began in March 2003, Russia had become a partner, a friend and even an ally of the United States in the global struggle against terrorism'.[45]

Such assurances and tolerance from Washington towards Russia were based on the assumption of shared interests in the fight against rogue regimes, terrorist organisations and militant extremist non-state actors, nuclear proliferation, the spread of weapons of mass destruction and other civilian-threatening military hardware accessible to hostile regimes and the terror groups they sponsored. Ultimately however the drift towards an authoritarian model in Russia led to a political schism with the West because the Moscow leadership became increasingly insecure about the way it was viewed and felt an ever greater need to project its power. Russia's Putin, widely encouraged to become stable and strong became obsessed with its own power. By becoming so, foreign policy under Putin, most notably in the Middle East, failed to fully evaluate the long-term impact on Russia's stability and security by inadvertently unleashing on its own doorstep new political, economic and military dynamics that were beyond its control or influence.

6

RUSSIA AND THE NEW REALITIES IN IRAQ

The US-led war on Iraq in 2003 was driven by a revolutionary zeal that characterised the spirit of the Bush administration at that time. Iraq became a battleground for fighting world terrorism, eliminating the threat of weapons of mass destruction in the possession of one of the world's most brutal dictatorships and, if that did not suffice, it was also to be a testing ground for regime change and nation-building. US foreign policy embarked on a precarious experiment to find out if it was possible to transform a conservative tribal society under authoritarian rule into a modern democratic state. Russia looked on with suspicion at such lofty aims. During the build-up to the war in 2003 a leading Russian academic wondered 'how should Russia respond to any conflict with Iraq considering its many years of alliance with Saddam?'[1] Contrary to the idealism in Washington the Putin leadership saw the invasion and occupation of Iraq as a quest to impose US leadership in the world by subjugating an influential state in the Middle East, which happened to be one of the world's largest oil producers.

As far as Putin and his supporters were concerned it was not in Russia's interest for the United States to succeed in Iraq. Controlling Iraq would have allowed the United States effective domination in the wider Middle East. In the geo-strategic puzzle of international rivalry Russia was already feeling constricted during Putin's first term, with NATO expansion in the West proceeding along, instability in the Caucasus making it susceptible to Western and Turkish influence, and the shadow of Chinese power encroaching ever wider in the Far East. Putin's dilemma was that he was not able to challenge the United States directly and it was widely and correctly anticipated that Putin would not support Saddam Hussein against the United States in a military confrontation because it would have reversed fifteen years of trust-building between Washington and Moscow. Aside from military limitations, Putin was keen to build Russia up as a rational world economic player. Defending Iraq would have isolated Russia in light of Saddam Hussein's terrible image in the world.

In actual fact, abandoning Saddam Hussein, as Russia eventually did, was not a difficult choice because Moscow's own experience of the Iraqi despot in decades of relations was not generally positive. Saddam Hussein's erratic behaviour over the years led him to misadventures and ultimately helped speed up the US aggression. Russia's goals were therefore reluctantly adjusted after the downfall of the Saddam Hussein regime to protect national and economic interests in Iraq in light of the new reality of the US occupation. Maintaining a foothold in Iraq and the region were important objectives for Moscow to uphold its international stature, especially when considering the emphasis on promoting Russia's energy and industrial-energy sectors. The war in Iraq and the insecurity it caused ultimately led Moscow to aggressively assert Russian influence in the post-Soviet space, resulting in a dual approach towards the United States so that 'even while discussing partnership on regional security issues with Washington, Putin and the Russian military were striving to create a CIS military alliance modelled after the USSR's relationship with its Eastern European satellites'.[2]

Russian foreign policy towards Iraq, as with the rest of the Middle East, can be divided into the pre-1996 and post-1996 eras under Yeltsin before the evolution in the Putin presidency. However, categorising Russian foreign policy into three distinct phases neglects the almost seamless transition from one phase to another. Thus while Kozyrev was foreign minister Russia began adopting a more independent line vis-à-vis the West from 1993 in light of the stiff opposition Yeltsin faced from conservative political opponents. The appointment of Evgenii Primakov as foreign minister in 1996 was an outcome of that progression and he in turn promoted and consolidated the centre ground of the political spectrum in foreign policy thinking that allowed continuity into the Putin era. Primakov was instrumental in establishing the basis of a pragmatic non-ideological foreign policy that was detached from the West.

In 1999, Putin inherited this approach to establish the framework of his foreign policy but with modification to fit the characteristics of his era by changing the emphasis from a fixation with classic geo-strategic concerns to include a special focus on Russia's economic interests. Primakov's appointment as chairman of the Russian Federation's Chamber of Commerce and Industry on 14 December 2001 appeared to be a move to marginalise him after the senior positions he previously held. However, in the context of Primakov's influence on Russian foreign policy and his Middle East expertise, in tandem with Putin's wish to raise the economic dimension in the country's international relations, this was a shrewd move to maximise Russia's international economic potential. Almost a decade later, on 12 November 2009, President Dmitry Medvedev underlined the new approach in a national address by stating that foreign policy was guided by pragmatism alone and the measure of its success was based on 'the improvement of the living standards of ordinary Russian citizens'.[3]

Saddam, sanctions and Yeltsin

For about a decade, beginning with Gorbachev's New Thinking until the mid-1990s, Russian foreign policy had significantly downgraded Iraq on its priority list. Epitomising this trend was the tacit Soviet endorsement of the US-led international coalition to liberate Kuwait from Iraqi occupation in August 1990. Moscow's central objective during the late 1980s and early 1990s was to improve relations with the United States and the rest of the Western world. Nonetheless, despite this phase of retreat the geo-strategic and economic importance of Iraq on the world scene remained an unavoidable reality. Iraq bordered Turkey and Iran, which were both major regional powers with a potential for substantial influence in the Caucasus and Central Asia. Iraq also bordered important Arab countries such as Saudi Arabia, Syria and Jordan as well as the small but oil-rich Kuwait.

Many analyses of Russian foreign policy underplayed the significance of Iraq for Moscow on the grounds that the United States, China, Germany and the rest of Europe were considered as having a far greater value due to their economic and military power. But from a regional context on a global scale the South West Asia portion of the wider Middle East was arguably equal in importance to other landmasses such as China to the east or Europe to the west in terms of Russian national security and economic potential. Iraq's centrality and impact on the region's political and economic affairs afforded it a special status by the Kremlin's decision-makers and the foreign policy retreat during the late 1980s and early 1990s was as a result of imposed political and economic realities rather than a matter of choice.

Russian policy towards Iraq was largely determined by the transitions it underwent during the 1990s and as Russia's economy deteriorated calls became more vociferous for prioritising the economic dimension in bilateral relations. In the early 1990s, when the liberal Westernisers in Moscow were dominant and the priority was placed on integration into the Western community, Iraq was considered as a nuisance topic that was being manipulated by the opposition hard-line communists and ultranationalists to highlight Yeltsin's international impotence. As relations with the West became strained and the pro-Western Kozyrev and his clique became discredited Russia moved to a more independent approach vis-à-vis the West on Iraq as well as other international issues. Yeltsin, however, resisted succumbing to the ideological anti-Western political opponents in Russia, represented primarily by the communists and neo-fascists and instead promoted the pragmatic centrist approach offered by the experienced Primakov. Thus from 1996, when Primakov became foreign minister, Russia undermined proposed solutions to the Iraq crisis determined solely by the United States and instead endorsed collective diplomatic counterproposals. Russia's preference was for the United Nations to play the leading role in resolving the problem of Saddam Hussein's non-compliance with the international community regarding weapons of mass destruction and the Iraqi people's humanitarian crisis caused by the UN-imposed sanctions.

Russia first revived economic relations with Iraq after the Soviet collapse in August 1993 by sending Deputy Minister for External Economic Relations Oleg Davydov to Baghdad. This modest overture risked being perceived as challenging the United States in Iraq at a time of a forceful US presence in the Gulf and Washington's aggressive drive to impose its economic influence in the region. As a result Moscow reiterated its general support for the West's anti-Iraqi coalition after the liberation of Kuwait, and to allay the fears of the other Gulf states Russia signed a bilateral agreement with Kuwait assuring the latter of its commitment to safeguarding its borders, independence and sovereignty.

Davydov's visit had opened the door for sustained long-term efforts by Russia to secure its share of lucrative contracts in Iraq and to establish an economic foothold in the Gulf region. In 1994 the Russian media intensified its focus on Iraq's economic potential, pointing to Baghdad's proposal 'to repay its debt to Russia—about $7 billion—immediately after the sanctions are lifted or eased'.[4] Such prospects were difficult to ignore in light of disappointment with Western promises of financial support and also the failure of rapid economic liberalisation to raise the declining living standards of the Russian people. Baghdad's promise of debt repayment was part of an attractive package luring major Russian participation into rebuilding the devastated economy as well as of military contracts to restore the capabilities of the severely weakened Iraqi armed forces. But Saddam Hussein's dangling of the economic carrot was accompanied with the condition that Moscow had an active role in fragmenting the international community's united position in the implementation of the severe UN-imposed sanctions regime.

The Russian leadership was well aware that overtly undermining sanctions and allowing Iraq to escape their impact would be perceived in the United States as an act of defiance. The collapse of the sanctions regimes would allow Saddam Hussein to claim a political victory in the Gulf and the wider Middle East despite the military defeat in 1991, creating the additional risk that this would be exploited by the unpredictable Saddam Hussein to embark on new military adventures. As Yeltsin's political position at home began weakening rapidly in 1995 due to economic turmoil, Chechnya's turning into a quagmire, and the increasingly rife corruption and crime, the hostile Russian Duma moved to paralyse the Russian President by voting on 21 April 1995:'To lift the sanctions against Iraq and set forth three goals for Russian policy: 1) to pressure the UN Security Council to repeal the embargo; 2) to collect Iraq's debt if the embargo was to be partially lifted; and 3) to support Russian business investment in Iraq and large-scale cooperation with that country.'[5] The timing coincided with yet another UN Resolution on Iraq which introduced a stringent mechanism, despite the hardships suffered by the Iraqi people due to the sanctions, offering limited humanitarian aid in return for oil sales. UN Security Council Resolution 986 stated that oil originating in Iraq could only be exported via pipelines in Turkey and that each transaction required prior UN approval.

The dire humanitarian crisis in Iraq was very partially eased and the Resolution did not provide a solution to the ongoing deadlock between

Baghdad and the international community. More specifically UNSC Resolution 986 did not directly address the issue of Iraqi cooperation with the international community, including cooperation with UN-sponsored nuclear weapons inspectors. The Duma's vote in April 1995 was a ploy to embarrass Yeltsin and highlight his lack of political influence on the international stage but it was also driven by leaders of the country's energy sector wanting to ensure Russia's share in Iraq in the post-sanctions era and by the defence sector elite mindful of the urgent need to modernise the Russian army's equipment and capabilities. The appointment of Primakov as foreign minister in 1996, with his nationalist credentials and sound reputation, was Yeltsin's response to neutralise much of the Duma's hostile manoeuvre. The second and third points of the Duma's demands in 1995 became the basis of Russian policy towards Iraq in the remaining years under Yeltsin.

In 1996 Russia and Iraq signed a multibillion dollar oil sector agreement that set off a chain of collaborative deals in the energy sector, including a $15 billion proposal to allow Russian drilling in the West Qurna and North Rumaila oilfields once sanctions were lifted. Primakov understood that it was unrealistic for Russia to unilaterally break the sanctions regime in defiance of the United States and his strategy in the following years was to encourage Saddam Hussein to gradually increase cooperation with the West without losing face while simultaneously trying to convince the United States and its allies to reward the Iraqi leader by partially easing the sanctions based on the level of compliance with UN demands. Thus Russia's vocal support 'for Iraq was of lower priority for Russian diplomacy than ensuring the primacy of the United Nations in the realm of international peace and security'.[6] Moscow's policy rejected Washington's absolutist all or nothing approach towards Iraq, and instead proposed a step-by-step process of targets and rewards as a solution to the deadlock.

The general political support in Russia for Primakov's style and approach allowed him to promote a more assertive foreign policy towards Iraq. The pragmatic Russian foreign minister was careful that, rather than pursue a unilateral approach, he utilised the United Nations Security Council (UNSC) as a forum to isolate the United States. The opportunity arose 'during the October 1997 crisis over arms inspections, [when] Primakov spearheaded efforts to erode Chinese and French support for the sanctions against Baghdad'.[7] Moscow argued that the UN's inspections for Iraqi Weapons of Mass Destruction should not continue indefinitely and that the UN Special Commission (UNSCOM) needed to set a deadline for its work in order to give the Iraqi people hope of an end in sight to the sanctions and provide the regime with an incentive to cooperate more meaningfully.

Russian pressure, along with European support, began to pay off with UNSC Resolution 1153 on 20 February 1998, which increased the amount allowed for essential goods to be imported to $5.256 billion worth of oil exports every 180 days. This was achieved despite a background of tensions between the Iraqi regime and UNSCOM, with Saddam Hussein refusing to allow access to his presidential palaces because he argued they symbolised national honour and sovereignty. The following month, Primakov played a leading role in mediation between Secretary-General Kofi Annan and Saddam Hussein that allowed for UNSC Resolution 1154 to accept a Memorandum of Understanding on the UN inspection of the Iraqi leader's residences and other sites. This mediation successfully averted a full-scale military confrontation between Iraq and the United States.

Primakov's success, although ultimately not long-lasting, capped a pattern of active diplomacy by Moscow on Iraq throughout the 1990s. Deputy Foreign Minister Viktor Posuvalyuk pointed out for example that: 'Russia did more for the normalisation of Iraqi-Kuwaiti relations than any other state.'[8] The claim typified the thinking in Moscow that Russia was capable of playing a constructive role in the Middle East and Primakov's ascendancy emphasised further that a balance to US power was an international necessity that allowed meaningful mediation to resolve conflict situations. There was also an honest expression of self-interest among Moscow's political elite. Russian policy towards Iraq may have began initially as a reaction to appease anti-Western political factions but it developed into a mainstream thinking which argued that Russia was losing the opportunity of billions of dollars worth of contracts while it fruitlessly waited for handouts from the United States.

Saddam's downfall

In the late-1990s Russia's emerging powerful business elite established an influential economic lobby within Yeltsin's ruling circle that sought to ensure that foreign policy did not overlook the prospect of highly rewarding construction and energy contracts in Iraq. This development merged harmoniously with Primakov's vision of a more active Russia in key regions in the world. Primakov's relative success in reasserting Russia's role in the Middle East and on the international stage helped pave the way for his appointment as prime minister in 1998 and his popularity continued to rise. This challenged Yeltsin's own credibility and authority as president as he became overshadowed by Primakov, who had become a strong and popular consensus candidate for the presidency after leading a vigorous anti-corruption drive and ably handling the country's economic crisis.

Yeltsin duly removed Primakov from his post on 12 May 1999 and following a very brief stint by Sergei Stepashin the unpredictable president appointed Vladimir Putin in August 1999 to lead the government. Putin immediately began laying the groundwork for his own political future by presenting a strongman image in terms of maintaining order at home yet reassuring the West that in world affairs and economic reforms he would offer continuity. Yeltsin's ailing health and widespread unpopularity meant that he was unable to maintain direct control of day-to-day political affairs, allowing Putin greater leeway and authority. This transitional period, from the latter half of 1999 until Putin began asserting his style on the presidency in 2002, witnessed continuing improvement in relations between Russia and the United States.

During the short period spanning Yeltsin's exit from national politics and Putin's first year in leadership Russia was more pliant on the Iraq inspections issue. This facilitated the adoption of UNSC Resolution 1284 on 17 December 1999 which established 'as a subsidiary body of the Council, the United Nations Monitoring, Verification and Inspection Commission (UNMOVIC)'[9] to replace the previous United Nations Special Commission (UNSCOM) charged with inspecting and preventing Iraq from rebuilding a weapons programme. UNSCOM was widely perceived as being unduly hostile towards the regime in Baghdad, thus UNSC Resolution 1284 was portrayed as a success for Russian efforts to abolish it. It also transpired that leading members of UNSCOM were on spying missions for the United States and Israel to consolidate further Moscow's claim that the previous inspection team had lost credibility. In fact, Primakov had described the behaviour of the pugnacious Australian head of UNSCOM, Richard Butler, as 'scandalous' and accused him of collaborating with Washington to create a crisis with Iraq.[10] UNSC Resolution 1284 also loosened the watertight UN sanctions regime by allowing Iraq greater flexibility in importing various forms of pre-approved humanitarian aid items and materials, in exchange for oil, than was initially prescribed by UNSC Resolution 986 on 14 April 1995. UNSC Resolution 1284 also implied acknowledgement of earlier efforts by Primakov to subtly offer the opportunity of a mechanism to be put in place linking the severity of the sanctions with the level of Iraq's cooperation with UNMOVIC, although this remained very far from what Russia and Iraq wanted.

Despite such concessions, by allowing UNSC Resolution 1284 to be adopted, courtesy of Russia's abstention on the Security Council, Putin's government had participated in giving UNMOVIC limitless powers as well as demanding that Iraq enabled 'UNMOVIC teams immediate, unconditional and unrestricted access to any and all areas, facilities, equipment, records and means of transport … as well as to all officials and other persons under the authority of the Iraqi Government whom UNMOVIC wishes to interview.'[11] This aspect of UNSC Resolution 1284 eventually became, if not the *casus belli*, then the manufacturer of the climate for the war in 2003.

Saddam Hussein rejected UNMOVIC's authority on grounds that its powers violated any semblance of national sovereignty, humiliated Iraqis and posed a direct challenge to the political elite in Iraq. Russia's collusion in such a Resolution was unusual. Aside from the consequence of incurring Iraqi and Arab displeasure there were dangerous implications regarding the rights of sovereign states vis-à-vis the international community. Moscow's political elite traditionally resisted interference in the affairs of a sovereign nation, a point firmly reasserted by Moscow (a decade later) to justify its defence of Syria's embattled Asad regime.

Russia's cooperation with the international community on UNSC Resolution 1284 was welcomed in the West but major hurdles reappeared when Iraq refused UNMOVIC unlimited access as demanded by the Resolution. As far as Washington was concerned this justified military action against Iraq and its obstinacy was considered as being enough proof of guilt by the US administration. In response, Putin argued for more patience and respect for Iraqi sovereignty, while at the same time Moscow sought to convince the Iraqi dictator to comply with international demands to avoid a military showdown. Russia had an obvious interest in avoiding such a scenario considering that the accumulation of years through the oil for food programme, based on UNSC Resolution 986 extending until Resolution 1284, meant that by '2000 all of Iraq's orders from Russia exceeded $20 billion',[12]

Regardless of Russian efforts, by 2002 it had become inevitable that the coming war would result in US military occupation of Iraq. A US-led coalition invaded and occupied Afghanistan in October 2001 and Moscow was already deeply concerned at the impact this could have on Central Asia and its southern rim. Allowing Iraq to fall under US occupation would leave Russia even more geo-strategically encircled and damage its prospects of reaping economic benefits from a lucrative market, further consolidating US global domination and undermining Russia's position in the wider Middle East. Yet according to one author writing in 2002 it became obvious 'that a long-term post-war US presence in Iraq would be unavoidable. As the US inexorably began moving towards war in fall 2002, others began to address the nettlesome issue of the "day after" in greater detail.'[13] To avoid this scenario, during the period from 2000 to 2003 Russia's efforts aimed to build international alliances that would undermine US justification and support for the occupation of Iraq in preparation for the new reality. In line with this strategy Putin recognised the value of improving relations with Turkey and Iran, which were both crucial in terms of reasserting Russia's presence in the Caucasus and fortifying its southwestern front. Iran became a particularly worthy substitute when considering the prospect of the loss of Iraq.

Putin's closeness with the United States, Turkey and Iran risked the wrath of Saddam Hussein, and his regime periodically implied that its displeasure with Russia's lack of support would result in the annulment of multibillion dollar contracts in the oil sector as well as in industrial and military opportunities. Yet the Bush administration's relentless pressure on Iraq and Saddam Hussein's narrowing options left him with little choice but to depend on Russia's support in the United Nations. Putin, until the war began in March 2003, found indirect benefits for Russia in the crisis because the threat of war increased oil prices, which in turn augmented desperately needed revenues into the economy. The no-war no-peace tensions between Iraq and the United States were advantageous as 'in January 2002, Russia had risen to first place among Iraq's main trading partners, leaving behind Egypt and France'.[14]

In political terms the brewing international crisis helped Putin divert attention away from authoritarian measures he was implementing to assert his presidency, as well as ferocious methods used by the Russian army to defeat Chechen insurgents in the Caucasus. Putin enthusiastically offered sympathy to the United States in the aftermath of the 11 September 2001 terrorist attacks and in turn the US media and Western leaderships portrayed the Russian leader as a young reformer who possessed a more sober approach than the flamboyant Yeltsin. Moreover, Russian efforts to moderate in dispute over Iraq improved Putin's image in Europe and he was seen as a positive element because of widespread European resistance to US military action against Iraq.

Russia aligned closely with Germany and France during this period because of shared suspicions about Washington's intentions and fears of imposing US hegemony in the Middle East and the world. In fact, Moscow's opposition to the war was less vocal than that heard among major European states such as France. As one analysis noted, during the build-up to war: 'US-Russian relations did not immediately suffer. In part, this was due to the fact that the leading forces opposing a US-British attack on Iraq were the French and Germans, and this provided diplomatic cover for Moscow,'[15] which appeared somewhat less antagonistic towards the Bush administration than Paris and Berlin. Putin revealed a glimpse of his political skills and qualities during the build-up to the Iraqi war by exploiting populist anti-war sentiments and maintaining Iraq's dependence on the one hand and subtly assuring the United States that it would ultimately not stand in its way if it brought down the Saddam Hussein regime.

As late as 29 October 2002, Kremlin political adviser Gleb Pavlovskii alluded that 'Putin's recent statement declaring an offensive against the organisers and financial supporters of international terrorism might include Saddam Hussein's Iraq,' and he accused Baghdad of 'conducting a hypocritical policy' of supporting 'this horrible business [of terrorism], the business of blood'.[16] This view was expressed in the context of the hostage drama at a Moscow theatre that month and while there were no official statements that revealed such antipathy towards the Iraqi regime the deliberate ambiguity from Moscow was intended to highlight Russia's eagerness to be seen as part of the Western family of nations fighting international Islamic terror. Western Islamophobia became also visible among sections of Russian society, which viewed Chechen rebel Shamil Basaev as its own Osama Bin Laden. This anti-Chechen and anti-terrorist wave made it easier for the Kremlin to align itself in 2002 with broad US policies.

The drama at the UN Security Council in the months preceding the war was accompanied by a media campaign in which the United States and Britain presented allegations as proven evidence that Iraq had resumed Weapons of Mass Destruction capabilities. US Secretary of State Colin Powell, in a poor performance at the UN Security Council on 5 February 2003, attempted to convince fellow members and the world through television pictures and questionable testimonies by dubious Iraqi exiles such as Ahmad Chalabi and Nouri al-Maliki that Iraq was developing weapons of mass destruction in violation of the various Security Council Resolutions. The urgency for war as presented by the United States and Britain did not seem to match the facts in the view of the sceptical Russians and French. Hans Blix, the experienced Swedish diplomat who was appointed to head UNMOVIC between 2000 and 2003 and who had previously led the International Atomic Energy Agency between 1981 and 1997 had plainly argued that there was no substantial evidence found that Iraq was developing weapons of mass destruction. Interviewed on television in 2004 by CNN reporter Christiane Amanpour, Blix stated that his team had conducted 'about 700 inspections and in no case did we find weapons of mass destruction'.[17]

Regardless of the conclusions reached by UNMOVIC the decision by Washington to invade Iraq was probably finalised in 2002 soon after President Bush began making the case for war in September during his address to the UN General Assembly. Regardless of strong international opposition and Moscow's concerns, a major ground offensive against Iraq became inevitable at the start of 2003. Putin made a last ditch effort to avert war by sending Primakov as a special envoy to Baghdad on 22 February 2003. At the time the visit was interpreted as a bid by Primakov to arrange a 'last-minute compromise deal, but he has since stated that he went to encourage Saddam to resign as leader, as this appeared to be the only way of avoiding another tragedy for the Iraqi people'.[18] Moscow's role was ultimately reactive and had no real impact on the final outcome. As one Russian political commentator pointed out during the approach to the war, 'Russia's position in this debate is not really being taken into consideration.'[19] Putin was all too aware of this fact yet the experience would mould his attitude towards Washington for his future years in power.

It was only upon the launch of the military operation to invade Iraq in March 2003 that Moscow openly and aggressively criticised the Bush administration but even this was done in order to save face with Russia's anti-US friends in the Middle East. Appearing too obsequious risked undermining trust in Russia by Iran and Syria and it would have damaged Putin's domestic image as an independent nationalist in the run-up to the 2004 presidential elections. As one author explained, 'If Putin had lost any of his credibility for throwing his support behind American intervention in Afghanistan, he certainly regained it all during his opposition to the war in Iraq.'[20] Putin's vocal criticisms of US actions helped to silence the anti-American factions in the Russian parliament and garner populist support among nationalist voters.

War and nation-building

If UNSC Resolution 1284 had established new parameters demanding Iraq's cooperation with the international community on the issue of weapons of mass destruction, UNSC Resolution 1441 adopted on 8 November 2002 provided Iraq with a 'final opportunity to comply with its disarmament obligations' under Chapter VII of the UN Charter, which sanctioned the use of decisive measures, including force, to ensure compliance.[21] The implication, by stating that this was a final opportunity, was that force would be used against Iraq and to further stress this point the Resolution ended by stating that Iraq 'will face serious consequences as a result of its continued violations of its obligations'.[22] Russia's role in allowing both resolutions to be adopted reflected Putin's willingness to show support to Washington until late 2002, despite the contradictory media rhetoric.

Moscow's deliberate ambiguity was highlighted by Russia's UN Ambassador Sergei Lavrov's official statement after the vote emphasising 'that the resolution did not contain any provisions for the automatic use of force and underlined that the sponsors of the text had affirmed that today'.[23] Lavrov's statement was not fully convincing because there were no realistic options available to deal with Iraqi non-compliance other than war since stringent sanctions were already in place and the oil for food programme was basically a humanitarian lifeline. While US Ambassador to the UN John Negroponte agreed with Lavrov that the resolution 'contained no "hidden triggers" and no "automaticity" with the use of force', he added in the same paragraph that in case of failure by the Security Council to act decisively against Iraqi non-compliance 'the resolution did not constrain any Member State from acting to defend itself against the threat posed by that country, or to enforce relevant United Nations resolutions and protect world peace and security'.[24] The formulation of UNSC Resolution 1441 was therefore a compromise between Moscow and Washington in which Russia did not want to be associated with any military action against Iraq through the UN but at the same time it tacitly acknowledged the right of the United States to take military action independently.

Armed with the new UN Resolution the United States and some of its key allies including Britain, Australia, Spain and Poland launched a massive military operation against Iraq on 18 March 2003. Operation Shock and Awe struck deep into Iraq through a combination of heavy aerial bombardment and rapid troop movement. The expectation was that such a show of force would lead quickly to the collapse of the Iraqi military structure and the downfall of the regime. The operation resulted in a high Iraqi civilian death rate because of the extensive nature of the aerial bombardment and long-range missile attacks. The primary aims of the war were successfully attained though and the regime disintegrated in April. Saddam Hussein temporarily escaped coalition troops and remained in hiding until he was captured towards the end of 2003.

Despite public opinion's displeasure that was expressed in Russia, Europe and the Middle East, the war appeared by April 2003 to be yet another indisputable example of US military power and diplomatic influence. Russia, France and Germany did not conceal their opposition to unilateral military action by the United States and its occupation of Iraq but they had been helpless to prevent it. Moscow's aims in light of the fact of a post-Saddam Hussein Iraq were to protect its economic obligations and interests that were established before the war and to preserve what had remained of Russian diplomatic influence in the broader Middle East. To do so however required the hastening of the US withdrawal from Iraq and in the process to minimise Washington's influence on the newly established Iraqi political leadership. These objectives formed the cornerstone of Russian policy towards Iraq thereafter under Putin and the emergence of a tenacious anti-occupation insurgency in Iraq expediently served Russia's objectives.

The Russian political leadership, epitomised by Putin, comprised hardened realists who came to grudgingly accept that the war was inevitable but even during the early period of US occupation. 'Moscow and its business circles still hoped that by cooperating with the Americans they would be able to preserve some of their economic interests in

Iraq.'[25] For most of 2003 Russia's official stance continued to outwardly present itself as a moderate opponent of US actions in Iraq and it supported Washington's transfer of powers from the military to the Governing Council of Iraq on 13 July 2003, which was widely viewed in the Middle East and among some Europeans as a puppet government. In light of the occupation, it was then noted that: 'Moscow and its oilmen fully grasp that Washington will now have leverage over the reconstruction of the Iraqi energy industry and thus a major card to play in determining global output and price levels.'[26] Yet vocal criticisms from the Kremlin were interpreted by the United States and in other Western states simply as part of Putin's desire to portray the hard-man image and to silence the communists in the Russian parliament. However, this underestimation of Moscow's behaviour and motives in the West failed to grasp a far more complex, stealthy and long-term policy that emerged, in which Russia actively sought to undermine the United States in Iraq and the Middle East, mainly through developing relations and coordinating with Iran and Syria.

The evolution of Russian policy towards the Iraq-US confrontation from a benign stance to an actively competitive one was due to several factors. During his early years as Russian president, Putin was keen to establish a positive rapport with the United States to secure international credibility for his own domestic political standing. The war on terror and militant Islam also saw a convergence of interests as Putin sought to impose Russian control over the recalcitrant Chechens and other Caucasian Muslim republics. When Putin took power Russia was still economically and politically as fragile as it had been under Yeltsin. Putin hoped, even as late as 2003, that by not antagonising the United States the Bush administration would not only spare Russia outward hostility and undermine its interests but that it would actually respect certain Russian spheres of influence, including a share of the windfall in the reconstruction of post-war Iraq.

President Bush's swaggering announcement on 1 May 2003 while dressed in military uniform that major combat operations had ended in Iraq was widely criticised as being premature. In reality events were slipping rapidly out of Washington's control and resistance to the US occupation in Iraq was gathering momentum. In addition, the threat of a civil war among the country's Shi'a, Sunni and Kurdish communities loomed. The consequences of the fragmentation of Iraq threatened to involve Turkey, Iran, Syria and Saudi Arabia in the conflict. Turkey opposed Iraq's Kurds from attaining independence because of the potential impact on its own large Kurdish community. Iran introduced large-scale and systemic support to Shi'a allies in Iraq whose political role and influence had amplified drastically after Saddam Hussein was deposed. According to one study of the consequences of the invasion, 'by liberating and empowering Iraq's Shiite majority, the Bush administration helped launch a broad Shiite revival that will upset the sectarian balance in Iraq and the Middle East for years to come'.[27]

After years of oppression by the Iraqi dictator the Shi'is were determined to maximise their political presence through powerful and well armed militias while the country's new political system and constitution were being defined. For Iran, more power for its Shi'a allies in Iraq equalled an extension of its influence in the Middle East and the oil-rich Gulf region. In turn, Iraq's Sunni community feared retribution by the empowered Shi'is and formed counter-militias. To complicate matters further Al-Qaeda fighters who had been forced out of Afghanistan began converging on Iraq and they contributed to some of the most horrific violence in attacks not only on US soldiers but also against non-Iraqi administrative and diplomatic officials, humanitarian aid workers and indiscriminately against Iraqi civilians.

Adding to the chaos was the controversial order by L. Paul Bremer, immediately upon his appointment on 23 May 2003 as US presidential envoy to Iraq, to disband the Iraqi army. Hundreds of thousands of Iraqi soldiers became unemployed and thousands of officers, many of whom enjoyed a degree of prestige and authority under the Saddam Hussein regime, were dismissed. Aside from humiliating the historically proud Iraqi army the move facilitated the ability of political groups and external states to recruit militia fighters and terrorists in Iraq. Mindful of the widespread criticisms Bremer later sought to defend himself in an article in which he stated that although it had 'become conventional wisdom that the decision to disband Saddam Hussein's army was a mistake... the policy was carefully considered by top civilian and military members of the American government. And it was the right decision'.[28]

But Bremer's order was widely interpreted as being part of a conspiracy to partition Iraq and facilitate control over its oil reserves in the north and south of the country. Moreover, some Arab commentators accused the United States of engineering a plot in which the dismantling of the army would serve to weaken the Sunnis, leading to their political marginalisation in Iraq and, consequently, in the rest of the Arab world while simultaneously promoting a strong Shi'a counterbalance. Iranian influence on Iraqi political life after 2003 became extensive and Iran 'built an impressive network of allies and clients, ranging from intelligence operatives, armed militias, and gangs to, most visibly, politicians in various Iraqi Shiite parties'.[29] Among them was the powerful Iraqi prime minister, Nouri Al-Maliki, whose reign became increasingly authoritarian. Tehran also supported powerful Iraqi Shi'a opposition figures, including Muqtada Al-Sadr and his powerful and autonomous militia the Mehdi Army.

Indeed, one of the lasting consequences of the US occupation of Iraq in 2003 was an intensifying confrontation between Sunnis, led by Saudi Arabia, and Shi'a led by Iran throughout south-west Asia. In the context of the clash of civilisations debate, if Muslims posed a threat to the Western world in the post-11 September world then for the conspiracy theorists what better way was there to counter the danger than by dividing the Muslim people and occupying them with intra-religious conflicts?

Regardless of these accusations, the United States was successful in its bid to topple the Saddam Hussein regime and install a new order in Iraq. The huge military campaign to invade Iraq was effective, with only 139 US troops killed, a small number considering the task at hand. However, the lofty goal of nation-building a prosperous, democratic and stable Iraq was not speedily accomplished. In part this failure was associated with the character of Iraq: 'The new Iraqi state was a backwater: it was weak, unstable, poor, and underdeveloped. The inhabitants were divided by tribal, ethnic, sectarian, religious, and regional differences.'[30] Tellingly, this was in fact a description of post-Ottoman Iraq that was inherited by the British in 1921, but almost a century later little had changed and the challenge of transforming Iraq into a secure and relatively democratic modern state was not overcome in the aftermath of the Saddam Hussein era.

Putin's second term and Iraq

Having overwhelmingly won a second term as Russian president on 14 March 2004, Putin found himself and Russia in a considerably stronger position vis-à-vis the United States than four years earlier. Moscow was long disenchanted with the United States over a range of issues, including NATO expansion and the proposed missile defence shield over Eastern Europe. Meanwhile, the Bush administration had become hostile towards a number of states that did not support the US invasion of Iraq and in December 2003, after months of 'hinting that countries that did not support the invasion of Iraq would pay a price' the US Defense Department released a list of countries it would allow 'to bid on lucrative contracts for rebuilding Iraq'.[31] Russia, France, Germany, and Canada were excluded from the list. Russia's Defence Minister Sergei Ivanov immediately responded to the announcement that Moscow expected payment of the $8 billion debt owed to it by occupied Iraq that was incurred during the Saddam Hussein era. Soon after winning control of the Russian parliament on 7 December 2003 Putin warned the United States in a live television broadcast against harbouring 'imperial ambitions'.[32]

Putin's behaviour occasionally caused bewilderment as the Russian president sometimes showed rather extraordinary signs of flexibility towards the United States over Iraq in the second half of 2004. This included Putin's assertion in June 2004 that Russian intelligence had warned the United States, while Saddam Hussein was still president, 'on more than one occasion that Iraq was preparing acts of terror in the US and its facilities worldwide'.[33] The statement was unusual in light of popular scepticism because it supported Bush's assertion that Saddam Hussein's regime posed a threat to US national security and subtly offered a justification for the invasion of Iraq despite Putin's claim that he had been against the war all along. Putin's revelation is only demystified when considered in the context of the upcoming re-election of George Bush later that year. Putin did not hide his desire to see Bush re-elected and there were many indications that the two men enjoyed a good personal relationship and political understanding. Despite the democratisation rhetoric, Bush was noticeably coy about discussing Russia's drift towards authoritarianism, including the tightening state control of the media and the marginalisation of opposition parties and figures. During a post-meeting press statement by Bush after meeting Putin on 8 June 2004 to discuss Iraq, the US president tellingly reflected: 'I always enjoy talking to my friend, Vladimir Putin. He's a strong leader who cares deeply about the people of his country and understands the issues that we face.'[34]

The meeting came on the day Russia voted in favour of UNSC Resolution 1546 that provided endorsement for the establishment on 30

June 2004 of the Iraqi Interim Government (IIG) under the leadership of Prime Minister Iyad Allawi. In view of the world media, Bush told his Russian counterpart: 'I appreciate your help, Vladimir, on getting that Security Council resolution through today.'[35] Although Moscow interpreted the transition of authority as a step in the right direction because it technically ended direct US rule of Iraq and transferred it to local actors, the IIG, like Allawi, were perceived as being US pawns. Nonetheless, in another gesture of cooperation with the United States, Putin warmly hosted Allawi in Moscow in early December 2004. During the meeting the prospect of Moscow's share of Iraq's economic rejuvenation was placed high on the agenda and Allawi's promises to award Russian companies lucrative contracts were partially fulfilled while 'Russia agreed to forgive 80 per cent of Iraq's debt.'[36] Despite the political and security uncertainty in Iraq at that time Putin was apparently content with Bush's assurances that the IIG was temporary until a permanent and a democratically elected government replaced it.

Legislative elections for a newly formed Iraqi National Assembly took place as scheduled on 30 January 2005. The elections were held in an atmosphere of extreme violence and although the Kurds and Shi'a participated in large numbers the Sunnis, who formed the backbone of the insurgency in central Iraq, boycotted the vote. The elected National Assembly was primarily charged with drafting a new constitution, which was ratified by a referendum in October 2005. Once again, the representation of Iraqi Sunnis was minimised in the face of a Shi'a-Kurdish understanding, leading to heightened fears of Iraq's disintegration. On 15 December 2005 general elections were held for the National Assembly, after its predecessor completed its role of drafting a constitution, and a new government was established under the leadership of Prime Minister Nouri Al-Maliki. The elected president of the Republic was Jalal Talabani, a long-time Kurdish opponent of Saddam Hussein.

On the surface, the democratic achievements in Iraq were commendable and there were high hopes that the country was heading towards stable rule. However, Washington had grossly miscalculated regional factors, including the geo-strategic ambitions of Syria and Iran. Pro-Iranian Shi'a parties dominated the National Assembly and the Maliki government. On the ground, Iranian-backed militias ruled southern Iraq as well as Baghdad's suburbs. In the north Kurds appeared to be heading towards creating an independent state while in the centre the

Sunnis felt marginalised and their voice became hijacked by foreign militant extremists. There was deep concern in Saudi Arabia and other moderate Arab Sunni states that Iranian influence in Iraq would launch wider Shi'a hegemony in the Gulf and the rest of south-west Asia. Considering that Syria, ruled by the Alawite Shi'a sect and which bordered Iraq to the west, was a close Iranian ally and the Shi'a Hezbollah was dominant in Lebanon, leading figures including King Abdullah of Jordan and President Hosni Mubarak of Egypt warned of a Shi'a crescent spanning the Middle East from Iran to the Mediterranean. Adding to these fears, on 14 February 2005 former Lebanese Prime Minister Rafiq Hariri was murdered in a massive bomb attack as his motorcade drove through central Beirut. Hariri was a towering Sunni figure in Lebanon who, by the time of his assassination, had acquired international stature. The billionaire tycoon was the driving force behind the economic revival of Lebanon following its thirty-year civil war and became a model of Sunni Muslim moderation. He was also close to the West and enjoyed particularly good relations with President Jacques Chirac of France. His elimination from Lebanese politics helped remove a significant counterbalance to the Shi'a Hezbollah and their Iranian and Syrian patrons in the country.

Russia's role in this regional shift during Putin's second term was highly significant. While maintaining relative pliancy over Iraq, Moscow focused its main attention on Iran in recognition of its ascending status. Iranian influence, in partnership with Syria, was not only restricted to Iraq but was considerable in Lebanon and among Palestinian factions. Russia therefore very intelligently continued to give the impression of cooperating with the United States over Iraq but simultaneously developed close relations with Iran and Syria and thus participating in the weakening of the US role in Iraq. Between 2005 and 2006 Washington's criticisms of Iran and Syria intensified as both countries were accused of allowing insurgents into Iraq in order to disrupt civil order and security. According to US counterterrorism coordinator Henry Crumpton, 'Iran supports Hezbollah. They are really the paymasters for Hezbollah who in turn are working with some of the Iraqis inside Iraq.'[37] Syria was also accused of allowing into Iraq Sunni insurgents with links to Al-Qaeda or former Iraqi Ba'thists, who were responsible for bloody terrorist attacks in order to cajole Washington into a compromise. The leadership in Damascus was the prime suspect in the Hariri assassination and had its own fears that it would follow the same fate as the Iraqi Ba'thist counterparts.

In 2006 Moscow hardened its international approach by preventing effective US measures from being taken against Syria and Iran, especially as the latter was also being accused by the West of developing a non-peaceful nuclear programme. Facing intensifying calls for withdrawal from Iraq in the Middle East and Europe, Bush's military adventure was being written off by many as a failure. Israel's failure to defeat Hezbollah in the 2006 war in Lebanon and the worsening situation on the Palestinian-Israeli front added to the demise of Washington's role as a Middle East's power-broker. However, it was the violence in Iraq and the rising death toll of US soldiers that struck the reputation of the United States most harshly on the international stage in the Bush era.

Moscow found an easy opportunity to exploit this weakened US position, allowing Russia to reassert its presence in the Middle East and strengthen its hand in negotiations with Washington on a range of global issues. Russia cunningly pursued its aims by continuing to refrain from lending vocal or material support to the Iraqi insurgents and quite often actually condemning the violence instigated by these groups. At the same time, Moscow's political elite encouraged a political solution for Iraq that included a multilateral approach involving many countries and particularly neighbouring Iran and Syria. Deputy Foreign Minister Alexander Saltanov, in 2006, emphasised Moscow's role in 'helping to concretise international aid for Iraq, through contacts with our friends in the region, the countries close to Iraq and then with the United States, Great Britain, France and Italy'.[38] An international conference called the International Compact with Iraq to provide economic support was organised in Sharm el-Sheikh, Egypt on 3 May and, significantly, it was attended by Iran and Syria in a sign of appeasement by Washington. But the gathering avoided political topics and did not involve direct talks between the United States and Iran and Syria. Russian efforts for a regional conference dedicated to defining Iraq's political future were stubbornly snubbed by Washington. In a televised interview at the end of 2007 Primakov reflected that: 'Iraq is a bleeding wound. We suggested from the beginning an international conference on Iraq with all its neighbours. However the US did not respond positively.'[39]

As an indicator of the friction between Moscow and Washington that had developed over Iraq, the Russian Foreign Ministry used particularly strong language to describe the televised hanging of former Iraqi dictator Saddam Hussein. On 31 December 2006 a spokesman for the ministry, Mikhail Kamynin, described the public execution as 'hasty and cruel, and shamelessly broadcast to the world'.[40] The key to the solution, according to Russia's foreign policy elite, was through national reconciliation endorsed by a regional conference. The Foreign Ministry statement warned that US intransigence was leading to a cycle of bloodshed and violence and placed on American shoulders 'the full weight of responsibility for what is happening in that country, and for the open disregard for the humanistic values they are zealously teaching others'.[41] In late 2007 the fragmentation of Iraq was a major preoccupation for regional and international leaderships, including Turkey, Saudi Arabia and Jordan. By then European public opinion also strongly objected to the US strategy in Iraq, leaving Washington isolated and Moscow in the mainstream, strengthening Putin's image in Russia and abroad.

The Iranian and Syrian positions were more obscure because while officially supporting unity, the division of Iraq offered new opportunities for expanding their regional hegemony and undermining the US and its allies. Unlike Iran and Syria, Moscow seemed to prefer preserving the integrity of Iraq because of genuine fears about the instability that the division of Iraq would cause. Syria's duplicity angered the Iraqi leadership and at times Prime Minister Maliki criticised Damascus for allowing terrorists to infiltrate across their shared borders while President Talabani simultaneously castigated the Syrian leadership for endorsing Turkish incursions into northern Iraq to attack Kurdish separatists. Talabani a Kurd himself, complained in October 2007, 'How could the president of an Arab country support military intervention against the Republic of Iraq? This is a very serious matter that hurts relations between the two countries.'[42]

Although Primakov had not officially spoken on behalf of the Russian Foreign Ministry or government since 1998 he continued to act as a foreign affairs adviser to Putin, who periodically dispatched him on special diplomatic missions throughout his presidency. Primakov warned late in 2007 that the violence in Iraq would deteriorate further between US forces and the various Shi'a militias, while 'neglect of the Sunnis also needs to be addressed by Washington and the international community'.[43] By bringing in Syria and Iran to discuss Iraq's future, Russia, as their diplomatic patron at the UN Security Council and on the international stage, was indirectly being brought into the equation as a bridge between them and the United States. Moscow calculated that the inclusion of international and regional powers in the political process diluted US political monopoly of Iraq. The linkage Primakov made between national reconciliation in Iraq and an international conference that included the participation of Iraq's neighbours was the cornerstone of Russian foreign policy during Putin's second term as president.

Back to economics

Russian policy towards Iraq, or rather the manipulation of the US invasion in 2003, had arguably achieved significant success by the time Putin completed his second term as president. With the United States weakened and searching for an honourable exit, Russia coordinated well with its regional friends Iran and Syria to regain a political foothold in the region. By 2007 Washington had been forced to undergo a major reversal in policy by talking directly with Iran to discuss Iraqi security. Doing so was recognition by the United States that it was unable to resolve the Iraqi problem unilaterally. The election victory of Barack Obama in 2008 only served to underline the US retreat and the new course of building partnerships for peace. This included what Obama described as resetting relations with Russia and respecting its voice in world affairs.

Russia's ability to emphasise its political role also improved its economic prospects in the region. Coordination with Tehran enabled Moscow to nurture relations with the Maliki government in order to allow Russian companies to compete in various Iraqi sectors, including energy and construction. On 19 September 2007 Iraq's Foreign Minister Hoshyar Zebari visited Moscow and discussed with his counterpart Sergei Lavrov the possibility of cooperation between Russia and Iran in the oil sector. The following year, in February 2008, Zebari met with senior Russian officials and during the visit Russia agreed to forfeit $12 billion, or 93 per cent of Iraq's debt. As a response, Zebari announced that 'the doors are open for Russian companies to work in Iraq', although he emphasised that they would have to compete on an equal footing with their international rivals.[44]

The cancellation of the debt was a gesture of appreciation towards greater Iraqi willingness to allow Russian companies major contracts in

Iraq. Russian firms in the electricity sphere alone had signed $500 million worth of contracts. Russia was particularly interested in the possibility that Iraq would reconsider bids by LUKOIL, which had its 1997 contract to explore and drill on the West Qurna-2 oil field cancelled by Saddam Hussein. In 2008 President Putin lobbied Maliki to upgrade economic relations, stating that Russian 'companies are ready to increase their contribution to the restoration and modernisation of the economic infrastructure of Iraq, primarily in the energy, oil and gas sectors where we have accumulated rich experience and made good arrangements'.[45] The plea by Putin was accompanied by a visit to Iraq by the president of LUKOIL, Vagit Alekperov, to attempt to revive the West Qurna-2 agreement.

At the end of his second term Putin noted that Russia had expanded its diplomatic missions in the post-Saddam Hussein republic. This included the establishment of a Consulate in the autonomous region of Kurdistan in November 2007, in Irbil and a proposed Consulate in Basra. Putin bluntly explained that he hoped that the opening of the Consulate in Irbil 'will become an important channel for facilitating cooperation with Iraqi Kurdistan' that would pave the way for Russian contracts in the Kirkuk oil fields.[46]

Soon after being elected for his third term as president in 2012 Putin appeared to have scored a major international achievement when media reports revealed that Russia and Iraq signed a staggering arms deal worth $4.2 billion as well as agreements in oil and transport. In October 2012 Prime Minister Maliki visited Russia and met his counterpart Dmitry Medvedev, who had obligingly yielded his presidential ambitions to allow Putin to return to the presidency that year. In that meeting both countries apparently surprised the international community, including the United States, by expressing a strong intention to revive bilateral relations and establish military ties after a dormant period from 2008. Moscow's move also followed Obama's declaration of military withdrawal from Iraq, leaving Maliki with greater confidence to pursue his own ambitions.

Analysts associated the Russian-Iraqi arms deal announcement as being connected to events in neighbouring Syria. Both countries were fearful that the success of the anti-Asad revolution would harm national interests and bring unwanted changes to the region. Maliki was, like Putin, vocal in his rejection of international intervention to topple the

Syrian regime although ironically his own position owed everything to similar intervention to topple Saddam Hussein. According to Russian sources, since 2003 'losses due to the termination of cooperation with Iraq have exceeded $8bn'.[47] As partial compensation, the Russian LUKOIL company was awarded the development of the West Qurna-2 field with an anticipated output of 95 million tons of oil a year. The reported $4 billion military sales created considerable confusion at the time, especially as it raised the possibility that Moscow was seeking to replace Syria with Iraq in the Middle East in a wider bloc that included Iraq. *RIA Novosti* defence analyst Konstantin Bogdanov concluded that although 'the post-Saddam government of Iraq is often viewed as a puppet of Washington', in fact 'that is not true: the new Shia-dominated government is trying to stick to its own independent policy line'.[48] This new independent line had taken Maliki much closer to Tehran, which had emerged as the greatest influence on Iraqi politics in contrast to the much publicised US retreat under Obama.

In the course of over thirteen years of effective control over foreign policy Putin appeared through skilful and opportunistic diplomacy to ensure that Russia adjusted well to the new realities that were forcefully imposed on Iraq. By projecting strength and expanding regional influence in cooperation with Syria and Iran, Iraqi leaders realised that it was erroneous to undermine the role of Russia as an important regional actor and economic partner. Moscow simultaneously avoided a confrontation with the United States and at the same time participated in weakening its position by aligning with anti-US forces in the Middle East. Obama's election victory in 2008 was a consequence of Bush's failure to deal decisively with Iran and Syria. Bush's vacillations between military action and engagement towards them in his second term left the door open for Russia to enter the fray in defiance of the bleak forecasts about Moscow's chances of regaining regional significance during Putin's first term as president.

Putin's critics in Russia and beyond pointed out that the popular uprisings in the Middle East and the revolution in Syria as well as the growing opposition to Maliki in Iraq in early 2013 served to highlight Moscow's narrow vision by consistently making wrong choices for short-term goals. Indeed, soon after the announcement of the $14 billion arms deal Maliki's office denied that such an agreement had ever been made and pointed instead to allegations of corruption in the Iraqi defence ministry. The Baghdad political establishment also recognised that despite the military withdrawal the United States remained a powerful political and economic actor in the region and the pragmatic Maliki wished to avoid displeasing Washington because of the arms deal with Russia. The remaining advocates of a Western-friendly Russian foreign policy could point out that the Soviet experience had taught Moscow that it was pointless to antagonise the West by linking national interests with fragile Middle East regimes.

7

THE SYRIA-LEBANON DILEMMA

As Yeltsin's strategists began their first draft of formulating foreign policy, Lebanon and Syria should have been allocated very little geo-strategic and economic relevance for Russia. Both countries did not directly border the former Soviet space and both were relatively small in terms of population, landmass and global economic impact. Yet Moscow exerted a great deal of effort, some would say disproportionately so, in diplomatic activity towards Syria and Lebanon from the mid-1990s. This was epitomised by Moscow's defiant defence of the Bashar Asad regime in a losing battle against popular rebellion that began in 2011, which antagonised important actors in the region and beyond. Two obvious reasons for Russia's position were the centrality of both countries in the ongoing conflict with Israel and, perhaps even more so, the special interplay between them and Iran. Syria was the inseparable regional ally of Iran in a bond dating back to the early 1980s. Hezbollah, an Iranian proxy militant group founded in the early 1980s was a powerful and often a decisive player in Lebanese politics. The relationship between Lebanon and Syria had been so intertwined since the 1970s that until 2005 Russia, much like the United States, viewed Lebanon only through the Syrian prism. The mass peaceful protests of 2005 forced the withdrawal of the 40,000 military force that had ensured Lebanese compliance to Syrian authority.

The popular anti-Syrian Cedar Revolution in 2005 forced Moscow to revise its approach and to play a balancing act in subsequent years as

Lebanon struggled to assert its independence from Syrian efforts to re-impose hegemony. Moscow ostensibly offered support for Lebanese independence as Lebanon, after all, was a founding UN member and a recognised sovereign state. Moscow's support for Lebanon's pro-democracy independence movement however risked antagonising its traditional partners Iran and Syria. Yet Moscow calculated that blatant Russian support for the anti-Cedar Revolution coalition, led by Hezbollah, would tarnish Russia in the club of pariah states and place it in contradiction of international law. Russian foreign policy, particularly in light of Primakov's influence, consistently sanctified the principle of sovereignty and downplayed the relevance of non-state actors, such as Hezbollah, and rejected external influence on any country by other states or blocs such as NATO. A few years after the largely peaceful Cedar Revolution, Moscow reverted to the same principle as the reason for rejecting external interference, including that of the UN Security Council, in Syria's violent uprising, which by mid 2013 had led to over 100,000 deaths, despite its own support for the regime and knowing that Iranian and Hezbollah militants were active participants in the military suppression of the uprising.

Moscow's paradoxical approach towards Lebanon and Syria was at least correct in recognising that the two countries were jointly at the heart of a complex web of international relations, which ultimately impacted Russia's relationship with the United States, Europe and the key countries in the Middle East. Syria and Lebanon were the remaining neighbours of Israel that did not sign a peace treaty with the Jewish state. In the 1990s, Russia took its first steps in a long-term project to present itself as a neutral but direct facilitator between Israel and its hostile neighbours. Under Putin, Russia's role mutated into a more pro-active Russian interference on behalf of Syria, Iran and Hezbollah to create a counterbalance not only to Israel, but ultimately the United States and its regional allies. Putin's critics in Russia and beyond emphasised that Moscow's alignment with Syria and Iran shaped the Western view of Putin and was an indicator of his true democratic credentials. Yet Putin belittled this factor and Russian foreign policy believed instead that the Iran-Syria-Hezbollah triumvirate formed a stalwart buffer against US influence and provided Moscow with the opportunity of a firm presence in the region.

Lebanon until 2004

Lebanon's modern history is filled with tragedy. Since independence from France in 1943 the country has struggled to survive due to regional and international rivalries manipulating internal divisions. Lebanese intellectuals and political thinkers have often repeated the quote dating back to 1950s that Lebanon's 'weakness is its strength and its strength is its weakness'.[1] The riddle is a simple one to solve. Most countries in the region after the Second World War had quickly become militarised, radicalised and homogeneous, as epitomised by the military coups in Egypt, Syria and Iraq in the 1950s. Lebanon, in contrast, remained culturally and religiously diverse and tolerant. Its political system was competitive yet liberal and largely pacifist. Beirut was known as the capital of press and political freedoms in the Middle East and was home to many political exiles from the region. This strength that made Lebanon somewhat unique in the Middle East also left it vulnerable to foreign interference and encountered repeated efforts to dominate it by ambitious neighbours. The first serious attempt was when Egypt's Gamal Abdul Nasser sought through the union with Syria to bring Lebanon into the fold in 1958. It was only President Camille Chamoun's attentiveness to the danger that prevented the scheme from succeeding by his timely request for US military assistance.

The division of Lebanon's political scene between liberal Westernisers and authoritarian anti-Western forces, usually with Soviet backing, ultimately facilitated the collapse of the Lebanese state in the 1970s. Threats to Lebanon's political system and national existence were accentuated in the 1960s when Palestinian fighters began entering Lebanon in large numbers to open a new front against Israel's northern borders. Lebanon became the most convenient location for Palestine Liberation Organisation (PLO) militants in the 1970s after Israel's other neighbours, Egypt, Jordan and Syria, all prevented Palestinian raids from their territories to avoid an unwanted war in light of the humiliating 1967 experience.

The Palestinian militants had become a destabilising factor in Jordan in the late 1960s, sparking genuine fears that with backing from Syria's Ba'ath regime, which was hostile to the conservative Jordanian government, they could overthrow the ruling Hashemite monarchy. Jordan's King Hussein's firm military response defeated the Palestinian revolt in September 1970 and tens of thousands of fighters were expelled, with many ending up in Lebanon. This confrontation, known as Black September, would in time become an important milestone on the path to Lebanon's civil war that officially started in 1976.

Lebanon's weak state structure and sectarian diversity were unable to withstand the weight of a well-armed, motivated and highly ideologised Palestinian movement. While the PLO was nominally led by the cunning Yasser Arafat, there were competing factions within the organisation, including the pro-Soviet Marxist Leninist Popular Front for the Liberation of Palestine led by George Habash, and off-shoots such as the Popular Democratic Front for the Liberation of Palestine led by Nayef Hawatmeh and Al-Sai'ka, which was a Syrian-manufactured group created intentionally to undermine Arafat's leadership. Coordination with these groups allowed Damascus a firm foothold in Lebanon and eventually in fulfilling a longstanding ambition to dominate the country under President Asad until his death on 10 June 2000.

Lebanon's plunge into Syrian, and thus potentially Soviet, influence concerned Israel and the West, particularly as superpower relations deteriorated after the Soviet invasion of Afghanistan in late 1979. The anti-communist leaderships in Washington and London in the 1980s openly espoused their combative ambitions on the international stage. The retreat of moderate forces in Lebanon and the ascendancy of Syria and the Palestinians there led to the Israeli invasion of Lebanon on 6 June 1982 in a massive operation that culminated in the occupation of Beirut. The military offensive led by Israeli Defence Minister Ariel Sharon involved the largest fighter jet battle ever recorded in the twentieth century with the Syrian air force, comprised of Soviet-made MiGs, suffering an overwhelming defeat with the loss of eighty-six jets while Israel did not record a single loss.[2] The June 1982 war in Lebanon also exposed Soviet impotence in its support for its Palestinian and Syrian allies. According to the Israeli academic Galia Golan, Moscow's policies highlighted 'contradictions [that] revolve around Moscow's willingness to provide arms and all-out support for the Arabs' positions, while being unwilling to approve of wars and risk intervention which might endanger Moscow's primary interest in avoiding military confrontation with the United States'.[3]

Israel's 1982 military offensive further complicated Moscow's already delicate position in Lebanon. Soviet relations with the Lebanese Communist Party had been badly damaged in the 1960s when an internal coup by young reformers overthrew the old guard, which was loyal to Moscow. George Hawi was among the reformist leaders who at the time insisted on the Lebanese Communist Party maintaining an independent line in local decisions. The Soviet leadership was not sympathetic to his perspective, and Hawi was accused of being a CIA agent by the prominent ideologist Mikhail Suslov.[4] Moscow instead invested in developing ties with Marxist Palestinian groups based in Lebanon in the late 1970s, which were to collaborate more closely with the Soviet Union. In the late 1970s relations with these leftist groups were utilised by Soviet intelligence 'to establish contact with Iranian opposition members and radical Lebanese Shi'ite groups, which also were training in Palestinian camps at that time'.[5] These connections proved to be significant, particularly as some of these militant Shi'a groups established Hezbollah in 1982. Hezbollah, translated as Party of God, was an extension of a global Shi'a awakening following the Iranian Islamic Revolution in 1979 under the spiritual and political leadership of Ayatollah Khomeini in Iran. Hezbollah and Iran, consumed in anti-secular religious fervour, viewed the Soviet Union as satanic as the United States and Lebanese Communist Party followers were regularly assassinated by Shi'a zealots.

The Soviet impact on Lebanese affairs diminished from 1982 until the early years of the Yeltsin presidency in the post-Soviet Union era despite Syria's re-emergence after the setback of the Israeli invasion and occupation of Lebanon. Asad had successfully managed to place himself in the position of leader of the resistance against Israel in Lebanon after 1982 by partnering Iran regionally and facilitating the training and arming of Hezbollah. Syria acquired further influence and legitimacy as a result of its support for the US-led coalition to liberate Kuwait from Saddam Hussein's Iraq in August 1990. Damascus was rewarded with Washington's tacit approval of Syria's occupation of Lebanon soon after the official ending of Lebanon's civil war.

The political balance in Lebanon remained fragile during the 1990s which enabled Asad to successfully market Syria's military presence in the war-ravaged country as being essential in maintaining peace and stability. Moreover, Asad had managed to convince the United States and Israel that his close ties to the Iranian leadership allowed him to maintain a leverage of control over Hezbollah. In the eyes of the West Syria had come in from the cold and even began negotiating peace terms with Israel in 1991. The rose-tinted glasses in Washington and other

European capitals failed to notice that Damascus was also helping its key Lebanese allies Hezbollah and the Amal Movement, both Shi'a, to grow into powerful militias over the course of the decade to act as its indigenous policemen under the pretext of resisting Israel's occupation of southern Lebanon. By allowing Lebanon's Shi'a, and particularly Hezbollah, to emerge as Lebanon's most dominant political and military actors in the 1990s Syria had also allowed Iranian influence to reach Lebanon and expand in the Middle East while delicately and patiently undermining the US role in the region.

Meanwhile, post-Soviet Russia in the early 1990s under Yeltsin adopted a more formal state-to-state diplomatic approach towards Lebanon and its post-civil war governments, downplaying relations with militia groups and non-state actors. Ostensibly, this pattern of state-to-state bilateral relations continued under Putin despite growing evidence that Moscow began since 2005 to support one coalition, led by Hezbollah, in favour of the Cedar Revolution coalition. Moscow's policy towards Lebanon suggested a repeated pattern of behaviour, except Soviet support in Lebanon for anti-Israeli and anti-Western Palestinian guerrillas in the 1970s was replaced under Putin by Russian support, via Syria and Iran, for anti-Israeli and anti-Western Shi'a militants.

Improving Russian-Iranian relations throughout the 1990s were mirrored by more positive interaction between Russia and Hezbollah but Yeltsin was initially reticent about elaborating these links because of the hostility that it could provoke from Israel and the United States. Iran's spiritual leader and successor to Khomeini, Ayatollah Khamen'i, was candid in his assertion that 'Hezbollah is the front line of the Islamic world in its fight with the Zionist enemy.'[6] Such assertions did not sit comfortably with Russia's bid to develop relations with Israel and the United States during Yeltsin's first years in office.

Because the 1990s were considered the decade of unrivalled American power, Hezbollah, Iran and Syria were all eager for Moscow to resume a balancing role in the Middle East to curtail the influence of Washington in the region. Hezbollah's spiritual leader Sheikh Muhammad Fadlallah declared in 1997 that it was time for Moscow to be more assertive in supporting 'Eastern countries, especially Arab and Muslim ones. This is the area where Russia can ...be the counterbalancing power to the West.'[7] Israel began to express concern about the growing contacts between Russia and Hezbollah from 1996 onwards and was particularly dismayed by Moscow's criticisms of Israel's military campaign, Operation Grapes of Wrath, against the Shi'a militant group in the spring of that year. This occurred a year after Foreign Minister Andrei Kozyrev had visited Lebanon hoping to involve Russia in Lebanon's large post-civil war reconstruction drive as well as to promote financial and business links. The Trade and Economy Cooperation Agreement, signed on 31 March 1995, was one outcome of the visit.

Kozyrev's successor Primakov invigorated Russian diplomatic activity in the Middle East by raising the profile of direct contact with Hezbollah. In December 1997 Russian Ambassador to Israel Mikhail Bogdanov had revealed that there were ongoing meetings with Hezbollah officials through the Russian Embassy in Beirut. During Primakov's visit to the Middle East in October 1997 Deputy Foreign Minister Viktor Posuvaliuk met with senior Hezbollah officials, including Shaikh Nai'm Kassem, who was the second most senior figure in the organisation's hierarchy. As part of the tour Primakov visited Israel, where reports revealed tensions in his meeting with then Prime Minister Benjamin Netanyahu. Primakov was hoping to relay news on missing Israeli airman Ron Arad, who disappeared in action over Lebanon in 1986 and was believed to be in Iranian captivity. Netanyahu did not welcome Primakov's efforts and instead relayed his disputing of 'the facts of the transfer of Russian weapons to Iran', as explained by Moscow, with the Israeli defence minister, Yitzak Mordechai, asking Russia to 'stop assisting Iran in developing surface-to-surface missiles and non-conventional weapons'.[8] Ambassador Bogdanov tried to allay Israeli concerns over growing contacts with Hezbollah by claiming that 'our cooperation with the organisation is meant to encourage restraint'.[9] Russia's attempts at playing a mediating role between Hezbollah and Iran on one side and Israel on the other were indicative of a dismissive attitude regarding Lebanon as a sovereign independent state. Hezbollah was a non-state actor that was not under the control of the government of Lebanon but was, rather, a proxy to Iran and Syria.

In April 1997 Prime Minister Rafiq Hariri visited Moscow to meet with his counterpart Victor Chernomyrdin, the first visit ever by a Lebanese head of government to Russia, to sign various trade agreements. The visit helped consolidate relations between Primakov and Hariri, who was an influential figure in the region due to his ties with the Saudi royal family as well as French President Jacques Chirac and other Western leaders. Hariri's significance was thus viewed in terms of enabling Russia to play a bigger role in the wider Middle East peace rather than specifically improving bilateral relations with Lebanon. The prevailing view in Moscow then was that 'Lebanon is not a country which can conduct its foreign policy independently,'[10] in reference to obvious Syrian hegemony.

Following the Israeli withdrawal from Lebanon in 2000 a Druze-Sunni-Maronite alliance emerged in opposition to Hezbollah's powerful arsenal of weapons which it preserved in order to maintain its absolute authority over large areas in the country. The anti-Hezbollah alliance also demanded the withdrawal of Syria's military forces because the pretext that it was a counterbalance to the Israeli occupation no longer existed. Despite the Israeli withdrawal from Lebanon in May 2000 in fulfilment of UNSC Resolution 425, which Soviet and Russian foreign policy had historically endorsed as the key to resolving Lebanese-Israeli differences, relations with Lebanon during Putin's first term continued to be dictated by the regional role of Syria, Iran and Hezbollah. Perceiving the US occupation of Iraq in 2003 as a common threat, coordination between Russia, Iran and Syria gained urgency, which in turn increased the importance of Hezbollah as a regional player from Moscow's perspective.

A decade after the civil war had ended the risk of internal strife in Lebanon diminished and the role of the Syrian army as peacekeeping forces became redundant. Moreover, the death of the ruthless Syrian President Hafez Asad in June 2000, after thirty years of rule, encouraged the Lebanese that there could be a softening stance by Damascus. In fact, Bashar Asad proved to be as dogmatic as his father in viewing Lebanon as a province of greater Syria and endeavoured to transform the country's traditional communal diversity into a centralised system subservient to Damascus. Lebanese-Syrian tensions escalated to the extent that by 2005, when Syrian forces were forced to withdraw, Moscow faced the uncomfortable choice between building relations with an independent Lebanese state or openly pursuing Russia's broader agenda of aligning with Iran and Syria to undermine the US presence in the region. During Putin's second term it became evident that Moscow preferred the latter at the expense of Lebanese independence and wider regional stability.

Putin and post-Hariri Lebanon

Lebanon's internal political situation became deadlocked from 1996 due to a power struggle between Hariri, who was an exponent of liberalising the Lebanese economy and integrating it with the West against Syria, which through its Lebanese allies sought to tighten its grip on its small neighbour and eliminate the influence of Hariri's international supporters. International neglect of the Lebanese file and tacit US support for Syrian hegemony indirectly served to prolong and escalate the friction. The US perspective towards Lebanon until 2005 was not actually very different from that of Russia. A US diplomat in Beirut expressed quite frankly when questioned that 'the United States did not have a Lebanon policy until 2005'.[11] It was a raw confession of what more senior US and Russian officials had been coyly and diplomatically implying for many years.

Hariri's regional and international stature had grown steadily since the early 1990s but he generally avoided openly antagonising Damascus due to the tacit international, and specifically US, recognition of Syrian dominance in Lebanon. Lebanese antagonism towards Syrian hegemony continued to intensify, however, and reached a crisis point on 3 September 2004 with the decision by the leadership in Damascus to extend the term of its loyal delegate President Emile Lahoud beyond his constitutional entitlement. Despite the heavy-handed methods Syrian security agents and their Lebanese allies used to force an amendment to the constitution, twenty-nine MPs out of the 128-member parliament from various sects, including Sunni Mosbah Ahdab, Druze Akram Shehayeb and Maronite Nassib Lahoud, courageously voted against the amendment, which was nonetheless forced through following a campaign of intimidation orchestrated in Damascus and implemented by its allies, led by Amal and Hezbollah.[12]

The rejection of Lahoud's presidential term extension had international support and resulted in UNSC Resolution 1559 on 2 September 2004, which called for the withdrawal of all foreign troops in Lebanon and for the Lebanese to govern their political affairs free from external influence. UNSC Resolution 1559 symbolised a major shift in Western policy towards Lebanon and the Middle East in general. The Bush administration, in light of its ongoing battle with international terrorism and the ideological conviction that unjust regimes encouraged and created terrorist groups, ceased endorsement of Syria's occupation of Lebanon on the grounds that it did not want to appear to be in collusion with an authoritarian system that did not differ much from the Saddam Hussein tyranny. US Ambassador to the UN John Danforth asserted Resolution 1559 was an international statement that Syria's continued military presence in Lebanon was 'wrong' and more significantly 'it would be very wrong of Syria to continue to interfere in the presidential electoral process in Lebanon'.[13]

Hariri's widely admired leadership in reconstructing Lebanon after the civil war, his political moderation and his Western-friendly economic policies allowed him to establish good relations with European states. France was particularly interested in Lebanese affairs because of historic ties dating back to the nineteenth century. Lebanon was officially part of the Francophone community and its Maronites traditionally looked to France as its international guardian. French support for Lebanon against Syrian hegemony facilitated the mending of relations between Paris and Washington following bitter diplomatic hostilities caused by divisions over Iraq. This US-French convergence against Syria created the possibility that the Middle East, not only in the Lebanese context, but more broadly, would evolve towards democratisation and also improved prospects for an Arab-Israeli peace. There were also expectations that by ending Syrian influence in Lebanon and weakening Hezbollah, Iran's and Syria's overall influence in the wider Middle East would be undermined.

In essence Hezbollah was a transnational ideological revolutionary movement manipulated by Iran and Syria to challenge the existing world order by military means. The traditional foreign policy elite in Moscow was unperturbed by Hezbollah, even though this radical movement could have been directed northwards towards Russia's southern rim. Putin's reign began in an atmosphere of hostility towards Islamic militancy in the Caucasus that had pierced the security of the Russian heartland and its own capital city. A decade earlier the Yeltsin leadership had warned that Islam was potentially the most effective unifier of the small and disparate ethnic minorities in Russia.[14] Yet Moscow's growing political endorsement and arming of Iran and its allies in the Middle East, indirectly to include Hezbollah, was based on the consideration from the late 1990s onwards that Sunnis, who made up the bulk of Russia's Muslims, were a distinct political entity from the Shi'is. The conclusions in Moscow were that while global militant Sunni Islam threatened Russian national security the Shi'a version did not, and would serve as a useful tool to undermine the West and its allies in the Middle East. It was observed that Moscow rejected 'Washington's view that Iran is a source of international terrorism'[15] and with major Sunni countries such as Turkey, Egypt, Saudi Arabia and Jordan being closely associated with the United States, Russia opportunistically presented itself as the patron of Shi'is in the Islamic world.

As a Sunni leader Hariri attained a measure of success in building relations with Moscow's leadership. Hariri first visited Russia to meet President Putin in October 2001, in the aftermath of the 11 September 2001 terrorist attacks, and later in March 2003, when both leaders expressed concern over the US occupation of Iraq. Moscow recognised that Hariri's international prestige and his connections with major Muslim leaderships in Saudi Arabia, Pakistan and Malaysia among others served Russian interests. Hariri considered that a resurgent Russia was valuable for promoting Lebanon's various regional causes and for the important role Moscow could play as an interlocutor between Lebanon on one side and Syria and Iran on the other. Yet Hariri's high-profile diplomatic presence on the world stage, including growing contacts with the Russian leadership, was viewed as an act of defiance by the leadership in Damascus, which had since the days under Bashar Asad's father, Hafez, imposed its will to speak on Lebanon's behalf in regional and international matters.

The forced extension of the Lahoud presidency in 2005 created a confrontational setting of a Western drive to contain the dominance of Iran and Syria in Lebanon. This disturbed the Russian leadership, which was already dissatisfied with the US occupation of Iraq. Yet at the time there was growing concern in the West that with the Shi'is emerging victorious in Iraq in the post-Saddam Hussein era the possibility that their Shi'a brethren would forcefully over-run Lebanon through the powerful and well-armed Hezbollah had become a genuine possibility. This scenario would have confirmed the forewarnings of the establishment of a Shi'a crescent spanning from Iran to the Levant.

On 14 February 2005 a huge bomb in the centre of Beirut killed Hariri as well as twenty-one others. The event marked a turning point in the history of Lebanon and to a large extent in the Middle East as a whole. In light of Syria's military occupation of Lebanon and its pervasive and omnipresent intelligence network involved in every detail of the country's political and security domains, the leadership in Damascus was the most natural suspect for most Lebanese. The norm from the 1990s on was that the Syrian regime not only imposed the president of Lebanon but also appointed the heads of the Lebanese army, intelligence and internal security forces and ensured the rapid promotion of its most loyal military officers to higher ranks. The Syrian regime, by virtue of its hegemony, also rewarded political allies handsome commissions on major economic projects and import licences to Lebanon to ensure that it was always able to depend on a large pool of politicians in Lebanese affairs. In light of deep and longstanding popular resentment and national humiliation it was unsurprising that the immediate popular reaction to Hariri's assassination was a massive show of anti-Syrian rage, which rarely in the country's history encompassed a coalition of all of its religious confessions. Hundreds of thousands of ordinary people took to the streets to participate in the Hariri funeral and more notably to demand Syria's withdrawal from Lebanon.

The significant political absentees from the pro-sovereignty rallies in the aftermath of Hariri's murder were Hezbollah and Amal, who not only remained detached from the emotional outburst but on 8 March 2005 organised, through a combination of sectarian appeal and intimidation, a massive street festival under the heading of 'Expressing our Gratitude to Syria'. The two parties presented the Shi'a community of Lebanon as being directly opposed to the pro-Hariri demonstrations a few weeks earlier. Hezbollah's message through its rally had both a national and regional impact. Hariri was an important and powerful Sunni figure not only in Lebanon but also in the Middle East, and his elimination seemed to be an attempt to tilt the overall balance of power in favour of the Iranian-Syrian axis and their proxies in the region. As a response to the 8 March gathering, a counter demonstration was organised in Beirut city centre on 14 March with a massive turnout to explicitly demand the withdrawal of Syrian troops from Lebanon and to call for the impeachment of its proxy president, Emile Lahoud. The Syrian army withdrew in April 2005 but Lahoud managed to remain in office until 2007, ensuring that Syria's network of allies in Lebanese political and security sectors continued to be active.

Despite occasional outbursts of localised violence and a chain of political assassinations targeting leading members of the 14 March movement a tense stalemate characterised Lebanese politics throughout

2005 until the summer of 2006. Russia's position during that period was characterised by ambiguity, as reflected by Foreign Minister Sergei Lavrov's statement regarding the demand for Syrian withdrawal that it was 'not an American view alone'[16] but was based on a UN Security Council Resolution. The implication was that Russia participated in the making of the Security Council Resolution 1559 in support of Lebanese sovereignty. At the same time Lavrov dampened enthusiasm by adding that 'it is a resolution which Russia, together with five other members of the Security Council abstained on'.[17] Russia's oscillating remarks were understandable considering that Lebanon's independence bid received broad European and Arab support which would have left Moscow isolated if it had taken an openly pro-Syrian stance.

Part of the ambiguity was influenced by the fact that key figures in the anti-Syrian alliance in Lebanon included the Druze leader of the Progressive Socialist Party, Walid Jumblatt, who, like his father Kamal, enjoyed historic political ties with Moscow. Other parties and political figures with ties dating back to the Soviet era, including leading members of the Lebanese Communist Party and Christian leftist figures such as George Hawi also joined the Cedar Revolution against Syria. History seemed to repeat itself. In the late 1970s the Soviet Union was forced to choose between supporting Syria or its Lebanese leftist allies after they clashed. Three decades later the Lebanon predicament for Moscow was decisively resolved after 2005, with Russia's position becoming less bashful about its preference for its longstanding relationship with Syria.

War and political crisis

On 12 July 2006 Hezbollah launched an attack inside Israel, killing two soldiers and capturing another two. A botched Israeli rescue attempt resulted in the killing of five more soldiers. Israel then launched a major military campaign against Hezbollah in Lebanon, partly to save face and in part because the initial Hezbollah attack broke previous tacit rules of engagement. From 2000 Israel considered attacks by Hezbollah within the Israeli-occupied Sheb'a Farms as tolerable and its response was usually relatively mild. However, on this occasion Hezbollah attacked soldiers in Israel proper and, more provocatively for the Israeli government, it also launched missile attacks on Israeli towns across the border from Lebanon.

The large quantities and sophistication of Russian military sales to Iran and Syria had rapidly caused high levels of alarm in Israel and the West before the outbreak of hostilities in 2006. Suspicions arose that advanced weapons were reaching Hezbollah as part of a broader agenda to dominate Lebanon and the region. US Secretary of State Condoleezza Rice warned during a meeting with a group of Arab journalists in February 2006 'that Syria, Iran and Hezbollah are a problem for the future course of Lebanon's development and also therefore the future course of the region'.[18]

The war during the summer of 2006 resulted in immense political and military ramifications, creating a seismic impact on the region. Until then doubts lingered about Hezbollah's true loyalties in light of Syrian withdrawal from Lebanon in April 2005 with many Western academics and observers continuing to believe that Hezbollah could be disengaged from its Syrian and Iranian patrons. One Western analysis in 2005 reflected that 'most of Lebanon's ethnic and religious communities want Syria to leave, and even some Lebanese Shiites joined the recent anti-Syrian protests'.[19] Typical of the naivety present among US and other Western observers, the commentator suggested that 'instead of trying to ostracise Hezbollah, Washington should focus on trying to get the organisation to stop pursuing its goals through violence'.[20] The cold reality of the war in the summer of 2006 showed that Hezbollah was an extremely well-armed organisation with global reach and unlimited ambitions working under tight Iranian and Syrian control. The Israeli ground offensive was efficiently halted on the southern Lebanese hills using advanced Russian-made anti-tank missiles, procured originally by Syria. It was only because of Iranian and Syrian support that thousands of Hezbollah rockets rained down on northern Israeli towns and settlements during the war. Moreover, Israeli sources revealed that listening posts manned by Russian and Syrian intelligence personnel on the Golan Heights provided information to Hezbollah during its clashes with Israel. Iranian intelligence personnel were also involved in coordinating with the Syrians in the new Russian-built communications centre on the unoccupied side of the Golan Heights.[21]

The war of 2006 was primarily due to regional and global factors rather than a local dispute between Hezbollah and Israel over the Sheb'a Farms. Significantly, the initial Hezbollah raid was carried out on the eve of the G-8 Summit in St Petersburg when it was anticipated that Washington and its Western allies would press Russia to endorse additional sanctions against Iran over its nuclear programme. Putin's friendly overtures to the West during the first term of his presidency became a distant cloud by the time of the G-8 Summit in St Petersburg in July 2006 and the deteriorating relations between Russia and the West coincided with the darkening political and security mood in the Middle East. Dmitry Trenin, director of the Carnegie Moscow Center, provided a starkly accurate analogy just before the start of the war, observing that Russia had seen itself 'as Pluto in the Western solar system, very far from the centre but still fundamentally a part of it. Now it has left that orbit entirely: Russia's leaders have given up on becoming part of the West and have started creating their own Moscow-centred system.'[22] Moscow's position during the war therefore was always going to stifle Western proposals on the end game of the war. As the war raged, Putin placed emphasis on an immediate ceasefire and to focus on the widely broadcast humanitarian impact on the Lebanese and Israeli populations and thus shelving discussions on possible sanctions against Iran.

Hezbollah's eventual success in impeding the Israeli assault in 2006 allowed Syria and Iran to make the political assertion to the West that no settlement in the Middle East would succeed without their blessing. The war effectively countered efforts to undermine Syrian and Iranian influence from 2004 through UNSC Resolution 1559, which sought to disarm Hezbollah and strengthen the Lebanese state. The assassination of Hariri in 2005, allegedly one of the figures responsible for UNSC Resolution 1559 and one of Lebanon's political heavyweights, was interpreted as being linked to the role of Hezbollah, its Syrian and Iranian patrons and the authority of the Lebanese state. The war in 2006 led to massive infrastructural devastation and the loss of over 1,200 lives on the Lebanese side but it strengthened the standing of Hezbollah and its patrons as a noble resistance to Israel's aggression, in part due to Russia's efforts to ensure a face-saving and speedy ceasefire. UNSC Resolution 1701 was adopted as a compromise to end the war by demanding an Israeli withdrawal from Lebanon and also to limit Hezbollah by calling on the Lebanese army to patrol the southern region bordering Israel, which Hezbollah had prevented in the past. The Resolution also dispatched a largely symbolic international observation force to monitor possible smuggling of weapons through Syria and by sea.

Following the 2006 war, efforts to restrain Hezbollah achieved little, considering that the democratically elected government of Fu'ad Siniora was pitifully helpless in the face of Lebanon's best-armed and well-funded military organisation. Moscow's ambiguous behaviour in 2006 and thereafter became a source of increasing concern not only in the West but rather understandably in Israel. In early 2006, several months before the start of the war, the head of Israel's military intelligence, General Aharan Zeevi-Farkash, criticised the use of Russian-made rocket-propelled grenades by Hezbollah in recent skirmishes. These weapons were first sold to Syria, with the insinuation that Russia would have known that their ultimate destination was Hezbollah, a claim that the Foreign Ministry in Moscow immediately denied.[23] An experienced Israeli commentator, pointed out that: 'Syria's centrality to the collection and transfer of intelligence to Hezbollah is based on separate agreements Damascus signed with Moscow and Tehran on intelligence cooperation,' and 'as happened with the significant numbers of advanced Russian anti-tank missiles procured by Syria and transferred to Hezbollah, Russia found itself operating indirectly in favour of the Lebanese Shi'ite organisation in matters of intelligence.'[24] Israeli accusations accompanied other serious allegations concerning the transfer of heavy weaponry from Russia to Hezbollah. In Spring 2003 there were claims that since 2002 Hezbollah had been acquiring SA-18 shoulder-fired anti-aircraft missiles, leading Israeli National Security Advisor Ephraim Halevy to ask the Russian government to halt the accessibility of such weapons to Hezbollah because of fears that they could target civilian airlines.[25]

Such apprehensions proved to be justified after Russian anti-tank weapons played a decisive role in the 2006 war, with television pictures transmitting their success in targeting Israeli tanks as they timidly trundled through the undulating Lebanese hills. Israeli Prime Minister Ehud Olmert's first trip after the summer 2006 war was to Russia to seek assurances from Putin that support for Syria and Iran would be curtailed but the response to such pleas was deliberately cool. Moscow continued to express its unwillingness to abandon Syria and by doing so it supported Damascus against international diplomatic pressure to halt its interference in Lebanese affairs. Olmert's visit coincided with strong statements by Israel's ambassador to Spain, intended to highlight his government's despondency with Western diplomatic efforts to engage Damascus by warning that 'Syria is not part of the solution. It is part of the problem.'[26]

Israel's efforts were fruitless partly because the country's political establishment was woefully fragmented over how to deal with Syria.

This was highlighted by Olmert's visit to Moscow in October 2008, his last overseas trip as prime minister, to convince the newly elected Russian President Dmitry Medvedev to abort further sales of sophisticated weapons to Syria. Hounded by financial scandals, Olmert was soon after forced to resign as prime minister but his reputation was equally tarnished by his failure to adequately deal with the growing power of Syria and Hezbollah, placing Israel's security at risk. Olmert had been one of the chief exponents of engaging Syria among Israel's political elite. Yet Russia continued to supply weapons to Syria, while newly-elected US President Barack Obama quickened the pace of courting the regime in Damascus, which indirectly further strengthened the position Hezbollah in Lebanon. Yet the policy of engagement not only proved worthless but also counterproductive in light of warnings that the regime could utilise chemical weapons in 2012.

Leaders of Lebanon's Cedar Revolution had repeatedly rang alarm bells that Hezbollah harboured a hidden agenda to invalidate the power-sharing formula in Lebanon outlined in the country's constitution, the Ta'if Accord signed in 1989, to enable more power to the numerically dominant Shi'is and potentially allow them to establish an Islamic state based on the Iranian model. Rodger Shanahan explained that: 'Although estimated to comprise 40 per cent or more of the population, [the Shi'a] are limited to 21 per cent of parliamentary seats and barred from becoming president or prime minister. Hezbollah initially opposed the 1989 Ta'if Accord because it failed to rectify this imbalance.'[27] The success of the Shi'is in Iraq after 2003 served as a model that could be emulated in Lebanon and this Iranian-led Shi'a resurgence was boosted by the prospect of Shi'a nuclear weapons in the hands of Iran. The strengthening of Hezbollah was endorsed by Syria because Damascus wanted to crush the Cedar Revolution movement to restore its influence in Lebanon. The Syrian leadership recognised that non-Arab Iran needed Syria as a bridge into Lebanon, establishing cooperation based on mutual interests between the two countries.

Russia's endorsement for the powerful Syrian-Iranian alliance was highlighted by *Newsweek* magazine in early 2006, pointing out that while Europe moved toward 'the tougher stance taken by the United States…a newly confident Russia has stepped […in] as middleman between East and West, reaching out to the region's untouchables—and making it clear that Moscow won't be taking orders from anyone.'[28]

Moscow's strategic endorsement of Iran and Syria raised fears that were expressed explicitly by Jumblatt and echoed by the monarchies of Jordan and Saudi Arabia, as well as Egyptian President Hosni Mubarak of 'Iranian plans to dominate the region with Syrian partnership ... to lead to the persianification of the region'[29] and eliminate the US counterbalance. Russian unease over NATO expansion in Europe, the invasion and occupation of Iraq and Afghanistan, competition in the energy sector over Eurasian pipeline routing and Washington's quest to spread democracy in Ukraine, Georgia and Lebanon fuelled strong motives to endorse Hezbollah and its regional patrons to undermine the United States in Lebanon and the wider Middle East. Joining forces with Syria and Iran was an important element of Putin's aspiration to place Russia on an equal footing with the United States.

Hariri Tribunal

The assassination of former Prime Minister Rafiq Hariri on 14 February 2005 came after more than a decade of competing political and economic objectives between him and the Syrian leadership. Tensions were contained until late 2004 because Hariri understood he was helpless in light of the Syrian regime's capacity for violence so he instead bought in the Syrian regime and its Lebanese allies into the economic and financial reconstruction of the country to promote stability and maintain a degree of political influence. When Lebanese economic growth slowed Hariri felt that Hezbollah's militant activities were not only unnecessary in light of the Israeli withdrawal from southern Lebanon in 2000 but were also harmful to investment and tourism opportunities in the country. The long-term success of Hariri's economic plans was heavily dependent on regional peace. As prospects for regional stability dimmed, by 2004 Hariri feared that Damascus was ready to impose its full authority over Lebanese affairs and to eliminate him completely from the political scene, relying completely on its loyal proxies instead. This was reflected in Syria's forceful extension of President Lahoud, widely considered a political puppet of the regime in Damascus who was also personally bitterly hostile towards Hariri.

Pro-Syrian politicians in Lebanon accused Hariri and his allies Marwan Hamadeh and Ghassan Salameh of being the authors of UNSC Resolution 1559, adopted on 2 September 2004, which sought to 'ensure the withdrawal of all non-Lebanese forces from Lebanon' (reference to Syria), and expressed concern 'at the continued presence of armed militias in Lebanon' (reference to Hezbollah).[30] Two of the three names implicated in the Resolution were assassination targets, while the third, Ghassan Salameh, was forced into exile for his own personal safety and he dared not return to Lebanon while the perpetrators of the Hariri assassination remained free to roam.

Immediately following Hariri's murder the United Nations sent a fact-finding mission led by Patrick FitzGerald, formerly a senior officer in the Irish police, who concluded that there was sufficient evidence to consider that the murder was politically motivated and was of interest to the international community. Consequently, UNSC Resolution 1595 was adopted to create a special investigative committee that was headed by Detlev Mehlis. His reports consolidated conclusions reached by the FitzGerald report and alluded to tense relations between Hariri and the Syrian leadership. Mehlis, a respected German prosecutor and judge, pointed to clear evidence of an orchestrated campaign to blacken Hariri's name by linking the former prime minister with corruption. Contrarily, the investigation found that corruption and cronyism was so rife among the Syrian-Lebanese security network the report presented the scenario that rather than being only politically motivated Hariri's murder was possibly sanctioned because he posed a threat to vested financial interests through his privatisation agenda.

Syria rejected Mehlis's claims and accused him of bias. When Damascus began stonewalling the investigation UNSC Resolution 1636 was adopted on 31 October 2005, which targeted Syria specifically in its demand for more meaningful cooperation, implicitly threatening the use of force. Moscow played a subtle role by not appearing to block the investigation into an international crime but simultaneously diluting or undermining the UN investigation efforts. In acquiescence to Syria's demands, for example, Mehlis was replaced by the Belgian prosecutor Serge Brammertz in January 2006, whose interim reports evaded any reference to names or evidence that implicated Syria. Several years later Brammertz was blamed by observers for stalling investigation efforts and indirectly making key evidence redundant. The damage caused to the investigation efforts by Brammertz was noted by his successor in 2007 Daniel Bellemare as well as Mehlis, who expressed his frustration to the media that so much progress made in the case had gone to waste. Suspicions arose in Lebanon that the great power games were trampling the course of justice. Washington's interest in seeking a deal with Damascus over Iraq and in facilitating nuclear negotiations with Iran were significant factors which, when linked to Russia's diplomatic support for Syria and Iran, made it feasible that there were furtive efforts to postpone potentially explosive conclusions relating to the Hariri investigations.

The Syrian government continued to provide very limited support and Brammertz's last report in November 2007 stated that the investigative commission 'will continue to request Syria's full cooperation in the discharge of its mandate'[31] as specified in UNSC Resolution 1636. Brammertz, however, also clouded the findings by requesting a complete forensic review of existing results and widened the scope of possible suspects to significantly absolve Syria. While Brammertz's impact was not decisive it was in part responsible for the delaying of the establishment of the Special Tribunal in Lebanon until 2013. Intriguingly, Washington praised Damascus for providing limited cooperation over Iraq and the Syrian regime resumed indirect negotiations with Israel through Turkish mediation at around the same time of Brammertz's final report.

The strengthening of Syria's hand vis-à-vis the investigative committee and easing of pressure by Washington on Damascus would not have been possible without Russia's collaboration. Russia intervened decisively on the UN Security Council in favour of Syria, undermining its claims that international law and diplomatic cooperation formed the cornerstone of its foreign policy. Brammertz, as the UN's chief investigator in the Hariri murder case, faced strong accusations regarding his personal ethics. Unlike Mehlis, who argued that the case was in the interest of international public opinion, Brammertz deliberately eliminated any transparency in the investigative process by arguing that secrecy would help the investigation efforts. Considering the expenses his team incurred, tens of millions of US dollars paid for by UN member governments, including Lebanon, there were doubts raised about accountability considering there was no end product to any of his reports. Yet in fairness to Brammertz it was highly unlikely that his actions took place in contradiction of UN Security Council directives and it was obvious that at the time US-Russian dynamics were far less harmonious than they were before 2005.

After 2006 the Bush administration changed course from a purely militaristic approach by acknowledging that ending violence in Iraq required a diplomatic solution that included other significant actors including Syria, Iran and Russia. The Israel-Hezbollah conflict in July and August 2006 strengthened the latter's standing and weakened the Lebanese pro-independence coalition, further consolidating the belief that Syria and Hezbollah were firmly lodged in Lebanese political affairs.

In May 2007 UNSC Resolution 1757 was passed after months of stalling caused by Moscow's unwillingness to allow the creation of an international tribunal with adequate authority to use force if necessary in calling witnesses and suspects under Chapter VII of the United Nations Charter. The tribunal would put suspects named in the UN investigation of the Hariri assassination on trial and obviously the court would have been ineffective without the mandate to compel states to submit to its requests. The Russian leadership stubbornly maintained that such tribunals violated traditional conceptions of state sovereignty, reflecting Syria's vociferous stance. Indeed, Moscow had its own reasons to be concerned considering accusations that Russian security agents were involved in assassinations outside of its territories, including the widely reported murder of Alexander Litvinenko in November 2006. There were suspicions by the Kremlin leadership that the Hariri tribunal could become a pretext by the West to overthrow the Syrian regime and further undermine Russia's role in the Middle East. Following intense diplomatic wrangling, Russia abstained from the Security Council vote but heavily criticised the adoption of the Resolution, despite the amendments that abandoned Chapter VII as a means to force cooperation by Syria, with Russia's UN Ambassador to the Security Council Vitaly Churkin complaining that the tribunal being formed 'by a unilateral decision of the UN Security Council damages Lebanese sovereignty' and violated international law.[32] Coincidentally, in the same month UNSC Resolution 1757 was approved, British authorities formally accused Russian national Andrei Lugovoi and demanded his extradition from Russia for questioning.

There was disappointment at Russia's lack of support for the international tribunal among leaders of Lebanon's Cedar Revolution. Saad Hariri, the son of the murdered former prime minister, and his allies, including Christian Maronite leader Samir Geagea increasingly recognised that Russia was not assisting their cause. Following a meeting on 17 April 2007 with Lebanese Prime Minister Siniora, a close political aide of Rafiq Hariri for many years, Russian Deputy Foreign Minister

Alexander Saltanov was blunt in endorsing Moscow's 'reservations about this tribunal, because we are wondering whether it will strengthen stability and normalise the situation in Lebanon or cause a new upheaval in the country'.[33] The statement was particularly harsh because it echoed Syrian threats to encourage its allies, including Hezbollah, to jeopardise stability in Lebanon should the tribunal formally accuse Syria's political leaders of involvement in the assassination. Hariri's son, Saad, was elected as an MP and headed the largest parliamentary bloc in May 2005 alongside his Cedar Revolution allies, paving the way for him to become prime minister in November 2009.

Moscow's dubious stances with regard to the UN investigation and tribunal led Saad Hariri and his allies to become increasingly reliant on the United States and the Bush administration for support. During the build-up to UNSC Resolution 1757 Syria's supporters in Lebanon forcefully shut down central Beirut's commercial area by erecting tents and declared their intention to topple the Siniora-led government by force. Syria's close ally Nabih Berri, who headed the Shi'a Amal Movement and was the speaker of parliament, prevented the legislative assembly from holding any sessions and thus left the country politically paralysed. To make matters worse the opponents of the Cedar Revolution government also blocked the scheduled election of the president in September 2007 and threatened civil war unless an agreed upon president was appointed. Using its proxies Syria's leadership effectively held the country to ransom and delivered the crystal clear message to the West that the fate of Lebanon's political future and its security could not be resolved if its demands were not recognised. Syria and Iran used similar tactics in Iraq with great effect.

Syria's principal aim was to evade liability in the Hariri assassination and to gain Western recognition for its special role in Lebanon. By 2008 Syria's tactics began producing noticeable successes, particularly with European countries. Under the leadership of Nicholas Sarkozy, France became a proponent of ending the isolation of the Asad regime. Sensing a sea change in Western attitudes, with both Bush and Chirac ending their presidential terms, the Syrian regime felt more secure and encouraged its allies in Lebanon to become bolder in their demands. At the end of January 2008 one of the main leaders of the Cedar Revolution at that time, Walid Jumblatt, visited Moscow to discuss specifically with Russia's foreign minister, Sergei Lavrov, the reasons for the delay in setting up the tribunal. Lavrov offered only vague general support for Lebanon although Jumblatt claimed that the Russian Foreign Minister promised that his government 'will contribute in expenses for the tribunal to aid its establishment'.[34] Moscow, however, viewed the tribunal with disdain and continued to develop relations with Damascus. A few months after the visit, Jumblatt abandoned the Cedar Revolution movement, in large part due to his realisation that Russian support for the Asad regime was strong and that Washington lacked the resolve to confront Russia over Syria and its role in Lebanon.

In May 2008 Hezbollah and its Lebanese allies, boosted by Syria's international diplomatic revival, unleashed their armed guerrillas into the streets of Beirut and the surrounding mountains to force the resignation of the Siniora government following a brief but intensive military offensive. International mediation to redesign the status quo in Lebanon led to an agreement being forged in Qatar's capital Doha, in which a so-called consensus government was formed that reinstated Siniora as prime minister but with Hezbollah and its allies acquiring a decisive one-third plus one of cabinet ministers. This ensured that it was impossible for proposals to be approved by the cabinet without opposition approval thus preventing any decisions from being taken by the Lebanese government on key issues such as the Hariri tribunal and the disarming of Hezbollah. The new arrangement formalised the restoration of Syrian influence in Lebanese affairs and also recognised Iran's powerful political role in Lebanese and broader regional affairs by granting Hezbollah an internationally endorsed veto in national political affairs.

Russian gestures to support the Lebanese state, such as its offer of ten MiG fighter planes in 2008, were largely a fig-leaf to disguise its role in the empowering of Hezbollah. The crippled Russian defence sector had been attempting since 1998 to offload 'about 600 surplus aircraft… offered worldwide at unprecedented low prices'.[35] Regardless, the offer of the MiG fighters was rather unsurprisingly formally withdrawn in 2010. Obama's first year as president was marked by more energetic efforts to appease Damascus, further aiding Russia's role in the extinguishing of the Cedar Revolution as the new US president abandoned Bush's universalism and aligned more closely with the relativist approach that Moscow had long marketed. As a result the international mood also changed and Britain went so far as to formally invite a Hezbollah MP Hussein Hajj Hassan to the Foreign Office to meet with officials in early April 2009.

The new path adopted by the West effectively restored Syrian and Iranian control over Lebanon and forced the humiliated prime minister Saad Hariri to meet President Asad, the man accused of ordering the assassination of his father, in Damascus. At the time Putin had temporarily made way for Medvedev to fill the presidential seat but he continued to effectively govern as a powerful prime minister until 2012, when he was re-elected as Russian president. Under Medvedev's presidency Russia's patronage was barely challenged in Lebanon and Syria as Obama oversaw a rapid retreat from the Middle East. In his first inauguration address in 2008 Obama had publicly offered 'the hand of friendship to oppressive regimes', music to the ears of the Kremlin leaders and their allies in Syria and Iran. For Lebanon, this looked for the time being like the end of the road for the pro-independence movement and its leaders.

Syria—historic background

A unique relationship existed between Moscow and Damascus from the 1950s. On the surface Soviet-Syrian and Russian-Syrian relations were remarkably consistent over the years. Between 1955 and 1986 Syria emerged as 'the largest non-communist buyer of Soviet weapons'.[36] While Jordan, Lebanon and Israel all gravitated towards the United States, Syria was seen as the Soviet Union's closest partner in western Asia. The relationship never reached the level of formal alliance but a Treaty of Friendship and Cooperation was signed in October 1980. Yet throughout the Cold War, despite the close relationship, Syria's iron ruler, President Hafez Asad, never neglected the value of maintaining communication channels and a close understanding with the United States. The wily Syrian leader was a recognised master at keeping his political options open.

US-Syrian coordination intensified and rapidly improved in the 1970s as Asad nurtured a deep understanding with the then influential secretary of state, Henry Kissinger. This relationship was so highly valued by Damascus that it was a principal factor explaining Syrian resistance to Soviet offers to sign a Treaty of Friendship and Cooperation, which both Egypt and Iraq had then signed. Asad also disappointed Brezhnev in the early 1970s when he undermined Soviet peace proposals to mediate in the Arab-Israeli conflict that could have granted

Moscow international prominence. Asad's motive was based on his conviction that any regional agreement was futile without Washington's consent. This established the basis of Syrian thinking and set the cornerstone of Syrian foreign policy thereafter. The tacit collaboration between Damascus and Washington allowed Syria to gain approval from the United States to enter Lebanon in the mid-1970s and to remain there after the end of the Lebanese civil war during the 1990s. In return, the Golan front between Syria and Israel remained quiet from 1974, sidestepping the regional political storms over the decades, implying an operational Israeli-Syrian understanding under US guidance to avoid direct war between the two countries.

It was during phases when US-Syrian relations underwent turbulent periods that Damascus turned to Moscow to consolidate its position. After Egypt signed the Camp David Peace Agreement with Israel in 1978, for example, Syria became 'alarmed by the upset of the regional balance of power', and 'beset by the mounting violent domestic opposition to his regime … Asad came to view a closer alignment with the USSR as an asset, rather than a liability.'[37] The Syrian leader pursued a clever strategy of touting the possibility of peace with Israel as a carrot to entice US political and economic support but there was never serious evidence that he had ever truly intended to sign a treaty as Egypt had done. A talented yet opportunistic political mind, Asad calculated that a peace treaty would likely spell an end to his regime because despite a faltering economy and stifled democratic rights and liberties, the confrontation with Israel was the foundation of the regime's justification for its existence and legitimacy to rule. As a member of the Alawite minority, Asad realized that normalising relations with Israel prior to a settlement of the Palestinian issue would have risked popular rebellion. Asad preferred instead to confront US pressure to sign a peace agreement with Israel during the late 1970s and 1980s even at the price of strained relations with Washington. Moreover, having successfully entered Lebanon without US opposition in the 1970s Asad had achieved a longstanding objective to broaden his regional influence without depending on Washington's goodwill.

Syria also compensated for its deteriorating relations with the West by cultivating relations with the outcast Khomeini regime in Iran. This placed Syria, with Soviet and Iranian backing, as the pivotal counterbalance to pro-US Arab states led by Jordan and Saudi Arabia for most of the 1980s. Yet ten years after re-aligning itself with the anti-Western front in consequence of the Camp David Agreement, Syria began reorientating its foreign policy towards the United States because of Gorbachev's overhaul of Soviet foreign policy. Asad took advantage of the Iraqi invasion of Kuwait in 1990 as an opportunity by siding with the Western alliance, erasing a decade of animosity in one act. To crown its return to international legitimacy Syria participated in the Madrid Peace Conference at the end of October 1991 under US and Soviet sponsorship. The timing was perfect for Syria because during the early 1990s Russia largely disengaged itself from the Middle East and was reduced to a minor international player.

After Syria joined the US-led alliance in the war against Iraq in 1990 President Clinton offered the Asad regime exceptional tolerance by turning a blind eye to human rights violations and tight authoritarian governance that differed little from the outcast rule of Saddam Hussein in neighbouring Iraq. Throughout his two terms in office Clinton also allowed Syria to consolidate its military and political presence in Lebanon, refusing even to consider it an occupation which, in comparison with the ideological Bush era appeared to be an embarrassing US collusion with the regime in Damascus.

Russian relations with Syria only began significantly improving in 1996, in line with Foreign Minister Primakov's efforts to re-establish a foothold for Moscow in the Middle East. Syria was Russia's natural choice, particularly as Iraq was then weakened and isolated under Saddam Hussein. Primakov used the route of reviving the stalled Middle East process as an entry for Russia into the region in parallel to promoting Russia as a valuable source of arms. Syria simultaneously did not want Washington and its chief regional ally Israel to dictate affairs in the Middle East and welcomed Russian overtures led by Primakov as well as European and United Nations participation to use as leverage in relations with the United States. During a visit to Moscow from 5–7 July 1999 Syria's President Asad endorsed Primakov's 'idea of a multipolar world and called for strenuous efforts to strengthen the role of the United Nations'.[38] However, President Hafez Asad ultimately prioritised relations with Washington and kept Russia on the fringes of regional peace negotiations. Another source of lingering frustration for Russia was the $12 billion dollar debt owed by Syria that was inherited from the Soviet era.

Damascus therefore relied on a policy of balancing relations between world powers to its advantage. One of the fruits of this approach was a $2 billion agreement in 1999 between Syria and Russia to sell highly sophisticated arms pending settlement of the debt issue. This was according to reports 'the first major military deal Syria concluded with Russia since the demise of the Soviet Union, marking the resumption of strategic cooperation between Damascus and Moscow'.[39] The deal marked the restoration of Russia as a major regional player.

Bashar's inheritance

Syria's Hafez Asad died in June 2000 after over thirty years of stern rule. Power was smoothly handed over to his son Bashar only one month after Putin's election as president in Russia. An indicator of the lingering frigid relations between Syria and Russia at that time was that Putin did not attend the internationally publicised funeral of the old dictator. Asad the younger had studied for a few years in England and was inexperienced in Syrian politics and military affairs until his father began grooming him for succession two years before his death. Western leaders had hopeful that the thirty-four-year old Asad would lead with an agenda to liberalise the rigid authoritarian rule in Syria.

The mood of optimism had blossomed when Israel withdrew its occupying troops from southern Lebanon in May 2000. The Israeli withdrawal removed a major obstacle in the way of the thus far elusive regional peace settlement. A year earlier Hafez Asad rejected Israeli Prime Minister Ehud Barak's offer to return all of the occupied Golan because of a dispute over 10 metres of land on the edge of Lake Tiberius, but peace in the Middle East seemed merely a nudge away. Western expectations that there would be more flexibility shown by the younger Asad, however, failed to recognise that Syria's intransigence over peace with Israel was more to do with its strategic and ideological motives in Lebanon, as well as domestic political restraints relating to the nature of the regime, and less to do with the status of the Golan. Re-gaining the Golan at the expense of losing Lebanon, which would have been a consequence of a bilateral peace agreement, was of little benefit to the Syrian elite because of deeply held fears among the ruling minority Alawite regime that the normalisation of relations with Israel would antagonise its own masses and the wider Arab and Muslim world as long as the Palestinians problem was not resolved.

As hopes of peace crumbled tumultuous regional and international events facilitated rapid improvement in Russian-Syrian relations during the first term of the Putin presidency. President Hafez Asad visited Russia in July 1999 to resolve the multi-billion US Dollar debts problem and facilitate the purchase of advanced weapons. In October 2000 Russian Foreign Minister Igor Ivanov travelled to Damascus to meet with his son Bashar to resume discussions his father had initiated and this was followed by more regular visits to Moscow by senior Syrian officials, including Foreign Minister Farouk Shara' in April 2001 and Defence Minister Mustafa Tlas the following month. As a gesture of Syria's goodwill towards Moscow during this phase, in 'September 2001, Damascus welcomed the pro-Russian Chechen leader, Akhmad Kadyrov'.[40] Bashar Asad was well groomed by his father to loyally grasp the wisdom of consolidating and nurturing the historic ties between Syria and Russia as a guarantee of self-preservation.

A marriage of convenience?

Syria's sympathetic outpouring to the United States in September 2001 led to a further warming in bilateral relations to augment Western expectations of reforms by the new leader in Damascus. As Moscow had manipulated the terrorist attacks against the United States to cast itself as similarly fighting terrorism in Chechnya, Damascus also presented itself as a secular regime holding back a tide of Sunni extremism in Syria. However, Asad's political honeymoon with the West ended dramatically in 2003 as a result of the US invasion of Iraq and in parallel the mounting Lebanese rebellion against Syrian rule. In Damascus, both developments were suspiciously associated with a wider agenda that was being pursued by the Bush administration that promoted regional democratisation and demanded Lebanese independence from Syrian occupation. As a result Russian-Syrian convergence thereafter reached peaks of intensive bilateral relations and military-strategic cooperation that was comparable to the highlights of the Cold War era. Putin's controversial support for the Syrian regime in 2012 and early 2013, while it stood accused of committing horrific widespread human rights abuses, indicated a centrality to Syria in Moscow's thinking that exceeded the worldview in Soviet times.

Syria and Russia, as well as Iran, concurred in 2003 that the US occupation of Iraq was a direct threat to their national interests and all opposed it fiercely. Damascus was highly suspicious that installing a new order after Saddam's downfall as part of a new wave of democratisation would encourage Washington to do the same in Syria. Russia and Iran shared the same concern in relation to their own context. Asad had tightened the Syrian grip on Lebanon since his father's death and promoted deeper bonds with Iran, allowing Hezbollah's military capabilities to grow beyond any stage in its history. Syria also, with Iranian help, exerted greater influence on radical Palestinian movements including Hamas. There was a Syrian, Iranian and Russian convergence in interests to make life difficult for the US troops in Iraq to safeguard their respective political ambitions and self-preservation taking into consideration that the leadership in Damascus 'awoke to 130,000 troops from an angry superpower parked on its eastern border. As Syria's Vice President, Farouq Al-Shara' noted, America was now Syria's neighbour.'[41]

In late March 2003, 'as the second week of the Iraqi war was drawing to an end the relations between Washington and Damascus worsened dramatically' with the former castigating the latter for allowing Sunni extremist fighters from around the Muslim world to 'cross into the country to join the fighting'.[42] Secretary of State for Defense Donald Rumsfeld echoed other official US warnings that Syria was actively supporting anti-US insurgents in Iraq. Even the typically more dovish Secretary of State Colin Powell repeated warnings to Damascus on 31 March by stating that in terms of its regional behaviour, 'Syria bears a responsibility for its choices and consequences.'[43]

Despite Powell's stern language it gradually transpired that the Bush administration was deeply divided on what to do about Syria. Initial American military success in Iraq was insufficient to disguise strong resistance to Washington's actions by European allies as well as Russia. Bush and his administration were in favour of exploiting the display of American power in the Middle East post-2003 by promoting democratisation because of the belief that longstanding authoritarian regimes had created fertile grounds for extremism and terrorists, who posed a threat to US national security interests. Bush's opponents rejected notions of exporting democracy and nation-building for being too idealistic. Even within Bush's inner circle senior figures, including Powell, preferred to appease and engage Damascus in a regional solution even while it was facilitating the killing of American soldiers in Iraq.

The internal political disputes in Washington and passionate European opposition to the US occupation of Iraq heightened confidence in

Damascus of winning its war of nerves with the Bush administration. Damascus, like Moscow, understood that it was unrealistic to attempt to halt the US military juggernaut from invading Iraq in 2003, which in the spirit of the campaign's name, Shock and Awe, was rapid and relatively brief. The occupation period, however, was inevitably more complex with a greater possibility that the United States would become deeply entrenched in the Iraqi quagmire. As the Syrians had hoped, the more ferocious and bloody the anti-occupation insurgency in Iraq became, the more the possibility of a military attack against it by the United States receded. Russia's political establishment and its Syrian counterpart gained belief that a messy and bloody security situation in post-Saddam Iraq could transform the US regional and international position from one of strength to one of weakness.

The European and anti-Bush US media argued with great success that the justification for the war that Iraq possessed weapons of mass destruction (WMD) was an outright invention. In reality, Bush and his administration were never able to present conclusive evidence that their suspicions regarding Iraq's weapons programme were accurate. A few Bush supporters and senior Pentagon officials, however, continued to maintain that Saddam Hussein did possess WMDs but that all evidence of their existence was eradicated under Russian supervision, adding that concealed materials were eventually shipped to Syria. John Shaw, a US government official for thirty years and former deputy undersecretary of defense specialising in international technology security argued as late as 2006 that Iraq's WMDs were smuggled out of Iraq 'by Russian Spetsnaz (special forces) units out of uniform', based on 'a flow of information from British contacts on the ground at the Syrian border'.[44] Controversially, Shaw claimed that his intelligence information revealed that former Russian Prime Minister Primakov stayed in Iraq between December 2002 and March 2003, immediately before the war started, during which time he 'Supervised the execution of long-standing secret agreements, signed between Iraqi intelligence and the Russian GRU (military intelligence), that provided for clean-up operations to be conducted by Russian and Iraqi military personnel to remove WMDs, production materials and technical documentation from Iraq, so the regime could announce that Iraq was "WMD free."'[45] This clean-up operation, it was argued, required the cooperation of Syria in ensuring a safe route out of Iraq. Both Syria and Russia denied that such a clean-up operation existed.

Despite the US occupation of Iraq, or perhaps because of it, Syria further fortified its position in Lebanon and began marketing the possibility in the summer of 2004 of forcing a constitutional amendment in the country's parliament to extend the presidency of Emile Lahoud, a loyal Syrian pawn among a large network of Syrian-made Lebanese political figures. The Bush administration's response was fierce in its support of Lebanese calls for independence, ending a longstanding policy by the Clinton administration of turning a blind eye to Syrian hegemony. The US Congress passed the Syria Accountability and Lebanese Sovereignty Restoration Act late in 2003 as a warning shot to Syria. On 11 May 2004 President Bush signed an Executive Order to implement the Syria Accountability Act to underline Washington's 'resolve to address the Syrian government's support for terrorist groups, its continued military presence in Lebanon, its pursuit of weapons of mass destruction, and its actions to undermine US and international efforts with respect to the stabilization and reconstruction of Iraq'.[46] The Act imposed sanctions including a restriction on military sales, a downgrading of US diplomatic representation in Damascus and a ban on direct flights between the two countries.

Undeterred, the Syrian regime defiantly bullied Lebanese legislators to extend President Lahoud's term in September 2004, which was immediately countered with UN Security Council Resolution 1559. Russia, having criticised both the Syria Accountability Act and abstained from Resolution 1559, claimed that antagonising the regime in Damascus would only undermine Lebanon's stability. As US pressure on Syria intensified, Russia energised its efforts to enter the Middle East stage as a counterbalance on Syria's behalf. The leadership in Moscow feared that the downfall of the Syrian regime would initiate a domino effect that would transform the Middle East into a US-dominated zone, further aggravating Russia's sense of encirclement. Yet in 2004 Putin was still unwilling to display outward hostility towards the United States due to a still disjointed foreign policy. One critic suggested that Putin's efforts to covertly support countries in the Middle East hostile to the Bush administration while he simultaneously endeavoured to build good relations with the United States during his first term were a result of 'Russia's weakness, chaotic policymaking, and lack of a coherent foreign policy strategy.'[47]

Yet 2005 revealed that Russia under Putin had established a coherent strategy with the aim of restoring influence in the Middle East. Syria thus became an attractive, and available, partner because the political leadership in Damascus was in need of a powerful international military patron with veto power on the UN Security Council. Following a meeting between Putin and Asad in Moscow on 24 January 2005 an observer noted that: 'Russian-Syrian relations improved dramatically. Russia has even agreed to sell an advanced air defence missile system to Syria over both American and Israeli objections.'[48] In later years it was Russia's contribution to modernising Syria's air defence system that prevented the implementation of a no-fly zone by Western powers to protect civilians from air strikes by the Syrian military between 2011 and 2013. Until 2005 Russia's reluctance to sell Syria advanced military weapons was a major obstacle to the improvement in bilateral relations.

As a consequence of Asad's visit, Moscow announced that it would write off most of Syria's longstanding debts and agreed to more flexible terms for repaying the remaining amount, estimated as some $3.6 billion.[49] With the resolution of the longstanding debt issue, 'Russia agreed to sell to Syria the Strelets air defence missile system, consisting of vehicle-mounted short range surface-to-air missiles' in a $100 million deal.[50] The deal naturally impacted the regional balance and potentially challenged Israel's air supremacy in the region. Yet Syria and Iran, facing intense pressure throughout 2005 and into 2006, became critical fortresses in Moscow's global geo-strategic outlook. Moscow considered that a militarised American foreign policy required a response in kind and Syria provided important options that were inherited from the Cold War era such as the naval port in Tartous, the only facility open for use by the Russian navy in the Mediterranean Sea to symbolise Russia's military reach in the post-Soviet era.

Negotiations to provide Russia with permanent naval bases on its sovereign shores were indicative of Syria's sense of isolation and Russia's greater regional ambitions. It emerged in 2007 that Russia agreed to write off Syria's outstanding debts, after it had forgiven 70 per cent in 2005, as part of the agreement to allow permanent Russian naval bases in Tartous and Latakia. In 2008, a British newspaper noted that: 'Tartous is being dredged and renovated to provide a permanent facility for the Russian navy, giving Moscow a key military foothold in the Mediterranean.'[51] Furthermore, Israel's security elite noted that the bases would upgrade radar and satellite monitoring capabilities and advance Syria's capacity to gather intelligence on Israeli military activities.[52] Securing the base complicated Russia's position in case of an Israeli or US military attack on Syria but there were suggestions that Moscow's drive to secure bases was specifically 'tied to American plans to deploy anti-missile bases across Europe directly along Russia's borders'.[53] This tit-for-tat approach, according to this argument, allowed for mutual retreat in any possible future negotiations on the issue.

In reality from 2004 Syria's extreme dependence on Russia for upgrading its military capabilities, also extended to diplomacy in warding off UN pressure. UNSC Resolution 1636, adopted on 31 October 2005, was significantly diluted following Russian threats to veto it altogether if it sanctioned strong measures, including military action, against Syria for non-compliance with the Hariri investigation. The Syrian leadership repeatedly and candidly declared that its ultimate strategy was to force the West to recognise that violence will escalate in the Middle East unless regional solutions were reached via Damascus, including Western recognition of Syria's oversight of Lebanese affairs. Asad and his allies in Lebanon were particularly heartened to hear these sentiments being echoed in European capitals and among Bush's political rivals in Washington.

Syrian self-assurance was bolstered when in the face of international and domestic pressure the Bush administration downsized its demand to merely seeking a modification in behaviour from Damascus rather than regime change, which contrasted with US policy towards Iraq under Saddam Hussein. The United States, haughty and proud during Bush's first term as president, had become battle-worn in Iraq during his second term. Syria took advantage to raise the pressure on Washington and flex its own regional muscles. Having assisted the flow of Al-Qaeda terrorists into Iraq to destabilise the country, encouraged its allies in Lebanon to smother the Cedar Revolution, and activated the Palestinian front to promote the schism between Hamas and the Palestinian Authority led by President Mahmoud Abbas, Syria produced a defiant show of its own weight in the Middle East despite the huge regional US military presence. Meanwhile, the high profile political assassinations in Lebanon continued, eliminating leading figures of the anti-Syria coalition without constraints or fear of retribution.

The war in the summer of 2006 was yet another indirect victory for Syria as the Israeli army's efforts to cripple Hezbollah and force the release of its captured troops ended in failure. Israeli officials had been persistently complaining to Russia before the war that mobile missile launchers sold to Syria were being transported to Hezbollah. Israeli suspicions were confirmed during the war, despite Moscow's assurances, as Russian-made rocket launchers were instrumental in halting Israel's ground attacks by targeting tanks and other armoured vehicles. With the ground assault floundering and the Israeli air force identifying limited targets because the Hezbollah fighters were embedded in civilian and residential areas, the Israeli military ran out of options and was forced to accept an internationally imposed ceasefire that was not favourable to the latter. Hezbollah flaunted its triumph and highlighted the Syrian regime's support in the war. As a result of the war US-Israeli military dominance in the region was further undermined, augmenting the demoralisation of the US military in Iraq on the other side of the Syrian border.

As an indication of Syria's re-emerging power and the Bush administration's floundering policies the US government sponsored the Iraq Study Group co-chaired by the influential former Secretary of State James Baker and Lee Hamilton, a thirty-year veteran serving as congressional sub-committee chair on European and Middle East Affairs to re-evaluate Washington's regional policies. The final report was released in December 2006 and although it focused on presenting a new approach to the 'grave and deteriorating' situation in Iraq it also offered a total revision of the Bush administration's handling of the broader Middle East situation.[54] According to the report: 'Syria should control its border with Iraq to stem the flow of funding, insurgents, and terrorists in and out of Iraq.' But as a striking admission of defeat it added that the US administration 'should try to engage them [Syria and Iran] constructively', despite stating that 'Syria is content to see the United States tied down in Iraq.'[55]

The Hamilton-Baker report was an emblematic announcement of defeat in the region as a whole but the victors were not Al-Qaeda but rather Syria and its regional partner Iran. Only two years earlier Bush had signed an Executive Order in May 2004 stating that: 'Syria has one of the most advanced Arab state chemical weapons capabilities and it is highly probable that Syria continues to develop an offensive biological weapons capability.'[56] These had been grounds for war against Iraq in 2003 but by 2006 Washington's acknowledgement that it had run out of options in the Middle East created a sense in Moscow that the unipolar era that Primakov warned about a decade earlier had ended. It can even be argued that due, to the consequences of the occupation of Iraq and the lack of strategic thinking by Washington, Syria and Russia combined to forcefully re-enter the Middle East as significant actors and bargain on better terms with the United States. The decline of US power was best epitomised by the success of Barack Obama in the presidential elections on a foreign policy platform that essentially rejected unilateralism and universalism, instead promoting dialogue with Syria and other former foes such as Iran.

Moscow remained cautious throughout about appearing to be openly siding with Syria because this would not only damage its relations with Israel, reverting to the short-sighted policies of the Soviet era, but also with important moderate Arab states such as Saudi Arabia, which was an economic force on the world stage and also an influential political and religious pole in the region. The Saudis considered Hariri's assassination to be a direct challenge to their authority by Syria and various sources indicated that King Abdullah of Saudi Arabia, along with President Jacques Chirac of France, asked Asad to ensure that Hariri would not be harmed. The elimination of Sunni Hariri from Lebanon's political scene created a Syrian and Iranian advantage and contravened the spirit of the Lebanese constitution that sought to maintain a balance of power among religious communities. Of particular concern to the Saudis was that, with the rise of Hezbollah's power, Syria and Iran created a powerful alliance that dictated events not only in the Levant but also in the oil-rich Gulf region where a significant Shi'a population lived.

Russian efforts to present itself as a neutral moderator in light of the 2006 war were belittled by *Newsweek* magazine, stating that: 'Moscow presents itself as the new "middleman" in the Middle East. But its role may actually be that of spoiler.'[57] In a climate of regional tension Russia's behaviour in the Middle East was placed once more under the spotlight in a way not seen since the Soviet era. In parallel to a precarious balance in the Middle East the relationship between Russia and the West over NATO expansion in Europe reached new levels of tension. Moscow also adopted an aggressively hostile stance in that period towards its former Soviet neighbours, particularly Georgia and Ukraine. Sensing the shift in the international balance of power, the leaders of the Cedar Revolution movement feared that Syrian efforts to return to Lebanon would be provided with Russian cover and that the political assassinations would continue without restraint or punishment. Among the most frequent Lebanese visitors to Moscow was Jumblatt, who told its leaders that it was 'in Russian interests to build good relations with Lebanon and convince the leadership in Damascus to stop interfering in Lebanon'.[58]

In September 2007 tensions mounted in Lebanon again over the election of a new president after Lahoud's extended mandate had expired. Syria's allies in Lebanon used various tactics, including street riots and the orchestrated paralysis of government institutions, to prevent the pro-Cedar Revolution parliamentary majority from electing a successor. The volatile situation resumed international pressure on Syria to allow Lebanon's presidential elections to take place peacefully but Russia again waded in on behalf of Damascus with the influential Primakov suggesting that despite continuing 'substantial leverage in Lebanon, Syria refrains from political intervention in the Lebanese presidential elections'.[59] Putin dispatched Primakov on a special mission to Syria on 7 November 2007 to explore options to resolve the political confrontation in Lebanon but also more significantly to discuss the possibility of reviving the Syrian-Israeli track of the stalled peace negotiations. Primakov noted that the Baker-Hamilton report had called on the United States to engage Syria and to increase efforts to reactivate the Arab-Israeli peace process. Because the Bush administration began low-level talks with the Syrians, who in turn initiated indirect negotiations with Israel over the Golan Heights by means of Turkish mediation, Primakov was hopeful that Russia would carve out a role in a newly developing regional process.

Primakov's visit to Syria took place two weeks after 'Israeli Prime Minister Ehud Olmert visited Russia and held talks with Putin…aimed at convincing Moscow not to sell Syria advanced anti-aircraft defence systems.'[60] Olmert's visit followed media reports of a major deal involving the sale of 'top-of-the-line fighter jets to Syria' worth $1 billion.[61] The sale included an unspecified number of MiG-29 aircraft and the advanced MiG-31Es, with sophisticated radar capable of intercepting several targets and flying three times the speed of sound. Russia's military sales were announced within months after the delivery of major anti-aircraft air defence systems that significantly enhanced Syria's capabilities, including mobile Pantsyr-SE1 that raised concerns they would be re-routed to Hezbollah fighters in Lebanon. Iran reportedly financed the deals in a reflection of the developing Iran-Syria-Russia triangle.[62]

Russian Foreign Minister Sergei Lavrov boasted in a meeting with his US counterpart Rice that 'it is counterproductive to isolate anybody', to underline the resurgent role of Syria in the Middle East.[63]

Syria flirts with the West

With hard-minded realism and regardless of its relationship with Moscow, the Syrian leadership always reached out to Washington in acknowledgement of the United States' superpower status, even during turbulent periods of US-Syrian relations, as a valuable prerequisite to the long-term survival of the regime. In the face of stiff pressure by Washington from 2003 the Damascus regime nonetheless resumed negotiations with Israel, through Turkish mediation, as a means to signal its intent for regional peace. The manoeuvre was a clever attempt to ease Washington's sense of fighting on too many fronts. As instability in Iraq and violence in Afghanistan persisted, Syria offered the façade of hope that an Arab-Israeli peace was possible and also implied that it was willing to terminate its partnership with Iran and co-operate over Iraq. With these soothing initiatives the young Asad managed to craftily neutralise potential US military action against Syria and in the process gained European support, so that by 2007 France under President Nicholas Sarkozy was openly mediating on behalf of the Damascus regime, despite the damaging accusations concerning its support for international terrorism and its role in destabilising Iraq and Lebanon.

The Syrian leadership was effective in highlighting to Washington its value in the region and, having made good use of Moscow by modernising the country's military capabilities, regaining a firm foothold in Lebanon and undermining the investigation into the murder of Hariri, Syria's rapprochement with the United States and the West became openly publicised in 2007. Washington and Damascus restored ties following the election of Barack Obama as US president in November 2008 and a US ambassador to Syria, Robert Ford, was appointed in 2010. With Obama seeming to bend over backwards to befriend the Syrian regime, for Russia this development seemed to present a re-enactment of old Soviet mistakes in which support and investment in dubious regimes was proven futile or offered little return. Obama's initiatives were short lived and ultimately backfired. Yet soon after, in 2011, President Asad faced the greatest challenge to his leadership of all.

Having largely pacified international efforts to undermine his rule the Syrian leader was forced to contend with the much more serious and damaging challenge of a widespread revolution from among his own population.

Until the start of the revolution Syria's behaviour was notoriously difficult to define for outsiders because of the regime's contradictory messages that allowed it to win over some sympathisers in the West. A study by David Schenker, a senior fellow in Arab politics at the Washington Institute for Near East Policy, who from 2002 to 2006 served in the office of the secretary of defense as country director for Syria, Lebanon, Jordan, and the Palestinian territories noted that Syria's political stances were typically opaque. Yet some in the West, as some Israeli politicians continued to do, were prone to only look at the positives in the duality of the Syrian regime's policies. It was clear, according to Schenker, that despite efforts by the United States and its allies to entice Syria to abandon its destructive role in the Middle East 'eight years after Hafiz Asad's son Bashar took power, Syria's relations both with Iran and its Lebanese terrorist proxy, Hizbullah, are even deeper'.[64] As significantly, Syria's relationship with Russia had become a strategic one with global consequences and was also impacted by internal political dynamics in both countries.

Yet until the outbreak of mass protests against the regime in 2011 there were voices in Western circles who believed that Syria had been unfairly maligned, that its regime's gross human rights record could be overlooked and, most naively, that it could be detached from the Iranian and Russian orbit to join the Western ranks. Among them was John Kerry, who was later appointed secretary of state in 2013 despite his unsuccessful stint as lobbyist for Damascus during Obama's first term. There were also prominent academics in the US such as Joshua Landis, or journalists including Seymour Hersh and Robert Fisk who promoted the regime, sometimes with dubious motives, as a model of secular civility in a region torn apart by religious extremism. The ambiguity was not unusual in light of the complex relationship Syria had with the West. For example, in September 2004, when US-Syrian relations stood at a particularly low point after the adoption of UNSC Resolution 1559, Assistant Secretary of State William Burns offered President Asad 'a deal ... In return for a cessation of terrorist infiltration across the Syrian border into Iraq, as well as some cooperation on other financial and military issues, the US government would relieve pressure on the Asad regime and no longer emphasize democratisation.'[65] The offer appeared incompatible with the administration's then obsession with regime change and democratisation, and discredits US policies as well as Western lobbyists on its behalf, especially as Syria declined to accept the terms, or at least demanded more in return, highlighting its commitment to its regional alliance with Iran and its growing confidence that Russia was a reliable partner and supporter.

Thus Syria's relationship with Russia during Putin's second term was very much influenced by the state of relations between Syria and the United States and also the growing strategic interplay between Damascus, Moscow and Tehran. The more hostile Washington became the more Syria allowed Russia to enter into the Middle East orbit as a counterbalance to the United States. When Washington lessened the pressure on Damascus in 2007 and with French and British help sought to appease the leadership, Syria readily announced its desire to co-operate. This point was not missed by Russian observers, with one commentator going as far as to say in April 2008 that 'Bashar Al-Asad is rushing to hug Washington.'[66] This comment was an immediate response to an interview of the Syrian president to an Arab newspaper that was reprinted in official Syrian papers. Of particular note to the Russian commentator was Asad's remark that 'the main role in the Middle East peace process belongs to the United States rather than Russia'. Asad added that 'the same was true during Soviet times', with the reasoning that 'Russia cannot exert pressure on Israel, nor could it do so in the past.'[67] This was a striking minimisation of Moscow's role by the Syrians regardless of whether Asad was genuine or he was craftily making a bid to rebuild damaged ties with Washington. The comparison with the Soviet era by Asad was most likely a deliberate insertion to remind Washington that Syria and the United States had a history of effective coordination, particularly over Lebanon and Iraq.

Asad welcomed Obama's victory in 2008 and responded favourably to his overtures for improved relations. But the reformed behaviour was not due to a sudden awakening that its activities of the past were wrong but rather because 2008 was a year in which new presidents were elected in Russia and the United States. The Syrian leadership calculated that there was a high possibility after the end of Putin's second term that Dmitry Medvedev would encourage an era of thaw between Russia and the

United States, which in turn would mean that Moscow was less likely to antagonise Washington over Syria. Medvedev cast himself as a reformer rather than a conservative, who was less hostile to Western ways. The leadership in Damascus thought it wise to keep its options open.

The presidential transitions in 2008 in Russia and the United States, while creating uncertainty, provided new opportunities. For Damascus, 2008 was a convenient year to exploit events until the maligned Bush era ended. This lull allowed Syria to build on its de facto control of Lebanon, evade answerability to the international tribunal and energise its Palestinian allies, which further consolidated its regional influence. This made it easier for the Syrian regime to impress on Washington that there was no alternative to a dominant Syrian role in Lebanese affairs. At the same time the Syrians continued to court the Russian leadership, with Asad meeting newly elected President Medvedev in August 2008 to discuss the sale of advanced anti-aircraft and anti-tank missiles and more controversially 'Iskander ballistic missiles that could threaten almost all of Israel'.[68] Russian officials had alluded in 2008 that the 'Iskander missile had been promised to Damascus in 2001, and only a personal request by Israeli Prime Minister Ehud Olmert to former President Vladimir Putin put a stop to its sale to Syria.'[69] Moscow repeatedly denied that it would provide Syria with any weapons that could dramatically alter the strategic balance in the region but from a Syrian point of view it confirmed that Russia's support would always be limited, further underlining the benefits of cultivating good relations with the United States.

Syria and the struggle for democracy

Russian diplomatic activity intensified markedly in early 2013 and included high-level meetings with the influential Lebanese political leader Walid Jumblatt followed a few days later by an official visit by President Michel Suleiman to Moscow. At the time the situation in Syria had become tragically deadlocked. With thousands of deaths recorded each month there seemed to be little hope in sight as US President Obama adopted a passive approach to the unfolding human catastrophe. Calls in the West for more assertive US action to end the Syrian crisis were being made for geo-strategic reasons and transcended morality as a motive. The Syrian opposition according to reports was being increasingly infiltrated by religious extremists, including the Nusra Front and the public mood in Syria had become more radical and vengeful because of perceived abandonment by the international community. Syria turned into a failed state, much like the Somalia of the 1990s, and not since independence did disintegration along ethnic and religious lines become such a distinct possibility.

Russian citizens in Syria, including 8,000 registered with the embassy in Damascus, found themselves in a highly vulnerable situation. Moscow's determined support for Asad placed them in direct danger of retaliation including kidnapping and murder by rebel fighters or by angry victims of the regime who suffered losses of their own. In this atmosphere, Russia began evacuating its citizens, sending chartered planes to Beirut in late January 2013. The evacuees were driven by bus to Lebanon before flying back to Russia because the fighting in Syria forced its major airports to shut down. Even as the aircrafts full of evacuees were flying out of Beirut, Lavrov publicly criticised the Syrian opposition for its 'obsession with the idea of the overthrow of the Asad regime' while admitting there were about another 1,000 citizens desperate to leave Syria.[70] Signalling a degree of confusion in Moscow, Lavrov denied that formal evacuation plans were being implemented because of concern the move would be interpreted as abandoning the Asad regime, yet just over a week earlier, in mid-January 2013, the Russian Consulate General in Aleppo was closed down by the foreign ministry after admitting that the Syrian government was losing control.[71]

Putin and Suleiman met on 23 January 2013 to discuss the impact of the Syrian crisis on Lebanon, coinciding with the first cohort of Russian citizens being evacuated via Beirut. Most striking about Suleiman's visit was the complete absence of any initiative or meaningful role by the United States at that time. Indeed, Obama had by then chosen not to get involved. Over 200,000 refugees had fled from Syria to Lebanon out of a total number exceeding 650,000 since the start of the uprising to escape the horrific violence in their country.[72] Suleiman asked Moscow to consider hosting a conference to provide material support to Lebanon and countries surrounding Syria who faced the massive influx of refugees. Intriguingly, during the visit the Russian proposal to arm Lebanon was raised again more than two years after Moscow had pledged to provide Lebanon with MiG fighters and other weapons. The promises then proved empty as both Russia and Lebanon retreated from the plan because of the regional and international consequences. But in 2013 Lebanon and other countries in the region had seen enough to believe the United States had effectively abdicated its influence and responsibilities, which allowed other players, namely Russia and Iran, to hold much greater sway in regional affairs.

The dynamics in relations between Russia, Syria and Lebanon became extremely complicated as a result of the wave of anti-regime uprisings that spread throughout the Middle East. Initially, the leadership in Damascus believed it would be immune to the revolutions that eventually toppled regimes in Egypt, Libya and Tunisia but by the summer of 2011 it too was facing a full-scale revolt. Strikingly, Moscow's position initially floundered, perhaps in part because President Medvedev at the time was not comfortable with aligning with what was widely considered as a brutal dictatorship and in part because the initially peaceful protests were a response to the torture and murder of a group of school children who had drawn anti-regime graffiti on a wall in the village of Deraa. The indecisiveness was quickly overcome though and Putin, as prime minister, and in 2012 as president, took the reins to assert an uncompromisingly pro-Asad position in response to Moscow's wider considerations.

Contemporary analyses emphasised arms sales and military factors such as the Russian naval facility in Tartous as basic explanations for Russia's unconcealed support for the Asad regime. Significant as they were, there were two less noted but arguably more compelling reasons for Moscow's stance that together revealed much about Russia's internal political character. The first and rather straightforward explanation was that Putin became quickly aware that the United States was not enthusiastic about regime change in Syria and while Washington dithered Moscow snatched the opportunity to make a show of an aggressive and unwavering posture that consolidated the impression of Russia resuming its great power status. This was a valuable image to uphold for Russia in terms of attracting new friends not on good terms with the United States or for bullying smaller neighbouring countries who may be considering escaping Moscow's orbit. Russia's ability to smother international action and render Washington impotent while the Syrian government orchestrated a sequence of massacres was Moscow's 'don't you dare' warning to disobedient countries, for example Georgia, that believe US protection can be relied upon. To assert that point, the survival of the Asad regime became linked to Russia's ability to determine international events and magnify its geo-strategic influence not only in the Middle East but also Eastern Europe, the Caucasus and Central Asia.

The second factor behind Russia's stance relates to the political system in Russia. Putin's re-election in 2012 was tainted by mass protests and declining support in the major cities of Moscow and St. Petersburg. It was predictable that Putin and his supporters would reject the principle of spreading democratic change in the streets and also with external intervention or support. Such nervousness was behind Russia's banning in 2012 of NGOs with external funding, or the law that limited street protests by imposing heavy financial fines on protesters in a country where average income was still in the bottom range of European countries. It was therefore largely an instinctive knee-jerk reaction by Russia to cling to the Asad regime that was not out of any particular love for it. Here Putin was at least partially sincere in his declaration that he had no personal sentiment towards the Syrian leader, but rather because Moscow was determined to ensure that any pro-democracy and pro-freedom protests failed. The survival of the regime in Syria became a political shield to prevent such dynamics from spreading to other countries including Iran and potentially to Russia at the end of the domino trail. Pro-Kremlin media and Russian academics virtually in unison described the so-called Arab Spring as a fiasco that only led to violence and in stability and mocked any suggestions that the protests led to more political freedoms and better representation and accountability.

This attitude in Russia was most passionately directed towards the Syrian example. Yet in reality Moscow's shared empathy for the Syrian government had been evident much earlier, from 2005, in the face of international criticism over Lebanon. This bond with the Asad regime had grown deep enough to undermine Putin's broader efforts to establish a meaningful presence in the region by negatively impacting the development of relations with very important regional actors such as Israel, Turkey and Saudi Arabia. Moscow's behaviour in defending the Syrian regime by allowing it to buy time and stalling UNSC measures, either with regards to Lebanon or to the popular uprising from 2011, cast serious doubts over Russia's true motives and its commitment to joining the international community as a constructive member. Russia's relationship with Syria provided the best evidence yet that there was a sinister component in foreign policy that Moscow kept hidden. As an example, in the summer of 2009 there was intense speculation that a reportedly hijacked Russian cargo ship loaded with timber, the *Arctic Sea*, was in fact smuggling a secret shipment of missiles bound for Syria. Soon after the ship was located it was widely suggested that the hijacking story had been invented by Russian authorities to cover up the trail of the cargo that was intercepted by Israeli authorities. Although Medvedev was president at the time the powerful Putin, as prime minister, was at the helm of a regime, dictating Russia's foreign policy and security agenda after 2008. The Russian cover-up and the incident as a whole did little for Moscow's international image and credibility, and highlighted that Putin's Russia remained trapped in a visceral reaction to defy and compete with the United States rather than to promote stability and democratic change in the region. Similarly, during the Syrian crisis Russian efforts to smuggle arms to regime forces were exposed, mainly by Turkey, on several occasions. Syrian opposition forces were particularly angered by Moscow's repeated denial or belittlement of massacres, murders and torture of protestors and its adoption of the regime perspective of events.

Russia's reputation in the Muslim world and in the West was hugely damaged by its unwillingness to encourage peaceful change in Syria and its alignment with the Asad regime. Turkey, Egypt and Saudi Arabia, all stalwart Sunni powers, were openly calling for Asad to step down and provided material support to the Syrian opposition. Yet Putin's Russia became a country where the ruling clique shared a kindred spirit with Asad's rule, dating back years before the uprising in Syria had started and the dynamics of these relations made it quite impossible for Moscow to reverse course. History may well come to show us that Russian policy towards Syria more than any other country exposed the hallmarks of the Putin era and the direction in which it took Russia.

8

THE ISRAEL PARADOX AND THE PALESTINIAN PROBLEM

Tyrannical regimes in the Middle East and global Islamic terrorists for decades often justified their actions by expounding vociferous complaints about Western double-standards in failing to address the humanitarian tragedy of millions of Palestinian refugees living in dismal conditions. Worse still, the West seemed particularly thick-skinned about the political aspirations of the Palestinian people for an independent homeland, offering Moscow a convenient opening to win wider Arab and Muslim support. According to one Russian observer commenting on the Soviet legacy of its support for the rights of the Palestinians, 'Russia is far from being a detached observer in the Middle East; indeed, the influential country enjoys the respect of the people in this region.'[1] Yet aside from claiming the moral high ground among Arabs and Muslims, Russia's political support for the Palestinians and its consistent endorsement for peace between them and Israel brought with it few tangible benefits and these were also lost due to Russia's support for the Asad regime under Putin.

An oft-repeated argument was that the resolution of the Palestinian problem would eliminate the political and socio-economic stagnation in the Middle East region. The ongoing Palestinian-Israeli conflict had become a symbol of Western injustice and inhumanity and thus offered both the Soviet Union and Russia a cause to exploit. The Palestinian people did not and could not offer Russia an immediate boost to the economy or provide a military-strategic advantage. Adopting the Palestinian cause in the 1990s however not only created a measure of popular support for Russia among Arabs and Muslims but it also facilitated relations with Iran and Syria as both countries thrived on anti-Western and anti-Israeli rhetoric. Russia's stated support for the rights of the Palestinians also dampened a potentially far more hostile reaction from Arab and Muslim countries during its military campaign in Chechnya in the 1990s. But such benefits had to be balanced with developing a meaningful relationship with Israel, which was a powerful regional actor offering opportunities of economic, cultural and technological cooperation. In addition, antagonising Israel with an overtly pro-Palestinian policy risked damage to relations with the United States and other Western countries, which Russia was very keen to avoid until about 2005.

Israel was a sought-after friend who was the enemy of another friend, the Palestinians. Faced with such a predicament the Russian political and economic elite became divided on the basis of competing ideological, strategic and economic goals behind policy making. The military-industrial complex for example held a generally pro-Arab position in order to promote weapons sales to anti-Israeli states and tacitly prolong the conflict. Russians in the modern financial sector and the oil and gas industries considered their country's interest to be in adopting a more balanced approach that would allow the development of relations with Israel as well as moderate, energy-rich Arab states such as Saudi Arabia and Qatar.

Ideologically, the Palestinian-Israeli crisis was perceived by some in Moscow as a classic East versus West conflict in which Russia was obliged to side with the Eastern Christian and Muslim Palestinians against Israel. Russia's geographic position on the front line of the Muslim world in Eurasia demanded a strategic placement of the country among the anti-Western bloc of nations, according to this Eurasian view of the world. This outlook became more pertinent while Putin was president because of the West's hostility to the Muslim world in the context of the 'War on Terror' and suspicions about Washington's motives. Putin's shifting behaviour reflected the debate by underlining the Kremlin's struggle to appease the contradictory internal and external pressures on Moscow's approach to the Palestinian-Israeli dispute.

Israel until Putin: a Background

Despite a turbulent relationship the Soviet Union never withdrew recognition of the state of Israel. The storminess of the Cold War, however, negatively impacted Soviet behaviour towards its own sizeable and important Jewish community, as Egypt and Syria, both under Moscow's military patronage in the 1960s, became more vitriolic in their anti-Semitic hostility towards Israel. In the competitiveness of US-Soviet rivalry Moscow endeavoured to prove its loyalty to its allies and show that it was a commanding superpower, and consequently relations with Israel drastically deteriorated.

There were finer nuances to Russian-Jewish relations that added to the tensions. Many of the founding settlers in Israel, helping to secure its establishment in May 1948, originated from the former Russian Empire and all had experienced or were indirectly impacted by the Pogroms and the deep-rooted anti-Semitism that peaked there around the turn of the twentieth century. In 1900 5.2 million of Europe's estimated 8.7 million Jews lived in the Russian Empire[2] and Jewish activists played leading roles in the Revolutions of 1905 and 1917, with Leon Trotsky (Lev Davidovitch Bronstein) perhaps the best known figure. Soviet Jews throughout the Soviet era continued to lead among their fellow communities in their contributions to art, literature and science, consistently ranking among the best educated segments of society. Nonetheless, the temptation for Jews to relocate to Israel, a Jewish homeland free from centuries of years of European discrimination and persecution was understandably great. The ideal of Israel, which transformed into reality in the mid-twentieth century, meant Jews could live in a country where they no longer felt as outsiders or as a guest minority.

The urge by Soviet Jews to leave to Israel became more widespread in the 1970s. This was viewed by the ageing and paranoid Brezhnevite regime in Moscow as an act of defiance and added to the already existing undercurrent of anti-Semitism among Russian and Ukrainian Slavs. Under Brezhnev there was more intense and advanced military support for Israel's enemies than ever before, particularly between 1967 and 1973. On the diplomatic front, the first Palestine Liberation Organisation (PLO) office to serve as diplomatic representation was opened in 1976 and Yasser Arafat was received publicly in Moscow by Brezhnev in 1977 after years of hesitation. In 1978 the PLO office in Moscow was granted diplomatic status, the year Egyptian President Anwar Sadat and

Israeli Prime Minister Menachim Begin signed the Camp David Accords. Moscow's political overtures were being made in light of infamous terrorist incidents such as the attack in 1972 on Israeli Olympic athletes in Munich by Palestinian groups linked with the PLO. While Israel and its Western allies labelled the PLO as a rogue terrorist organisation the Soviet Union was granting its leadership diplomatic respectability. Soviet apologists suggested that this was to compensate for the lack of direct military support that was provided by Moscow to the Palestinians to allow it to be an effective mediator.

The Soviet leadership had consistently attempted to convince the PLO to acknowledge the legal right of the state of Israel to exist in order to remove a major hurdle that would allow the activation of the peace process. But the decade preceding 1985, the year Mikhail Gorbachev assumed the position of general secretary of the Communist Party of the Soviet Union, was a particularly low period of Soviet-Israeli relations. In the early 1980s the Cold War détente had become a distant memory and the Middle East mutated into a far more radicalised and polarised arena. In the late 1970s the Khomeini-led revolution in Iran, the Soviet invasion of Afghanistan and the Egyptian switch to the Western camp after signing a peace treaty with Israel left little room for compromise. The PLO was divided between the radical and belligerent pro-Syrian factions and Arafat's Fatah movement. This was a reflection of the intense animosity between Arafat and Syria's Hafez Asad, which played out in the military confrontation between Palestinian and Syrian forces in Lebanon's civil war. Soviet foreign policy reached a point of disarray by the time of Brezhnev's death in 1982 because it had alienated the West, antagonised Israel and failed to keep its own allies in line. Israel's rejection of Moscow as an effective mediator in the Middle East appeared to be justified, especially as in the 1970s and 1980s the Soviet Union was barring hundreds of thousands of Jews, unofficially termed refusniks, from emigrating.

As Gorbachev and his foreign minister, Eduard Shevardnadze, set about to end Soviet isolation it was obvious to them that readjusting policy towards Israel was of paramount importance. As a gesture of goodwill, among the first reforms of the Gorbachev era was to ease restrictions on Soviet Jews to allow them to leave to Israel, initially via Vienna and other European cities because no direct relations or flights existed between the two countries. In 1986 contacts between Soviet and

Israeli officials were resumed for the first time since 1967, eventually leading to full diplomatic ties between the two countries in October 1991. The time lag since the initial contacts was due to internal resistance to Gorbachev over concerns that premature recognition would leave traditional Soviet friends feeling betrayed. Eventually, the establishment of relations was justified on the basis that it would allow the Soviet Union to play its role as co-sponsor of the Madrid Middle East Peace Conference that first convened on 30 October 1991. In practice it reflected the weakened position of the Communist Party hardliners and the emergence of new forces of influence in Soviet and, soon after, Russian politics.

In 1992 a new Russia was born and the Soviet Union ceased to exist. This created an opportunity for a new basis of relations with Israel and President Yeltsin and his reformist foreign minister, Andrei Kozyrev, energetically distanced themselves from Soviet policies and made deliberate efforts during 1992 and 1993 to make up for lost time in relations with Israel. Among the most effective actions Russia took in favour of Israel in the region during those initial years was not to do anything at all. In other words, by yielding to US leadership in the peace process and informing the Palestinians and Syrians that Russia would not act as a military counterbalance to Israel and the United States in the Middle East Arafat and Asad realised that the peace process was the unavoidable route to ending their international isolation.

Yeltsin and Kozyrev's emphasis on building friendly relations with the West that was initiated by Gorbachev in the late 1980s indirectly facilitated the Palestinian-Israeli agreement reached in 1993. Moscow's political disengagement at the time was paralleled by an active economic thrust towards finding new partners in the Middle East. Bilateral Russian-Israeli trade grew rapidly so that by 1995, after crossing the $500 million mark, Israel became Russia's second largest trading partner in the Middle East after Turkey.[3] Moscow's new policies towards Israel, however, eventually encountered major limitations in the same way as Russia's efforts towards the United States reached an impasse. The initial progress in developing economic relations stalled, with Russia's first ambassador to Israel, Alexander Bovin, reminiscing that during 'my five and a half years in Israel, I didn't implement a single large Israeli-Russian project'.[4]

While prodding the Palestinians in the early 1990s towards reaching a settlement with Israel, arguably to the advantage of the latter, Moscow was simultaneously carefully constructing relations with Iran. According to the Rabin government that was formed in 1992 the Iranians had emerged as the single most dangerous threat to the security of Israel. In confirmation of such fears, the United Nations arms register in October 1994 noted that Iran had emerged as 'Russia's largest arms customer'.[5] Rabin relayed his concerns to Yeltsin and Kozyrev on his visit to Moscow on 24 April 1994, the first ever by an Israeli prime minister since the creation of Israel. The Russian leadership offered verbal assurances but did not deny that Iran was earmarked as an important long-term economic partner. Co-operation with Tehran was geo-strategically wise considering that Iran bordered the unstable Caucasus region and shared a coastline on the Caspian Sea.

Russian-Iranian cooperation, despite Israeli complaints, resulted in positive outcomes for Moscow. Tehran supported the Armenians, Russia's historic allies, against the Azerbaijanis in their war in the Caucasus and co-operated with Moscow in curtailing the civil war in Tajikistan. Yeltsin's Russia had little to lose in abandoning the Palestinians but much to gain in building a solid relationship with Iran. The balancing of relations between Iran and Israel became the major challenge under Yeltsin and later throughout the Putin era.

In the early 1990s Russia faced the embarrassing situation of being the major source for the burgeoning number of Jewish settlers in disputed territories. Arab and Muslim public opinion associated the Yeltsin-Kozyrev era with Western support for Israel and the deterioration of the Palestinian humanitarian crisis. Russian foreign policy under Yeltsin therefore lost prestige among the Arabs while it failed to gain Israel's confidence because of Moscow's developing relations with Tehran.

During the latter half of the 1990s the Middle East peace process began to falter and violence increased with a new uncompromising government under Benjamin Netanyahu in Israel renewing settlement expansion. In response, Hamas and other violent Palestinian factions began a wave of suicide bombings inside Israel, killing dozens of innocent civilians. In this setting Foreign Minister Primakov, Kozyrev's successor, set a new course of strengthening ties with both Iran and Hezbollah and a special envoy to the Middle East, Viktor Posuvaliuk, was appointed to improve Russia's position among Arab and Muslim countries. Foreign Ministry officials flew regularly to Lebanon in 1996 and in the following years to meet with senior Hezbollah officials. While refusing to condone acts of terrorism, Primakov offered justifications for Palestinian frustration which further irritated Israeli public opinion.

As a balancing diplomatic manoeuvre Primakov visited Israel in October 1996 to meet with Prime Minister Benjamin Netanyahu, who had annulled previous peace agreements with the Palestinians. Despite low expectations, as a 'gesture of goodwill' Netanyahu facilitated 'the transfer of ownership to the Russian Federation of a number of Jerusalem-based real estate facilities that had previously belonged to the former Soviet Union and the Russian Orthodox Church'.[6] The move was largely aimed to ensure that Russian hostility would be contained and to allow Israel to preserve some influence on Moscow's behaviour in the Middle East. Israeli complaints to the authorities in Moscow in late 1997 about contacts with Iran and Hezbollah were explained according to the Russian Ambassador to Israel, Mikhail Bogdanov, as being in Israel's interest. According to Bogdanov Russia was maximising its diplomatic leverage to restrain Hezbollah and that Moscow was using its contacts with Tehran to find out more about the fate of abducted or missing Israeli military personnel. However, there was a noticeably more critical tone towards Israel by Moscow following a round of fighting between Israel and Hezbollah in April 1996 when Primakov actively sought to play a mediating role. This dualistic approach was part of Primakov's strategy of rebalancing the Russian role by winning back the trust of Israel's adversaries to allow Moscow to change their behaviour in concert with Western powers that have influence over Israel.

During Yeltsin's last years in office, in light of the conflict in Chechnya, Russian public opinion was prone to being more sympathetic to Israelis rather than Palestinians because of the shared imagery of Islamic terrorism. This was relevant in light of Hamas and Islamic Jihad attacks on civilian targets in Israel at that time. As an interesting indicator of attitudes, one study found that the 'former Caucasophobia turned into Arabophobia' among Russian Jews who relocated to Israel. The author noted that: 'If Jews—members of a well-educated urban minority, quintessentially victims of ethnic hostility—subscribe so eagerly to such stereotypes then it is not all that surprising that xenophobia is prevalent among Russian intellectuals.'[7] Putin was among the new elite who on several occasions betrayed an underlying negative personal attitude towards Muslims, particularly during his handling of the Chechen war.

There was a growing transnational relationship between Russia and Israel throughout the 1990s by virtue of the large Russian-Jewish community in Israel which maintained its old habits and language and found it difficult to integrate with older Jewish communities. During the 1990s nearly 700,000 Soviet Jews migrated to Israel and the figure grew to over 1 million in 2012, comprising about one in seven of the Israeli population. Since Russian speakers were a major segment of Israeli society, the largest Russian-speaking community outside the former Soviet space, the 'Russian-speaking Jews have emerged as a prominent interest group' in Israel.[8] Furthermore, Russia opened its borders to Jews who wished to leave, so unlike during the Soviet era families who emigrated could still return regularly to visit relatives or friends on a regular basis. This helped in maintaining bonds between Russia and Russian Jews in Israel. One leading Russian-Jewish figure, Vladimir Jabotinsky, describing his community's view of Russia, remarked: 'I do not know if many of us love Russia, but many, too many of us, children of the Jewish intelligentsia, are madly, shamefully in love with Russian culture, and through it with the whole of the Russian world.'[9] This would not be the first or last paradox in relations between Israel and Russia.

Putin and Israel

Lilia Shevtsova, in a portrayal of the Russian president, wrote that: 'Putin behaved like an agent in enemy territory, letting no one learn his true intentions—if in fact he had any.'[10] It would not be unfair to apply this rather poetic brushstroke to Putin's behaviour on the Middle East scene in general, and with regard to Israel in particular during the first term of his presidency. The contradiction of Putin's policy approach towards Israel was succinctly noted in an article published in the winter of 2005. The article's opening statement boldly declared that the 'Russian government remains the greatest facilitator for Iranian nuclear ambitions. It has had close ties to terror-sponsoring regimes such as Syria and Saddam's Iraq.'[11] In the following paragraph however the article declares that: 'Under Putin, Russia has not only declined to adopt Western Europe's increasingly shrill anti-Israel posture, but in many ways he has actually tilted Russian policy in Israel's favour, at least with respect to the Israeli-Palestinian conflict.'[12] That Putin could be described as pro-Israel and at the same time supporting and endorsing Israel's most dangerous regional threats, including Iran, was riddled with inconsistency. Yet it is this Israel paradox that provides telling insights into Russia's behaviour towards the Middle East and Putin's style on the international scene.

Soon after Putin's election as Russian president in 2000, the Camp David II Summit was held in July bringing together PLO Chairman Yasser Arafat and Israeli Prime Minister Ehud Barak under the personal mediation of US President Bill Clinton. Although Russia endorsed the event and was nominally a co-sponsor of the ongoing peace process it was excluded from the meetings held between 11 July and 25 July. The Camp David II Summit was a rare opportunity to resolve the Israeli-Palestinian dispute, in part because Clinton was very keen to end his presidency in its final year with the achievement of being termed global peacemaker. Barak had also indicated a genuine commitment to a comprehensive resolution after he withdrew Israeli troops from south Lebanon and he also offered Syria to return the Golan Heights according to the 1967 borders. Yet despite such positive indicators the divisions between Israel and the Palestinians stubbornly persisted and had become more complex over time. Among the most contentious points of dispute was the status of Jerusalem, which Israel claimed was its united and eternal capital, while Palestinians wanted the eastern part of the city as their own capital. Moreover, Israeli public opinion was unwilling to allow the depopulation of all existing settlements in the West Bank while the Palestinian leadership insisted on the right of all refugees to return. Moscow was noticeably detached from these issues and remained so during further efforts in 2000 to find a breakthrough, including at the Sharm Al-Shaikh gathering in October that was organised by the United States and Egypt, where Israeli-Palestinian talks were again conducted without Russian participation.

The failure of the peace efforts on the Syrian and Palestinian fronts and a new violent uprising, known as the Al-Aqsa Intifida that broke out in late September 2001, proved to be a decisive political blow to Prime Minister Barak and he was replaced by the hawkish Ariel Sharon in March 2001. In this setting Putin visited Israel in May 2001 with the purpose of improving bilateral relations. Sharon praised Putin during the visit and suggested that Russia's position had become more sympathetic to the Israelis than the Europeans. Attitudes in Russia had become more flexible towards Israel in the early Putin years and 'with the exception of a small number of left wing and nationalist papers, most of the Russian media were…generally more pro-Israeli than in Western

Europe, and the Russian public, while alarmed about the events, remained largely detached and neutral'.[13] In light of the terrorist attacks in the United States in September 2001, Putin sought to present Russia as a comrade-in-arms with the Western world and Israel fighting against barbaric Islamic terrorism. It was not missed by observers at the time that Putin's close identification with Bush against Islamic terrorism was bold 'even to the extent of welcoming (to the chagrin of the Russian military establishment) closer American ties with other Soviet successor states in the pursuit of what he was quick to identify as a common enemy'.[14] Israel was a seeming natural partner in this global struggle.

Israeli opinion-makers supported the vision of forming a broad alliance, with commentators such as Ariel Cohen warning that: 'The ideological expansion of radical Islam cannot be stopped without the cooperation of the US, Western Europe, Russia, India, Israel and other countries.'[15] Putin was nonetheless forced to restrain his participation in this coalition and heed the calls of domestic interest groups to maintain good relations with the Arab and wider Muslim world. According to one Russia analyst, among those unhappy with a warming of relations with Israel were 'pro-Arab elements in Russia's Foreign Ministry and in the increasingly influential secret police who hope to restore the close ties Moscow had in the Arab world in Soviet times'.[16] Only months before 11 September 2001 'Muslim deputies in the Duma created their own separate parliamentary caucus claiming the defence of the Palestinian people as one of its major goals.'[17] Internationally, coordinating too closely to Israel antagonised important partners such as Iran and damaged economic interests in the Middle East as well as risked alienating Russian and neighbouring Muslims.

The nature of the strategic US-Israeli alliance further hindered efforts to improve relations with Israel because critics argued that Russia would always play second fiddle. Efforts to stimulate military cooperation between Israel and Russia, for example, ended in failure because of commitments that 'Israel must clear with the United States any significant transfer of advanced technology. Domestically, the Israeli government is under pressure to stay away from military-technical cooperation with Russia until there is convincing evidence that Moscow is not leaking nuclear and missile technologies to Iran.'[18] The Russian-Israeli rapprochement eventually reached its peak in 2002 and from then on Moscow's slant became more evidently and consistently unfavourable. A discernible turning point can be traced to April 2002 when the Israeli military launched an operation against the Palestinian town of Jenin, in an act of collective punishment, which resulted in high civilian casualties and was accompanied by the imposition of a blockade on the town's residents that prevented the supply of basic humanitarian aid. In response, the tone of criticisms from Moscow became acutely more severe while the United States maintained its unquestioning support for Israel in the face of international outrage. This coincided with Russian displeasure with Israel for placing Palestinian leader Yasser Arafat under house arrest from the end of 2001 and Moscow's rhetoric became more vigorous in its criticisms after his residential compound was placed under siege and shelled to a bare skeleton by the Israeli military in September 2002.

There were three compelling reasons for Russia to adopt a stronger anti-Israeli position at that time: First, the image of Arafat and the residents of Jenin being blockaded while enduring heavy shelling by the powerful Israeli military gained strong international public, including European, sympathy; Second, by not explicitly supporting the Palestinians Russia risked burning all its bridges with the Arab and Islamic world, which was already offended by the US anti-Islamic rhetoric in its war on terrorism; Third, there was a broad view that Sharon's actions were not driven by a rational political agenda but by a personal and vindictive vendetta against his long-time foe Arafat. Moscow's leadership recognised that it was dangerous to be associated with emotional behaviour rather than a well-defined strategic line in dictating policy. Russia also did not want to be perceived as being outdone by the Europeans in terms of political and humanitarian sympathy with the Palestinians. Taking note of these factors Putin smelled an opportunity to take advantage of the raging international anti-Americanism in Europe and other parts of the world including the Middle East that swelled during the Jenin Siege following the diminishing tide of sympathy for the United States since September 2001. Russia sought to present itself as the defender of international justice and the protector of the weak as an alternative to Israeli violations and US double-standards.

As Russian foreign policy under Putin began hardening its tone towards Israel the United States and Britain coincidentally began an aggressive campaign to justify war against Iraq. Moscow thus identified the need to form a significant alliance of nations to counterbalance US ambitions in the Middle East, including plans to occupy Iraq, and this specifically required support from Arab and Muslim countries, which in turn led to a cooling of relations with Israel. A noticeably hostile attitude resumed in the Russian media and by political observers close to the government, with one regular commentator, as president of the Institute of Middle East Studies, noting that Sharon's 'actions show that Israel's former pride in its democratic institutions actually veiled traditions of clan authoritarianism that are quite a match for the neighbouring Arab states'.[19]

As a result of this changing regional atmosphere Putin's re-election in 2004 took place in a distinctly different setting with regard to Israel than when he was first elected as president. The US-led occupation of Iraq and the continued violence there compounded the worsening relations that were developing between the West and Russia over NATO expansion plans. In light of these developments, one analysis argued that: 'Beginning in 2005, Russia has made a major effort to increase its influence in the region. This is in part a counterweight to NATO's expansion eastward and in part a response to Russian reverses in Georgia and Ukraine. Russia has also signed major arms agreements with both Syria and Iran—agreements that have greatly exacerbated tensions in the region.'[20] Russia's active and aggressive increase in its arms sales and delivery to Syria and Iran became a cause for serious concern in Israel. Russia's ongoing support for Iran's nuclear programme was more widely being seen as a deliberate effort to change the strategic balance in the region. More troubling for Moscow was Israel's developing relations with Georgia and Azerbaijan, two countries making an active effort to break away from Russia's orbit. A Russian, Syrian and Iranian alliance, if fulfilled, not only would surround US troops in Iraq but could also threaten Israel's existence through the proliferation of advanced missile technology to its regional enemies.

Throughout Putin's second term Israel continued to place the Iranian nuclear issue at the top of its security agenda. While Iran vehemently denied its intention to create nuclear weapons, arguing that its programme was only intended for peaceful purposes, the fierce anti-Israeli language emanating from Tehran and the military support the regime was providing to Hezbollah, Hamas and Syria suggested that there was a belligerent intent by the Iranian regime. Israel's leadership and public shared the perception that the country simply couldn't afford to believe

Iran, and by the same token Russia, about the peaceful nature of the nuclear programme. Aside from posing a direct threat there was also the possibility that Iran could arm proxies with smaller but lethal dirty bombs to threaten Israel, particularly via Hezbollah in Lebanon. Even the scenario of Iran possessing nuclear weapons without using them because of the fear of retaliation would still be highly problematic for Israel. By joining the nuclear club the regime would broaden its popular support, 'thereby increasing its legitimacy and longevity. Iran might be further empowered to pursue its regional interests…[and] Iran's nuclearisation might spur an expensive arms race that would drain resources away from more productive purposes in the Israeli economy.'[21] That would make Israel's long term future dependent on consistently reliable large-scale Western support in the face of open-ended hostility by its neighbours.

In July 2006 Israel confronted evolving threats by retaliating to a Hezbollah raid on its northern border with a major military campaign in Lebanon. The Hezbollah raid was timed to coincide with a G8 Summit meeting in St Petersburg, Russia, that was preceded by strong language and threats between the United States and Iran regarding the latter's nuclear programme. In Lebanon it was widely suggested that Hezbollah's timing was intended to divert attention away from Iran during the Summit, when US President Bush was expected to put pressure on Putin to agree to further sanctions on Iran. Regardless of the legitimacy of arguments that the war was deliberately instigated by Hezbollah for such motives, the outcome was successful from Iran's point of view because Putin was able to turn the tables on the United States by demanding that Israel halt its military campaign with immediate effect. Eventually, Israel succumbed to international pressure for a ceasefire without achieving any of its objectives, including crippling Hezbollah's military strength in Lebanon. In fact, Hezbollah emerged stronger politically and the victory it claimed consolidated further the alliance between Syria, which was vital in facilitating the arming of the military Shi'a group as well as in terms of providing it with political support in Lebanon, and Iran. It also allowed Putin to feel confident that his policy of supporting Iran and Syria in the region was a correct one because it curtailed US power on the international stage and enhanced Russia's own prestige by allowing it to be on the winning side.

Israel's setbacks in Lebanon were a personal humiliation for Prime Minister Ehud Olmert, who was hurried into war in July 2006 and then hurried into a ceasefire in August 2006. Perhaps to counteract the criticisms from his political opponents Olmert embarked on a more proactive effort to negotiate with Syria, claiming that his intention was to split its partnership with Iran. Because those adequately familiar with Syrian politics recognised that Damascus was highly unlikely to change its behaviour and its alliances, Olmert's actions were most likely a cynical attempt to rescue his personal reputation, especially as he was concurrently facing corruption charges in Israel. The dubious motives for the proposed Israeli-Syrian peace negotiations in 2007 led Primakov to ask: 'Is Israel's call for peace with Syria yet another diversion?'[22] The questionable motives for announcing these talks were also directed at Syria and in November 2007, despite a long absence from the Foreign Ministry, Primakov was dispatched to Syria by Putin to convince President Asad to not disrupt Israeli-Palestinian peace efforts.

While political and security differences between Russia and Israel, particularly over Iran, became more apparent there was simultaneously a steady growth of direct trade that crossed the $1.5 billion mark in 2007 in addition to 'over a billion [US dollars] in energy deals'.[23] Israel became particularly interested in importing Russian gas in light of the Arab and Iranian boycott while Russia sought to extend pipelines from the Black Sea via Turkey to the southern resort of Eilat. After a slight downturn due to the banking crisis in 2008 trade picked up again so that Israel emerged as a major economic interest in the Middle East for Russia. It is of significance that Russia's three main trade partners in the region, Turkey, Iran and Israel, are all non-Arab countries.

On 25 June 2012 Putin met with Netanyahu to discuss further expanding bilateral trade with emphasis on technology and energy, particularly gas. With trade figures at over $3 billion, Putin's visit was timed to build on the existing positives in bilateral relations and also, significantly, to redress some of the differences that had arisen in the previous decade. This was largely due to the transformations in the Arab world, which were marked by a political surge by Islamist parties such as the Muslim Brotherhood in Egypt. In Syria too, the opposition was dominated by Islamist groups and the Palestinian Hamas, which was an offshoot of the Muslim Brotherhood, evacuated its headquarters in Damascus in sympathy with the anti-Asad uprising.

Russia's support for the Asad regime upset relations with the Palestinians and in all cases Islamist parties were historically regarded with suspicion in Moscow. The deterioration of relations with the Arab world thus forced Moscow to revise its approach towards Israel and Putin's visit in 2012 consolidated shared interests: 'Topping that list is a shared sense the Russia and Israel alone fully understand the menace of Islamic extremism. Israel believes it confronts extremism on a daily basis and Putin sees it as a serious threat to Russia's territorial integrity emanating from the restive northern Caucasus region.'[24] Both Israel and Russia viewed the downfall of the Asad regime as being unfavourable because of the unpredictability of what could follow. Popular Arab conspiracy theories and media insinuations frequently suggested that Asad had been able to survive the fierce revolt for so long because of Russian-Israeli collusion.

The transformations in the Arab world during Putin's third term therefore required a Russian rethink of its strategic relationship with Israel. Yet Moscow continued to ignore Israeli requests to limit Russian arms sales to Syria and its proxy Hezbollah. From Israel's standpoint, 'specifically disturbing was Putin's continued refusal to put Hamas and Hezbollah on Russia's list of terrorist organisations, allowing money to flow freely from Russia to two of Israel's worst enemies'.[25] This led one analysis to conclude that: 'Israel's biggest existential threat is not from its Arab neighbours but rather from a global power seeking to establish its own interests in the Middle East. In other words, Israel's neighbours only become a threat once they obtain outside patronage making them bold, organised and armed enough to strike at Israel from all sides.'[26] Israel had become resigned to the fact that Russia would continue to support Iran, but pragmatism prevailed to allow bilateral relations to flourish in areas of mutual benefit. Neither Russia nor Israel wanted a return to the blind Soviet era enmity that had been so damaging to both parties.

The Palestinian angle: a background

The displacement of the Palestinians was arguably the single most forceful influence on regional politics in the second half of the twentieth century. The authoritarian regimes of Syria, Iraq and Egypt from the 1950s all adopted the Palestinian cause to legitimise their grip on power and to justify their regional behaviour. In Jordan, Palestinian refugees collided with the monarchy in a bloody conflict that climaxed in 1970.

This led to the forceful ejection of Palestinian militias and their families from Jordan, mostly to Lebanon, where the large influx of armed Palestinian refugees tilted the sectarian balance away from the Christians and dragged the country into a bloody civil war. From 1967, Palestinian guerrillas organised themselves to attack Israel from across all its borders, including the occupied West Bank and Gaza and most infamously some factions initiated terrorist campaigns against Jews around the world and in pro-Israeli nations, which involved the hijacking of airlines and bombing of civilian targets. The Palestinian issue became the cause unanimously adopted by Arab governments as well as their political opposition rivals to guarantee popular support. The existence of the Palestinian diaspora scattered in limbo came to symbolise Western racism in its careless discard for Arab and Muslim opinion with millions of refugees continuing to live in miserable camps, without citizenship and identity and no end in sight to their plight.

In Soviet times Khrushchev and his successors until the end of the Soviet era considered themselves as the patrons of the underdog. The Palestinians and their Arab supporters considered the Soviet Union as a vital outlet that gave their voices access on the global stage, particularly on the United Nations Security Council. Until 1967 Gamal Abdul Nasser, Egypt's president, aspired to lead the Arab renaissance and through his fiery anti-Israeli and anti-Western speeches during the 1960s promised to return Palestinians to their homeland by military means. With Egypt and Syria heavily armed by the Soviet Union it was only a matter of time before a major war would break out. In June 1967 Israel surprised its enemies by launching a massive pre-emptive air strike, wiping out Arab military capabilities and ensuring dominance of the Middle East skies. With such an advantage, the resistance of the Arab armies collapsed and Israel extended territories under its control. Most significantly Israel augmented its partial control of Jerusalem with the Eastern quarter of the capital, thus enabling it to unite the religiously significant city under its control.

The character and the dynamics of the Arab-Israeli conflict changed dramatically after 1967. Essentially, the Arab states realised that Israel was a permanent fixture in the Middle East due to the limitless political and military support it received from the United States and the West in general. The Soviet Union, while breaking off diplomatic relations, also tacitly supported Israel's existence by its vocal demand for a peaceful settlement with the Palestinians. UNSC Resolution 242, adopted unanimously including the Soviet Union in November 1967 after the war in June, demanded a 'just and lasting peace in the Middle East' and affirmed the right of all states to live in secure borders. The defeat of Egypt and Syria in 1967 turned out to be a major setback for the Soviet Union. Gradually, Egypt and Syria moved away from the Soviet orbit and Cairo completely severed ties after shifting to the pro-Western camp in the mid-1970s after the Yom Kippur War in October 1973. Syria also opened tacit channels of coordination with Washington during the 1970s because President Hafez Asad recognised that the Soviet Union's effectiveness was limited by its desire to avoid a direct confrontation with the United States. In light of this the Arab states also became less inclined to confront Israel directly, leaving the Palestinians to fight on their own through military units known as Feda'iyin to wage raids on Israel.

Soviet-PLO relations improved markedly as a result of Syrian and Egyptian orientation towards the West with Palestinian leader Yasser Arafat being received publicly in 1977 for the first time in Moscow in a manner befitting a head of state. The event symbolised Soviet desperation to maintain a degree of influence in the region having failed to establish firm state-level alliances in the Middle East as a whole. The confused Middle East foreign policy under Brezhnev and Soviet Foreign Minister Andrei Gromyko forced Moscow to play a balancing act between the PLO and Syria, who were locked in a bitter military feud to control Lebanon. The Soviet invasion of Afghanistan in December 1979 created additional tensions between the Soviet Union and the Muslim world. Saudi Arabia, the spiritual centre of Islam, had emerged as a major financial backer of the Palestinians due to the oil boom in the 1970s and it had also become the focal point of Muslim resistance to the Soviet invasion and occupation of Afghanistan. It was little wonder that Gorbachev's New Thinking in Soviet foreign policy emerged largely as a reaction to the befuddled Brezhnev era.

From the Palestinian perspective the Gorbachev era dealt a heavy blow to their aspirations. Gorbachev had allowed Soviet Jews to leave in the tens of thousands each year and most typically they settled on occupied land in the West Bank. By doing so, Palestinian claims of statehood and the return of their refugees diminished with every flight full of Soviet Jews. When Arafat complained during his stay in Moscow in

1988 about his fears for the future of his nation, 'Gorbachev lectured visiting PLO chief Yasser Arafat that Israel was also concerned about its security and borders.'[27]

A central component of Gorbachev's New Thinking was to extract the Soviet Union from regional conflicts that did not offer any tangible economic and political gains and that were of little significance to the national security of the country. The Israeli-Palestinian dispute was a classic example of costly political and economic investment purely for ideological purposes during the Cold War rivalry. Eventually, Moscow calculated that there was more to be gained from good relations with the United States than with the Palestinians, who were effectively abandoned in the late 1980s by the new approach. Gorbachev's detachment from the Palestinian side in the conflict resulted in Arafat's renunciation of terrorism and for the first time he offered a vocal recognition of Israel as a state and partner for peace. As a result of Arafat's modified stance and the US-Soviet warming of relations the Madrid Peace Conference opened on 30 October 1991. Despite the compromises, Arafat was vetoed by Israel from attending the conference, which for the first time kick-started the Palestinian-Israeli peace process. Arafat was represented by the pacifist Dr. Haidar Abdul Shafi, further underlining the argument that under Gorbachev, 'Soviet diplomacy played a significant, if unadvertised, role in bringing about a more moderate Palestinian position on the Middle Eastern settlement.'[28]

The Palestinians during the Yeltsin years

In 1992, the first year of Yeltsin's presidency post-Soviet Union, Moscow's official line 'did not mention Palestinian rights or the Israeli occupation'.[29] Russia's general disengagement from the Middle East was a consequence of Foreign Minister Kozyrev's focus on bettering relations with the United States and the West. Throughout 1993 Moscow deliberately took a back seat in formal Arab-Israeli peace negotiations, which tellingly took place in the hallways of the State Department in Washington DC. The leadership in Moscow was oblivious to the secret Oslo talks and appeared surprised when the outcome was publicly announced. The result of the secret talks, the Declaration of Principles, was signed between Arafat and Israeli Prime Minister Yitzhak Rabin in September 1993 on the White House lawn, with Bill Clinton basking in the glory of the role of peacemaker. The September 1995 Israeli-Palestinian Interim Agreement was an implementation document of the Oslo-inspired Declaration of Principles of 1993, which among other things established the Palestinian National Authority under Arafat's leadership following a partial withdrawal of Israeli forces from the West Bank and Gaza. The agreement allowed for Palestinian self-rule after legislative elections although there was no Israeli commitment on the creation of a Palestinian state. According to the Interim Agreement final status issues such as the fate of Jerusalem would be resolved at a later date.

In September 1994, one year after the signing of the Oslo Declaration of Principles in Washington DC, Arafat's first meeting with President Yeltsin took place in Moscow to discuss bilateral relations. The Russian leadership welcomed Arafat to give further encouragement to the Israeli-Palestinian peace accord and also to provide endorsement to the Palestinian leader in light of fierce criticisms from radical Palestinian groups Hamas and Islamic Jihad. In turn, Arafat hoped that the meeting would initiate a process of re-engagement with Russia as a long-term counterbalance to the United States and his Arab and Muslim opponents, including Iran. As a seasoned political player, Arafat was correct to invest his efforts early in the Yeltsin presidency because Russian foreign policy began shifting away from the pro-Western tilt in the second half of the 1990s.

Primakov's appointment in 1996 confirmed the process of transition in which Russia once more began seeking to play a significant role in the Middle East independently from the United States. In February 1997 Arafat was invited to Moscow as head of the Palestinian National Authority. Primakov offered Arafat unequivocal support and expressed strong criticism of Hamas and Islamic Jihad, both of which refused to renounce violence, thus also joining the West in condemning Palestinian terrorism. But Moscow was also subtly diverging from the Israeli position under Prime Minister Benjamin Netanyahu who blamed Arafat for terrorist attacks by accusing him of failing to curtail them. Netanyahu's unconcealed agenda was to annul the Oslo agreements and aggressively rebuild settlements in the disputed territories in order to change the demographic landscape before the scheduled final status talks with the Palestinians were held. This was supported by the veteran and highly influential Israeli political figure Ariel Sharon, who served in the Netanyahu government in the 1990s as Minister of National Infrastructure.

Netanyahu and Sharon wanted to humiliate Arafat, who was a figure of hate for many Israeli Jews. Primakov deftly presented Russian foreign policy as moderate by rejecting political violence and fiercely supporting the peace process while the United States, in fear of antagonising Israel, appeared to be a negative element that failed to uphold existing peace agreements by supporting extremist Israeli leaders.

Primakov, this time in his role as prime minister, visited Arafat in Ramallah in October 1998 to openly advocate statehood for the Palestinians but Russia's approach remained 'cautious because it did not want to antagonise either Israel or the United States.'[30] This balanced diplomacy was put to the test on 4 May 1999 when the final status negotiations over the Occupied Territories were scheduled, but deliberate Israeli procrastination in the process prevented discussions. In response, Arafat travelled to Moscow on 5 April 1999 to seek Russian support for a unilateral declaration of Palestinian statehood. Russian Foreign Minister Igor Ivanov however responded coolly and the leadership in Moscow informed the Palestinian leader that the act would be counterproductive. Sharon, as foreign minister, travelled to Moscow one week after Arafat and praised Russia's role in convincing the Palestinian leader to postpone the declaration of independence.

While Primakov's policies in the Middle East were being widely praised in Russia, rivalry between the president and the prime minister intensified. On 12 May Yeltsin felt sufficiently concerned over Primakov's growing influence in the Russian political establishment to remove him from his post as prime minister. Yeltsin's decision was endorsed by Western governments and the Western media had widely labelled Primakov as pro-Palestinian and anti-Western but in reality, while he was a driving force in Russia's active return to the Middle East during the late-1990s he also developed good relations with Israeli political leaders, including more hawkish, right-wing figures such as Netanyahu and Sharon. The Western simplification of the Yeltsin-Primakov rivalry failed to consider that the president of Russia enjoyed essential powers in foreign policy that formed a lynchpin of Russia's various political forces and trends. Primakov's initiatives were therefore carried out in tandem with Yeltsin and both leaders consistently presented Russia as a balanced player in the Palestinian-Israeli dispute. Russian foreign policy during this period was not untypical of Western European states such as France and Germany, both of which were at times even more critical than Moscow of Israeli policies towards the Palestinians.

Putin and the Palestinians

Yeltsin's sudden resignation at the end of 1999 and Putin's promotion from prime minister to acting president signalled another new variation of Russian policy towards the Palestinians. Putin was a part of a new generation of politicians and 'thirty years younger than Primakov, he had not been a high-ranking official in the Soviet state apparatus'.[31] The implication was that Putin did not suffer from the traditional anti-Israeli prejudice and pro-Palestinian sympathy that was common in the old Soviet establishment. Indeed, the Chechen experience and the rise of Islamic terrorism in Russia in the late 1990s were offered as reasons why Putin, the man from European St. Petersburg, was likely to feel less empathy with the Palestinian cause. According to one pro-Israeli analysis, published in 2001, 'Unlike the Russian position under Primakov, Putin's Russia was not only even-handed; he even seemed to tilt toward Israel as the crisis developed.'[32]

This latest crisis among many in Palestinian-Israeli history referred to the failure of efforts by US President Clinton to conciliate differences over final status arrangements between Arafat and Prime Minister Ehud Barak between 11 July and 25 July 2000, resulting in an outbreak of violence that peaked in September that year.

The causes of the Al-Aqsa Intifada, sometimes called the Second Intifada, were hotly disputed. Israelis blamed Arafat for rejecting a generous offer by Barak at the Camp David Summit in July for a viable Palestinian state that included much of the West Bank and all of the Gaza Strip, but the Palestinians responded that there was little compromise displayed by the Israelis on the key issues of Jerusalem, which Israelis insisted would remain as the unified capital of Israel as well as effectively maintaining sovereignty over the religious sites in the city. Barak also remained vague on the right of Palestinian refugees to return and refused to set a mechanism to adequately compensate those who would be prevented from returning to areas under Israeli sovereignty. Adding fuel to the fire was the provocative visit by Ariel Sharon on 28 September 2000 to the Temple Mount, also a holy site for Muslims in which Israeli forces imposed heavy-handed measures to keep Palestinian worshippers away. Sharon was on a campaign to be elected to the post of prime minister but Palestinians considered this event as the spark of the Al-Aqsa Intifada because it symbolised Israeli arrogance in forcefully imposing their sovereignty, both religious and political, over the Palestinians.

The official Israeli view accused Arafat of deliberately manufacturing the violence in light of the stalled negotiations to raise the stakes and gain more favourable terms for the Palestinians. Soon after the failure of the Arafat-Barak talks in Camp David, from which Russia was excluded, Arafat had announced that he would unilaterally declare Palestinian independence on 13 September 2000 and on 11 August he took the pre-emptive measure of travelling to Moscow to gain Russian backing. Once again Russian Foreign Minister Igor Ivanov rebuffed Arafat and advised him to exercise 'extreme caution' to ensure that 'this step should guarantee the achievement of the Palestinian-Israeli [peace] settlement'.[33] This came in the context of Putin's view that only bilateral negotiations can achieve a lasting peace to help formalise Palestinian aspirations.

In 2001 Putin was keen to establish good relations with newly elected US President George Bush and by doing so Russian statements largely agreed with the West in condemning Palestinian violence. The 11 September attacks further unified Moscow and Washington against terrorism and left the Palestinians feeling increasingly isolated. Between 2001 and 2005 there were several large-scale terrorist attacks against Israelis by Hamas and Islamic Jihad, including: 'The death of 11 people in the Jerusalem district of Beit Israel on March 2, 2002; 22 people killed at Tel-Aviv's Central Bus Station on January 5, 2003; and 11 people killed when bus No. 19 was bombed in Jerusalem on January 29, 2004.'[34] Although Israeli military operations against the Palestinians also intensified there was a common perception in Washington and Moscow that terrorism could not be allowed to be seen as a successful method to achieve political aims. The Putin leadership, until late 2002, was particularly keen to assert this point in light of Russia's own war in Chechnya.

In May 2002 Russia was invited to join the Quartet on the Middle East—USA, Russia, EU and UN—to mediate in the Israeli-Palestinian dispute in recognition of its amenably pro-Western anti-terrorist stance. The Quartet was meant to be a fairer honest broker compared to the failed US monopoly on that role and its main achievement was the Road Map for Peace announced on 30 April 2003 and adopted by UNSC Resolution 1515 on 19 November 2003, with Russian and US support. But Israeli Prime Minister Sharon treated the Road Map disdainfully and bypassed the internationally endorsed peace proposal by unilaterally withdrawing from Gaza. Sharon's government also began constructing a security wall along the frontiers of the West Bank in a one-sided designation of Israel's borders.

The reaction by Russia's leadership to Arafat's death on 5 October 2004 was sympathetic, particularly following Israel's military siege of his compound, and Foreign Minister Sergei Lavrov laid a wreath on the long-time Palestinian leader's tomb during his visit to the Occupied Territories on 23 November of that year. By then the mood was already changing in the relationship between Russia and the United States in light of the occupation of Iraq and differences over European defence plans. Following Putin's re-election in March 2004 Russia aligned with European Union support for Palestinian and Arab rejection of the unilateral Israeli plan to build a so-called security wall between Israel and the West Bank. Although Bush was the first US president to openly endorse the creation of a Palestinian state alongside Israel, Washington's passive role towards Israel's deliberate devaluation of the Road Map for Peace intensified anti-American sentiments in the Middle East and to some extent among Europeans. Washington's marketing of the Road Map for Peace in 2003 and subsequent lack of action to implement it in the following years created the widespread impression that the plan was a temporary diversion intended to diffuse criticisms of the war on Iraq.

In April 2005 Putin was 'the first world leader to visit the Palestinian Authority in Ramallah since [Mahmoud] Abbas had taken over as its leader on January 9, 2005'.[35] In a symbolic gesture of support for the Palestinian leadership Putin laid a wreath on Arafat's tomb. Eventually, Washington and other European capitals followed Putin's example in providing political support for Abbas in light of the growing challenge by Hamas. One of the enduring consequences of the US-inspired plan was the demand for Palestinian general elections. Following Arafat's death the PLO's dominant role in national politics became seriously challenged by Hamas, particularly as after decades of promises and negotiations the PLO had delivered the Palestinian diaspora very little in tangible terms.

The impoverished Palestinians of Gaza were radicalised and considered the wealthy political elite around Arafat as being corrupt. On 26 January 2006 Hamas won a large majority of the Palestinian parliament in national elections and this result apparently, despite the floundering reputation of the PLO, 'stunned US and Israeli officials'.[36] Putin added a further element of surprise by immediately congratulating Hamas for their parliamentary success and extended an invitation to their leadership to visit Moscow. In a single political act, Moscow not only snubbed the West, which was seeking to isolate Hamas and its newly formed government, but also Palestinian President Abbas and the PLO, running against the grain of a long history of bilateral relations.

A Hamas delegation visited Moscow in March 2006, and again in March 2007, in defiance of the West, Israel and moderate Arab states such as Egypt and Saudi Arabia. These developments signalled a significant departure from Russia's policy towards the Palestinians and Israel from the 1990s and early Putin era and implied a more aggressive approach in Middle East affairs. A sensationalist headline in the Russian newspaper *Pravda* announced: 'USA cuts funds to Palestine, Russia prepares to deliver arms to Hamas.'[37] Seen in the context of Russian support for Iran and Syria it appeared as if Moscow and Putin were endorsing extremist forces in the Middle East and effectively seeking to alter the existing balance of power in the region.

In late June 2006 Israel launched a major military campaign deep into Gaza following the abduction of Israeli Corporal Gilad Shalit and the killing of two other soldiers in a scenario not dissimilar from the Hezbollah raid a few weeks later on 12 July 2006 that sparked a major war in Lebanon. In both conflicts the outcome damaged Israel's image of impregnability because of the failure to rescue its abducted soldiers and ultimately left Hamas and Hezbollah in a stronger position. Concurrently, Russia had in 2006 acted firmly to protect Iran and Syria, the military and political patrons of Hamas and Hezbollah, from international sanctions. Putin's gamble of supporting Hamas was ruthless but well-timed, while US policy in the Middle East was in disarray in light of international criticisms of its controversial occupation of Iraq and its lack of action against Israel's demolition of regional peace efforts. In light of these developments by the end of 2006 Washington was forced to announce that it would rethink its strategic approach towards the Middle East, with Bush adopting much of the Hamilton-Baker Iraq Study Group Report that called for negotiations with Syria and Iran. By reaching out to extremist forces and the patrons of Hamas, the United States dealt a serious blow to the credibility of Abbas and other moderate forces in the Middle East. This was magnified by Moscow's approaches to Hamas.

With the PLO's Abbas as president of the Palestinian National Authority and Hamas controlling parliament and consolidated with military superiority in Gaza, two Palestinian loci of political authority became a reality for the international community to consider. While the West and Israel continued to reject any engagement of Hamas, terming it a terrorist organisation, Russia had deftly placed itself in a position to mediate in the bitter rivalry between Hamas and the PLO, which escalated into open clashes from 2006. Putin not only manoeuvred to place Russia as a bridge between competing Palestinian factions but also enabled Moscow to act as an available mediator between the United States and the Palestinian political leaderships including its radical factions.

In 2007 Primakov offered a knowledgeable assessment of the Palestinian landscape and Russia's role in it in light of the changes in the regional balance of power during 2006. Primakov recognised that Egypt, Saudi Arabia and Jordan were supportive of Abbas, while Syria and Iran were pro-Hamas. Palestinian and regional deadlock led Primakov to offer three scenarios. The first was the military defeat of Hamas, which Primakov dismissed as an unrealistic option considering that numerous Israeli efforts in the past had not only failed but also tended to make Hamas more popular among Palestinians. A second scenario he described was the calculated preservation of the status quo with the aim that the Israeli and Western embargo on Gaza would turn Palestinians against Hamas. 'Evidently, a "black and white" game is being played—a rich West Bank and a poor Gaza,'[38] in reference to the US-led boycott of Hamas representatives. Primakov's third scenario however was particularly interesting because it proposed 'invigoration of the Palestinian-Israeli peace process, with the Palestinian side represented by the Fatah leadership. Creation of a Palestinian state in the West Bank with the subsequent inclusion of Gaza could be put forward as an "intermediate goal".'[39] In the long run this scenario would lead to the creation of a Palestinian-Jordanian confederation to form a stronger state than a proposed landlocked entity between Jordan and Israel. Most notably, Primakov stated 'that Russia could accept any solution that would suit both sides of this long-running bloody conflict'.[40] Indirectly, this approach also implied a comprehensive Middle East solution that left Hamas to burn in their own flames of isolation. This view reflected Primakov's conservatism that shunned militant religious groups as stable partners in the making of Russian foreign policy that served national interests. Intriguingly, it also suggested that Putin's expedient approach towards Hamas and the wider region diverged from the basis established by Primakov in the 1990s.

Moscow's courting of Hamas between 2006 and 2007 was largely tactical rather than strategic. Russia had little influence over Hamas and no real interest in seeing the group dominate Palestinian politics. Hamas was part of a broader strategy that incorporated Syria, Iran and Hezbollah, in undermining the United States in the Middle East and restoring an important voice for Russia in regional and international affairs. Conversely, Moscow was also keen not to allow a deterioration in its relations with Israel and also with Saudi Arabia, Egypt and Jordan, which were involved in an intense regional struggle to resist Iranian-Syrian hegemony in the region that was vividly mirrored in Lebanon and among the Palestinians. While in Lebanon this conflict took on a sectarian nuance as Shi'a Hezbollah challenged a Sunni-Druze-Christian majority, in the Palestinian Authority it was reflected in the PLO-Hamas schism. These divisions had become particularly pertinent following the Iraq war in 2003 and the transfer of political power in Baghdad to the Shi'a community, indirectly strengthening Iran in the region. Russia's blatant advances towards Hamas in 2006 and in early 2007 risked antagonising much of the Sunni Muslim world as a consequence.

On 26–27 June 2007 Moscow once more readjusted its policy when Foreign Minister Lavrov visited President Abbas to help him consolidate his position in light of his internal feud with Hamas. Soon after, during the visit of Palestinian Authority President Mahmoud Abbas to Moscow on 31 July 2007, Putin referred to him as the 'legitimate leader of all Palestinians'.[41] The statement came in the context of Hamas taking full military control of Gaza a month earlier in June to further undermine the political authority of Abbas. Moscow's manoeuvres were in part linked to efforts by the Kremlin leadership to host a conference on the Middle East. Russian policymakers considered that such an event would add prestige to Russia's role as an international diplomatic arbitrator and reaffirm the country's influence in the Middle East. Nonetheless, despite Lavrov's public announcement during the Annapolis Middle East Conference on 27 November 2007 that stated Russia's desire to host a follow-up gathering in Moscow, the response was cool from the other attendees, except the Palestinian Authority leader Abbas. Hamas and its chief sponsor Iran demanded a boycott of the meeting. Russia expressed hope of a Middle East Conference in Moscow for a few months more but eventually gave up after its calls continued to be rebuffed.

Abbas visited Moscow again on 17 April 2008 to meet with the Russian president in an effort to revive the peace process and ultimately to consolidate the traditional political links between Russia and the official Palestinian government. Abbas offered Moscow the carrot that he would act as chief supporter and promoter in the region to encourage the United States to agree to host a Middle East conference in Russia. This occurred one month after Lavrov's visit to Syria where he met the Hamas leader Khaled Mish'al, upsetting both the Israelis and Abbas. Moscow's justification for the trip was that it was mediating between not only Israel and the Palestinians but also in helping the competing Palestinian factions to resolve their disputes to form a united front.

Abbas visited Moscow once more in December 2008 to meet with the new Russian president, Dmitry Medvedev, as tensions erupted between Israel and the Hamas-ruled Gaza. During the Israel war on Hamas in late 2008 until early 2009, the Russian media was not particularly sympathetic to Hamas. More significantly, Medvedev offered no diplomatic initiatives, allowing Egypt to take the lead in the ceasefire negotiations with Israel which required bringing the Palestinian factions closer together to ensure a viable and lasting agreement. Moscow's deliberate inaction during the crisis was a reflection of its lack of real diplomatic influence over Hamas.

Prime Minister Putin met Abbas on 7 April 2009 in Moscow to reassure him that Russia did not consider Hamas as the legal representative of the Palestinian people. At the same time Hamas's links with Iran and Syria meant that Moscow could not ignore the militant group's regional impact. The dichotomy was ended with the Arab uprisings, particularly in Egypt and Syria. Hamas refused to support the Syrian regime and vacated its headquarters in Damascus soon after the protests began in 2011. The new Egyptian president, elected in 2012 with strong Muslim Brotherhood backing, took a firm stance against the Asad regime and was cautiously suspicious of its ally Iran. Hamas's main leaders followed and condemned the Syrian regime's use of cruel and sometimes indiscriminate violence against civilians. Hamas had never formed the core of the Iran-Syria-Hezbollah axis although Damascus and Tehran highly appreciated the symbolic value of its endorsement because of the sentimental support in the Arab and Sunni street for the Palestinian cause. Hamas's shift towards the Sunni mainstream, which also helped its reconciliation with Abbas, undermined Russia's efforts to gain Palestinian sympathy and more notably placed Moscow on the side of the Shi'i-Alawi alliance in the Middle East, which was considered a menace by the majority Sunnis.

The Israeli elections in January 2013 merely confirmed the feeling that the opportunity for Israeli-Palestinian peace was more distant than at any time in the history of the conflict. The Israeli parliament, the Knesset, contained more right-wing, anti-Palestinian MPs than ever. Meanwhile the Arab world was undergoing internal turmoil and this further weakened the Palestinian leadership's bartering position. Russia's disdain for the popular demands among the Arab public for political freedoms was perceived negatively among Palestinians and the wider Arab world. Moscow's self-promotion as the defender of the underdog, dating back to Soviet times, was perceived as being hypocritical. The ambiguity in Russia's behaviour left many doubts about Putin's true intentions. While Moscow's foreign policy leadership consistently maintained that its actions were always motivated by the desire to become a viable mediator between Israel and the Palestinians, critics countered that Russia had persistently yet tacitly fuelled divisiveness and extremism to further its own wider selfish interests, often without real concern about the impact of such policies on the people most affected by the Israeli-Palestinian conflict. Russian technological expertise allowed the Iranians to develop their nuclear programmes; Russian arms continued to flow in support of Asad's Syria; and all the while Russia cultivated and expanded its trade and economic relations with Israel. Support for the Palestinians was in reality little more than a useful device in a global game of influence to enhance Russia's, and specifically Putin's, prestige.

9

SAUDI ARABIA AND JORDAN

ROYAL OPPORTUNITIES

Foreign policy under Putin was driven by economic interests as well as geo-strategic considerations. A cornerstone of New Thinking under Gorbachev was that the one-sidedness of Soviet foreign policy in the Middle East in its support for radical anti-Western regimes and groups narrowed Moscow's opportunities. The ideological framework of Soviet foreign policy also limited prospects of expanding international trade relations that would have benefited the domestic economy. With the aim of eradicating these perceived flaws New Thinking paved the way for diplomatic and economic relations that had been virtually frozen during the Cold War. This approach continued in post-Soviet Russia and was most manifestly visible in the development of relations with two traditionally Western-oriented countries in the Middle East: Jordan and Saudi Arabia.

Saudi Arabia, as the world's most significant oil producer, offered obvious economic attractions. Further still, Saudi Arabia's status as the spiritual homeland for the world's Muslim population, including Muslims living within Russia and in the bordering post-Soviet space, added to its international weight. In the energy-rich Gulf region Saudi Arabia was the main counterbalance to Iran. Though smaller in terms of size and economy, Jordan hosted important Caucasian, including Chechen, communities, and its Hashemite monarchy enjoyed an unrivalled heritage in the Middle East. Moscow also recognised Jordan's role as a key outpost of US and British security interests in the Middle East and as an experienced interlocutor in the Israeli-Palestinian dispute.

Yeltsin and Putin displayed a strong will to improve relations with the two monarchies and the interest was mutual, with one Jordanian diplomat commenting in 2007 that: 'Moscow still has many strings to pull and Putin is determined to do just that in the absence of some more conciliatory moves from the US with regard to Russia's own strategic security concerns,' adding that, 'without Russia, Washington may not succeed in bringing its policies in the Middle East to fruition'.[1] The remark highlighted a reciprocal desire by the leaderships in Amman and Riyadh to engage a better respected Russia, which had become more assertive in the region by the time of Putin's second term. Moscow's interventions in defence of Iran and Syria validated the perception that Russia had become once more a world power with regional influence that could not be ignored. Putin was determined to take these relations to new levels of co-operation but such efforts were hindered by the evolving political and religious regional complexities that were made more problematic by Russia's growing presence in the Middle East.

Russia and Jordan in the 1990s

King Hussein of Jordan, an important US ally in the region, was universally recognised as an astute and pragmatic political operator. The king's attributes were not missed by successive political leaderships in Moscow and even at the height of the Cold War diplomatic channels between the two countries were active. In June 1976 Russia provided Jordan, which hoped to reduce its dependence on the United States, with a SAM air defence system that was then the first major military transaction between the two states. From the Soviet viewpoint, Jordan was a valuable conduit in the Israeli-Palestinian peace process and King Hussein was a rare Arab voice that was listened to in the West, as well as in Israel. For Jordan, relations with the Soviet Union from the 1970s gained greater urgency for the purpose of restraining Syria, which was its principal foe in the region. With the deterioration of US-Soviet relations in the early 1980s, King Hussein made two visits to Moscow in 1981 and 1982 to complete military deals including the purchase of SAM-8 missiles in response to Washington's refusal to sell similar weapons to Jordan. Differences between Amman and Washington also arose in 1990 due to Jordan's lack of support for US military action to eject the Iraqi military from Kuwait. King Hussein argued for a diplomatic solution, rather than military action, to resolve the crisis to avoid undesired repercussions. In part, this reflected Amman's concern over the large Palestinian population in Jordan which largely sympathised with Saddam Hussein.

There was a general concurrence of views between Russia and Jordan on the key issues affecting the Middle East. Both were strongly supportive of the Israeli-Palestinian peace process, opposing violence from both sides as a means to achieve a breakthrough and the two countries agreed that the conflict was the root of the region's problems. Jordan had a strong interest in the resolution of the Palestinian problem because the radicalisation of the Palestinians and intransigence by the Israelis ultimately threatened the future of the monarchy. Moscow considered relations with Jordan, a moderate Arab state that served as an intermediary between the Palestinians and the Israelis, to be a useful component for its own aspirations to act as a regional peacemaker. This convergence of views implicitly suggested that Jordan and Russia agreed that the limp US willingness to press Israel to compromise undermined regional stability.

In the 1990s both Jordan and Russia had shared interests in preventing the downfall of the Saddam Hussein regime in Iraq. The Jordanian leadership feared that turmoil in Iraq would result in Iranian and Syrian hegemony in the region in addition to warnings by officials in Amman that an Iraqi civil war would destabilise the security of neighbouring countries. With a hostile Syria to its north, a fragmenting Iraq to its east and the Israeli-Palestinian conflict on its western border, Jordan was in a particularly fragile location and viewed the adventurism of Washington's policies as needlessly undermining national security. Despite this outlook the shrewd King Hussein remained essentially pro-Western throughout the 1990s but he never closed the door in the face of an active Russian role in the region in order to preserve an effective counterbalance to the United States. These examples highlighted the relative independence Jordan enjoyed and allowed the post-Soviet leaderships in Moscow to inherit a sound framework for improved relations.

The pro-Western outlook by Yeltsin and Kozyrev promoted optimism and enthusiasm for developing relations with moderate states such as Jordan to reflect and symbolise the distancing of the new Russia from the

Soviet era. In October 1992 the Russian Federation and Jordan successfully resolved the debt owed to the Soviet Union following a high-level delegation visit to Amman led by Foreign Economic Relations Minister Petr Aven. In contrast to protracted debt negotiations between Russia and Syria, Russian media noted the 'exceptionally friendly tone of the talks, in which Jordan's King Hussein also took part'.[2]

Bilateral relations faced their first major challenge by the outbreak of war in Chechnya in 1994. The Chechen community in Jordan was staunchly loyal to the Hashemite monarch and Moscow was unhappy with Amman's apparent sympathy with the Chechen cause. Recognising the need not to allow the issue to undermine the mutual interests of both countries, King Hussein encouraged his government and media to practice a 'strict ban on pro-Dudaev [then Chechen President Djokar Dudaev] propaganda in Jordan'.[3] By 1996 Moscow became more comfortable with Amman's stance regarding Chechnya and this allowed Foreign Minister Primakov to actively pursue his goal of strengthening ties with all major Arab countries and build a balanced Russian foreign policy in the region. In this setting Jordan's role was considered as being essential considering its central location and Primakov expressed particularly complimentary personal praise for King Hussein in recognition of his unique influence on regional affairs.

Making good use of longstanding political connections and detecting the growing Arab differences with Washington, 'Primakov was in a position to easily outbid the US for the Arab side's favour. During a November 1996 tour to the region, Primakov served as a middleman between Jerusalem and Damascus while simultaneously strengthening ties with both Palestinian leader Yasser Arafat and Jordan's late King Hussein.'[4] In October 1997 Primakov proposed, following one of many meetings with King Hussein, systemising coordination with Jordan to revive the stalled peace process in the region and asserted that there was agreement between them on the need for 'synchronised efforts in all directions—Palestinian, Syrian, and Lebanese'.[5] For much of the late 1990s Primakov and King Hussein were in agreement that Washington's inflexible position towards Iraq was counterproductive. Regular military strikes on Iraq and the tough sanctions regime created a deteriorating humanitarian crisis and further radicalised Jordanian and Palestinian public opinion and undermined King Hussein's policy of maintaining friendly relations with the United States.

Over time Jordan's ageing ruler endured growing frustration at Washington's neglect of his warnings and advice with regards to the Israeli-Palestinian dispute and Iraq. The experienced monarch feared that at best the United States was insensitive and lacking finesse to understand the Middle East and at worst that Washington pursued a hidden agenda that sought to purposefully destabilise the region. Towards the end of his reign King Hussein sent a personal message via Crown Prince Hassan to Primakov upon his appointment as prime minister in September 1998 that indicated a tone of genuine respect and a desire for a more active Russian role: 'His Majesty King Hussein has asked me to convey to his dear friend and brother his warmest congratulations on the confidence the Russian people have placed on you as prime minister.'[6] King Hussein's death on 7 February 1999 witnessed an equally impassioned tribute by Primakov and the Russian establishment in a mark of respect and acknowledgement of a decades-long relationship that was based on mutual understanding of regional and bilateral challenges.

Putin and Jordan

After 1999 bilateral relations between Jordan and Russia were highly influenced and regularly tested by the Israeli-Palestinian dispute and the rise of Hamas, the war in Iraq, Russia's second war in Chechnya and the growing ambitions of Iran. King Abdullah was King Hussein's successor to the throne in 1999 and he efficiently and rapidly asserted his style and leadership on Jordanian politics and the region. While remaining Western-orientated, King Abdullah proved remarkably consistent in pursuing his father's policies, which included maintaining pragmatic and productive relations with Moscow. Jordan's new King was particularly keen on promoting Russian investment in his country and more generally on upgrading bilateral economic ties. Putin and King Abdullah in their first years in leadership shared similar characteristics in terms of youthful dynamism, pragmatism and an outspoken urgency for reforms to modernise their countries without relinquishing a steely, almost visceral, resolve to rely on security forces to impose law and order to protect their political authority and national stability.

King Abdullah's first official meeting with President Putin took place in Moscow on 28 August 2001 during the build-up to the Second Palestinian Intifada in late 2000. The two leaders, through official statements, expressed agreement on a variety of regional issues including the Palestinian-Israeli conflict. Putin praised the Jordanian monarch for his 'consistency and far-sightedness'.[7] Amman and Moscow both endorsed the US-proposed Mitchell Plan, including its urging of Arafat to crack down on Palestinian militants as a precursor for the re-initialisation of the peace process. The two leaders emphasised the need to resolve the deadlock in Iraq by downgrading the stiff sanctions to ease the humanitarian hardships faced by many in the country. After meeting Putin the Jordanian King asserted his hope that the visit would 'provide the necessary means to cement bilateral ties and to promote various joint projects, especially in trade and investment'.[8] By the time Putin made his historic trip to Amman in February 2007, the first by a Russian leader to Jordan, King Abdullah had visited Moscow and met the Russian president seven times.

Less than three months after his first visit to meet with Putin, King Abdullah travelled to Moscow again on 22 November 2001 for more discussions with the Russian president on the Palestinian-Israeli conflict but this time the meeting took place in the context of the Al-Qaeda attacks on the United States in September and the subsequent launching of the US-led war on Afghanistan to oust the Taliban. There was strong support from both leaders for the US war on terror and Russia's leadership was particularly pleased with Jordan's official policy of criticising radical Islamist insurgents in Chechnya and associating them with Al-Qaeda. Amman, like Russia and the United States, had its reasons to be deeply concerned about growing Islamic extremism and the danger it posed to the security of Jordan. Al-Qaeda, Hamas and Hezbollah all viewed Jordan and its ruling monarchy as being treacherous for signing a peace agreement with Israel in 1994.

Primakov, serving as President Putin's special envoy, was dispatched on several occasions to Jordan between May and June 2001 to help initiate a Palestinian-Israeli peace dialogue based on the Mitchell Plan, which demanded a halt to the construction of Israeli settlements in Occupied Territories as well as an end to violence from both sides. The trend to extremism from the Israeli and Palestinian sides led to escalating violence that threatened to involve other countries in the region and the internal stability of neighbours such as Jordan. There was therefore a mutual Russian-Jordanian interest in promoting a more vigorous approach to ease Palestinian-Israeli violence and speed up peace negotiations towards a final settlement. Washington's continued lethargy in terms of applying pressure on its ally Israel raised Moscow's value for Jordan, and virtually all other Arab states, as an alternative power in the region when it came to reaching a fair and balanced peace between the Palestinians and Israelis. There were other differences with the United States too, most striking of them all being the war and invasion of Iraq in 2003, which Jordan and Russia considered as reckless adventurism. But during Putin's first term Russia and Jordan were fully supportive of Washington's war against Al-Qaeda-affiliated terrorist groups around the world.

In a significant coincidence, while King Abdullah was on a visit to Russia in early September 2004 a group of Muslim and Arab terrorists took control of a school in Beslan in North Ossetia and held over 1,100 hostages. The hostage-takers demanded a Russian troop withdrawal from Chechnya following Putin's launch of a second major military campaign to pacify the breakaway republic. The ensuing effort by Russian forces to free the hostages led to 330 deaths, including 156 school children. The Beslan tragedy that began on 1 September 2004 and described by Putin as a 'total, cruel, full-scale war' on Russia by 'international terrorism',[9] left a deep imprint on Russian public opinion. The visit by the Jordanian monarch at that time could have been embarrassing, considering that ties between Chechens in Jordan and the insurgents in the northern Caucasus were widely documented. King Abdullah's reaction to the Beslan tragedy was managed with great skill and Amman took sides with Moscow in light of the Islamisation of the Chechen conflict and tied this to its own struggle with Islamic extremists.

Hundreds of Jordanians had joined the Mujaheddin in the 1980s to fight the Soviet occupation in Afghanistan and many of them continued their struggle elsewhere after the Soviet withdrawal in 1989. During the 1990s, some of the most radical and influential insurgents in the Caucasus were ethnic Chechen Jordanians, including Shaikh Fathi, who led an Islamic combat unit known as Jama'at that rivalled the secular Chechen resistance forces and was 'based on a detachment of militant veterans of wars in the Middle East, Afghanistan and Tajikistan'.[10] Shaikh Fathi was succeeded following his death in 1997 by 'Abdurrakham, another ethnic Chechen from Jordan and the religious leader of all of Chechnya's Jama'ats'.[11] The Muslim insurgents had tried since the late 1990s to expand the war throughout the northern Caucasus, mainly into Dagestan, often leading them to clash with local Chechens who wished to keep the character of the war as a national struggle for independence from Russian domination.

Jordanian support for the Chechens was largely humanitarian and was provided by individuals or groups through unofficial channels to their ethnic counterparts in the Russian Federation but there was little else and official support was deliberately stifled. A year and three months after the Beslan incident, on 9 November 2005, Al-Qaeda claimed responsibility for the bombing of three major hotels in Amman that become known as Jordan's 9/11. The attack sought to destabilise Jordanian security and to discredit King Abdullah, whose authoritarian rule was accepted by his people largely on the basis that he offered them relative stability and security in a region swamped by conflict. Putin reacted quickly to express support for the Jordanian monarch and strongly condemned the terrorist attack, reaffirming that the two countries were united confronting the same threat of radical Islamist militants.

Jordan's regional policies consistently and historically called for moderation and opposed militant solutions. In light of this, during Putin's second term the main challenge to Jordanian-Russian relations arose from Moscow's increasingly hostile stance towards the West and its menacing support for Iran and Syria and their allies Hezbollah and Hamas. After the US invasion of Iraq and the downfall of the Sunni Saddam Hussein regime King Abdullah in 2005 was the first high-profile political figure to warn of an Iranian-inspired Shi'a crescent being formed in the Middle East. This referred to Iran's growing influence spanning across Iraq, where Shi'is had emerged as the dominant political force, to Syria ruled by an Alawite Shi'a splinter sect and reaching Lebanon where Shi'a Hezbollah was the most dominant political force. Moreover, although a predominantly Sunni Palestinian group Hamas was rapidly falling under the Syrian-Iranian orbit. Hamas openly challenged the secular Fatah movement for dominance and Amman's political leadership recognised that the emerging political confrontation would have negative consequences for Jordan because of its government's close cooperation and endorsement of the secular Palestinian leadership led by Mahmoud Abbas. The murder of the influential Lebanese Sunni leader Hariri on 14 February 2005 only added to the sense that the Shi'is led by Iran were in the ascendancy in the region.

The US war on Iraq in 2003 undermined Jordan's extremely vulnerable position by strengthening the Syrian-Iranian axis, particularly as the leadership in Amman refrained from publicly criticising the US occupation of Iraq in order not to antagonise the Bush administration. As the insurgency in Iraq became more violent Jordan's King Abdullah struggled to defuse local anti-US sentiments while maintaining his country's strategic relationship with Washington. However, instead of taking Jordan closer to Russia the political leadership in Amman, including King Abdullah, was dismayed and concerned by Putin's strong support during 2005 and 2006 for Iran and Syria, as well as Hamas and Hezbollah. Moscow was seen to be directly contributing to the escalation of regional tensions by taking sides, which was a noticeable shift in approach from its policies during the 1990s and early Putin era when Russia actively presented itself as a mediator. There was additional frustration felt by the Jordanians at the failure to increase the volume of bilateral trade between the two countries despite Amman's openly expressed desire for Russian investments in the Kingdom. Putin and King Abdullah met on 18 August 2005 in the Black Sea resort of Sochi, primarily to upgrade trade relations but also to discuss the latest developments in the Middle East with the situation in Iraq topping the agenda. The reality for Jordan was that polarisation undermined a decades-long policy of promoting stabilisation because it was considered as safeguarding national security.

As regional violence intensified Moscow called for an international conference on the Middle East that was a diplomatic retort to US unilateralism in the handling of the Iraqi file, particularly from 2003. The Russian proposal hoped to include Iran and Syria in the process yet the two countries were considered by the West as actively fuelling violence in Iraq by allowing insurgents and weapons through their borders. Iran and Syria faced broad criticisms and US pressure over a range of other issues at the time. Syria in particular was under intense pressure in light of the murder of Hariri and despite its military withdrawal from Lebanon in April 2005 Damascus continued to negatively interfere in Lebanese internal affairs and was the prime suspect in a spate of assassinations and bombings targeting the Cedar Revolution supporters. The significance of the timing of the Russian proposal for a Middle East conference therefore was because it came at a period of heightened suspicion in Moscow that the Bush administration was planning a military attack to destroy the Iran-Syria axis.

Russia's proposal to invite Iran and Syria to attend an international conference was perceived by their regional competitors as a capitulation to the terrorists in Iraq and their backers, and strengthened the impression that Moscow was prodding Washington to bargain with them. King Abdullah was perturbed by Putin's actions but he nonetheless adopted cautious diplomacy to ensure that Russia's position remained approachable and balanced. During his visit to Moscow and Sochi in 2005 King Abdullah declared emphatically that 'we need Russia, we need its leadership in the Middle East. And again this is an opportunity for me to see the president [Putin] and to bring our countries closer together.'[12] Yet despite this Moscow's posture in the Middle East in 2006 became more defiant and belligerent towards the United States. Russia's invitation to Hamas leaders for a meeting with Putin in 2006 following Palestinian parliamentary elections was a stunning break from the traditional line adopted by Moscow of endorsing the PLO and Fatah president Mahmoud Abbas, who was strongly supported in Amman and in Western capitals. By refusing to cooperate with the international boycott of Hamas, which had not renounced violence and refused to recognise Israel, Russia appeared to deliberately widen the schism in the Middle East by supporting the rejectionist Iranian-Syrian axis and their proxies.

Putin's audacity in 2006 was an important factor in strengthening the resolve of Iran and Syria in the face of US pressure and arguably played a significant part in allowing Hezbollah in Lebanon the confidence to launch the raid on Israeli soldiers in July that set off the war during that summer.A regional cold war threatened to explode that year as tensions worsened between Saudi Arabia, and its ally Egypt, and Syria and Iran. In this climate Jordan cleverly portrayed itself as an intermediary out of fear that its internal security would be shaken by neighbouring Syria and Shi'a-dominated Iraq. In light of the apparent loss of US morale and confidence after 2005 Amman sought to prevent Russia from decisively tipping the balance in the region towards Damascus and Tehran by encouraging Moscow to play a moderate role.

Putin's unprecedented visit to Jordan and Saudi Arabia in early 2007, the first ever by a Russian or Soviet leader, was part of a readjustment of Russia's behaviour in the region. Part of the purpose of the tour was to reassure countries that feared the rise of Iran that Russia remained a neutral player that was interested in developing political, military and economic relations throughout the Middle East. Putin arrived in Jordan on 9 February 2007 and met King Abdullah to emphasise areas where the two countries shared similar regional objectives, including a two-state solution to the Palestinian-Israeli conflict and the eradication of extremism. A joint statement pointed to the importance and 'readiness to use the potential of Russian-Jordanian bilateral relations to promote collective international efforts' in resolving regional 'problems on a firm international legal basis'.[13] The latter reassured Jordan by indicating that Russia rejected hostile or expansionist actions by Iran, Syria or its proxies that threatened existing states. As an indication of the increasingly co-operative political relations between the two countries, the Moscow-backed president of Chechnya, Ramzan Kadyrov, visited Jordan in August 2007, turning the page on Russian concerns over Jordanian support for Chechen separatists.

Putin's visit in the region though was primarily geared towards promoting Russian foreign economic policy and this converged with Jordan's wider aims of attracting investment and economic development. Before the visit, the Jordanian ambassador to Russia, Abdullah Kurdi, said that: 'Jordan, with its limited economic possibilities can be attractive for Russian investors due to its geographical location, favourable investment climate and general stability, as well as its developed financial infrastructure, skilled personnel and high educational level, including thousands of graduates from Soviet and Russian universities who fluently speak Russian.'[14] The aspirations though were never fulfilled despite the optimistic official pronouncements by both parties. Many of the bilateral agreements were small scale, such as a joint venture for selling and servicing Kamaz trucks operating in Jordan from 1997 and the building of power grids. Primakov, as Chairman of the Russian Chamber of Commerce and Industry, visited Jordan in February 2004 to initiate the establishment of a Russian-Jordanian Business Council but bilateral trade had barely exceeded $100 million each year.

On his visit to Russia in August 2005 King Abdullah attended the Moscow International Air Show to purchase 'two IL-76MF Russian military transport planes, in a deal reportedly worth more than US$100m'.[15] Other deals included Russian investment in Jordan's tourism industry, including the construction of hotels on the Dead Sea and in supplying rolled steel and chemical products to the Kingdom. An agreement in 2006 was signed to assemble KA-226 helicopters in Jordan as well as flight training by Russian pilots. During Putin's visit in 2007 a contract was signed for the construction of a plant in Jordan to assemble

Lada automobiles, but such highlights were rare and in relation to other countries in the region the Hashemite Kingdom had much less to offer Russia in economic terms than Turkey, Israel, Iran or Saudi Arabia.

Jordanian pragmatism nonetheless prevailed and political relations continued to be exceptionally stable, despite Russia's more imposing approach from 2005. A Jordanian diplomat noted that despite the dangerous support for Tehran and Damascus provided by Moscow, which included the supply of advanced weapons, there was confidence that Putin ultimately had a strategic interest in preserving a balance of forces in the region as part of a wider strategy of limiting US global power. 'Thus Iran and Syria are only pawns in a much bigger game and are used to challenge US hegemony in the Middle East in order to ensure Russian hegemony in its own neighborhood,'[16] or so it was hoped.

During Putin's visit to Jordan on 27 June 2012, very soon after the start of his third presidential term, regional instability was once more prevalent due to the Arab uprisings. The Jordanian monarch faced dangers to his leadership not only from regional turmoil but also from his own internal opposition, whose bulk was the same Muslim Brotherhood ideology that had succeeded in gaining power in Egypt and Tunisia. Moscow's overall position from 2011 was highly sceptical of the Arab Spring and the official Russian media mocked Western optimism that the popular uprisings were democratising the Middle East by highlighting the examples of Egypt and Tunisia, where the Muslim Brotherhood governments faced violent counter-revolutions in the early months of 2013. Jordan was therefore generally content in the knowledge that Russia was antagonistic towards the Muslim Brotherhood and its regional ascendancy and was comforted by Moscow's nervousness about radical change in the region although ironically Amman was supportive of the Syrian revolution. Amman and Russia's leadership shared a paramount interest in maintaining an overall strategic balance in the region and a loathing for the Muslim Brotherhood, which was resentful of Russian support for Iran and the Syria regime. In turn Russia highly valued Jordan's role as a diplomatic base from which it could promote its role as an intermediary in regional disputes and for its pragmatic approach that contained the rise of the Muslim Brotherhood. Thus over many years of political and geo-strategic trials and challenges relations between Putin and King Abdullah were kept cordial and functional due to the intensely pragmatic core in the character and nature of both leaders.

Saudi Arabia until Putin

After years of bitter rivalry between the communist state and the Wahhabi Kingdom, Gorbachev's New Thinking in foreign policy and the Red Army withdrawal from Afghanistan combined to create momentum for the establishment of diplomatic relations between the Soviet Union and Saudi Arabia in September 1990. A month earlier Iraq's invasion of Kuwait sped up the process because Saudi Arabia was keen to guarantee Soviet support to counter the threat posed by Saddam Hussein's regime. The establishment of relations was a significant event considering that for decades the two countries were ideologically speaking poles apart. The puritanical Wahhabi society prevented successive kings, including dominant personalities such as King Faisal, from establishing relations with an atheist country. Mutual hostility was compounded by Soviet support for radical Arab governments, including the Egyptian Nasserite regime, that were secular in nature and challenged the Saudi royal family for regional influence.

In early 1979 a window of opportunity was opened for improved bilateral relations when the Shah in Iran was toppled by a popular revolt during a period when Western media were waging a negative campaign against Saudi Arabia's conservative society. Many among the Saudi elite formed suspicions that whenever there were Western and particularly US demands to purchase expensive weapons or when a dispute over oil prices arose the media coincidentally highlighted the backwardness of Saudi society, while arguably more tyrannical regimes in the region were conveniently forgotten. Riyadh was particularly frustrated at US refusal to sell the Kingdom advanced fighter jets and at Washington's failure to stifle the Iranian Islamic Revolution. The negative view of Washington among Saudis in the late-1970s led Primakov, then Director of the USSR Institute of Oriental Studies, to feel that there were 'no insurmountable obstacles to the development of normal Saudi-Soviet relations'.[17] Hopes were quickly dashed however with the Soviet invasion of Afghanistan at the end of 1979, which brought the Red Army closer to the warm waters of the Gulf.

In response to the invasion the Saudi Kingdom was the first country to announce a boycott of the 1980 Olympic Games in Moscow, later followed by the United States and other countries. For the rest of the decade Saudi Arabia became the leading Muslim country that supported the insurgency in Afghanistan by providing financial support, fighters and ideological training that was so extensive that Riyadh could justifiably claim chief responsibility for the Soviet retreat in 1989. Among Gorbachev's priorities after 1985 was the mending of badly damaged relations with Saudi Arabia caused by the Afghan war in recognition of its influential role in the Middle East and the wider Muslim world.

Gorbachev's efforts laid the groundwork for Yeltsin to expand relations with the kingdom, which was viewed by the new democratic Russian leadership as an attractive source to attract foreign investments during a phase of economic crisis. During a tour of the Arab Gulf states in search of new markets in May 1992, Foreign Minister Kozyrev regretted the negative consequences of traditional Soviet ties with Iran, Iraq and Libya and suggested that the new Russia would rather 'deal with stable, moderate regimes, and these are the ones with which we are trying to develop military cooperation'.[18] Saudi banks extended loans of $250 million to aid the Russian economy but overall there was little progress made in developing bilateral economic relations under Yeltsin. Riyadh remained concerned, despite Kozyrev's statement, about Russia's military support to its principal Gulf rival Iran. In the late 1990s the Saudi government was also frustrated by Russia's efforts to attempt to assist Saddam Hussein back into the international fold despite him harbouring deep animosity and a vengeful attitude towards the Kingdom. Further strains in bilateral relations were caused by a deeply held view that was reflected in the Saudi media and among the powerful religious community that Russia pursued an anti-Islamic agenda, pointing to the war in Chechnya and Moscow's support for Serb-led massacres and ethnic cleansing of Bosnian Muslims in the Balkans as evidence.

Putin and Saudi Arabia

One of the defining features of Putinism was the strong emphasis on Russian nationalism with specifically Slavic and Orthodox Christian characteristics. Over the course of time, the Putin era projected a resemblance to nineteenth century Tsarist Russia and its motto of Autocracy, Orthodoxy, Nationalism. Putin's first presidential election success was often associated with a reaction against Islamic terrorism that threatened not only the Caucasus but also Moscow and other Russian cities. Russian officials avoided characterising the war in Chechnya as a national struggle and instead blamed it on Islamic extremism. Very few Russians questioned the imperialist past in terms of the subjugation of non-Russian and non-Orthodox peoples, taking for granted their inclusion into the Russian Federation. Such widespread views required the creation of an enemy that was alien to the traditional values in Russia and with a moral code that was universally rejected.

Typically the term Wahhabism became synonymous in Russia with the Sunni militant Islam associated with the Taliban and other Muslim militants that emerged from Afghanistan in the 1990s, in the same way the West used the term Al-Qaeda to describe worldwide Sunni Islamic terror networks. In political terms the anti-Wahhabism conveniently enabled a distinction to be made by Russia's policy makers between the Shi'a militant Islam backed by Iran and radical Sunni Muslim groups. Yet widespread strong anti-Islamic sentiments emerged in Russia in the 1990s as a precursor to Putin's rise and these became prevalent in the media as well as among the ruling political and Christian religious class. One Orthodox Church viewpoint reflected that 'a Muslim society has a value foundation that is completely different from a Christian society, which is based on the Christian teaching of human dignity'.[19] The rector of St Petersburg Theological Academy and College, Bishop Konstantin, went further by describing Islam as 'a religion of aggression and war' and an expression of 'eastern brutality'.[20]

Because the Wahhabi branch of Islam was historically associated with Saudi Arabia difficult hurdles for Russian-Saudi relations prevented significant progress in bilateral relations, which on the whole remained tense until 2003, the year of Crown Prince Abdullah's visit to Moscow in September. Chechnya was a lingering sore point, with persistent Russian claims that 'Saudi foundations … were providing Chechen rebels with the funding that allowed them to continue their resistance.'[21] Senior Russian officials, including Putin, also had persisted in reminding audiences that the majority of the hijackers during the 11 September 2001 attacks in the United States were Saudi nationals. In turn, Riyadh felt that Moscow's handling of the Chechen issue was severe and uncompromising and compelled it to maintain a cool posture towards it.

In 2003 regional developments led to a sharp turnaround in Saudi-Russian relations and consequently Putin took great care to balance his colourful anti-terrorism language by presenting Russia as a friend of the Islamic world. The basis of this transformation was the US invasion of Iraq, which was opposed by Moscow and Riyadh. Although Saudi ruler

King Fahd lived until August 2005, Crown Prince Abdullah was effectively in charge in 2003 and thereafter due to the ailing health of the monarch. When separate terrorist attacks by extremists struck Russia and Saudi Arabia in May 2003, 'Putin portrayed Moscow and Riyadh as victims of a common enemy.'[22] In November 2003, only a few months after Crown Prince Abdullah's visit to Moscow, another major terrorist attack struck the Saudi capital Riyadh, causing twenty-two deaths and well over a hundred injuries.

In October 2003 Putin attended the Organization of Islamic Countries Summit despite strong popular anti-Muslim sentiments in Russia in light of terrorism associated with the Caucasus. Russia's high-level participation was motivated by shared concerns over the US invasion of Iraq. Significantly from the Saudi standpoint, Abdullah, as Crown Prince and later as King, increasingly lent a sympathetic ear to advisers who warned that Washington was tacitly endorsing a Shi'a revival in the region to keep the Muslim world fragmented and the Kingdom and its oil reserves under the heel of the United States. The Saudi political establishment was particularly sensitive to the emergence in the United States of mainstream journalists such as Seymour Hersh and a number of academics associated with political think-tanks who were driven by a suspiciously anti-Saudi agenda. This lobby sought to present the Iranian-backed Shi'a and their Syrian partners as a benign alliance, or implicitly as victims of a widespread extremist Sunni sea in the Middle East. These authors claimed that the Saudi royal family was directly accused of sponsoring a range of extremists groups, including Al-Qaeda.[23]

In this atmosphere political relations with Russia were viewed by Saudi policy makers as a matter of survival in the face of a pervasive campaign in the West encouraging dialogue with Iran and Syria, while exaggerating the Saudi influence on Al-Qaeda-associated groups. The influence of pro-Iran and pro-Syria lobbyists in the United States laid the groundwork for President Obama's policy towards the Middle East during his first term.

Crown Prince Abdullah's visit to Russia from 2–4 September 2003 took place in the context of Saudi opposition to the occupation of Iraq because of fears that by removing Sunni Saddam Hussein the Shi'is would take political control of the country. Although Saddam Hussein was not trusted by the Saudis and relations with Iraq had been characterised by hostility since the late 1980s, Riyadh tolerated the Iraqi leader because he was seen as a shield against Iranian and Shi'a expansion. The downfall of Saddam Hussein eventually opened the floodgates of Iranian influence into the Arab world, notably in partnership with Syria to dominate Lebanon and the Palestinian Hamas movement. Iran and Syria also held the key to stability in Iraq in the post-Saddam era. Due to Riyadh's displeasure, it was not until the summer of 2007 that Saudi Arabia re-opened its embassy in Baghdad, reflecting its concerns about Iranian influence in the country. The Saudi leadership's anxiety over Iranian influence and the US occupation of Iraq forced a greater urgency in improving relations with Russia.

Yet Russian military support for Iran was a menace to Saudi Arabia's national security and a nuclear-armed Iran was potentially the single most dangerous challenge to the Kingdom. Tehran insisted that its nuclear programme was a peaceful one. However, the Iranians emerged as a major power in the Gulf region primarily because of Russia's development of its nuclear facilities, sales of advanced weapons and political support on the international stage. With the growing influence of hardliners within the regime, the Iranian military was able to boast its own production of long range missiles capable of carrying nuclear warheads as well as Russian-designed submarines which threatened civilian and commercial shipping through the strategic Strait of Hormuz between the Arabian Peninsula and Iran. Saudi Arabia had a sizeable Shi'a population of its own living mainly in the oil-rich north-eastern region and who, with agitation directed by Iran, threatened the unity of the Kingdom. Furthermore, Iranian threats to destroy Arab oil supplies if attacked by the United States led the government in Riyadh to recognise the need for Russian understanding and cooperation in limiting Iran's regional influence.[24]

The Iranians benefitted directly from Russian support and indirectly because of US policies in the region, which allowed Tehran to dangle the carrot of dialogue not only over the nuclear issue but also to offer itself as being on the same front as the West against Sunni extremism. In light of Saudi-Iranian tensions, Russian Foreign Minister Sergei Lavrov travelled to the Kingdom for his first ever visit and following his meeting with King Abdullah on 21 May 2006 he attempted to reassure the Saudi leadership that Russia was only interested in allowing Iran to develop a peaceful nuclear programme. Soon after the visit, when pressed in an interview to a Saudi newspaper on Moscow's unwillingness to allow strong UN Security Council Resolutions to be adopted against Iran, Lavrov admitted that Tehran needed 'to eventually answer extremely serious questions, whose results have long been known to the IAEA [International Atomic Energy Agency]', but he added that the Iranian government 'continues to cooperate with the IAEA although it still has not replied to all the questions asked'.[25] Leading Russian analyst and director of the Center for International Security, Institute for World Economy and International Relations Alexei Arbatov acknowledged in 2006 that Russia's behaviour on the international stage 'effectively negates the prospects for the UN to provide legal grounds for sanctions or military enforcement measures against Iran'.[26] Arbatov noted that 'precisely for these reasons'. and in light of US military entanglement in Iraq, 'Tehran perceives its political position to be strong enough to rhetorically challenge Washington with immunity.'[27]

Saudi-Iranian rivalry intensified following the assassination of Lebanese former prime minister, Rafiq Hariri, on 14 February 2005. Hariri, although a Lebanese, also acquired Saudi citizenship in the 1980s and since the end of the Lebanese civil war had been considered in Riyadh as a Sunni safeguard and balance to the rising power of Shi'a Hezbollah and Iranian hegemony. The elimination of Hariri from the delicate Lebanese political equation was considered as a direct Iranian-Syrian provocation against them and in the context of the rise of the Shi'is political power in Iraq the murder was interpreted as a direct challenge to Sunni Arabs under the spiritual and often financial leadership of the Saudis. Following Syrian and Iranian orders, loyal groups in Lebanon began a campaign of inciting revolt against the Saudi government, particularly after the July war in 2006 when the government in Riyadh apportioned part of the blame for the fighting with Israel on Hezbollah.

Lebanon's largely unregulated media was habitually utilised by regional governments to undermine rivals. Syrian and Iranian influence and management of major television networks, specifically their news and current affairs programming, and newspapers in Lebanon, was significant. Lebanese satellite television channels, including al-Manar, NBN, OTV and al-Jadeed, were outspoken Syrian and/or Iranian mouthpieces. Another important channel, LBC, while presenting itself as more balanced had pro-Syrian politicians in Lebanon, including Suleiman Franjieh who was a personal friend of Bashar al-Asad, as a major shareholder. Only two major television channels in Lebanon, Murr TV and Future, were funded by pro-Cedar Revolution figures. Lebanese media impact went beyond the borders of the small country and enjoyed popularity in the Arab Gulf because of the relative social freedom the country enjoyed. The Saudis viewed the onslaught of propaganda against them by pro-Syrian and Iranian television channels in Lebanon as a direct challenge to national security. The pro-Hezbollah Iranian-funded channel al-Manar, for example, incited Shi'is in the eastern region of Saudi Arabia to revolt and in 2012 and 2013 regularly stoked Shi'a hostility in Bahrain against the pro-Saudi Sunni ruling monarchy. Pro-Syrian channels such as al-Jadeed or the Aouni OTV were more aligned with the approach favoured in Damascus, which constantly portrayed Saudi Arabia as the exporter of Wahhabi terrorism.

Another disturbing element for the Saudis of this lively Lebanese media scene was that many Western correspondents reporting on the Middle East tended to be based in Beirut because of its more liberal social scene and comfortable climate. Some noteworthy reporters such as the American Pulitzer winner Seymour Hersh and Britain's Robert Fisk, who lived in Beirut for over thirty years, waged fierce crusades against Saudi Arabia and offered a more rose-tinted view of Iranian and Syrian policies in the region. One of the most significant sources of information for these writers was Lebanese journalist and former Minister of Information Michel Samaha, who was arrested and imprisoned in August 2012 after being caught in possession of large quantities of explosives that were provided by Syrian intelligence with the intention of murdering Christians, including senior religious figures, in Sunni Muslim areas.[28] The Syrian motive was driven by the same purpose of showing, had Samaha not been caught due to sophisticated police work, not only the Lebanese but also Western audiences that Saudi-backed Sunnis were blood-thirsty terrorists while Damascus and Tehran were being unfairly portrayed as being dangerous.

Saudi insecurity about regional and Western perceptions made it very important to gain at least a degree of Russian understanding and cooperation in the region. Yet Putin's behaviour in 2006 was not appreciated by the Saudis and by their allies in Lebanon because Russia stalled repeated attempts to pass UN Security Council Resolutions that could have forced Syria to halt its interference in Lebanon, including the steady supply of heavy weapons to Hezbollah. Moscow also undermined proposed UNSC Resolutions to demand Syrian cooperation with the

UN tribunal that was established in 2005 to bring Hariri's killers to justice. When in May 2008, only a little over a year after Putin's historic visit to Saudi Arabia, Hezbollah militants and their allies entered and forcefully occupied West Beirut, a predominantly Sunni quarter, it appeared as more evidence of the Shi'a ascendancy in the region and Russian complicity in this development because Moscow had repeatedly blocked concrete efforts to support the Cedar Revolution government led by Prime Minister Fu'ad Siniora in order to undermine the position of the United States and its allies in the Middle East. Hezbollah's military intervention in 2008 to further assert its political hegemony dashed Saudi hopes that Russia could play a positive role in the Middle East and to a large extent Riyadh's political elite lost confidence in Putin's intentions and promises thereafter. This perception among the Saudi political elite became more deeply embedded a few years later as a result of Russia's forceful support of Syria's regime after 2011 despite Riyadh's energetic efforts to convince Moscow to revise its stance.

Hezbollah's forceful occupation of Beirut in 2008 had greatly undermined the image of Saudi Arabia as the patron of the Lebanese Sunnis. Saudi-Russian differences also sharpened over the Palestinian-Israeli dispute as well as over intra-Palestinian rivalry. In 2002 King Abdullah had announced an Arab-Israeli peace initiative that offered a comprehensive settlement to resolve all disputed land issues involving Lebanon, Syria and primarily the Palestinians that rivalled the agenda of the confrontationists, led by Iran and Syria, who doubted that a peaceful settlement could ever be achieved and advocated a violent struggle as the only path. In sum, the Saudi initiative offered Israel peace with all the Arab and Muslim states once a fully viable Palestinian state, including a capital in East Jerusalem and a just outcome for the millions of displaced refugees was recognised by the Israelis. The PLO and the Palestinian National Authority endorsed the initiative.

Although Iran and Syria did not officially reject the initiative until 2009, both states until then were lukewarm in their reaction to it by presenting it as a weak compromise. At the March 2009 Arab League Summit in Doha, Saudi Arabia finally acquiesced to regional criticisms by announcing that the peace plan would expire after a limited period of time if a positive Israeli response was not forthcoming. Opposition to the plan in the region was fuelled by Iranian-Syrian regional ambitions to manipulate popular anger, which were checked by Saudi Arabia's peace proposal that was an alternative to the rhetoric of confrontation. Both Iran and Syria rejected a settlement that they did not have a role in initiating and the success of the Saudi peace plan would have marginalised their roles in the Middle East. Hamas, the Palestinian group rivalling the PLO, rejected a peace with Israel although ostensibly it endorsed the Saudi initiative, insisting that it was the Israelis who were undermining progress by building more settlements and creating new realities that would eventually make it impossible to establish a viable Palestinian state.

Throughout the Putin era the Middle East was strategically divided between a group of nations led by Saudi Arabia and an alternative bloc under Iranian guidance, and this division was widened after the tilting of Iraq towards the Shi'a alliance after 2003. The rivalry was reflected in the political struggle for dominance among Palestinians. The Palestinians were split into two main political groups, although there remained many independent smaller factions, with one led by the PLO and the other by Hamas. Fighting between the PLO and Hamas increased in frequency until 2006, when legislative elections created a wide schism between a Hamas-controlled parliament and a PLO-led presidency and government, following President Mahmoud Abbas's election victory in January 2005. Eventually, clashes between the two factions resulted in Hamas's control over the Gaza Strip which administratively broke away from the mainland Palestinian territories on the West Bank. To avert deterioration in the crisis and mitigate Iranian-Syrian interference Saudi Arabia played a central role in mediating between Hamas and the PLO and attained temporary success in February 2007 by sponsoring the Mecca Agreement. This agreement, after lengthy and difficult negotiations, was considered a major breakthrough for the Saudis, although Qatar and Egypt were also active in mediation efforts because it initially appeared to be charming Hamas, whose leaders were then based in Damascus, away from the Syrian and Iranian orbit.

Hostilities between the Palestinian factions however resumed within months and the failure of the Mecca Agreement was blamed on Syrian and Iranian foul play to maintain their grip on the reins of the Palestinian cause due to its high emotional appeal among Arabs and Muslims. Again, Saudi suspicions about Russia's role were heightened, particularly because Moscow's historic relationship with the Palestinians could have been more actively imposed to force the two factions to reconcile. Considering the Palestinian reliance on Moscow in international diplomacy and the tight US-Israeli alliance, Russia, more than any other country on the UN Security Council, had the authority to play a decisive role in the implementation of the Mecca Agreement. Instead, Russia played a passive role and allowed Syria and Iran to enjoy vigorous determination of events on the ground. As with the King Abdullah Middle East peace initiative it was strategically vital for Iran and Syria to undermine the Saudi role in the region.

Open hostility between the Palestinian rivals was vividly illustrated during the Israeli campaign in Gaza in early 2009 when senior Hamas officials accused their Palestinian political rivals in the West Bank of betrayal and collusion with the enemy. Moscow's relationship with Saudi Arabia was constantly tested during this period because Iran and Syria had evidently evolved into key geostrategic partners in the region. An early indicator was Putin's surprise move of inviting Hamas leaders to Moscow in January 2006, which was a sharp break from its traditional policy of supporting the PLO and the Palestinian National Authority. The visit was obviously going to antagonise Saudi Arabia as well as Israel and the United States. Initially, there was difficulty in understanding Putin's desire to associate Russia with a militant Islamist group while offending more stable traditional nation-states. Moscow's justification was that it intended to facilitate reconciliation between the rival factions, which seemed reasonable in 2007 because combined Russian and Saudi efforts would have facilitated the approach to the Mecca Agreement in February of that year. Hamas leaders were invited to Moscow and encouraged to establish a united Palestinian front while the Saudis convinced Mahmoud Abbas to acknowledge a power-sharing formula with Hamas. Coincidentally but significantly, the Saudi-brokered arrangement came within days of Putin's historic visit to Saudi Arabia.

Putin's trip to Saudi Arabia in February 2007 was obviously geared towards reassuring Riyadh that Moscow was not partnering Iran against the Kingdom. Russia sought to improve relations with Saudi Arabia because of its recognised influential role in the region and also because of the access to the US political leadership enjoyed by the government, particularly the administration of George Bush. This factor was also recognised by Tehran when in January 2007, 'Iran's top nuclear negotiator, Ali Larijani, delivered a letter from Supreme Leader Ayatollah Ali Khamenei and President Mahmoud Ahmadinejad to King Abdullah asking him to ease US-Iranian tensions.'[29] Putin's trip to Saudi Arabia the following month was highly anticipated by both parties, with the Kingdom expecting an accommodating Russian approach on a variety of regional issues and the Russian leadership was equally hopeful of reaching a new level of bilateral economic cooperation. King Abdullah remarked that he looked 'forward to expanding [...] cooperation' between the two countries 'by signing agreements for the protection and promotion of investment, air transport and avoidance of double taxation. We also want to expand our cooperation in research, education and technology.'[30]

The veteran Russian Middle East expert Vitalii Na'umkin also noted soon after Putin's Middle East trip that Russia would launch six satellites for the Saudis.[31] High oil prices during 2007 allowed Saudi Arabia and Russia to rapidly build a huge reserve cash surplus that was available for investment into various projects. The two energy-producing giants expressed mutual desire to improve coordination in this area and this opportunity was studied during Putin's visit. The Russian delegation included Alexei Miller, the head of Gazprom, and Vagit Alekperov, representing LUKOIL. In the words of one observer: 'Moscow and Riyadh, as major oil exporters, are tacit allies in seeking to keep world oil prices high.'[32] The trend of high energy prices made Saudi Arabia a particularly attractive potential consumer of Russian goods and services but it also created an impetus for the two countries to protect common interests in a highly unstable regional climate.

Putin's keenness to open up new Arab markets was made apparent during his first years as president and Primakov's appointment to lead the Russian Chamber of Trade and Industry was central to this policy. Following the first-ever Russian-Saudi Economic Forum in Moscow in 2003 a growing convergence between Russia and Saudi Arabia saw a breakthrough in 2004 with a variety of agreements, including a concession to LUKOIL, the Russian oil company, for a multi-billion dollar agreement spanning forty years for 'prospecting rights and geological works, as well as the opportunity to develop natural gas and gas condensate fields on an area of 30,000 square kilometres in the Rub Al-Khali desert'.[33] The project, called Luksar, resulted in committed investments worth $4 billion and following an agreement between LUKOIL and Saudi oil giants Aramco Corp, 'they have 80 and 20 per cent in the joint venture, respectively'.[34]

Beyond the expected realm of economic cooperation Russia attempted to sell Saudi Arabia nuclear reactors for peaceful energy purposes as well as 150 T-90 tanks. High oil prices and regional dangers had promoted Saudi Arabia to rank as one of the world's largest purchasers of arms, according to a report by the US Congress, and Moscow was keenly interested in a share of the $3.4 billion the Kingdom allocated for weapons in 2006, placing it second only to India.[35] In 2007 Putin 'indicated Russia's willingness to sell helicopters, build rocket-propelled grenade (RPG) factories, provide sophisticated anti-aircraft systems—the Carapace (*Pantsyr*), TOR M1, and Strelets'—and offered Saudi Arabia the 'opportunity to join the Russian satellite navigation system, GLONASS'.[36] The visiting Russian Federation delegation to the Kingdom in 2007 accompanying Putin, which included President of Tatarstan Mintimier Shaymiev, also very eagerly promoted a project to build a railway connecting the religiously significant cities of Mecca and Medina.

Despite the conflicting regional ambitions bilateral trade relations between the two countries witnessed steady growth in the Putin era, at least until the Arab Spring. In the nine years between 1997 and 2006 Russian exports to the Kingdom grew in value from $112 million to $693 million, an increase of 533 per cent, with Russia climbing from thirty-fourth largest exporter to Saudi Arabia, to twenty-fourth throughout the decade. By the time of Putin's visit to Saudi Arabia Russian exports had crossed the $800 million figure, double the $400 million level in 2005.[37] Early Saudi warmth for a strong Russia in the Middle East was evident, in part because of Riyadh's displeasure at confused US policies and strategies in the region, which only seemed to strengthen Iran, Syria and Hezbollah. This culminated in 2007 when Putin was awarded the Kingdom's highest honour, the Abdul-Aziz Order for Services to Islam, as recognition of the new role Russia was playing in the region and as a message to the United States that alternatives existed on the global level.

Nonetheless, progress in bilateral relations did not quite match Moscow's expectations in penetrating Saudi markets and trade or in terms of encouraging Saudi investments, which remained modest compared to other regional powerhouses including Turkey and Israel. The Iranian regional ascendancy was the basis of Saudi cautious nervousness and Putin's visit to the Kingdom in February 2007 was overshadowed by Riyadh's serious concerns about Russian ambiguity, with fears that it was covertly strengthening Iran and Syria to enhance its regional and international standing vis-à-vis the United States. The Saudi leadership hinted that by tangibly diminishing support for Iran the leadership in Moscow could expect lucrative contract awards including the right to explore and produce natural gas near Ghawar. The linkage between economic co-operation and Russia's support in containing Iranian influence in the region became particularly lucid during Putin's visit in 2007 to Saudi Arabia. Politically, King Abdullah also offered support for Russian participation on regional issues including Iraq and the Palestinian-Israeli conflict, contrary to US preference.

In the year Medvedev was elected president, 2008, Moscow endeavoured to maintain a practical balance between Saudi Arabia and Iran in the hope of keeping both relationships intact. In July 2008 the influential head of the Saudi National Security Council, Prince Bandar, met Putin, then prime minister, to discuss the rise of Iranian and Syrian influence and to ensure Russian co-operation under newly elected President Medvedev. Reports indicated that the two countries signed a major military agreement worth over $2 billion based on discussions initiated in 2007. During Bandar's visit speculation mounted that the Saudi purchases were enticements aimed at distancing Moscow from Tehran, leading Prime Minister Putin's spokesman to respond that suggestions 'that Russia's relations with Saudi Arabia with regard to military technological co-operation may in any way be linked to the Russian-Iranian dialogue are out of place and untrue'.[38]

The courtship continued to dither during Medvedev's presidency and in many respects reached a cul-de-sac in 2009, partly because it became obvious that Russia was not going to abandon Iran and Syria and also in part due to the nature of the dual leadership in Russia. Putin's rhetoric became more uncompromising and solidified the view of a fortress Russia, while Medvedev gave the impression of being the softer partner who was closer in mindset to the reformists of the early 1990s. The charade proved largely meaningless by the time the Arab uprisings swept across the Middle East, unveiling the true picture of Russia's regional allegiances and confirming what the Saudis had long suspected. Moscow's foreign policy under Putin was strategically fixed: 'Russia intends to benefit from the weakening of the US in the region, in order to present itself as a counterweight to Washington.'[39] As long as this was the mindset in Moscow, the Saudis believed, Russia would continue to expend all its efforts to strengthen and consolidate the Iran-Syria bloc in the region.

Saudi Arabia was further disturbed by Russia's behaviour in response to the Syrian revolution. Not only did Moscow doggedly defend the Asad regime but the high level of military support and co-operation over the previous years, which had previously been downplayed by Russia, became more evident. One of the main justifications provided by the Obama administration for ignoring pleas for a military intervention in Syria to avert a humanitarian crisis was that the country had developed extremely advanced air defence systems provided by Russia which was bolstered by Russian technical and logistical support. Saudi anger, at the popular and elite levels, was difficult to contain. Putin sporadically attempted to diffuse this hostility by claiming that Russia was not interested in the person of Bashar al-Asad, who was particularly despised by the Saudis, who felt that he had betrayed them after years of attempting to accommodate him. Soon after starting his third term as president Putin sought to downplay differences with Saudi Arabia and claimed in one interview that while Moscow enjoyed good relations with Iran and Syria 'we also get on very well with Saudi Arabia. I have cultivated a warm personal relationship with the Custodian of the Two Islamic Shrines [King Abdullah].'[40] The statement was delivered not long after a strong Saudi rebuke of a series of statements by officials in Moscow on Shi'a unrest in the country's eastern province and implying that the Kingdom was supporting terrorists in Syria. The Saudi response asserted that the 'Russian accusations are based on false assumptions reported by the Syrian media,'[41] marking the lowest point of relations in over a decade. The reference to the Syrian media was also an intentional slight because mainstream Russian news and government sponsored channels such as the Arabic version of the *Russia Today* network virtually emulated official Syrian regime interpretations of news reporting of regional events as well as of the popular uprising.

The stagnation continued in 2013, with reports that Saudi businessmen revoked contracts with Russian firms and that chamber of commerce offices in Riyadh were closed down. The souring of Saudi-Russian relations to this extent was not foreseen only a few years earlier. According to one analysis in 2007: 'Moscow can talk to both conservative and radical Arab regimes, to Sunni and Shi'ite alike, to Israel and Hamas, and to Iran. This gives her a flexibility that the USA does not have.'[42]

Russia's engagement of Saudi Arabia under Putin gave the impression that diversified economic and political options had been made available that elevated Russia's tangible involvement in the region. The two countries shared a common goal in controlling the worldwide global market that could have also led to rapid progress in relations. The opportunities missed by Russia to better cultivate relations with Saudi Arabia, while in part not helped missed by complicated regional dynamics, were undoubtedly due to the nature of Putin's world outlook and the core principles of Russian foreign policy that was crafted during his second term. This represented Russia's abandonment of an integrationist international approach and the adoption of a posture based on confrontation that paralleled growing authoritarianism combined with rising energy revenues for Putin's system.

10

IRAN, TURKEY AND THE FRAGILE SOUTH

Iran and Turkey emerged as powerful magnetic poles for Muslims to gravitate towards in the post-Soviet space as they sought to form their identities in the 1990s. Turkey offered the model of secular modern Islam that contrasted sharply with the revolutionary religious Shi'a version offered by Iran. In turn, Moscow's leadership appeared genuinely concerned that the two states harboured expansionist aims in Russia's southern backyard in Central Asia and the Caucasus and was uncertain about their impact on the significant Muslim populations of the Russian Federation. Perhaps to allay Russian fears a senior advisor to Tatarstan President Mintimer Shaimiev proposed the idea of Euro-Islam in 1998 which 'organically combines Muslim values with the values of liberalism and democracy…'[1] According to this idea Muslim Tatarstan, a major component of the Russian Federation, gained little from orientating itself towards large external Muslim powers and would be better served by integrating with the dynamic and prosperous European civilisation in tandem with Orthodox Russia. Despite Shaimiev's efforts to reassure Moscow the rise of Putin in 1999 confirmed that there was lingering uncertainty about Russia's future as a unified country and its identity. In the eyes of many Russians 'there was no consensus on what Russia's national borders should be; nor was there a distinct national consciousness'[2] when Putin became president and this boldly underlined the national security necessity of establishing a clear understanding about the spheres of influence along its southwestern rim with Turkey and Iran.

By virtue of their sizeable territorial mass, large populations and indispensible geo-strategic locations Turkey and Iran were widely viewed as states of major significance in the international order. Dominating the geographic edges of the north and east of the Middle East, these two non-Arab Muslim countries historically exerted a strong influence on their Arab neighbours and established themselves as regional powers. Iran was the inheritor of a great Persian civilisation while Turkey represented Sunni Turkic culture and was the successor of the long-dominant Ottoman Empire in the Middle East. Iran's 1.6 million square kilometres landmass was double that of Turkey but its population of 66 million is smaller than the latter's 76 million.[3] Recent forecasts have suggested that the population in each country will surpass 80 million before 2050. The two countries directly bordered the former Soviet Union and after 1991 became significant players in Central Asian and Caucasian affairs, consequently placing them high on the priority list among Russia's elite foreign policy makers.

Historical background—Iran and Russia

A long history of antagonistic relations existed between Persia and the expanding Russian Empire, which in the latter half of the nineteenth century embarked on a series of military campaigns that captured the prominent Central Asian cities of Tashkent, Bukhara and Samarkand. The Russian expansion ultimately defined Iran's current northern border. Soviet relations with Iran were typically strained as a result of disparate ideological orientations and this was compounded by competing geo-strategic ambitions. Until 1979 Iran was a politically conservative and a staunchly pro-Western monarchy that despised and was hostile to Soviet communism. After the Second World War, Stalin attempted to maintain a Soviet foothold in northern Iran on the basis of a wartime agreement with Britain to create zones of influence to ensure that the government in Tehran did not ally itself with Nazi Germany. Western pressure forced Stalin to eventually retreat in 1946 in what was perhaps the first glimpse of the Cold War era. Iranian communists, however, continued to agitate against the ruling Shah until the 1970s but in 1979 a radical Shi'a clique seized power in a revolution led by Ayatollah Ruhollah Khomeini, who had been in exile in France, along with other radical clerics. Khomeini's rhetoric was fiercely anti-communist despite the contribution of communists and other leftists to the popular uprising that led to the eventual downfall of the Shah.

The radical clerics who ruled Iran adopted a harsh anti-Western rhetoric and their leader Ayatollah Khomeini established a model of governance that transferred ultimate power to a council of religious jurists who guided the state institutions of the country, including its parliament, presidency and military. The new regime crushed rival communists by executing or imprisoning thousands of party members soon after seizing power. The new ideology and leadership that dominated in Iran became a major source of concern for Moscow in the 1980s, especially as it espoused the expansion of militant and radical Islam on the Soviet Union's southern border. Moscow's policy makers at that time faced the simultaneous ascendancy of Jihadists in Afghanistan and radical Shi'is in neighbouring Iran spanning the borders of six of the fifteen largely Muslim Soviet republics. The revival of political Islam in the region posed a serious challenge to the integrity of the Soviet Union as well as to the survival of secular pro-Soviet states in the Arab world. In turn, the occupation of Afghanistan since1979 had created fear in Tehran of growing Soviet encroachment that did not subside until the withdrawal of the Red Army towards the end of the 1980s.

Despite mutual suspicions during the first decade after the Iranian Revolution the complexities of the Cold War and the Middle East arena created opportunities for Soviet leaders to build positive relations with Iran because of its belligerent hostility towards the United States, which Khomeini infamously tarnished as the Great Satan. An anti-Western Iran counterbalanced the military weight of NATO-member Turkey in south-western Asia and rivalled Sunni Saudi Arabia, which was the chief sponsor of Jihadis operating in Afghanistan. Ideological differences between Iran and the Soviet Union still made it impossible to establish close relations but shared concerns and goals led to increasing levels of co-operation, particularly as isolated Tehran recognised the benefits of Soviet support while the West provided backing to Saddam Hussein's Iraq during the Iran-Iraq war in the 1980s.

Due to the pragmatism in Soviet policy initiated by Khrushchev in the 1960s Moscow had already began actively pursuing the strategy of tolerating and cooperating with anti-communist regimes such as the Ba'th in both Syria and Iraq as long as they acted to limit US penetration into those areas. The prospect of improved Soviet-Iranian relations, however, was ultimately stifled in the late 1980s because Gorbachev's New Thinking required Moscow to pursue better relations with the West and Israel. Gorbachev also endeavoured to build relations with Saudi Arabia, Iran's major Islamic foe which had been funding much of Saddam Hussein's military in its eight-year war with Iran. It was only after the death of Ayatollah Khomeini in June 1989, who was feverishly ideological and who espoused an atmosphere of permanent revolution, that the long-term military, economic and diplomatic relationship between Tehran and Moscow flourished.

The president of Iran who succeeded Khomeini in 1989 was the pragmatic and skilful diplomat, Ali Akbar Rafsanjani. He led a faction within the ruling elite which espoused realism in Iranian foreign policy based on the tactic of promoting a truce with the West to allow Iran to exploit its economic resources and expand its military capabilities to better confront external threats and internal challenges to the regime. The pragmatic wing further argued that the development of good relations with Moscow would help utilise the Soviet seat on the UN Security Council as an important tool to protect Iran from the adoption of damaging Western-backed international measures and other forms of diplomatic pressure.

On 5 November 1989 the Soviet Union and Iran signed a preliminary agreement to establish military technical co-operation, but Iranian hopes for rapid diplomatic successes were largely hindered in the late 1980s and early 1990s because of Moscow's eagerness to join the Western family at that time. When in the mid-1990s Russia's relations with the West became more frosty and opposition to the Yeltsin-Kozyrev pro-Western foreign policy intensified Moscow began to consider Iran as a lucrative diplomatic, economic and military prospect. The pace of co-operation between Tehran and Moscow then quickened in the course of the decade so that by the end of the 1990s, as the first fruits of the 1989 military-technical agreement, Russia had sold Iran 'twenty-six MiG-29 fighter planes, more than 1,000 T-72 main battle tanks, more than 1,500 BMP-2 armoured combat vehicles, and three Kilo-Class diesel submarines'.[4]

As Russia's political leadership harmonised its perspectives on national interests and international risks in the 1990s towards a more pragmatic approach Moscow paid more attention to Tehran's regional political influence and its military reach into the heart of the Middle East conflict, through Hezbollah in Lebanon and its alliance with Syria. Iran's clout was also evident over Palestinian groups such as Islamic Jihad and Hamas, which both relied on Syrian intelligence and Hezbollah to provide technical, intelligence and media support. Most importantly for Moscow though was growing acknowledgement of Iran's role in, and connections to, Central Asia and the Caucasus. During the 1990s Moscow shifted towards a more geo-strategic Eurasian emphasis and increasingly Iran would become a defensive shield in Russia's southern region. This point was often repeated by pro-Kremlin Russian commentators with the outbreak of the Syrian revolution in 2011 to justify Moscow's concern that the collapse of the Asad regime would be followed by instability in Iran. According to this view Russia considered Iranian stability a red line because of the impact that turbulence there would have on countries bordering Russia.

Yet in the 1990s progress was initially slow in improving bilateral relations between Iran and Russia with an Iranian newspaper analysis in 2007 summarising that although 'this period is seen as Russia's period of change and transition, Russia's co-operation with the United States was a major concern for Iran. Based on this, mistrust remained as one of the significant characteristics in the relations between the two countries.'[5] The cultivation of Russian-Iranian relations was made easier as the Iranian brand of Islamic rule went through a phase of approachable pragmatism under Rafsanjani, allowing greater co-operation in facing unilateral US actions and decisions and resulting in the perception that 'if the enemy of one's enemy is automatically one's friend, then according to this line of reasoning Iran is Russia's natural ally in the region'.[6] Realignment of Russian strategic thinking from 1996 further facilitated the establishment of meaningful political, economic and military co-operation between Iran and Russia.

The necessity for Moscow and Tehran to co-operate in the Caucasus and Central Asia opened up more complex and multi-dimensional Russian-Iranian relations. Iran's constructive role in the Armenia-Azerbaijan conflict and the civil war in Tajikistan were well received in Moscow and rather than 'backing the emerging Taliban movement in neighbouring Afghanistan, Tehran opposed it, mirroring Russian concerns'.[7] Russia and Iran also agreed on preventing a Western foothold in the Caspian Sea basin, with the two countries sharing a substantial shoreline with other neighbours in the Caucasus and Central Asia. As disputes among the Caspian Sea littoral states over access and shipping rights remained unresolved, the possibility that smaller states such as Azerbaijan would encourage Western involvement on their behalf continued to concern Moscow as well as Tehran. The political class and media in Russia generally praised Iran's role on various issues considered vital for Russian national security leading the Duma to urge Yeltsin in 1998 to pursue a more vigorous policy of partnership with Iran. Moscow's shift from a pro-Western to a Eurasian mindset at that time helped raise Iran's profile among policy makers and in light of the anti-Sunni Wahhabi atmosphere in Russia when Putin became acting president it became inevitable that Russian-Iranian cooperation would increase further.

Putin and Iran

A psychologically slanted interpretation suggested in 2006 that 'marked by a defiant nationalism', Iran and Russia 'have much in common. Energy wealth gives them a sense of unique opportunity, the conviction that time is playing in their favour, and that they can now redress the humiliations they have suffered from the outside world.'[8] The US invasion of Iraq in 2003 and its regional consequences undoubtedly brought Moscow and Tehran closer together as Russian-Iranian strategic and military co-operation directly challenged the United States and its dominant role in the region. But Russian-Iranian rapprochement was not only a reaction to the policies of the Bush administration in the Middle East because 'Putin, under pressure from the military industrial complex, resumed conventional arms sales to Iran in December 2000,'[9] abrogating a previous understanding signed in 1995 between Washington and Moscow on the issue. With this act Putin took bilateral relations with Iran to a much higher level of military and diplomatic co-operation in the following years despite fears in the West and Israel as well as among Arab states that the government in Tehran was pursuing a nuclear weapons programme as part of a massive remilitarisation agenda and that Russia was surreptitiously aiding Tehran's regional ambitions.

The revitalisation of relations between Iran and Russia under Putin was based on international developments and experiences in the 1990s, such as the rise of the Taliban in Afghanistan and disappointment with the West in general but there were also strong internal economic motives that were considered. The rise in oil prices in the late 1990s meant that Iran's dollar cash flow had improved, making it an attractive potential customer for Russian exports. The still undiversified Russian economy depended on the weapons industry as its most practical and realistic export source. Moscow's justification for selling weapons to Iran at the time was made easier because President Mohammad Khatami was a moderate. Khatami's efforts to promote dialogue with the West even created the possibility for some Western states to resume arms sales and other exports. Some Russian analysts warned that Moscow was in danger of being left behind and 'persistent calls by Washington to terminate Russian exports to Iran were portrayed by these circles in Moscow as being motivated by the desire of American corporations to save future opportunities in the Iranian market for themselves'.[10] The urgency that was felt in Moscow of maximising the potential of the Iranian market was due to 'a growing realisation in the military-industrial complex that the list of potential customers was getting too short'.[11] China and India, while very large and lucrative partners, were insufficient as such a narrow market weakened the Russian hand in negotiations over contractual terms and undermined national security by providing the two Asian giants with weapons that could be used against the country of the original supplier.

The US invasion and occupation of Iraq in 2003 created in Tehran and Moscow a shared feeling of encroachment that demanded growing collaboration. On 1 May 2003 Bush prematurely declared that the war in Iraq was over and that US triumph had been achieved, with only 139 American soldiers killed since the war began in March. While this was to some extent true Washington had catastrophically failed in devising a post-Saddam strategy for the country. After Saddam Hussein a new political reality emerged in Iraq that enabled Iran to establish a firm foothold in the country. The Shi'is formed the largest sect in Iraq and the US occupation empowered them to play a decisive role in the country's new constitution and political system. Powerful Shi'a militias emerged, including Muqtada Sadr's Mehdi Army, with received decisive support by the Iranian Revolutionary Guards. Beyond military support a contemporary assessment noted that all of Iraq's dominant Shi'a parties 'attract voters by relying on vast political and social-service networks across southern Iraq that, in many cases, were created with Iranian funding and assistance'.[12] Iranian backing for the insurgency in Iraq against

US troops was evident as part of a regional alliance with Syria that aimed to assert a new hegemony and undermine Western influence. Indeed, observers noted that Iran's sway in Iraq meant that it 'has emerged as the main victor from the war'.[13]

Moscow had vociferously argued since Primakov became foreign minister in 1996 that the United States was wrong to act on the basis that it was the world's sole superpower. The US National Security Strategy of 2002 'arrogated the right to itself of pre-emptive military action',[14] without necessarily consulting with other important powers. By aligning its strategic interests with Iran Russia's regional status was significantly enhanced. Initially, Iran appeared concerned by the ambitious and belligerent behaviour by the United States, caving in to pressure and agreeing to accept the terms that allowed short notice access to nuclear facilities by the International Atomic Energy Agency (IAEA) as well as temporarily suspending uranium enrichment. Moscow was also initially stunned at the high-handed approach by the Bush administration. The military and political entanglement of the United States in Iraq however allowed the leaderships in Iran and Russia to claim a moral victory after the relentless international criticisms of the unilateralist approach by Washington.

Russian convergence with Iran over Iraq during the US occupation was an essential element of a broader strategic objective prevalent in Moscow to curtail US supremacy in the international system. Ostensibly, Moscow had little interest in allowing Iraq to become an Iranian puppet state and rather contrarily, Russia should have had more reasons to be concerned that the ascendancy of Shi'a power would aggravate the danger of militant Sunni extremism in the Middle East. While Russia was able after 2001 to skilfully manipulate Al-Qaeda terrorism to justify its own war in Chechnya and present itself as an ally of the West, the Moscow leadership recognised the danger that the Sunni insurgency in Iraq could inspire and mobilise Sunnis in and around Russia. In some respects the motor 'driving the relationship between Russia and Iran is their common concern about Sunni Islamic radicalism'.[15] To a greater extent, both Iran and Russia were able to exploit Western hysteria over Al-Qaeda terrorism during Putin's first term to divert attention from their own regional agendas by promoting the value of dialogue and co-operation with the West against terrorism.

Putin's determination to stamp his authority on foreign policy was immediately apparent and one of his first appointments in 2001 was

Alexander Rumyantsev, a scientist, 'as head of the Ministry of Atomic Energy (Minatom), replacing Yevgeny Adamov, who had the habit of trying to make nuclear deals with Iran without Kremlin approval'.[16] Adamov was charged and convicted in 2008 of corruption charges. The nuclear sector was at the core of relations between Iran and Russia. In a television interview broadcast on 1 January 2008, Primakov noted that Russian-Iranian relations were long considered a high priority for Moscow, reflecting the view of a strong pro-Iranian lobby in Russia that portrayed Iran as a barrier to Western influence on its southern borders. The influence of this lobby was highlighted when in March 2001 an Agreement on the Foundations for Bilateral Relations and Principles of Cooperation was signed between Russia and Iran.

Concurrent with the agreement in 2001 Iran purchased 'thirty military transport planes and thirty MI-8 military transport helicopters'.[17] Yet Primakov attempted to downplay the relevance of military sales and focused instead on the pragmatic and tactical nature of Russian relations with Iran. The former prime minister, whose influence behind the scenes in policy making continued under Putin, sought to explain Russo-Iranian co-operation by stating: 'I don't agree with those on the left and right who say that Iran and Russia are strategic partners because a strategic partner for Russia has to have complete harmony with Russia's interests and Iran does things that do not comply with our views.'[18] The message confirmed Moscow was pursuing a broader national security agenda where Iran was more of a means rather than an end.

Moscow recognised that Iranian sway in the Middle East transcended beyond Iraq and was also significant in Lebanon through its proxy militia Hezbollah. The US occupation of Iraq, high oil and gas prices and an Israeli disregard for the furthering of the peace process with the Palestinians all played into Iranian hands as pragmatic voices in the Middle East became submerged in a tidal wave of belligerent and hostile political speeches in the region as a whole. This emerging hegemony that Iran was acquiring resulted in intensified friction with Saudi Arabia, which feared that Tehran was paving the way for a transformation of the region by manipulating the anti-Western and pro-Palestinian sentiments among the Arab populations.

The assassination in Lebanon of the Sunni leader Rafiq Hariri on 14 February 2005 occurred a few months before Iranians elected Mahmoud Ahmadinejad as president in June. Ahmadinejad, with outspoken anti-Western views, had defeated his pragmatic rival Mohammad Khatami in controversial elections. While the connection between the two events was not immediately obvious, in time they pointed to a belligerent tide and uncompromising polarisation sweeping the Middle East. Hariri was a powerful but moderate Sunni figure in Lebanon who contrasted sharply with the militant rhetoric of Iranian-sponsored Hezbollah and the assassination resulted in tense Sunni-Shi'a relations in Lebanon that threatened to escalate into a full-scale civil war. The turmoil in Lebanon was magnified when Hezbollah sought to extract from the outcome of the war with Israel in the summer of 2006 demands for more power for the Shi'is in the country's political system at the expense of the Sunnis and Christians. Israel's attempt to contain Hezbollah was repelled by the Iranian-backed group, which received long-range missiles from Iran that targeted cities in central Israel. Hezbollah fighters also received training in Iran to match Israeli troops in close range combat in Lebanon's southern villages.

Israel's failures in the summer 2006 war in Lebanon tilted the regional balance of power in favour of Iran, as well as Syria, and further illuminated US limitations in the Middle East. Inside Lebanon the war led to a bitter confrontation between Hezbollah with its pro-Syria allies against a coalition of Christians, Sunnis and Druze under the Cedar Revolution banner, leading to a power vacuum in 2007 that prevented the election of a president to fill the post in 2008. With Hezbollah's backing the Shi'a speaker of parliament used his position to prevent any legislative meetings from taking place. In addition, with the resignation of the Shi'a ministers from the Cabinet the legitimacy of the government was challenged by Hezbollah, Iran and Syria with their supporters in Lebanon demanding a redesigning of the national political system. In other words, all constitutional centres of authority had been left paralysed.

The Lebanese crisis was directly blamed on Iranian and Syrian efforts to impose a regional hegemony. Russia's role during this phase subtly strengthened Tehran's position by blocking US efforts to impose harsher international sanctions on Iran. Moscow also made it clear that any military action against Iran would be considered as a direct threat to Russian national interests and security. Russia's support for Hezbollah and Iran in Lebanon seemed to contradict its sporadic claims that it supported the Cedar Revolution. Moscow also antagonised Israelis from across the political spectrum by defending Iran, which used its proxy

Hezbollah to launch rocket attacks against Israel's population. Putin's diplomatic cover for Iran's proxies in Lebanon also angered the Saudis who feared that the demise of the Sunni role in Lebanon, in accompaniment to Sunni demise in Iraq after the downfall of Saddam Hussein, would set off a Shi'a domination of the region.

Putin's Russia was caught in the midst of a tense struggle for supremacy between Iran and moderate Sunni Arab states as well as between escalating belligerence between Iran and Israel and its Western supporters. Iran's alliance with Syria was extremely profitable because the ruling regime in Damascus enjoyed many tentacles of influence with Lebanese and Palestinian groups. Although Arab speaking, Syria's political leaders belonged to a minority Alawi sect that had some bonds with Shi'a interpretations. Thus Syria was to a large extent a vital bridge for the non-Arab Iranian elite to access and influence Arab Shi'is and Palestinian groups who were connected with Syrian security organs. In fact, it was through Syria that Iran was also able to establish links with Hamas and to provide it with support, angering Saudi Arabia, Egypt and Jordan who feared that Tehran was abducting the Palestinian cause to acquire widespread popular Arab support to further undermine their governments.

Moscow's association with Tehran was meticulously manipulated by Putin during his second term in office in his battle over the installation of missile defence shields in Eastern Europe as well as other points of friction, including Russia's dispute with Georgia. Partnering a rising Iran in the region enabled Putin to exploit the weakened US position in the Middle East as a result of the Iraqi occupation to glamorise Russia's rejuvenated world status. Among the controversial actions of Putin's leadership was Moscow's role in diluting Western pressure on Tehran to allow international nuclear inspectors full access to Iran's nuclear programme. The construction of the $800 million Bushehr nuclear plant, contracted to Russia in the Yeltsin era, was intended for peaceful purposes but eventually suspicions arose that Tehran was pursuing more sinister aims. From October 2000 when 'Moscow…stepped up its efforts to complete the Iranian nuclear reactor at Bushehr (work on which had languished under Yeltsin)'[19] a new trend was established and more dangerously 'Russia—the soothing or indignant pronouncements of its leaders notwithstanding—according to many experts and officials in the area remains the world's leading source of WMD-related items and expertise proliferation.'[20] Putin and his state apparatus resiliently endorsed the Tehran regime and defended Iran's right to pursue a peaceful nuclear programme by arguing that there was little evidence that Tehran was secretly acquiring technology for nuclear weapons.

Highlighting Moscow's determination, Putin insisted that Tehran's assurances convinced 'Russia that Iran indeed does not intend to produce nuclear weapons and we will continue to develop relations in all sectors, including peaceful atomic energy.'[21] Emphasising patient negotiations as the only means to resolve Iran's dispute with the West, 'Russia (together with China) promised to veto any UNSC Chapter VII resolution imposing sanctions—to say nothing of the use of military force.'[22] Russia's resolve was tested in late 2004 when Iran began its uranium enrichment process to take its nuclear programme to a more advanced stage. To deflect Western pressure Russian Foreign Minister Sergei Lavrov travelled to Tehran in October 2004 to convince the Iranian leadership to show flexibility in order to prevent tougher UN Security Council Resolutions that would embarrass Russia. Nonetheless, Moscow remained adamant that it would not compromise its role as contractor for the Iranian nuclear programme, particularly in light of the potential financial gains for Minatom, which governs the national nuclear industry. The Bushehr plant was one of several planned reactors, up to twenty according to Tehran, and its successful completion was expected to promote Russian nuclear expertise to a wider international market in a multi-billion US dollar export sector.

Moscow's strategic support for Iran was shrewd and carefully managed to pre-empt growing international pressure and to avoid possible damage to Russia's wider policy in the Middle East. Putin modified his stance in April 2005, appropriately announcing during his visit to Israel that he proposed that Iran place all its nuclear facilities under the safeguards of the IAEA. Iran rejected the proposal and instead called for direct negotiations with the United States on the issue, otherwise it threatened to withdraw from the nuclear Non-Proliferation Treaty altogether. Russia did not want its close coordination with Iran to jeopardise its diplomatic ties with other countries in the region, particularly Israel. The surprise victory of hardliner Mahmoud Ahmadinejad in the Iranian presidential elections in June 2005 threatened to embarrass Putin, coming soon after his visit to Israel. Months after his election victory, in October 2005, Ahmadinejad suggested in a lecture to students that Israel 'must be wiped off the map'.[23] Yet Ahmadinejad's bellicose speeches did not deter Moscow from maintaining extensive relations with Tehran and Russia's dogged support for Iran in the face of widespread international criticisms reached such an extent that following Ahmadinejad's election victory, one article in a Russian newspaper asked provocatively if 'Russia Won the Elections in Iran?'[24]

In February 2006 Moscow proposed to host Iranian uranium enrichment in Russia as a safeguard that the Iranian nuclear programme would receive limited fuel quantities to preserve its peaceful nature. In a bid to offset a tough Western response Putin suggested that Russia would be one of several countries that could establish uranium enrichment centres under the supervision of the IAEA. Tehran again rejected the offer, contending as ever that Iranian sovereignty was being violated by placing its nuclear programme at the mercy of international agencies and foreign countries. In 2006, as media speculation intensified that Washington was planning a military strike against Iran's nuclear facilities Putin began demanding that Iran 'conform fully' to its international nuclear obligations but tempered this by endorsing 'the legitimate rights of the Iranian people to develop a nuclear-electric programme that is reliable'.[25] Moscow strongly endorsed a multilateral framework of negotiations with Tehran over the nuclear issue based on a 5 plus 1 formula, comprising the five Security Council Countries and Germany, as an alternative to sanctions and possible military action. Russia's proposal received broad European sympathy in light of the lingering friction with the United States over Iraq and Putin subtly benefitted from worldwide mistrust of Washington's aims.

The negative political ramifications of Russia's role in shielding and developing the Iranian nuclear sector included criticisms by the United States, Israel and other Arab countries, but the Russian leadership nonetheless saw political advantages to be gained because the crisis improved Moscow's diplomatic positioning by enabling it to demand compromises in return for any positive role it played in defusing the crisis. The anti-Bush atmosphere prevailing in Europe from 2003 encouraged the Russian leadership not to acquiesce. Internally, an indicator of Putin's toughened stance was the dismissal of Rumyantsev in 2005 as head of the Ministry of Atomic Energy and his replacement by the security services-supported Sergei Kiriyenko. This coincided with an agreement in February 2005 that allowed Russia to provide Iran with nuclear fuel following a dispute from September 2003 'over who would pay for the return of the spent fuel from the reactor, with Iran demanding that Russia pay for it and Moscow refusing'.[26]

Two years later in early 2007 a dispute over delayed payments by Iran resurfaced which led to a pause in the construction work in the Bushehr plant. There were suspicions that the suspension of work was not unrelated to diplomatic pressure being placed on Russia. Rahman Qahremanpur, a member of the Iranian parliament's National Security and Foreign Policy Committee, confessed that 'our relations with Russia are not in a normal state right now, because Russia is under intense pressure by the Americans to cut its ties with us'.[27] The dispute was eventually resolved in late March but the suspicions over the incident remained as conspiracy theories suggested that the whole confrontation was deliberately exaggerated by Moscow to give the impression that there was a genuine problem with Tehran. Despite the awkwardness of Russia's co-operation with Iran in terms of wider relations with the international community, Moscow calculated that this was not significantly harmful to national interests. On the contrary, for one analyst: 'Weapons sales, in addition to nuclear power and space co-operation, have become yet another important way to maintain the perception of Russia as a great power.'[28] The developing nuclear industry was seen as an important source of income and employed thousands of high-level scientists who would otherwise be tempted to live and work abroad. Iran had also emerged as a geostrategic lynchpin holding Russia's south together and an opinion became more prevalent in Moscow that persistent US threats to launch a military campaign against Iran belied a greater ambition by Washington and its allies to weaken and isolate Russia. The advantages of supporting Iran's nuclear programme far outweighed the disadvantages of Western, Arab and Israeli complaints.

Putin's toughened stances on a variety of issues in the Middle East during his second term, not least Iran, raised disturbing questions about Moscow's long-term objectives. A popular opinion maintained that Russia had no interest whatsoever in Iran becoming a military nuclear power because its influence would then be projected not only in the Middle East but also in Central Asia and the Caucasus, which Moscow would obviously be opposed to. There were other contrary indicators that Moscow saw benefits in such a development, especially as ever more damning evidence transpired that Tehran was going through the threshold required for a peaceful programme. During the tough years of bargaining at the United Nations Security Council in 2005 and 2006 one author noted that: 'Moscow was far more reluctant than the other powers to contemplate any form of sanctions against Iran if Tehran were, indeed, found to be developing nuclear weapons.'[29] In 2007, Ukraine's populist leader Yulia Tymoshenko openly accused Russia of strengthening Iran's hand in the nuclear crisis so that 'the sanctions now imposed by the Security Council are so tepid that they are unlikely to be effective'.[30] Ahmadinejad's blatant and vocal belligerence, including his warning in early 2007 to Britain and the United States, the 'enemies' of Iran, that 'the path you have chosen will not lead to your salvation or guidance … [but to your] destruction'.[31] only added to the sense that Russia's behaviour lacked any genuine shared concerns with the West and the United States in particular that Iran's intentions were peaceful.

UNSC Resolution 1696, adopted on 31 July 2006 in the midst of war in Lebanon between Hezbollah and Israel, failed to threaten any serious measures for non-compliance and in time proved favourable to Iran and its Lebanese proxy. Russia's role on the Security Council allowed Tehran to divert attention away from its own nuclear dispute with the United Nations by focusing on Hezbollah's war with Israel in Lebanon in 2006, implying Moscow's compliance with Iranian tactics. Public Iranian rejection of the Russian proposals regarding uranium enrichment pointed to Moscow's limitations in influencing Tehran's behaviour and conformed to reports that when Putin and Ahmadinejad met in New York in September 2005 the Iranian president bluntly told his Russian counterpart not to consider proposing any concessions by the Iranians. However, Putin was known to be a shrewd politician and there was a strong likelihood that Russia's doomed uranium enrichment proposal was made with the expectation that it would be rejected in order to deflect Western pressure on itself in light of accusations that Moscow was an integral part of a strategic triangle including Iran and Syria to weaken the US and its allies in the Middle East.

In light of the 2006 war in Lebanon Iran had emerged as an expanding if not expansionist power in the region, when also considering its established influence in Iraq and the determination to proceed in the nuclear programme. In all its schemes Russia proved to be a useful partner. Russia's stifling of various proposed UN Security Council Resolutions on these issues resulted in mounting forewarnings that either the United States or Israel would unilaterally use military action to curtail

Iranian power. In February 2007 a report by the IAEA claimed that in violation of previous agreements Iran had continued with its uranium enrichment programme, later confirmed by Tehran on the grounds that it was fulfilling its sovereign right not to succumb to international pressure. After the report was released speculation mounted about a US airstrike against Iran towards the end of the Bush presidency.

Russia continued to deflect pressure on Iran by Washington and in October 2007, Putin warned 'we should not even think of using force in this region'.[32] This unambiguous message was made by Putin during his stay in Iran, the first trip by a top Kremlin official to Tehran since Stalin's visit in 1943. Typical of Putin's style, the visit was under the guise of a broader meeting comprising the Caspian Sea states, but the event was used to solidify and bolster bilateral relations with Iran, where the Russian president met both President Ahmadinejad and the supreme leader, Ali Khaminei. Within two weeks of Putin's visit Foreign Minister Lavrov travelled to Iran on 31 October 2007 in a bid 'to talk sense into Tehran', according to the Russian media.[33] In mid-December, however, and in defiance of Washington Russia began delivery of nuclear fuel for the Bushehr plant with Russian officials claiming that the shipments would not be used for military purposes. When Putin as prime minister, met Ahmadinejad in July 2008 he re-emphasised Russia's enthusiasm for Iran to complete the construction of the nuclear plant as soon as possible, in defiance of international concerns.

The victory of Barack Obama in the US elections was received with relief and as a welcome break by the Russian leadership. Not only had Obama claimed that he wished to reset relations with Russia but in his inauguration speech he offered 'the hand of friendship' to oppressive regimes, including Iran and Syria, to make room for dialogue. Pressure was relieved during the parallel terms of Medvedev and Obama on Moscow and the likelihood of military action against Iran subsided. When Putin was elected back to the presidency in 2012 speculation had been growing that Israel would take unilateral action against Iranian nuclear facilities. Russia's pro-Iranian position was made more glaring in its support for the Asad regime, Tehran's strategic ally, against the popular uprising. After the hiatus, Putin returned in 2012 to show more than ever before as Russian leader that he would ruthlessly pursue his policies without any obligation to appease the international community and that he perceived the international order in a manner that was reminiscent of the Cold War era.

Iran: arms and trade

Moscow's growing bilateral relations with Iran included large-scale military sales further indicating that there were no worries in the Kremlin about Iran's rising power and influence. Yeltsin temporarily had caved in to US pressure not to sell advanced weapons to Iran but as soon as 'Putin became president he angered Washington by abrogating the Gore-Chernomyrdin agreement in November 2000 and resuming arms sales to Iran'.[34] Putin's action was an early statement that Russia would be looking after its own interests and that it had lost faith in pursuing pro-Western policies. President Khatami travelled to Moscow in March 2001 'to sign a new $6.5 billion arms deal. Among the weapons systems Iran was interested in were MiG-29 fighter planes and the S-300 anti-aircraft system.'[35] The deal was augmented in 2006 when Russia sold over $1 billion-worth of Tor-M1 modern air-defence systems, 'capable of protecting a target from up to 48 incoming planes or projectiles to a range of six kilometres',[36] and other military hardware to Iran. Russian media reports confirmed in early 2007 that half of the twenty-nine Tor-M1 missile systems bought by Iran had arrived and were being stationed around Iran's nuclear sites.

In late 2008, there were claims of more advanced weapons being sold to Iran by Rosoboronexport, the national arms export agency of Russia, including long range S-300 missiles. Denials by Kremlin officials did not ease Washington's concerns that these missiles threatened the security of US troops in Iraq and Afghanistan and would disrupt the regional balance of military power in the region. In March 2009, Russia's official state media confirmed that a contract to sign S-300 missiles to Iran had been signed and that it 'is being gradually executed'.[37] Israel's government spokesman Yigal Palmor revealed in 2008 that a delegation had been sent to Russia and 'we were told that Russia is keeping their promise to [Prime Minister] Ehud Olmert that Russia wouldn't do anything to jeopardise Israel's security'.[38] In 2010 President Medvedev signed a decree halting sales of long-range S-300 missiles to Iran, which directly threatened other countries in the Gulf region including Saudi Arabia as well as Israel, partly in response to international pressure.

Soon after Putin was re-elected president of Russia in 2012 hints and rumours resurfaced in Moscow that sales of the S-300 missiles to Iran would resume, especially as the collapse of the Asad regime looked more imminent. An official close to the Russian Defence Ministry reflected

Russian fears by suggesting that the 'fall of the Syrian government would significantly increase the chances of a strike on Iran' before adding that resumption of 'S-300 shipments to Iran may be a very timely decision'.[39] A Russian think tank close to the Kremlin, the Centre for Analysis and Strategic Technologies, estimated that Russia forfeited revenues worth over $1 billion by pausing the sale of S-300 missiles to Iran after 2009.[40]

Russian non-military trade with Iran also recorded significant growth under Putin. Russia's charge d'affaires in Tehran, Aleksei Dedov, noted a 43 per cent increase in the volume of trade between 2003 and 2004 alone to exceed $2 billion annually and underlining that: 'Russia views Iran solely as its regional partner, and not as a challenger.'[41] This was a significant improvement on the average $600 million annual turnover of the mid-1990s. An agreement was also reached in 2005 to unify the power grids of the two countries.[42] The rise in energy prices between 1998 and 2006 increased Iranian revenues from oil and gas from $11 billion to $40 billion annually. Yet despite this additional spending power of the Iranians, overall, bilateral trade aside from the energy and military sectors remained unimpressive, with 'Iran's share in Russian foreign trade not exceeding 1 per cent' in 2008 with a turnover of '$3.7 billion, mostly accounted for by Russian exports ($3.3 billion)'.[43] In comparison, Russian trade with Israel in 2007 was at three times the size and with Turkey trade was five times the size of that of Iran, reaching over $20 billion annually. Co-operation with Iran in the technology field was also negligible when compared to other major Asian countries, highlighted by minor projects such as the launching in October 2005 of a Russian-Iranian satellite Sina-1 to allow the transmission of Russian television programmes. By 2010 Russian trade with Iran did grow to $4.2 billion but a telling comparison revealed that in the same year bilateral trade between China and Iran was at $30 billion and grew to $40 billion in 2011.[44] China was reliant on Iran for providing its energy needs but its expanding economy also increased its capacity to replace Russia, particularly in the technology and industrial sectors.

The attraction of establishing closer economic ties with Iran was not helped by Tehran's unreliability in paying for goods and services provided by Russia. According to one estimate: 'Of the nearly $5 billion that Russia earned from arms exports to Iran in the 1990s, only about $1 billion was paid in cash.'[45] In early 2007 Iran halted its cash transfers to Russia as a form of pressure by Tehran to ensure that Moscow continued to play the role of reliable partner in its struggle with the West over its nuclear programme. Iran exported pistachios and other food products to Russia but another major obstacle to trade was that 'Freight between the two countries is possible only via the Serahs border crossing in Turkmenistan, where the wheels of the train have to be changed, since the railway tracks have a different gauge in the former Soviet Union.'[46] The failure to maximise the trade potential between the two countries was a result of a mutual reticence to view the other as an enduring strategic partner, further bolstering the view that each country saw the other as an instrument to further national goals in a broader setting.

The long-proposed prospect of an Iranian-Russian-Qatari gas troika, which would have effectively monopolised the world's gas market, was openly discussed by Russian and Iranian policy makers in 2008 and 2009 but the idea failed to materialise because of Moscow's caution about the repercussions of such a move. Despite the statement by president-elect Medvedev on 16 April 2008 that 'we support the idea of building an organisation of gas-producing countries',[47] Russia was careful not to sacrifice its multilateral efforts in the Middle East by placing all its eggs in the basket of an ultimately unstable regime in Tehran.

Turkey and Russia until Putin

From the onset of the Cold War, Turkey became a vital cog in NATO. Joining the defence alliance in 1952, Turkey was the only NATO member directly bordering the Soviet Union that provided the possibility of opening a military ground offensive on its soft southern underbelly. The politically dominant military leadership in Turkey was extremely hostile towards leftist political parties and brutally targeted communist party members in the country. Throughout the Soviet era Moscow was critical of the banning of the Turkish Communist Party and irritated Ankara by supporting the rights of the Kurdish separatists.

A visit by Soviet President Nikolai Podgorny to Turkey 1973 reflected the atmosphere of US-Soviet détente at the time, culminating in the 1978 Understanding on Good Neighbourliness and Co-operation but relations remained largely strained until Gorbachev's New Thinking dominated Soviet foreign policy during the late 1980s. The simultaneous emergence of the politically agile Turgut Ozal in Turkish politics facilitated a rethink of bilateral relations and his first visit to Moscow in

1986, as prime minister, marked a significant change in Turkish attitudes. Ozal, who became president of Turkey in 1989, was a proponent of strengthening relations with Moscow in order to diminish Soviet backing for the Kurds and also importantly to restrain Syria, which supported radical Kurdish separatists. The Syrian-Turkish territorial dispute over the Hatay Province, also known as the Sanjak of Alexandretta, a historic region in the northern Levant with a significant Arab-speaking population, regularly threatened to lead to a military confrontation between the two countries during the 1980s. Ozal hoped that the pacification of Moscow would be translated into forcing Syria to tone down its claims to the disputed territories and discourage it from using the Kurds as pawns to force Turkey into a settlement.

Among Ozal's enduring achievements was the expansion of bilateral trade relations so that during the Putin era Russia became Turkey's most important trading partner in the world after Germany. This development marked a remarkable change in perception and interaction compared to the Cold War. Turkish reevaluation of its northern neighbour was reciprocated because from the 1980s the Soviet leadership considered it important to consolidate its vulnerable southern borders, particularly in light of the rise of Islamic extremism in Iran and Afghanistan, by building solid relations with secular Turkey. Thus despite ongoing political challenges confronting the two countries in the 1990s, such as the conflict between Armenia and Azerbaijan, there was great emphasis to ensure continued improvement in relations that reflected the high importance Turkey and Russia afforded each other in the post-Soviet era.

The two countries shared similarities in that they were remnants of former larger empires and 'like Russia, Turkey has Caucasian, Balkan, Middle Eastern and European identities and different interests at stake in all of these regions'.[48] Like its Ottoman predecessor, Turkey was a natural geographic barrier to Russia's expansion south towards the Middle East. In the post-Soviet era the growing significance of the transit of oil and gas transformed Turkey into an important battleground for supply routes from East to West. Within weeks of the lowering of the Red Flag from the Kremlin, Turkish Foreign Minister Hikmet Cetin flew to Moscow on 20 January in 1992 to initiate a dynamic reciprocity in high-level visits that year, including a visit by Kozyrev to Ankara in February and President Suleiman Demirel's visit to Russia on 25–26 May 1992.

These visits established a framework of understanding on a variety of issues and included a renewed commitment to the principles of good neighbourliness and co-operation agreed upon in the late-1970s. On 25 June 1992 Yeltsin visited Istanbul to represent Russia in the Black Sea Economic Co-operation Summit, which included first time participation by leaders of the newly independent former Soviet states. Diplomatic visits and activities maintained a similar momentum for the remainder of the 1990s and included a two-day visit to Russia by Prime Minister Tansu Ciller on 8 September 1993, while Russian Prime Minister Viktor Chernomyrdin travelled to Turkey on 15 December 1997. This was the first visit by a Russian prime minister to Turkey since the Soviet era. The high-level diplomatic visits in four years between 1992 and 1996 produced fifteen separate agreements and protocols on political, economic, military and cultural matters and although there was a short lull in the late 1990s the vibrancy quickly resumed under Putin.

Turkish-Russian politics and trade

Among the most impressive success stories in twenty years of post-Soviet Russian foreign relations was the dramatic turnaround in Russian-Turkish economic ties. This was achieved despite lingering suspicions in Moscow that Turkey's political elite harboured hidden ambitions to acquire influence in the Caucasus and Central Asia on the basis of a Turkic connection. Putin inherited a pattern of improvement in bilateral relations after a difficult start under Yeltsin and a blip of tensions that emerged between Russia and Turkey between 1996 and 1998 when Foreign Minister Primakov endorsed the prospect of installing S-300 missile systems on the Greek-Cypriot portion of the island. The Turkish military strongly rejected the move as a direct challenge to national security and implied the threat of force to prevent their installation.

Throughout the 1990s, while Russia was undergoing military reductions in terms of troop numbers and equipment Turkey was rapidly expanding its military capabilities. The election of Necmettin Erbakan as Turkey's first Islamist prime minister in June 1996 created added unease in Moscow because he had expressed sympathy with the Chechen cause. Primakov's floating of the possibility of installing the S-300 missiles in Greek-Cyprus appeared to be a manoeuvre to remind Erbakan of Russia's reach. The Russian leadership was suspicious about Turkey providing logistical support to Chechnya during and after the 1994–1996 war, which considerably weakened Moscow's grip on the recalcitrant Caucasian republic.

In 1999, relations began improving rapidly again after Erbakan was pressured into resigning in mid-1997 by the Turkish military and Russia withdrew plans to install the missiles in Cyprus. This détente occurred in parallel to a warming of relations between Greece and Turkey. The positive atmosphere was made possible by Ankara's general active pursuit of a co-operative policy towards Moscow at the time Putin was elected president in 2000 in line with the adopted strategy of 'normalisation with the neighbourhood, a concept developed by Ahmet Davutoglu—an influential advisor to PM [Recep Tayyip] Erdogan and FM [Abdullah] Gul—[which] helped the convergence to come about'.[49] Davutoglu, with a similar pragmatic diplomatic mindset to that of Primakov in Russia, was later named Turkish minister of foreign affairs in May 2009.

In response to Russia's financial crisis in 1998 Moscow could ill afford the deterioration of relations with Turkey and co-operation resumed with greater urgency. The blatant pro-Western approach in Russia had subsided when Putin was elected in 2000 and a new pragmatic nationalist policy dominated but this did not hinder the improvement of relations with Turkey but rather helped promote them because Russian disappointment with the detached West necessitated greater priority being afforded to influential countries closer to home. In his bid to promote better bilateral relations, 'Putin lamented the fact that a Russo-Turkish political agreement lags behind economic ties'[50] in light of the power the two countries possessed to counter threats in the Middle East and Central Asia. The new policy initiated by Primakov encouraged a multi-polar world and close co-ordination with large Eurasian states, including China, India, Iran and Turkey, placing them at the heart of Russian national interests.

The positive developments were first materialised in an action plan signed in New York in November 2001 by Foreign Ministers Ismail Cem and Igor Ivanov outlining trade and tourism as the backbone of long-term relations between the two countries. The plan, entitled From Bilateral Relations to Multidimensional Relations, created mechanisms of co-operation ranging from fighting terrorism to co-ordination on Caucasian and Central Asian Affairs. A positive outcome of this transformation, for Turkey at least, was Russia's closing down of the office of the PKK, Kurdish Workers Party, in Moscow and an asylum request by Kurdish rebel Abdullah Ocalan was refused, leading to his eventual capture by Turkish authorities.

The US war on terror and the invasion of Iraq further added to Turkey's significance for Moscow because of its strategic location, leading one veteran expert of Russian foreign policy to claim, in the context of the Iraq war in 2003, that 'Only three countries in the region are of primary significance to Moscow, and these are Iran, Iraq and Turkey.'[51] Moscow's efforts to consolidate relations with Turkey were boosted by rising Turkish nationalism and sense of affinity with fellow Muslims, which was energised by Bush's declared war on terror and the invasion of Iraq, both perceived among ordinary Muslims as a war on Islam. The political and economic policy elites in Turkey considered 'enhanced relations with Russia as a counterweight to ties with the EU and the United States, should Ankara run into problems with Washington with regard to the war in Iraq or with Brussels during EU accession talks'.[52]

The perceived snobbery by the EU in the handling of Turkey's application for membership created a popular resentment by Turks and, more significantly, hostility transpired towards the West by nationalist elements among Ankara's rising political and security leaderships. As a reflection of this trend, 'In March 2002, the secretary general of the Turkish National Security Council, General Tuncer Kılınç, declared that Turkey should form an "alliance" with Russia.'[53] Turkey, like Saudi Arabia, was opposed to the invasion of Iraq not out of any particular sympathy for Saddam Hussein but because of predications that it would drastically alter the delicate regional balance, taking into account all its religious and ethnic intricacies. Saudi Arabia's primary concern was the influence Iran would acquire because of the strengthening of the Shi'is but for Turkey there was also a deep anxiety that the war would unleash a widespread Kurdish uprising launched from the independent Kurdish entity in northern Iraq.

Ankara was particularly nervous because of public debates in Washington about dividing Iraq into three autonomous entities based on schemes by hawkish members of the Bush administration to reformat the Middle East. This implied the carving of existing nations to accommodate disaffected minorities. Iraqi Kurdish leaders had been working closely with Washington during the 1990s on ways to topple the Saddam Hussein regime and after the invasion they openly presented themselves as US allies. Iraqi Kurdistan in the post-Saddam era enjoyed unprecedented autonomy and this breathed new separatist hopes for Kurds in neighbouring countries, including Syria and Turkey. The traditional political stalwarts of Iraq's Kurds for decades, Massoud Barzani who became president of the Kurdistan Regional Government and Jalal Talabani who became president of Iraq, displayed caution by not challenging internationally recognised borders and they distanced themselves from radical Kurdish movements in Turkey and Syria. Ankara nonetheless blamed the Iraqi Kurdish leadership for sheltering PKK rebels who had conducted military operations in Turkey. Tension between Iraqi Kurdistan and Turkey resulted in frequent shelling by the Turkish army of Kurdish targets within Iraq and fighting escalated so that in late 2007 the Turkish parliament authorised its government to approve cross border military operations for one year to hunt down PKK militants in northern Iraq.

Despite military clashes on the Iraq-Turkey border the leadership in Ankara acted with relative restraint in light of the US occupation of Iraq. A former Indian Ambassador to Turkey noted that: 'March 2003 was a watershed when the Turkish Parliament rejected the government motion (with 2/3rd majority in the Parliament) to allow' the US army 'to open a second front against Iraq from Turkish soil'.[54] Four months earlier Turks had elected an Islamist government that took the country away from the staunchly secularist past it was known for but the new government was keen to show it was moderate and sought to reassure both Moscow and Washington that it was a stable force in Turkish politics. It continued the strong rejection of Kurdish separatism by former governments and at the same time emphasised the importance of the country's strategic alliance with the United States. The Islamist leadership even actively developed relations with Israel while it vocally supported the Palestinian right to statehood.

Turkey's new orientation nonetheless endeavoured to tone down excessive reliance on the United States after several episodes that led to disillusionment, particularly regarding Washington's support for the Kurds and over the Congressional support for the Armenian genocide. Ankara actively promoted good relations with its neighbours, including Greece, Syria and Iran specifically as a counterbalance to US unreliability. Annoyance at Washington's evident support for Kurdish autonomy and its strategic shortsightedness which had strengthened Iran in the region was compounded by a sense in Ankara that the United States had after 2006 become weak in defending moderate forces in the Middle East as well as pro-democracy movements in Central Asia. To further irritate the Turks the Bush administration failed in October 2007 to prevent the US Congress from formally acknowledging the Armenian genocide as a historic fact. Turkey's foreign minister, Abdullah Gul, warned Washington in response that 'as the elected government of democratic Turkey, we would not be able to remain indifferent'.[55] In a climate of growing Turkish disenchantment with the United States Ankara and Moscow downplayed their main differences over Russia's longstanding support for the Kurds.

Russia and Turkey also overcame a historic dispute over the Straits of the Bosphorus and the Dardanelles, Russia's naval gateway out of the Black Sea and into the world. Moscow was aware that 'up to 25 percent of Russian foreign trade to the Mediterranean [passed] through the Black Sea Straits'.[56] Turkey had long claimed that unrestricted shipping through the Straits posed an environmental hazard, particularly to the 11 million population of Istanbul. Ankara argued that the narrow straits were located on densely populated coastal cities and, if shipping was left unregulated, especially with regard to nuclear warships, would create risk on a catastrophic scale. Turkey insisted on the terms of the Montreux Convention of 1936 that allowed it to control access of military ships from other nations while maintaining the principle of the freedom of shipping for cargo and trade. Tensions first emerged in July 1994 when Turkey introduced restrictive measures and again applied further restrictions in December 2002 that led Russian Prime Minister Mikhail Kasyanov to protest in May 2003 that 'decisions to change cargo transit rules should never be taken unilaterally'.[57]

Differences over the Straits were submerged after 2003 in recognition of mutual political interests and under Putin there was special emphasis on developing the economic sector. Few examples better illustrated Putin's added dimension of raising the priority of economic relations to foreign policy than that of Turkey, which aside from the financial meltdown in 1998 had witnessed a consistent growth rate in bilateral trade since the end of the Soviet era. Moscow successfully nurtured the emergence of Turkey as a major trading partner in the region and as a comparative example, Russia's volume of trade with Armenia, Azerbaijan and Georgia in the Caucasus in 1996 'was less than 5 per cent of the 1991 trade figures, and for Central Asia only about 10 per cent' whereas trade with Turkey grew by over 50 per cent in the same period.[58] Under Putin the growth rate in the value of bilateral economic relations was even more impressive, with the volume of trade doubling between 2003 and 2004 to reach almost $10 billion annually.[59]

Following Putin's historic visit to Turkey in December 2004 there were four meetings between the Russian president and Prime Minister Erdogan in 2005 and in that year the volume of bilateral trade reached an all-time high of $15 billion with the goal being set to reaching over $25 billion in 2008.[60] Tourism was a particularly flourishing sector and by 2010 Russia overtook Germany in the annual number of tourists visiting Turkey. The growth rate continued on target and when Putin met with Erdogan in December 2012 Russia was Turkey's largest trading partner 'mainly in Russia's favour…The two countries boast that two-way trade will triple to some $100 billion in the coming years'.[61] Impressively, the meeting took place with the backdrop of the violence in Syria dominating international affairs as Moscow and Ankara stood at opposite ends of the spectrum, with Turkey supporting the popular revolution. Russia also conveniently overlooked the deployment of Patriot missiles in Turkey across the border with Syria, which in other circumstances could have been an unacceptable disruption to the military balance in the region.

Economic relations between the two countries were diverse, yet central to these ties was the construction of a new energy transportation infrastructure to deliver gas to the European Union and the Mediterranean Sea. The geo-strategic significance of this new energy infrastructure was immense and consequently Russian-Turkish relations were marked by contradictions in the Putin era with regard to the gas pipelines issue. Turkey's strategic position was unrivalled in terms of pipeline routes and according to one study in 2007, 'Ten producers, with 35.5 percent of global gas reserves, are or might potentially be interested in using Turkey as a transit country to the EU.'[62] Turkey's largest share of gas imports arrived from Russia followed by neighbouring Iran. The gas network project known as Blue Stream took Russian gas via 1,250 kilometres of pipelines under the Black Sea, emerging in Samsun on the Turkish coast and reaching the capital Ankara. From there it was planned to extend the route to the Eastern Mediterranean, potentially supplying Israel and Lebanon as well as other states in the Middle East. The gains from the

Blue Stream venture with Turkey were offset by direct competition as Russia looked for alternative outlets. Russia initiated work in 2009 for a South Stream project that extended the pipelines network from below the Black Sea to southern Europe through Bulgaria. As a result of these and other projects Russia in the Putin era had expanded an energy pipeline infrastructure bridging Asia and Europe to empower Moscow in its strategic bargaining position vis-à-vis Europe and the West in general.

Western governments promoted trans-Turkish pipeline routes from the Caspian Basin countries to undermine a Russian monopoly of energy supplies to Europe and promote diversification of suppliers and routes. Chief among Moscow's objections was the Baku-Tbilisi-Ceyhan pipeline, taking Azeri and Kazakh oil to the West, because it was considered 'as a challenge to its status in the Caspian basin and an obstacle to its oil trade'.[63] Turkey's heavy dependence on Russia for gas, accounting for half of its total gas imports since 2004, complicated matters further because Ankara preferred not to antagonise Moscow by challenging its regional energy strategy.[64] Alexei Miller, as Gazprom Chief Executive Officer, accompanied Putin to Turkey in December 2004 to enhance strategic co-operation in the gas sector so that during Putin's second term, sources suggested that Turkey imported 65 per cent of its natural gas and 20 per cent of its oil from Russia.[65] The contradictory role of Turkey as a major energy-dependent customer and energy transportation rival was deftly handled by Moscow and Ankara in order to allow development of bilateral relations to flourish. In 2012 Turkey not only reached agreement for Russia to build a second pipeline through its territories but also to construct its first nuclear power facility.

Beyond economics Russia's foreign policy elite rated Turkey as a military power that required special consideration. Turkey boasted a 'military establishment that is the largest in the region with approximately 625,000 active duty military personnel' instantly making it a 'formidable military actor even without considering its critically important ties to NATO'.[66] Turkish military spending more than doubled to $6.8 billion in 1996 from a decade earlier and continued to grow steadily while post-Soviet Russia struggled to maintain expenditure on the basic infrastructure of its armed forces.[67] Consequently, under Putin there was an increasing trend towards developing military coordination, beginning with the naval Black Sea Force that was formed in April 2001 and comprised Turkey, Russia, Romania, Bulgaria and Georgia. Significantly the venture was 'the first time Turkey and Russia [were] participating as part of a joint military contingent in 500 years of bilateral relations.[68] As a further gesture of mutual trust in 2008 a Russian and Turkish military band performed together in the Kremlin, a minor but symbolically meaningful event.

The leadership around Putin was keenly aware that while the Russian army was demoralised the Turkish armed forces grew by 20 per cent in the 1990s and became 'capable of fielding within a short period of time over 1 million troops'.[69] Such factors encouraged Russia under Putin to sell Russian arms to Turkey and also to work on joint military-industrial projects, of which a showpiece was the $4.5 billion deal involving attack helicopters built in partnership with Israel. This was a major breakthrough considering that a 'request that NATO markets be opened to Russian-manufactured weapons was rejected by the NATO negotiators' under Yeltsin.[70] Turkey was a force to be reckoned with but Moscow also understood Ankara's problems, such as Kurdish separatism, a fragmented Iraq and a difficult Syrian regime and all these problems created useful opportunities for closer co-ordination.

As a result of the pragmatism shown by both leaderships, bilateral co-operation adopted an approach that focused on shared national security interests based on stabilisation rather than conflict. With Ankara's defence elite diversifying its arms suppliers to include Russia and promoting interdependence on the political and economic fronts, the image of Turkey as a NATO wedge driven into Russia's southwest region faded during the Putin era to the extent that the two countries began exploring geo-strategic partnerships, particularly with regards to the Caucasus and Central Asia. Putin's visit to India in December 2004 preceded his visit to Turkey in the same month, during which notions of a Eurasian foreign policy in the midst of concerns about US hegemony were revived. It was duly noted that: 'Primakov was obsessed with the idea of strategic alliance among Moscow, New Delhi, and Beijing. But some political analysts seem to believe that it would be unwise to underestimate Ankara's potential to become Russia's strategic partner as well.'[71] The security relationship followed the lead of trade relations and 'in 2008 Medvedev stated that Turkey is becoming Russia's "Strategic Partner" and in 2010 Turkey officially struck Russia from its "list of external security threats"'.[72] Such propositions were an indication that Russian-Turkish relations had come a long way under Putin.

Rivalry in the Caucasus and Central Asia

Despite the initial Western orientation, Russia after 1991 could not neglect building relations with the countries of the former Soviet Union, taking into consideration 'economic links, finances, transportation, military facilities, troops and not least the fate of some 25 million ethnic Russians residing outside the Russian Federation'.[73] It was unsurprising therefore that the initially exclusive Western outlook by Moscow's foreign policy elite rapidly faltered. Russia's relations with its Central Asian and Caucasian neighbours, which became sovereign independent states free to pursue their own foreign policy, took on a greater significance when factoring in Turkish and Iranian behaviour and ambitions. In the mid-1990s, while the war in Chechnya was raging, a festering suspicion emerged in Moscow that sinister forces were at play on its southern border with the intent of undermining the unity of the Russian Federation. To reassure Moscow, Iran took particular care to co-operate with Russia on a wide range of issues including the civil war in Tajikistan, the Armenia-Azerbaijan war and the dispute over the Caspian Sea. In contrast, taking note of historical experience and its dominant regional role, Turkey in the early 1990s was 'viewed by Russia as a traditional geopolitical rival in the Caucasus and Central Asian region'.[74] Another observation noted that suspicion prevailed of 'an expansionist aspect to Turkey's penetration of the South Caucasus and Central Asia ... [that was] common to large parts of Russia's defence establishment'.[75]

Despite the challenging mutual perceptions, bilateral relations between Turkey and Russia reached ever higher levels of co-ordination and economic interdependence. The urgency to resolve the historical competitiveness in the Caucasus and Central Asia became all the more compelling for the stability of a vast region stretching from the Black Sea to China, especially in view of the trilateral dynamics involving Iran. During Putin's presidency until the second half of 2002 Moscow adopted a Western-leaning approach when 'in the summits in Rome in May 2002 and Moscow in June 2002, the United States, NATO and Russia formally agreed to work toward a co-operative security regime throughout the CIS'.[76] But the election victory of the Islamist AK party in November 2002 led to a re-evaluation in Moscow that Turkey would revitalise pan-Turkism and pan-Islamism on its southern rim.

Significantly, when the Federation Treaty was signed on 31 March 1992 all of Russia's republics signed except Chechnya and Tatarstan, both with strong Turkic-Muslim associations. The success of the Islamist AK party in Turkey clashed with the character of the Putin presidency at the time, which placed heavy emphasis on the Slavonic and Christian character of Russia when the 'demonisation and continued repression of the Chechens'[77] threatened to spill over to other Muslim peoples in the Russian Federation and the post-Soviet space. The dynamics of relations with Turkey in the context of the Caucasus and Central Asia also had global implications. Turkey was perceived in Moscow as the Western Trojan Horse in southwestern and central Asia, and thus Iran was considered a useful obstacle to such goals. Moscow's dilemma was that if Iran became too strong and influential, radical Islam would spread into the Central Asian republics and the Caucasus and eventually also undermine the integrity of the Russian Federation.

During Putin's first term, apparent Russian retreat in Central Asia was speeded up by the 11 September 2001 attacks in the United States. Washington's aggressive anti-terrorism policy, instigated by the invasion of Afghanistan and the toppling of the Taliban, naturally heightened Washington's interest in the bordering Central Asian republics. In September 2001 the US Congress granted Uzbekistan $25 million for weapons and in January 2002 Washington committed to Uzbekistan '$100 million of the $4 billion that Congress has allocated for fighting terrorism'.[78] In December 2001, neighbouring Tajikistan allowed the US-led coalition to use an airbase at Kulob, 40 kilometres from the Afghan border to fight against the Taliban. Kyrgyzstan also permitted use of an airbase on its territory that remained in operation although its future was in April 2010 placed in doubt following the uprising that toppled President Kurmanbek Bakiev. With the US invasion of Iraq in 2003 further consolidating the impression of American hegemony, commentators during Putin's first term concluded that: 'September 11 has had the effect of rendering the erosion of Russian influence and power in the region more visible.'[79]

Russia's position in the Caucasus during Putin's first term encountered similar retreat, despite Moscow's energetic efforts to project an image of power through its second war in Chechnya. Azerbaijan and Georgia brazenly detached themselves from the Russian orbit and marketed themselves as an extension of the Western community with the Baku-Tbilisi-Ceyhan pipeline serving as a physical spine to the strategic road from the Caspian Sea to the West via Turkey. Only Armenia, a perennial enemy of the Turks and in conflict with Azerbaijan, presented itself to Russia as a reliable ally. In order to further consolidate a strategic balance Armenia also nurtured relations with Iran, historic rival of Turkey in the Caucasus. Russian-Iranian relations therefore emerged in the Caucasus, and to some extent in Central Asia, to serve as a strategic balance to the US-Turkish coalition.

These developments consolidated conclusions in the Russian National Security Concept that was released on 17 December 1997, which warned that the main potential threat was 'the deployment by great powers, or by their coalitions, of armed forces in regions close to Russia's borders'.[80] Moscow proved to be diplomatically adept under Putin in eroding this threat and transforming the polarised scenario until 2002 by strengthening bilateral relations with Turkey and promoting a level of interdependence which, by the second term of the Putin presidency undermined Azerbaijan and to a larger extent a more defiant Georgia to bolster Russia's overall standing in the region. This was starkly emphasised when Russian troops entered Georgia in the summer of 2008 and barely a whimper of opposition was heard in Iran or Turkey. The nurturing of relations with Turkey in spite of the historic challenges signalled a triumph of Russian diplomacy built over the course of the decade and was a vindication of Putin's emphasis on economic relations, as highlighted by the Turkish example, as a cornerstone of national geo-strategic interests. The consolidation of relations with Turkey in particular assisted in safeguarding Russian unity and reasserted Moscow's dominant role in Central Asia and the Caucasus. This success was further underlined considering the trend towards regional fragmentation prevalent in Russia during the late Yeltsin era.

Similar motives intent on bolstering security on its southern rim explained Russian efforts to nurture good relations with Iran during the Yeltsin and Putin presidencies. Iran's growing influence in the Middle East through its alliance with Syria and support for Hamas and Hezbollah led Russia's elite to develop and upgrade relations with Tehran under Putin because it indirectly meant that Russian global reach and influence would also be expanded. This was a primary aim of Putin's because it solidified Russia's image as a global player which, in turn, restored a sense of national pride by enabling Moscow to appear as a more effective balance to the United States. This approach did not negate the argument that Russia's relations with Iran were guided by concerns on its door step in the Caucasus and Central Asia. On the contrary, the projection of global power strengthened Russia's position vis-à-vis its smaller and more vulnerable neighbours.

A similar argument with a strategic emphasis suggested that Iran was an important Eurasian pole that added weight to Primakov's 1998 proposal for an alliance with China and India to counter US power and NATO expansion by creating strong multi-polar alliances in the international system. Iran's strategic location on the northern Gulf and its rich abundance in oil and gas was particularly significant in the East-West balance of the international system. There was nonetheless a persistent counter claim that: 'Russia's primary interest in Iran has involved the latter's proximity to the Caucasus and Central Asia region, not its position in the Persian Gulf.'[81] In reality though, Tehran's capabilities proved to be limited in the Caucasus and Central Asia. The main concern with Iran in the 1990s was its influence in Persian Tajikistan but there continued to be a strong pro-Iran lobby in Moscow that pointed to its role as an important barrier to Western penetration not only in the Middle East but also the Caspian Basin.

Iran displayed generous sensitivity to Russian insecurity over national fragmentation and bordering threats and this was highlighted when in 1999, as war with Chechnya re-ignited for a second time in a decade, Iranian President Khatami expressed to visiting Foreign Minister Igor Ivanov 'his government's respect for Russia's territorial integrity'.[82] Iran also showed itself to be largely co-operative with Russian efforts to resolve the conflict in Tajikistan because Tehran was more concerned about attaining backing from Moscow in the face of US pressure over a range of issues, chief among them being the country's nuclear programme. Russian and Iranian convergence of interests was similarly evident on Afghanistan, particularly after 2001, as both countries considered US and Pakistani intervention and influence there as undesirable. Moscow and Tehran were both eager to stifle the possibility that Afghanistan would become a pro-Western launching ground for interference in Central Asian and Iranian affairs.

The energy aspect of trilateral relations between Iran, Turkey and Russia and its geo-strategic impact on Central Asia and the Caucasus was as complex and crucial as territorial and ethno-religious factors. Kazakhstan, Azerbaijan, Turkmenistan and Uzbekistan enjoyed significant oil reserves while Turkmenistan possessed large gas fields followed by

Kazakhstan and Uzbekistan, with Azerbaijan in fourth place. The quantity of energy reserves in the Caspian Basin was disputed but the littoral states, Russia, Iran, Azerbaijan, Kazakhstan and Turkmenistan, could not agree on a framework of demarcation for the landlocked sea. After sixteen meetings the special working group of Caspian states concluded in January 2005 that it could not even find a common agreement on the legal status of the sea and the issue remained open-ended thereafter.

The dispute was somewhat more multifaceted than typical reporting about whether the Caspian Sea was defined as a sea or a lake because in both cases there were differing interpretations of law governing the way it should be divided. There was likewise a general but simplistic tendency to place Russia and Iran on the same side of the dispute against Azerbaijan because until 1991 the sea was divided between Iran and the Soviet Union. Initially there was some alignment in Russian and Iranian interests over the Caspian Basin, with the two countries stressing the value of pre-1991 treaties. Tehran and Moscow were also determined to hinder US influence in the Caucasus and Central Asia and 'neither [was] keen on seeing Azerbaijan flourish as an independent state, Iran for fear that it would exert a pull on Iran's own sizeable Azeri minority'.[83] Iran and Russia shared the view that the division of the undersea Caspian on the basis of national delineation among the five littoral states was not in their interests, in part because it would pave the way for separate military agreements that would allow external countries to enter and partly because it would leave 'the vast majority of the sea's hydrocarbons in the hands of Azerbaijan, Kazakhstan and Turkmenistan'.[84]

To Iran's displeasure, in 1998 Russia shifted from insistence on common sovereignty over the whole of the sea after 'strong lobbying by the oil industry forced the Russian government to gradually move towards a compromise approach'.[85] This left Iran isolated, particularly after it had adopted a more belligerent posture towards Azerbaijan but it too eventually presented a compromise solution by accepting the principle of national delineation while insisting on the division of the seabed resources equally among the five surrounding countries, giving Iran a 20 per cent share even though it only had 12 per cent of the seashore. By then Moscow had accepted the principle argued by Azerbaijan, Kazakhstan and Turkmenistan of delimiting the sea based on national shorelines although differences continued on the method of outlining median lines and whether the entire sea should be divided or in parts by separating the seabed, surface and water mass.

Thus while Russia favoured the division of the seabed alone, leaving the surface available for common use, Iran considered that the whole sea should be divided. Consequently, during Putin's first term as president Russia and Iran did not share the same view on the Caspian Sea status as was sometimes reported. Putin and Iranian President Khatami met in March 2001 in an effort to prevent an escalation of the dispute and an agreement was reached between them 'not to recognise any borders in the Caspian Sea until its legal status was resolved'.[86] In July of 2001 and a few months after the meeting Iran massed troops on the border with Azerbaijan and deployed a naval vessel to sabotage oil exploration missions sponsored by BP-Amoco. This resulted in tacit Turkish and US warnings to Iran to respect Azerbaijani sovereignty or face military consequences. In 2002 the first summit-level meeting of all five states took place in Turkmenistan to attempt to resolve the issue but the 'talks ended without any progress in settling the dispute about the legal status of the sea'.[87] In August of that year Russia celebrated 280 years of Peter the Great's Caspian campaigns with a naval show of power that included 'sixty ships and 10,000 troops'.[88] The exhibition merely underlined the volatility of the Caspian region and the unresolved differences among the littoral states.

Moscow's position drew closer to that of Tehran's after 2003, particularly as the other three states contesting the Caspian Sea were insistent on a technical demarcation process based on existing shorelines that was to their advantage because of the uneven division of resources of the Caspian and the nature of its geographic shape. However, relations remained uneasy and soured considerably in 2012 when Russia accused Iran of using fake companies to acquire a 25 per cent stake in the strategically important Astrakhan Port. Russian officials even went so far as to threaten to take the matter to the United Nations as a violation of the sanctions regime but the Kremlin overruled Russia's economic lobbies that were seeking to limit Iranian competition in view of broader joint interests with Tehran.

Ultimately though, according to one opinion 'both Iran and Russia are on the losing end of the Caspian equation' that divided seabed and sea surface sovereignty on the basis of the existing shorelines.[89] Russia was ultimately not interested in aggravating the disputes over the Caspian basin because its regional influence was unrivalled and Moscow's greater fear was that the radical Iranian regime, confronted with the challenge of a growing impoverished population 'may be inclined to use military force in the Caspian Sea to reinvigorate their lost authority and galvanise public support'.[90] This risked Western intervention in the Caspian which would undermine Moscow's strategy and core objectives in the region.

Because of the disputes over the Caspian Sea and the energy wealth hidden in natural reserves, as well as the securing of routes for the free transportation of oil and gas, it was unsurprising that 'the most important rivalry in the Southern Tier is the one that is evolving between the United States and Russia, which has at its centre issues of oil and gas transportation'.[91] A shared sovereignty settlement was preferred by Moscow because it excluded the United States and NATO from the Basin and both Russia and Iran were not in favour of a Western-sponsored trans-Caspian pipeline that would bypass both countries. A division of sovereignty approach, conversely, opened the door for Western and US entry into the disputed region. Natural gas, unlike oil, was more difficult and requiring expensive pipeline networks to transport it became a particularly contentious product in international relations. Instability stemming from Caspian Sea rivalries was potentially disruptive to West European demand and could damage relations between Russia and NATO. Yet Russia under Putin considered itself as the rightful security master of the former Soviet landmass and actively sought to stifle any opportunity for the United States and NATO to access a foothold in the region by imposing its own peace.

The construction of a coherent Russian foreign policy from 1996 was definitive in terminating the heavy emphasis on Western orientation and moving towards fostering regional relations closer to home. According to one observer, 'Political leaders of all movements from ultra-nationalist to communists philosophise about geographical space as the most important determinant of the nation's development, and the foreign policy of all states is interpreted almost exclusively in geopolitical terms.'[92] One of the key aims of this new policy was 'denying, as much as possible, non-CIS states and NATO any military-security access or engagement in the Caucasus and Central Asia'.[93] As in the example of the Caspian disputes, including tensions between Iran and Azerbaijan, 'a conflict could easily expand beyond the borders of the Caspian littoral to Turkey and other states'.[94] Relations with Turkey and Iran thus, while important in the Middle East context for enhancing Russian global influence, also became a crucial component of Russia's immediate national security objectives and maintaining strong relations and a degree of influence with the two states became a paramount goal.

11

CONCLUSION

REVOLUTIONS, TYRANTS AND PUTIN

The election of Dmitry Medvedev as Russian president in the spring of 2008 was a stage-managed event, reminiscent of the hollow elections during Soviet times. Medvedev inherited a more centralised state, with a pyramid-like political structure. Russian nationalism and orthodoxy became informal doctrines to be obediently followed by the mainstream and there was little tolerance of fringe or minority opinions that threatened authority. The security agencies, loyal to Putin, surfaced to enforce the unity of the peoples of the Federation. The media was brought under a tight leash, independent journalists were marginalised and many were murdered in mysterious circumstances. Wealthy and powerful opponents of the Kremlin leadership risked exile, faced imprisonment or worse. The economy was also more tightly controlled as the Putin-led clique took direct control of every major sector.

Four years later Medvedev was unceremoniously shoved aside when he finished his term, allowing Putin to return to the top of the pyramid and lead directly from the top. The emphasis on the power and centralisation of the state reflected itself in foreign policy. Russia began to demand respect on the world stage to erase the memory of humiliation that characterised the Yeltsin era. Putin's foreign policy was guided by more than wounded pride as economic factors became highly prioritised. Oil and gas, military sales, nuclear expertise, banking and finance and other important sectors of the economy demanded a Russia that was outward looking and competitive. By 2005 'Russia captured almost one quarter of the arms market in the developing world.'[1] It was not workable in Putin's mind to be a tiger at home and a mouse abroad. In addition to this there was that lingering suspicion among Russians and their politicians that the West was not to be trusted.

Yet, perhaps typically, Russia under Putin remained an enigma. There was another side to Putinism beyond the view of a centralised state with pseudo-imperialist ambitions. Putin himself respected the constitutional limit on his presidency and gave way to a younger and politically softer candidate, without significant links to the security services and who was generally more digestible for Western leaders. Society and culture also witnessed rapid development as more Russians travelled abroad and enjoyed access to the latest technological gadgets. Middle-class Russians were able to get the latest international and local news, even on their national television channels such as *RTR*'s 24-hour news channel, with relative objectivity. Of course there were taboos, such as any criticism of the president or prime minister (when Putin held that post), but Russians in the opposition could access the internet for independent discussion and get news about their leader's failings from international sources. Young people also had the option of disengaging from politics and living in a vibrant pop culture or alternative sub-cultures. Russian social developments at least quashed any comparisons between modern Russia and the Soviet Union.

Under Putin, US-Russian relations were characterised by a degree of competition for resources and influence but they never transcended into direct confrontation. Moscow was keen to promote co-operation with the West where possible, as long as Russia's security, economic and political concerns were respected. Putin was successful in convincing the West, sometimes forcefully, that Russia required a wider berth in international affairs than was the case under Yeltsin. This was typified in late 2011 and 2012 when Russia blocked international efforts to support the revolution in Syria by preventing the United Nations Security Council from taking decisive action. Despite the brutal crackdown by the Syrian regime and the risk of upsetting a horrified Western public opinion, Moscow explicitly offered Syria's Asad a lifeline for political survival because of fears that its interests in Syria and in the region would be undercut in case the regime was overthrown.

CONCLUSION: REVOLUTIONS, TYRANTS AND PUTIN

The double-headed eagle

Considered in pre-Christian times to be an expression of power, the double-headed eagle came to symbolise a political vision towards the East and the West in post-Byzantine Orthodox Russia. In the early 1990s Yeltsin's Russia had a pro-Western focus, preferring to ignore its gigantic landmass beyond the Ural Mountains or south of Volgograd. Strong ideological and nationalist opposition as well as Washington's unilateralism under President Bill Clinton forced Yeltsin to fully revise foreign policy thinking. Yeltsin still resisted the siren call of the anti-Western lobbies, including the strong Communist Party. Instead, Yeltsin resorted to a centre-ground era of pragmatism and the promotion of a multi-polar world approach between 1996 and 2000. Evgenii Primakov was architect-in-chief of this policy and during his tenure as foreign minister and then prime minister he reformed Russian foreign policy to align with the new perspective.

The double-headed eagle aptly symbolised the contradictions in Russian political thinking. Indeed, there is something almost comical about this mythical creature that doesn't quite know where to look. Primakov asserted that it was natural for Russia to widen its scope of vision considering its geographic milieu and the global threats it faced. Critics complained that Russian strategy merely avoided making an honest choice about national ambitions and the country's place in the world. Promoting a multi-polar world was on the surface a neutral but realistic approach that took into account international rivalry but it also placed Russia in a position to undermine the West and prolong conflicts in the developing world.

Russia's duplicity was made obvious in the Middle East and most notably over Syria. From late 2011 Moscow appeared to successfully apply Primakov's vision of multi-polar balance to the West by partnering with China as well as to some extent India, South Africa and Brazil to stall Western efforts to support the Syrian revolution. This stance had its drawbacks because it potentially undermined Russia's relationship with Turkey, much of the Arab world as well as major European countries including France. There was international consensus supporting an end to the violence and oppression in Syria and Putin appeared to spearhead a group of emerging powers that endorsed state terror and choked democratic change. This perception, although open to debate, was undoubtedly made more relevant during the build-up to the presidential elections in Russia in March because of growing domestic opposition to Putin.

Between 2000 and 2002 Putin pursued pragmatic Western-friendly policies. After 2003 the Russian eagle discernibly turned its gaze from West to East. While remaining on the whole pragmatic, Russia became aggressively competitive towards the United States and Europe. This attitude first peaked in 2006, with Putin apparently seeking to weaken and humiliate the United States. On a general level Russian foreign policy also sought to rebuild damaged relations with the wider Muslim world and this required a new focus on the major issues of the Middle East. This new direction by Russia was aided by the unpopular US-led occupation of Iraq.

Russian behaviour in the Middle East is best understood in the context of powerful internal factors and the evolving international system. Understanding these drivers of foreign policy-making revealed a deep underlying continuity from the mid-1990s. Internally, the state of the Russian economy was fragile during the Yeltsin era and thus was initially hopeful of a Western bail-out. When it became obvious that this was not forthcoming Moscow realised that it would have to pursue an independent and self-centred economic approach, which included building relations with nations offering potentially lucrative markets. The Middle East was a natural target area in this regard. Under Putin, as energy became a crucial source of income for the Russian state, it became important to develop relations with oil- and gas-producing countries. There were also other lucrative economic attractions, such as military sales, nuclear energy and major projects requiring investment that raised the priority of the Middle East and South-West Asia in particular.

On a security level, Russia's relations with the Muslim world were considered as paramount in light of the conflicts in the Caucasus and terrorist threats. Relations with the Muslim world and in particular Iran and Turkey also became vital for safeguarding the unity and security of the Russian Federation. A hostile Turkey or Iran undermined the post-Soviet borderlands and potentially facilitated the infiltration of armed groups and dangerous elements into Russia itself. Thus after an initial phase of strong anti-Muslim sentiments under Putin that was fuelled by the war against Caucasian separatists, Moscow began a concerted effort to pacify the Muslim world by building friendly relations not only with Turkey and Iran but also Saudi Arabia and Jordan among others.

Russia's foreign policy was also influenced by external developments on the international stage. NATO's expansion and plans to install missiles in Eastern Europe, US unilateral actions in the Balkans and later in the Middle East all led to a sense of encirclement by Moscow's political elite. While the West turned its gaze to China, which also posed a long-term threat to Russian security, a strong feeling prevailed in Russia that their country was being belittled and deliberately humiliated. The response under Putin was tough but measured. The Middle East, more than anywhere else, provided an opportunity to undermine the United States and reassert the image of Russia as an important and decisive global player.

From the beginning of Putin's second term as president Moscow brazenly aligned itself with Iran, Syria and Hezbollah by sending weapons and defending them in forums of international diplomacy, including the UN Security Council. Meanwhile, the United States found itself increasingly entangled in Iraq and its policies in Lebanon and on the Palestinian-Israeli track were left in tatters. The victory of Barack Obama in the US election in 2008 was to some extent considered an American acknowledgement of weakness, if not defeat, in its Middle East policies. Obama's retreat from his promise to revive Israeli-Palestinian talks in one year and his inept paralysis in response to the Syrian crisis only highlighted his massive failures in Middle East politics.

Despite negative elements to Russia's behaviour in the Middle East the foreign policy domain has witnessed credit-worthy stabilisation. This process began in the late-1990s with the victory of pragmatism and centrism over pro-Western idealism and anti-Western hysteria. The revival of a national—not necessarily nationalist—foreign policy is based on the view that the policy of the Russian Federation must reflect the mainstream of public opinion, which also feels a strong sense of national pride. A good foreign policy was seen as one that upholds and defends the security of the Russian Federation and this inevitably raised the value of building good relations with neighbouring regions and the promotion of national economic interests.

Russia's Middle East policies, compared to the United States, led to better results because to some extent they were aimed at goals unconnected to the specifics of Middle East politics. For example, support for Iran's nuclear programme was linked to Western plans to extend the NATO nuclear shield closer to the Russian border in Europe. Moscow's message was obvious: Expansion of NATO's nuclear capabilities in Europe will be matched by Russia's support for nuclear expansion in the Gulf and other parts of the Middle East. Moscow was looking to strike a deal with the United States and Putin was well aware that Washington never gave anything without asking for something in return. In this case the trade-off was between Iran and Eastern Europe.

Moscow and the Middle East domino effect

The spark for the Arab revolutions was a single incident that could have been scripted by Victor Hugo. In December 2010 a young university graduate in Tunisia called Mohammad Bouazizi, frustrated at the lack of employment opportunities due to widespread corruption and general nepotism and favouritism, took up selling vegetables to earn a living. Apparently failing to meet local bureaucratic requirements the police, with typical roughness, confiscated his cart. The financial implications of this act for this already impoverished young man led him to beyond rage and he set himself on fire. Almost immediately after the incident hundreds of youths in Tunisia took to the streets, smashing shop windows and vandalising cars.[2]

The so-called Arab Spring, or more generally the political uprisings that swept across from the Maghreb to the Gulf, created a major challenge to the Russian political establishment and posed uncomfortable home truths for Russia itself. It so happened that these tumultuous events mirrored the build-up to Putin's re-election to the presidency in 2012 after a four-year hiatus. Long considered as living in the most politically backward regions in the world, Arabs appeared to be joining the historic march towards democracy. Yet Russia was seemingly going in the opposite direction. Because of constitutional amendments that extended the term of the Russian president from four to six years, Putin had the potential to remain in office as president for another two terms or twelve years barring additional constitutional amendments to extend his rule further. While in the Middle East people were burning effigies of the likes of Libya's Mouammar Qaddafi, Tunisia's Zein Al-Abidine Ben Ali, Egypt's Hosni Mubarak and Syria's Bashar Asad, dominant political godfathers in their societies, Russians were expected to huddle under the giant shadow of Putin's statue.

A significant number of Russians however began to defy the world view presented by the Putin regime. Open protests became more widespread, particularly after the disputed legislative elections of December 2011. But the cause of the protests carried broader grievances than a rejection of dubious practices to boost the results of the elections. Russians began to debate whether they were on the road to authoritarian rule, in a country where corruption had become more widespread, opposition voices were being intimidated and silenced, and the influence of the security services had become reminiscent of the Soviet-era KGB. Perhaps the greatest concern was that a national vision for Russia did not exist beyond the figure of Putin himself. The system was built around him and Russia's rich and proud society seemed to come second. That largely explains why a common chant of defiance for Russian oppositionists became '*Rossiia bez Putina!*'—'Russia without Putin!'.

The emergent widespread Russian opposition in 2011 was not sudden and had been festering for some time. In his first term Putin was supported by a wide spectrum of Russians, including liberal pro-Western reformers, pragmatic centrists and anti-Western nationalists. He skilfully balanced his tough leader image that largely subdued Chechnya and imposed law and order with a liberal pledge to reform the economy, open up society and in foreign policy to build trust with the United States and other West European countries. From the beginning of his second term Putin began his drift to authoritarianism and centralisation and with it Russian foreign policy became more defiant of the West and generally more belligerent towards neighbouring countries. He gradually revealed that he cared less and less about the West and even began expressing disdain while he increasingly displayed his affinity for the Russian security services, particularly as a tool to govern by eliminating his rivals. With each step in that direction, liberals and pro-Westerners abandoned Putin as he made himself more reliant on the pillars of anti-Western nationalist opinion and the security services.

Very few Russian observers doubted that Putin enjoyed and continued to enjoy a high degree of popular support, although how much is open to question. What became apparent though was that the peak of popularity he enjoyed had passed and from about 2010 was heading on a downward slide. In 2009 Russia's economy endured a significant slowdown after a run of fruitful years due to high energy prices. Despite an omnipresent Putin publicity machine official figures were forced to concede that unemployment had risen that year to six million and that Prime Minister Putin's opinion polls ratings had declined, albeit to a still generous 74 per cent.[3] In the presidential elections of 2012 Putin's support, according to disputed official figures, barely scraped 64 per cent.

Putin's political machine and parliamentary bloc, that lost its majority in the December 2011 elections, was purposefully titled United (One) Russia, but the Russian ruler had by his own actions become a divisive figure. A major characteristic of the Putin-dominated system was that the only broad opposition continued to be the Communist Party while liberal parties were virtually extinguished. This created the impression that Putin was the most viable and moderate option available. The danger of playing this game was that only the communists and other ultranationalists would have the official platform to take over after Putin, who often echoed their foreign policy rhetoric to gain popularity.

The return of Putin to the presidency following elections in March 2012, despite significant opposition and the loss of popular support in Moscow and St. Petersburg, suggested that Putinism still defined the nature of Russian politics. But this was a very different Putin to the Putin of a decade before when he had enthusiastically promoted partnership with the United States and a diversified and constructive foreign policy on a global level.

The Syria case

There are few better examples of what Russia has transformed into under Putin than Moscow's behaviour in the midst of the Syrian revolution from 2011 to 2013. Russia's almost frantic efforts to prop up the Asad regime in Syria baffled many observers. Why would Moscow stubbornly defy the international community and align with a regime that had embarked on a campaign of brutal repression?

The uprising in Syria erupted as President Medvedev was seeing out his term in office. There were early indications that Medvedev, considered more liberal than Putin, was not prepared to defend the Asad regime. Overall, Medvedev's real impact on both domestic and international affairs between 2008 and 2012 had been minimal. Russia's tough position in support of Syria generally took time to develop and there was uncertainty in Moscow at first about how to react to the Syria crisis. Medvedev's and Russia's initial hesitancy to express outright support for Asad therefore was not because of personal differences with Putin but were in part linked to the debate over when the Syrian revolution began.

Opposition to the regime of Bashar Asad had been brewing for more than a decade and there were ongoing sporadic clashes, particularly in eastern Syria, in previous years. Eastern Syria, known as Al-Jazeera (Mesopotamia), was largely populated by Kurds seeking greater autonomy. Russia's traditional position dating back to the Soviet era was sympathetic to the Kurds and Moscow largely attempted to maintain neutrality in the political dispute between Damascus and Syria's Kurdish minority. By the end of January 2011 eastern Syria and its major cities Qamishli and Hasakeh had become the most unruly parts of the country yet the Russian position remained typically restrained on the issue. In early March events took a dramatic turn after Syrian security agents in the southern city of Der'a abducted, tortured and murdered fifteen children, the youngest being nine-years-old, who had allegedly written anti-regime graffiti on a wall. This inept and gratuitous handling of the incident and the failure to appease clan elders in Der'a, which is located in the historic and proud Houran region, was compounded by the military assault on mourners and protesters who were demanding that officials responsible for the death of the children be brought to justice. Eventually, widespread rage and sympathy for Der'a stormed across Syria. What had started as low-level regional tensions in eastern Syria transformed into a national revolution.

As the uprising in Syria gained momentum and the violence increased in the second half of 2011 the international community began to put pressure on Asad to step down as president, with US President Barack Obama doing so in August of that year. In the context of the demise of longstanding rulers in Tunisia, Egypt and Libya Moscow suddenly and possibly unexpectedly began facing the prospect of losing Syria. Putin's decisive and visceral reaction to this was to doggedly defend the Asad regime to the extent of even supplying the Syrian government with arms, also providing training and intelligence support to crush the uprising. Typical of his brilliant opportunism which helped consolidate his reign for so many years, Putin did this in part because he sensed a weakness and indecisiveness in the Obama administration that quite simply allowed him to get away with it. There was added value in terms of timing as Putin geared up for the December 2011 legislative elections and the presidential elections in March 2012. Putin could act out the role of defender of Russian pride and international interests in front of his audience on the international stage. As Russian reformers increasingly turned against Putin he in turn entrenched himself among the anti-Western traditionalists.

There were many analyses attempting to make sense of the Russia's determined support for Syria, which included defiantly vetoing UNSC Resolutions that plans for humanitarian efforts, because of fears that the end result would be the end of Asad and his regime. Explanations included typical references by commentators to valuable arms sales, the naval facilities and economic interests. Moscow was also justifiably concerned about the nature and character of Syria and the rest of the region in a post-Asad scenario and in particular there were fears expressed in Russia about the rise of extremist Islamist governments. Without doubt all of these were significant factors but none of them were important enough to place the image and reputation of Russia under such risk of damage.

The smug face of Vitaly Churkin, Russian ambassador to the UN, as he brazenly raised his hand as seen on television screens across the world to reject a proposed Security Council Resolution to stop the violence in Syria in light of thousands of documented deaths and human rights abuses, raised the ghastly spectre of the Cold War. There were even reports that Churkin had thuggishly threatened an Arab envoy during closed door deliberations. Russia's foreign minister, Lavrov, similarly antagonised the Syrian opposition by virtually adopting the official Syrian explanation of the violence on the ground. There seemed to be so little logic in undermining relations with Turkey, Saudi Arabia and the wider Muslim world, largely united on the demand for Asad to leave power, for Asad's Syria. Indeed, Russian economic interests in Syria were relatively small compared to Turkey and other regional economies. Perhaps also pertinently there were concerns that Putin would antagonise Russia's own Muslim populations. Moscow concerns throwing away a decade of carefully constructed relations in the Middle East.

There were some calculations that upon winning the presidential elections in March 2012 Putin would correct the Russian position and cooperate with the West once more for an amicable solution to the deadlock on Syria. That would have been the classic Putin of old: balancing between the Russian psychological obsession with national pride that is filled with anti-Western suspicions and practical realities that required modernisation, reform and a pragmatic approach to international affairs. Yet the Russian position did not offer any compromises and indeed there were new reports of more weapons shipments to the Syrian regime as the UN recorded death toll reached over 75,000.[4]

The reasons for Putin's intransigence on Syria went beyond bilateral economic relations or any single cause. Events in the Syria case confirmed, as this book has hopefully shown, that Putin merely pursued a long-established trend to re-impose Russia's global influence by undermining that of the United States. This was significantly speeded up in 2005 and 2006, during Putin's second term. The concept of the multipolar world, first introduced in Russian foreign policy thinking by Primakov in the 1990s, reappeared with gusto as Russia joined forces with China, India, Iran, Brazil and South Africa to stifle Western efforts. In April 2012 Russia made great show of the BRICS (Brazil, Russia, India, China and South Africa) Summit in India, touting the potential of a rival non-dollar currency for economic development and boosting trade volumes with members to top $500 billion annually by 2015.[5] The Russian media's extensive coverage of the event clearly intended to show that a new power balance existed in the world order that did not include the United States and often rather misleadingly represented Russia as the leader of this still disjointed grouping.

Russia was to be, Moscow's decision-makers hoped, the rope that bound the BRICS together, and to other countries such as Iran that have an interest in diminishing US power to form a formidable global alliance. Washington's retreat from world affairs, and particularly the Middle East, under Obama encouraged Russia to press on with greater assertiveness, particularly in Syria. According to one American commentator writing at the end of March 2012, if successful in eventually surviving the internal challenge to his rule, Asad will 'owe not only his allies, Iran and Russia, but the White House as well…the Obama Administration has come to the Syrian president's rescue—not because of any love for Assad, but because Obama wants to stay on Russia's good side'.[6]

Putin's quest for greater global influence paralleled his restless hunger for more power at home. This was associated with the internal challenges the political system faced. According to one definition, 'Putinism is an informal social contract by which ordinary Russians have given Putin their unquestioning political support in return for rising living standards and increased national self-respect after the post-Soviet humiliations of the 1990s.'[7] As it became difficult for Putin to deliver on providing rising living standards for most people the system increasingly emphasised national self-respect to compensate. Similarly, state corruption and a crooked legal system only humiliated the ordinary Russian citizen at home who was not connected to men in Russia—and they were usually men—in positions of influence.

The concern is now about where Putin's order will lead Russia. While Putin remains relatively astute, pragmatic and cautious in his international manoeuvres the Syrian example highlights a longer trend towards confrontation as long as the West allows him the leeway to do so. The domestic political situation appears to be unravelling as Putin is arguably finding it difficult to maintain his ability to balance the competing forces of Russian politics, making the system more fragile than at any time since the Yeltsin era. The difference between Putin and his predecessor is that Putin showed no willingness to harmonise Russia with the international community and took to exploiting international crises to uphold his system. Supporters of Putin claimed that there was no alternative to Putin and he has himself cleverly led many Russians and the outside world to believe that a strong and confident Putin is a strong and confident Russia. The popular uprisings in the Middle East however showed us that no country's fate can be tied to that of one man.

In that respect Putin's tight embrace of the Asad regime to prevent its downfall had even deeper meaning than exploiting Russia's traditional national pride, geo-strategic fears and anti-Western sentiments. It was a psychological urge by his clique to protect its own survival. How could Moscow accept notions of people power and a universal right to form a genuine political opposition? Most sinful for Putin and his loyal political elite, how could Russia tolerate the idea that the international community could have the right to violate the sovereignty of a state to prevent the repression of a people by their government? The wrangling over Syria has revealed a deep cultural schism between Russia and the West and possibly also began to show us with much more clarity Putin's true inner values and psyche. The Russian elite's ability not only to cynically manipulate the crude and appalling violence in Syria but to become the chief provider of arms for it indicates a mindset that shows how far Russia has drifted from the West and, more tellingly, brings Putin's personality and his KGB heritage to the fore. The Putin order has crossed the point of no return and there are fleeting but visible signs that grave dangers lurk in the international system in the coming period.

NOTES

1. INTRODUCTION

1. 'Rice says Mideast is threatened by Iran-Syria-Hezbollah nexus', *Naharnet*, 20 February 2006. http://www.naharnet.com/domino/tn/NewsDesk.nsf/getstory?openform&40EA87BCCC296240C225711B0033B29C, last accessed 20 February 2006.
2. Reddaway, Peter and Dmitry Glinski, *The Tragedy of Russia's Reforms: Market Bolshevism Against Democracy*, Washington DC: United States Institute of Peace Press, 2001, p. 169.
3. Bidder, Benjamin, 'Nuclear threats and busty ladies in the race of second place in Russia', *Der Spiegel Online*, 28 February 2008. http://www.spiegel.de/international/world/0,1518,538403,00.html, last accessed 17 February 2010.
4. Karny, Yo'av, *Highlanders: a Journey to the Caucasus in Quest of Memory*, New York: Farrar, Strauss and Giroux, 2000, p. 252.

2. THE COLD WAR AND THE DEMISE OF MIDDLE EAST NATION-STATES

1. The Sykes-Picot Agreement, 1916. http://www.yale.edu/lawweb/avalon/mideast/sykes.htm, last accessed 15 July 2007.
2. *The Sunday Express* on 4 January 2004 and in *The Guardian*, 15 January 2004. http://www.guardian.co.uk/comment/story/0,3604,1123787,00.html, last accessed 15 January 2005.
3. Brown, Derek, 'What have the Arabs ever done for us?', *The Guardian*, 15 January 2004. http://www.guardian.co.uk/comment/story/0,3604,1123787,00.html, last accessed 15 January 2005.
4. Hyde, Marina, 'This week', *The Guardian*, 17 January 2004. http://www.guardian.co.uk/diary/story/0,3604,1125212,00.html, last accessed 18 January 2004.

5. Keylor, William R., *The Twentieth Century World: an International History*, New York: Oxford University Press 2nd Edition, 1992, p. 267
6. Keylor, William R., *The Twentieth Century World*, p. 270.
7. Keylor, William R., *The Twentieth Century World*, p. 271.
8. Ulunian, R.A., 'Soviet Cold War perceptions of Turkey and Greece', *Mezhdunarodnyi Istoricheskii Zhournal* (International Historical Journal), 20, 2002. http://history.machaon.ru/all/number_02/analiti4/3/index.html. last accessed 26 January 2004.
9. Ulunian, R.A., 'Soviet Cold War perceptions of Turkey and Greece'.
10. Kramer, Mark, 'The role of the CPSU International Department in Soviet foreign relations and national security policy', *Soviet Studies*, 42, 3, July 1990, p. 430.
11. Dagan, Avigdor, *Moscow and Jerusalem*, London: Abelard-Schuman, 1970, p. 81.
12. *Cold War International History Project (CWIHP)*, memorandum of a conversation between Soviet Ambassador to Egypt D.S. Solod and Egyptian Prime Minister G. Nasser—Archive of the Foreign Policy of the Russian Federation (hereafter AVPRF) fond 087, opis 17, papka 34, delo 5, listy 190–192 obtained and translated for CWIHP by Guy Laron, Woodrow Wilson International Center for Scholars. CWIHP.org
13. *Cold War International History Project (CWIHP)*.
14. Dagan, Avigdor, *Moscow and Jerusalem*, p. 114.
15. Vassiliev, Alexei, *Russian Policy in the Middle East: from Messianism to Pragmatism*, Reading: Ithaca Press, 1993, p. 62.
16. Kramer, Mark, 'The role of the CPSU International Department in Soviet foreign relations and national security policy', p. 431.
17. Kramer, Mark, 'The role of the CPSU International Department in Soviet foreign relations and national security policy', p. 431.
18. Farid, Abdel Magid, *Nasser: The Final Years*, Reading: Ithaca Press, 1994, p. 24.
19. Mooney, Peter, *The Soviet Superpower: the Soviet Union 1945–1980*, London: Heinemann Educational, 1982, p. 142.
20. Breslauer, George, 'Introduction', in George Breslauer (ed.), *Soviet strategy in the Middle East*; Boston, Ma.: Unwin Hyman, 1990, p. 5.
21. *Time Magazine*, 'The Middle East: persuasion amid peril', 7 September 1970. http://www.time.com/time/magazine/article/0,9171,902699,00.html, last accessed 14 August 2006.
22. These are classified Arabic transcripts of minutes of the meetings between President Sadat of Egypt (and his foreign and defence ministers) with members of the Soviet elite, including Brezhnev, Kosygin, Podgorny, Gromyko, Andrei Grechko (defence minister), Ponomarev and others. The transcripts were kept by the Egyptian president's information secretariat and were made available to me.

23. Petro, Nicolai and Alvin Z. Rubinstein, *Russian Foreign Policy: from Empire to Nation State*, New York: Longman, 1997, p. 9.
24. Daniels, Robert V., 'Evgenii Primakov: contender by chance', *Problems of Post-Communism*, 46, 5, September/October 1999, p. 29.
25. Kramer, Mark, 'The role of the CPSU International Department in Soviet foreign relations and national security policy', p. 434.
26. Kramer, Mark, 'The role of the CPSU International Department in Soviet foreign relations and national security policy', p. 435.
27. Kramer, Mark, 'The role of the CPSU International Department in Soviet foreign relations and national security policy', p. 436.
28. Heller, Mark A., *The Dynamics of Soviet Policy in the Middle East: Between Old Thinking and New*, Tel Aviv University: Publications of the Jaffee Center for Strategic Studies, 1991, p. 50.
29. Kuvaldin, Viktor, (Gorbachev policy adviser 1989–91), 'From Cold War to new world order' in Gorodetsky, Gabriel (ed.), *Soviet Foreign Policy 1917–1991: a Retrospective*, London: Frank Cass, 1994, p. 193.
30. Heller, *The Dynamics of Soviet Policy in the Middle East*, p. 76.

3. YELTSIN AND THE DECADE OF TRANSITION

1. Khripunov, Igor, 'Russia's weapon's trade: domestic competition and foreign markets', *Problems of Post-Communism*, 46, 2, March/April 1999, p. 39.
2. Moser, Robert G., *Unexpected Outcomes: Electoral Systems, Political Parties and Representation in Russia*, Pittsburg: University of Pittsburg Press, 2001, p. 1.
3. Malcolm, Neil, 'Foreign policy making' in Malcolm, Neil, Pravda, Alex, Light, Margot and Roy Allison (eds.), *Internal Factors in Russian Foreign Policy*, Oxford: Oxford University Press, 1996, p. 118.
4. Dunlop, John B., 'Russia: confronting a loss of empire 1987–1991', *Political Science Quarterly*, Winter 1993–4, p. 615.
5. Moser, Robert G., *Unexpected outcomes*, p. 13.
6. Khripunov, Igor, 'Russia's weapon's trade: domestic competition and foreign markets', p. 45.
7. *BBC SWB*, 29 April 1994.
8. Arbatov, Alexei, Chapter 4, 'The vicissitudes of Russian politics', in Baranovsky, Vladimir (ed.), *Russia and Europe: the Emerging Security Agenda*, Oxford: Oxford University Press, 1997, p. 110.
9. Daniels, Robert V., 'Evgenii Primakov: contender by chance', *Problems of Post-Communism*, 46, 5, September/October 1999, p. 27.
10. Khripunov, Igor, 'Russia's weapon's trade: domestic competition and foreign markets', p. 39.
11. Khripunov, Igor, 'Russia's weapon's trade: domestic competition and foreign markets', p. 41.

12. Khripunov, Igor, 'Russia's weapon's trade: domestic competition and foreign markets', p. 41.
13. Ivanov, Igor, *New Russian Diplomacy: Ten Years of Moscow's Foreign Policy*, Washington DC: Brookings Institution Press, 2002, p. 8. http://site.ebrary.com/lib/aub/Doc?id=10063832&ppg=20
14. Karny, Yo'av, *Highlanders: a Journey to the Caucasus in Quest of Memory*, New York: Farrar, Strauss and Giroux, 2000, p. xiii.
15. Shevtsova, Lilia, *Putin's Russia*, Washington DC: Carnegie Endowment for International Peace, 2003, p. 198.
16. Elbaz, Michel, 'Dangerous liaisons: covert "love affair" between Russia and Hezbollah', *Axis Information and Analysis*, 24 May 2005. http://www.axisglobe.com/hezbollah1.htm Primakov also considered China as a potential key ally that could strengthen Russia's international standing.
17. *The Guardian*, 10 January 1996, p. 5.
18. Daniels, Robert V., 'Evgenii Primakov: contender by chance', p. 29.
19. E. Shevardnadze, lecture by Georgia's former president at the Royal Institute of International Affairs, London, 16 February 1995.
20. Golan, Galia, *Moscow and the Middle East: New Thinking on Regional Conflict*, London: Pinter, 1992, p. 338.
21. Karny, Yo'av, *Highlanders*, p. xvii.
22. Reddaway, Peter and Dmitri Glinski, *The Tragedy of Russia's Reforms: Market Bolshevism Against Democracy*, Washington DC: United States Institute of Peace Press, 2001, p. 2.
23. Reddaway, Peter and Dmitri Glinski, *The Tragedy of Russia's Reforms*, p. 2.
24. Reddaway, Peter and Dmitri Glinski, *The Tragedy of Russia's Reforms*, p. 34.
25. Reddaway, Peter and Dmitri Glinski, *The Tragedy of Russia's Reforms*, p. 35.
26. Pushkov, Aleksei, 'Kozyrev's foreign policy: what should replace it?' *Moscow News* (*The Current Digest of Post-Soviet Press)*, 20 December 1995, p. 6.
27. Nikitenko, Evgenii and Nikolai Pikov, 'Duga Nestabil'nosti' (The arc of instability), *Nezavisimaia gazeta*, 4 December 1996, p. 5.
28. Reddaway, Peter and Dmitri Glinski, *The Tragedy of Russia's Reforms*, p. 37.
29. Baranovsky, Vladimir (ed.), *Russia and Europe*, p. 46.
30. Qimao, Chen, 'Sino-Russian relations after the break-up of the Soviet Union,' in Chufrin, Gennady (ed.), *Russia and Asia: The Emerging Security Agenda*, New York: Oxford University Press, 1999, p. 288.
31. Malcolm, Neil, 'Russian foreign policy decision-making' in Shearman, Peter, *Russian Foreign Policy Since 1990*, Oxford: Westview Press, 1995, p. 27.
32. Reddaway, Peter and Dmitri Glinski, *The Tragedy of Russia's Reforms*, p. 499.
33. Reddaway, Peter and Dmitri Glinski, *The Tragedy of Russia's Reforms*, p. 113. The authors were fiercely critical of Yeltsin throughout their work, either questioning his personal integrity or at other times portraying him as under the mercy of cynical financial gangsters.

34. Payne, Laura, 'U.S.-Russia security relations', *Foreign Policy in Focus*, 3, 26, September 1998, p. 1. http://www.fpif.org/pdf/vol3/26ifusru.pdf
35. Reddaway, Peter and Dmitri Glinski, *The Tragedy of Russia's Reforms*, p. 95.
36. Shiraev, Eric and Vladislav Zubok, *Anti-Americanism in Russia from Stalin to Putin*, New York: Palgrave, 2000, p. 38.
37. Arbatov, Alexei, 'Is a new Cold War imminent?', *Russia in Global Affairs*, 2, July–September 2007. http://eng.globalaffairs.ru/numbers/20/1130.html
38. Reddaway, Peter and Dmitri Glinski, *The Tragedy of Russia's Reforms*, p. 602.

4. FROM SEEPING TERRORISM TO CREEPING AUTHORITARIANISM

1. Sakwa, Richard, 'Putin's leadership: character and consequences', *Europe-Asia Studies*, 60, 6, August 2008, p. 881.
2. Walker, Shaun, '"Time" names "dangerous" Putin as Person of the Year', *The Independent*, 20 December 2007, http://news.independent.co.uk/europe/article3266592.ece, last accessed 20 December 2007.
3. Ivanov, Igor, *New Russian Diplomacy: Ten Years of Moscow's Foreign Policy*, Washington DC: Brookings Institution Press, 2002, p. 166.
4. Ivanov, Igor, *New Russian Diplomacy*, p. 2.
5. Walsh, Nick Paton and Ewen MacAskill, 'Putin lashes out at "wolf-like" America', *Guardian Unlimited*, 11 May 2006. http://www.guardian.co.uk/russia/article/0,,1772175,00.html
6. Karny, Yo'av, *Highlanders: A Journey to the Caucasus in Quest of Memory*, New York: Farrar, Strauss and Giroux, 2000, p. 47.
7. 'Leading Mufti calls for an end to xenophobia', *Radio Free Europe/Radio Liberty Newsline*, 1 August 2007. http://www.rferl.org/content/article/1143923.html, last accessed 2 February 2008.
8. Lynch, Dov, '"The enemy is at the gate": Russia after Beslan', *International Affairs*, 85, 1, 2005, p. 143.
9. Malashenko, Alexey, 'Into the labyrinth of Russia's intensifying Islamism', *The Daily Star* (Beirut), 21 April 2006, p. 6.
10. Staalesen, Atle, Chapter 11, 'Orthodoxy and Islam in post-Soviet Russia: opposing confessional cultures or unifying force?', in Kolstø, Pål and Helge Blackkisrod (eds), *Nation-building and Common Values in Russia*, Lanham, Boulder, Oxford: Rowan and Littlefield Publishers Inc., 2004, p. 311.
11. Karny, Yo'av, *Highlanders*, p. 47.
12. Malashenko, Alexey, 'Into the labyrinth of Russia's intensifying Islamism', p. 6.
13. Hahn, Gordon M., *Russia's Islamic Threat*, New Haven and London: Yale University Press, 2007, p. 1.
14. Malashenko, Alexey, 'Into the labyrinth of Russia's intensifying Islamism', p. 6.

15. Malashenko, Alexey, 'Into the labyrinth of Russia's intensifying Islamism', p. 6.
16. *CNN.com*, 'Putin calls for stronger army', 10 May 2006. http://www.cnn.com/2006/WORLD/europe/05/10/russia.putin.address/index.html, last accessed 11 May 2006.
17. Moser, Robert G., *Unexpected Outcomes: Electoral Systems, Political Parties and Representation in Russia*, Pittsburg: University of Pittsburg Press, 2001, p. 152. The descriptions of the blocs have been modified to make them relevant to the foreign policy debate. For full elections results see also Organization for Security and Cooperation in Europe's Office for Democratic Institutions and Human Rights report published on 13 February 2000. http://www.osce.org/documents/odihr/2000/02/1454_en.pdf, last accessed 18 March 2009.
18. Legvold, Robert, 'Russia's unformed foreign policy', *Foreign Affairs*, 80, 5, September/October 2001, p. 70.
19. Mendelson, Sarah E., 'The Putin path', *Problems of Post-Communism*, 47, 5, September/October 2000, p. 3.
20. Reddaway, Peter and Dmitri Glinski, *The Tragedy of Russia's Reforms: Market Bolshevism Against Democracy*, Washington DC: United States Institute of Peace Press, 2001, p. 614.
21. Tsygankov, Andrei P., 'Russia's international assertiveness: what does it mean?', *Problems of Post-Communism*, 55, 2, March/April 2008, p. 39.
22. Khripunov, Igor, 'Russia's weapon's trade: domestic competition and foreign markets', *Problems of Post-Communism*, 46, 2, March/April 1999, p. 41.
23. Freedman, Robert O., 'Putin, Iran, and the nuclear weapons issue', *Problems of Post-Communism*, 53, 2, March/April 2006, p. 39.
24. Sánchez-Andrés, Antonio, 'Arms exports and restructuring in the Russian defence industry', *Europe-Asia Studies*, 56, 5, July 2004, p. 689.
25. Bukkvoll, Tor, 'Arming the Ayatollahs: economic lobbies in Russia's Iran policy', *Problems of Post-Communism*, 49, 6, November/December 2002, p. 33.
26. Colton, Timothy J. and Michael McFaul, *Popular Choice and Managed Democracy: the Russian Elections of 1999 and 2000*, Washington DC: Brookings Institute Press, 2003, p. 13.
27. Kolstø, Pål and Helge Blackkisrod (eds), *Nation-building and Common Values in Russia*, Lanham, Boulder, Oxford: Rowan and Littlefield Publishers Inc., 2004, p. 2.
28. Karny, Yo'av, *Highlanders*, p. 172.
29. Parfitt, Tom, 'Putin silent as fiercest critic is murdered', *The Guardian*, 9 October 2006. http://www.guardian.co.uk/frontpage/story/0,,1891012,00.html, last accessed 26 December 2007.
30. *Moscow News*, 'US Rice meets Russia's Lavrov, says Russia must do better', 2 February 2005, http://mosnews.com/news/2005/02/07/ricelavrov.shtml, last accessed 21 February 2006.

31. Rumsfeld, Donald H., 'America's alliances are more flexible than ever before', *Daily Star* (Beirut), 15 May 2006. http://www.dailystar.com.lb/article.asp?edition_id=10&categ_id=5&article_id=24428#, last accessed 16 May 2006. The *Daily Star* published this commentary in collaboration with Project Syndicate (www.project-syndicate.org).
32. Putin's speech at the Munich Conference on Security Policy on 10 February 2007 in Tsygankov, Andrei P., 'Russia's international assertiveness: what does it mean?', p. 39.
33. Yavlinsky, Grigory and Viktor Kogan-Yasny, 'Passive isolationism endangers Russia but also the West', *Daily Star* (Beirut), 4 July 2007. http://www.dailystar.com.lb/article.asp?edition_id=10&categ_id=5&article_id=83514, last accessed 4 July 2007.
34. Yavlinsky, Grigory and Viktor Kogan-Yasny, 'Passive isolationism endangers Russia but also the West'.
35. Arbatov, Alexei, 'Is a new Cold War imminent?', *Russia in Global Affairs*, 2, July–September 2007. http://eng.globalaffairs.ru/numbers/20/1130.html, last accessed 30 November 2007.
36. Arbatov, Alexei, 'Is a new Cold War imminent?'.
37. Arbatov, Alexei, 'Is a new Cold War imminent?'.
38. Charap, Samuel, 'The Petersburg experience', *Problems of Post-Communism*, 51, 1, January–February 2004, p. 61.
39. Arbatov, Alexei, Chapter 4, 'The vicissitudes of Russian politics', in Baranovsky, Vladimir (ed.), *Russia and Europe: The Emerging Security Agenda*, Oxford: Oxford University Press, 1997, p. 87.
40. Ivanov, Igor, *New Russian Diplomacy*, p. 7.
41. Tyldum, Guri and Pål Kolstø, Chapter 2, 'Value consensus and social cohesion in Russia', in Kolstø, Pål and Helge Blackkisrod (eds), *Nation-building and Common Values in Russia*, Lanham, Boulder, Oxford: Rowan and Littlefield Publishers Inc., 2004, p. 48.
42. Lukyanov, Fyodor, 'Debates about values', *Russia in Global Affairs*, 3, July–September 2005. http://eng.globalaffairs.ru/numbers/12/935.html, last accessed 30 November 2007.
43. Bogaturov, Alexei, 'The sources of American conduct', *Russia in Global Affairs*, 1, January–March 2005. http://eng.globalaffairs.ru/numbers/10/821.html, last accessed 30 November 2007.
44. Bogaturov, Alexei, 'The sources of American conduct'.
45. Bogaturov, Alexei, 'The sources of American conduct'.
46. Putin's speech at the Munich Conference on Security Policy on 10 February 2007 in Tsygankov, Andrei P., 'Russia's international assertiveness: what does it mean?', p. 41.
47. Karny, Yo'av, *Highlanders*, p. 270.

48. Kolstø, Pål and Helge Blackkisrod (ed.), *Nation-building and Common Values*, p. 20.
49. Podberezsky, Igor, Chapter 3, 'Between Europe and Asia: the search for Russia's civilizational identity', in Chufrin, Gennady (ed.), *Russia and Asia: The Emerging Security Agenda*, New York: Oxford University Press, 1999, p. 36.
50. Moshes, Arkady, 'Reaffirming the benefits of Russia's European choice', *Russia in Global Affairs*, 3, July–September 2005. http://eng.globalaffairs.ru/numbers/12/942.html, last accessed 30 November 2007.
51. Moshes, Arkady, 'Reaffirming the benefits of Russia's European choice'.
52. Moshes, Arkady, 'Reaffirming the benefits of Russia's European choice'.
53. Kolstø, Pål and Helge Blackkisrod (ed.), *Nation-building and Common Values*, p. 11.
54. Talbott, Strobe, Lyne, Roderic and Koji Watanabe, 'A trilateral view of a changing relationship with Russia', *Russia in Global Affairs*, 4, October–December 2006. http://eng.globalaffairs.ru/numbers/17/1073.html, last accessed 30 November 2007.
55. Talbott, Strobe, Lyne, Roderic and Koji Watanabe, 'A trilateral view of a changing relationship with Russia'.
56. Tsygankov, Andrei P., 'Russia's international assertiveness: what does it mean?', p. 48.
57. Khripunov, Igor, 'Russia's weapon's trade', p. 39.
58. Kisriev, Enver, Chapter 5, 'Republic of Dagestan: nation-building inside Russia's womb', in Kolstø, Pål and Helge Blackkisrod (eds), *Nation-building and Common Values*, p. 141.
59. Putin's speech at the Munich Conference on Security Policy on 10 February 2007 in Tsygankov, Andrei P., 'Russia's international assertiveness: what does it mean?', p. 44.
60. Reddaway, Peter and Dmitri Glinski, *The Tragedy of Russia's Reforms*, p. 78.
61. Colton, Timothy J. and Michael McFaul, *Popular Choice and Managed Democracy*, p. 58.
62. Sakwa, Richard, Chapter 1, 'Regime change from Yeltsin to Putin: normality, normalcy or normalization', in Ross, Cameron (ed.), *Russian Politics under Putin*, Manchester: Manchester University Press, 2004, p. 21.
63. Sakwa, Richard, 'Regime change from Yeltsin to Putin', p. 21.
64. Sakwa, Richard, 'Regime change from Yeltsin to Putin', p. 20.

5. A COHESIVE FOREIGN POLICY FOR A DISORDERED WORLD

1. Freedman, Robert, 'Reviving the Cold War in the Middle East?', *The Daily Star* (Beirut), 3 December 2007. http://www.dailystar.com.lb/article.asp?edition_id=10&categ_id=5&article_id=87176, last accessed 3 December 2007.

2. Colton, Timothy J. and Michael McFaul, 'America's real Russian allies', *Foreign Affairs*, 80, 6, November/December 2001, p. 47.
3. Hassan Nasrallah's speech eulogising Imad Mughniyeh was televised on Hezbollah's TV station *Al-Manar*, on 14 February 2008, one day after the assassination. Mughniyeh's direct military command of Hezbollah activities was elaborated upon by Nasrallah in a follow up speech on 22 February 2008, also on *Al-Manar* television station.
4. *Naharnet*, 'Report: 5,000 Hizbullah fighters joined Asad's forces in Damascus fighting', Beirut, 7 January 2013. http://www.naharnet.com/stories/en/67353-report-5–000-hizbullah-fighters-joined-assad-s-forces-in-damascus-fighting, last accessed 8 January 2013.
5. Malashenko, Alexey, 'Into the labyrinth of Russia's intensifying Islamism', *The Daily Star* (Beirut), 21 April 2006, p. 6.
6. Goldgeier, James M., *Power and Purpose: US Policy Toward Russia After the Cold War*, Washington DC: Brookings Institute Press, 2003, p. 2.
7. Freyer, Wesley A., *Prospects for collective security in the Western hemisphere*, published on the internet and supported by a Fullbright-Garcia Robles Grant, 1993. http://www.wtvi.com/wesley/collectivesecurity.html, last accessed 6 March 2006.
8. Khasanova, Gulnara, Chapter 10, 'Nation-building and values in Russian textbooks', in Kolstø, Pål and Helge Blackkisrod (eds), *Nation-building and Common Values in Russia*, Lanham, Boulder, Oxford: Rowan and Littlefield Publishers Inc., 2004, p. 272.
9. Billington, James, *Russia in Search of Itself*, Washington DC: Woodrow Wilson Center Press, 2004, p. 90.
10. *Radio Free Europe/Radio Liberty Newsline*, 'Putin wants deeper friendship with Islamic world', 14 March 2008. http://www.rferl.org/content/article/1144072.html, last accessed 30 November 2008.
11. Arbatov, Alexei, 'Is a new Cold War imminent?', *Russia in Global Affairs*, 2, July–September 2007. http://eng.globalaffairs.ru/numbers/20/1130.html, last accessed 30 November 2007.
12. Lynch, Dov, '"The enemy is at the gate": Russia after Beslan', *International Affairs*, 85, 1, 2005, p. 144.
13. Lo, Bobo, *Russian Foreign Policy in the Post-Soviet Era: Reality, Illusion and Mythmaking*, Gordonsville VA: Palgrave Macmillan, 2002, p. 7. http://site.ebrary.com/lib/aub/Doc?id=10044885&ppg=18
14. Evans Jr., Alfred B., 'Putin's legacy and Russia's identity', *Europe-Asia Studies*, 60, 6, August 2008, p. 902.
15. Saltanov, Alexander, *30 Days*, Catholic Church monthly interviewed by Giovanni Cubeddu and Pierluca Azzaro, October 2006. http://www.30giorni.it/us/articolo.asp?id=11640, last accessed 18 January 2008.

16. Khasanova, Gulnara, 'Nation-building and values in Russian textbooks', p. 277.
17. Arbatov, Alexei, 'Is a new Cold War imminent?'.
18. Arbatov, Alexei, 'Is a new Cold War imminent?'.
19. Payne, Laura, 'US-Russia security relations', *Foreign Policy in Focus*, 3, 26, September 1998. http://www.fpif.org/briefs/vol3/v3n26fsu.html, last accessed 13 March 2006.
20. Bowker, Mike, Chapter 14, 'Conflict in Chechnya', in Ross, Cameron (ed.), *Russian Politics under Putin*, Manchester: Manchester University Press, 2004, p. 255.
21. Glendinning, Lee, 'Poland and US sign missile defence deal', *The Guardian*, 20 August 2008. http://www.guardian.co.uk/world/2008/aug/20/poland.usa, last accessed 20 August 2008.
22. Goldgeier, James M., *Power and Purpose*, p. 5.
23. Colton, Timothy J. and Michael McFaul, 'America's real Russian allies', p. 47.
24. Reddaway, Peter and Dmitri Glinski, *The Tragedy of Russia's Reforms: Market Bolshevism against Democracy*, Washington DC: United States Institute of Peace Press, 2001, p. 62.
25. Reddaway, Peter and Dmitri Glinski, *The Tragedy of Russia's Reforms*, p. 70.
26. Polikanov, Dmitry and Graham Timmins, Chapter 12, 'Russian foreign policy under Putin', in Ross, Cameron (ed.), *Russian Politics under Putin*, Manchester: Manchester University Press, 2004, p. 229.
27. Arbatov, Alexei, 'Is a new Cold War imminent?'.
28. Bogaturov, Alexei, 'The sources of American conduct', *Russia in Global Affairs*, 1, January–March 2005. http://eng.globalaffairs.ru/numbers/10/821.html, last accessed 30 November 2007. The author wrote the article in his capacity as Deputy Director of the Institute of International Security Studies at the Russian Academy of Sciences and Editor-in-Chief of the journal *Mezhdunarodniye Protsessy*.
29. Saltanov, Alexander, *30 Days*, interview in Catholic Church monthly.
30. Speech by Foreign Minister Sergei Lavrov in Moscow on 24 March 2007 in Tsygankov, Andrei P., 'Russia's international assertiveness: what does it mean?', *Problems of Post-Communism*, 55, 2, March/April 2008, p. 41.
31. Rumer, Eugene, *Dangerous Drift: Russia's Middle East Policy*, Washington DC: Washington Institute for Near East Policy, Policy Paper 54, 2002, p. 79.
32. Evans Jr., Alfred B., 'Putin's legacy and Russia's identity', p. 905.
33. Arbatov, Alexei, 'Is a new Cold War imminent?'.
34. Arbatov, Alexei, 'Is a new Cold War imminent?'.
35. *Naharnet*, 'Nasrallah acknowledges giving financial support to militant Palestinian factions', Beirut, 27 April 2006. http://www.naharnet.com/domino/tn/NewsDesk.nsf/getstory?openform&EF1DFD9616E3F907C225715D003F8FC7, last accessed 29 April 2006.

36. Osborn, Andrew, 'Russia becomes larges arms seller to Third World', *The Independent*, 31 October 2006. http://news.independent.co.uk/europe/article1943298.ece, last accessed 1 April 2009.
37. *RIANovosti*, 'Russian arms sales at $12 bln in 2012', 17 December 2012. http://en.rian.ru/trend/russian_arms_export/, last accessed 12 January 2013.
38. *BBC Online*, 'Russia names terrorist groups', 28 July 2006. http://news.bbc.co.uk/2/hi/europe/5223458.stm, last accessed 1 November 2006.
39. *Novosti* (Russian News and Information Agency), 'Russia's Putin says too early to talk about Iran sanctions', 17 July 2006. http://en.rian.ru/world/20060717/51471883.html, last accessed 1 November 2006.
40. Dubnov, Arkady, 'A hot G8: Middle East is focus of St. Petersburg Summit', 17 July 2006, p. 1. From *The Current Digest of the Post-Soviet Press*, 58, 29, 16 August 2006. http://www.currentdigest.org/index.cfm/article/3CA931EB-7E90–9BD4-CF30558A23CB90FC, last accessed 4 March 2008.
41. Rahr, Alexander, 'Why Schroder loves Russia', *Russia in Global Affairs*, 4, October–December 2004. http://eng.globalaffairs.ru/numbers/9/709.html, last accessed 21 July 2007.
42. Rahr, Alexander, 'Why Schroder loves Russia'.
43. Socor, Vladimir, 'Russia poised to lead an evolving cartel of gas-exporting countries', *Eurasia Daily Monitor*, 4, 70, 10 April 2007. http://www.jamestown.org/programs/edm/single/?tx_ttnews%5Btt_news%5D=32667&tx_ttnews%5BbackPid%5D=171&no_cache=1, last accessed 7 July 2009.
44. Berman, Ilan, 'Russia and the Mideast vacuum', *IASPS Papers in Strategy*, Washington DC: Institute for Advanced Strategic and Political Studies, 12, June 2001, p. 3.
45. Goldgeier, James M., *Power and Purpose*, p, 314.

6. RUSSIA AND THE NEW REALITIES IN IRAQ

1. Mirsky, Georgy, 'The Baghdad puzzle', *Russia in Global Affairs*, 2, July–September 2007. http://eng.globalaffairs.ru/numbers/2/462.html, last accessed 30 November 2007. Dr Mirsky wrote this article in his capacity as a professor at the influential Institute of World Economy and International Affairs.
2. Blank, Stephen, 'The post-Soviet states and the post-Saddam Middle East', *Middle East Review of International Affairs*, 7, 2, June 2003, p. 61.
3. *Russia Today* TV, address to the Federal Assembly of the Russian Federation, 13 November 2006.
4. Guseinov, El'mar, '"Irak nadeetsia podkupit" Moskvu', (Iraq hopes to bribe Moscow), *Izvestiia*, 13 July 1994, p. 24.
5. Freedman, Robert O., 'Russian policy toward the Middle East under Yeltsin and Putin', *Jerusalem Viewpoints*, 461, 2 September 2001. http://www.jcpa.org/JCPA/

Templates/ShowPage.asp?DRIT=2&DBID=1&LNGID=1&TMID=111&FID=443&PID=0&IID=1125&TTL=Russian_Policy_Toward_the_Middle_East_Under_Yeltsin_and_Putin, last accessed 11 April 2007.

6. Dannreuther, Roland, Chapter 2, 'Russia and the Middle East', in Carter, Hannah and Anoushiravan Ehteshami (eds), *The Middle East's Relations with Asia and Russia*, London and New York: Routledge Curzon, 2004, p. 29.
7. Berman, Ilan, 'Russia and the Mideast vacuum', *IASPS Papers in Strategy*, 12, Washington DC: Institute for Advanced Strategic and Political Studies, June 2001, p. 8.
8. Kreutz, Andrej, *Russia in the Middle East: Friend or Foe*, Westport, Connecticut, London: Praeger Security International, 2007, p. 84.
9. Official United Nations website. http://www.un.org/Depts/unscom/Keyresolutions/sres99–1284.htm, last accessed 11 August 2008.
10. Kreutz, Andrej *Russia in the Middle East*, p. 89.
11. Official United Nations website.
12. Kreutz, Andrej *Russia in the Middle East*, p. 89.
13. Hashim, Ahmad, 'Saddam Husayn and civil-military relations in Iraq: the quest for legitimacy and power', *Middle East Journal*, 57, 1, Winter 2003, p. 38.
14. Kreutz, Andrej, *Russia in the Middle East*, p. 94.
15. Freedman, Robert O., 'Russian policy toward the Middle East under Putin: the impact of 9/11 and the war in Iraq', *Alternatives* (Turkish Journal of International Relations), 2, 2, Summer 2003. http://www.alternativesjournal.net/volume2/number2/putin.htm, last accessed 9 January 2008.
16. *Radio Free Europe/Radio Liberty Newsline*, 'Influential analyst hints Moscow might join anti-Hussein coalition', 1 November 2002. http://www.rferl.org/content/Article/1142792.html, last accessed 14 August 2008.
17. Powell, Bonnie Azab, 'UN weapons inspector Hans Blix faults Bush administration for lack of "critical thinking" in Iraq', *UC Berkeley News*, 18 March 2004. http://berkeley.edu/news/media/releases/2004/03/18_blix.shtml, last accessed 14 August 2008.
18. Bowker, Mike, *Russia and the Islamic World*, Aldershot, England: Ashgate, 2007, p. 100.
19. Mirsky, Georgy, 'The Baghdad puzzle'.
20. Tsygankov, Andrei P., *Russia's Foreign Policy: Change and Continuity in National Identity*, New York, Oxford: Rowan and Littlefield Publishers Inc., 2006, p. 141.
21. Official United Nations website.
22. Official United Nations website.
23. Official United Nations website.
24. Official United Nations website.
25. Kreutz, Andrej, *Russia in the Middle East*, p. 103.
26. Blank, Stephen, 'The post-Soviet states and the post-Saddam Middle East', p. 63.

27. Nasr, Vali, 'When the Shiites rise', *Foreign Affairs*, 85, 4, July/August 2006. Database: Academic Search Premier.
28. Bremer III, L. Paul, 'How I didn't dismantle Iraq's army', *New York Times*, 6 September 2007. http://www.nytimes.com/2007/09/06/opinion/06bremer.html, last accessed 16 August 2008.
29. Nasr, Vali, 'When the Shiites rise'.
30. Hashim, Ahmed, 'Saddam Husayn and civil-military relations in Iraq,' p. 12.
31. Tully, Andrew F., 'Iraq: analysts say exclusions from contracts could hurt US', *Radio Free Europe/Radio Liberty Newsline*, 11 December 2003. http://www.globalsecurity.org/wmd/library/news/iraq/2003/12/iraq-031211-rferl-172001.htm, last accessed 9 January 2008.
32. *Indiainfo.com*, 'There were no terrorists under Saddam Hussein', 18 December 2003. http://news.indiainfo.com/spotlight/usiraqwar/18putin.html, last accessed 17 August 2008.
33. *BBC News*, 'Putin says Iraq planned US attack', 18 June 2004. http://news.bbc.co.uk/2/hi/americas/3819057.stm, last accessed 18 August 2008.
34. *The White House* official website, 'President Bush, President Putin discuss Iraq', 8 June 2004. http://www.whitehouse.gov/news/releases/2004/06/20040608–27.html, last accessed 18 August 2008.
35. *The White House*, 'President Bush, President Putin discuss Iraq'.
36. Kreutz, Andrej, *Russia in the Middle East*, p. 105.
37. *Naharnet*, 'State Department says Hezbollah is supporting anti-US groups in Iraq', 29 April 2006. http://www.naharnet.com/domino/tn/NewsDesk.nsf/getstory?openform&F7BC36C84500B3ACC2257161002F5060, last accessed 2 May 2006.
38. Saltanov, Alexander, *30 Days*, Catholic Church monthly, interviewed by Giovanni Cubeddu and Pierluca Azzaro, October 2006. http://www.30giorni.it/us/articolo.asp?id=11640, last accessed 18 January 2008.
39. Interview with Evgenii Primakov on *Rossiya Al-Yaum* (Russia Today) TV, broadcast on 1 January 2008 in a review of the Middle East in 2007.
40. *Radio Free Europe/Radio Liberty Newsline*, 'Widespread criticism of execution of former Iraqi dictator', 3 January 2007. http://www.rferl.org/content/article/1143784.html, last accessed 20 January 2009.
41. *Radio Free Europe/Radio Liberty Newsline*, 'Widespread criticism of execution of former Iraqi dictator'.
42. *Radio Free Europe/Radio Liberty Newsline*, 'Iraqi president criticises Syria's stance on Turkish incursions', 22 October 2007. http://www.rferl.org/content/article/1143977.html, last accessed 8 September 2009.
43. Interview with Evgenii Primakov on *Rossiya Al-Yaum* (Russia Today) TV, broadcast on 1 January 2008 in a review of the Middle East in 2007.
44. *RIA Novosti*, 'Iraq says Russian firms will not get business privilege', 12 Febru-

ary 2008. http://en.rian.ru/world/20080212/99008694.html, last accessed 19 August 2008.

45. Eckel, Mike, 'Putin: Russia wants more work in Iraq', *USA Today*, 24 March 2008. http://www.usatoday.com/news/world/2008–03–24–566797666_x.htm, last accessed 19 August 2008.
46. Eckel, Mike, 'Putin: Russia wants more work in Iraq'.
47. *The Voice of Russia*, 'War over: Russia is back in Iraq', 9 October 2012. http://english.ruvr.ru/2012_10_09/War-over-Russia-back-in-Iraq/, last accessed 13 January 2013.
48. *The Voice of Russia*, 'Al Maliki buys Russian weapons and defends Syria against Turkey',10 October 2012. http://english.ruvr.ru/2012_10_10/Al-Maliki-buys-Russian-weapons-and-defends-Syria-against-Turkey-verbally/, last accessed 13 January 2013.

7. THE SYRIA-LEBANON DILEMMA

1. The origins of this remark remain unclear but it dates back to the 1950s.
2. Golan, Galia, *Soviet Policies in the Middle East from WWII to Gorbachev*, Cambridge: Cambridge University Press, 1990, p. 127.
3. Golan, Galia, 'The Soviet Union and the Israeli action in Lebanon', *International Affairs* (Royal Institute of International Affairs), 59, 1, Winter 1982–1983, p. 16.
4. Interview with Karim Mroue, former General Secretary of the Lebanese Communist Party, in *Russia Today Arabic* (*Rossiia Al-Yaum*) TV channel, broadcast on 13 January 2010.
5. Elbaz, Michel, 'Dangerous liaisons: covert "love affair" between Russia and Hezbollah', *Axis Information and Analysis*, 24 May 2005. http://www.axisglobe.com/hezbollah1.htm, last accessed 16 Feb. 2006.
6. Hamzeh, Ahmad Nizar, *In the Path of Hezbollah*, New York: Syracuse University Press, 2004, p. 146.
7. Comments made to the Russian daily newspaper *Zaftra* in early 1997, quoted in Elbaz, Michel, 'Dangerous liaisons'.
8. *BBC News*, 'Missing aviator Ron Arad dead, Primakov tells Israelis', 27 October 1997. http://news.bbc.co.uk/1/hi/world/monitoring/16740.stm, last accessed 11 September 2008.
9. Elbaz, Michel, 'Dangerous liaisons'.
10. Interview with Vitalii Na'umkin in Moscow in 1996. Na'umkin was then head of the Institute of Oriental Studies in the Russian Academy of Sciences.
11. Gathering of small group of students and academics interviewing Ryan Gliha, US Cultural Attache in Beirut on 15 December 2006.
12. Assaf, Nayla, 'Lebanese MPs give Lahoud 3 more years', *Daily Star* (Beirut), 4 September 2004.

13. United Nations website. http://www.un.org
14. Moser, Robert G., *Unexpected Outcomes: Electoral Systems, Political Parties and Representation in Russia*, Pittsburg: University of Pittsburg Press, 2001, p. 80.
15. Bukkvoll, Tor, 'Arming the Ayatollahs: economic lobbies in Russia's Iran policy', *Problems of Post-Communism*, 49, 6, November/December 2002, p. 31.
16. *The Guardian*, 'Moscow calls for Syria to leave Lebanon', 3 March 2005. http://www.guardian.co.uk/world/2005/mar/03/russia.syria, last accessed 7 October 2008.
17. *The Guardian*, 'Moscow calls for Syria to leave Lebanon'.
18. *Naharnet*, 'Rice says Mideast is threatened by Iran-Syria-Hezbollah nexus', 20 February 2006. http://www.naharnet.com/domino/tn/NewsDesk.nsf/getstory?openform&40EA87BCCC296240C225711B0033B29C, last accessed 20 Feb. 2006.
19. Byman, Daniel, 'Hezbollah's dilemma', *Foreign Affairs*, 13 April 2005. http://www.foreignaffairs.org/20050413faupdate84277/daniel-byman/hezbollah-s-dilemma.html, last accessed 21 March 2006.
20. Byman, Daniel, 'Hezbollah's dilemma'.
21. Schiff, Ze'ev, 'Hezbollah received intel from Russian-Syrian listening post during war', *Ha'aretz.com*, 4 October 2006. http://www.haaretz.com/hasen/spages/769512.html, last accessed 6 October 2006.
22. Trenin, Dmitri, 'Russia leaves the West', *Foreign Affairs*, 85, 4, July/August 2006. Database: Academic Search Premier.
23. *Israel Insider*, 'Russia rejects Israel's claim that Hezbollah used Russian rockets', 1 January 2006. http://web.israelinsider.com/Articles/Briefs/7408.htm
24. Schiff, Ze'ev, 'Hezbollah received Intel from Russian-Syrian listening post during war'.
25. *Middle East Intelligence Bulletin*, 'Hezbollah reportedly acquires SA-18 SAMs', 5, 4, April 2003. http://www.meib.org/articles/0304_l2.htm
26. *Naharnet*, 'Israel Ambassador to Spain: Hezbollah still armed thanks to Syria', 18 October 2006. http://www.naharnet.com/domino/tn/NewsDesk.nsf/Lebanon/6CFDEE7463489A90C225720B00480103?OpenDocument
27. Shanahan, Rodger, 'Hezbollah's dilemmas', *Mideast Monitor*, 1, 1, February 2006. http://www.mideastmonitor.org/issues/0602/0602_4.htm
28. Matthews, Owen (with Anna Nemtsova in Moscow), 'Past as prologue: Moscow presents itself as the new "middleman" in the Middle East. But its role may actually be that of spoiler', *Newsweek International*, 27 February 2006. http://www.msnbc.msn.com/id/11436739/site/newsweek/
29. Jumblatt television interview on *Lebanese Broadcasting Company* with Marcel Ghanem, on the programme 'Kalam Al-Nas' ('what people say'), on 30 March 2006.
30. United Nations website. http://www.un.org/Depts/unscom/Keyresolutions/sres99–1284.htm, last accessed 11 August 2008.

31. Ninth Report of the International Independent Investigation Commission, November 2007, headed and presented by Serge Brammertz. The report was authorised by UNSC Resolutions 1595 (2005), 1636 (2005), 1644 (2005), 1686 (2006), 1748 (2007).
32. *RIA Novosti*, 'Russia says planned Hariri tribunal affects Lebanon sovereignty', 31 May 2007. http://en.rian.ru/russia/20070531/66382412.html, last accessed 9 October 2008.
33. *RIA Novosti*, 'Moscow unopposed to intl. tribunal on Lebanon ex-PM's death', 17 April 2007. http://en.rian.ru/russia/20070417/63830929.html, last accessed 9 October 2008.
34. *Al-Mustaqbal* Lebanese daily newspaper, 'Hezbollah denies links with "Black Sunday" results' (hizballah yatanassal min nata'ij 'al-ahhad al-asswad'), 2861, 30 January 2008. http://www.almustaqbal.com/storiesprintpreview.aspx?storyid=272883, last accessed 30 January 2008.
35. Khripunov, Igor, 'Russia's weapon's trade: domestic competition and foreign markets', *Problems of Post-Communism*, 46, 2, March/April 1999, p. 46.
36. Kreutz, Andrej, *Russia in the Middle East: Friend or Foe*, Westport, Connecticut, London: Praeger Security International, 2007, p. 16.
37. Karsh, Efraim, 'Soviet-Syrian relations: the troubled partnership', in Light, Margot (ed.), *Troubled Friendships; Moscow's Third World Ventures*, Royal Institute of International Affairs, London: British Academic Press, 1993.
38. Kreutz, Andrej, *Russia in the Middle East*, p. 23.
39. Davis, Douglas, 'New arms deal between Syria, Russia threatens Israel', *Jewish Telegraphic Agency*, 5 February 1999. http://www.jewishsf.com/content/2module/displaystory/story_id/10522/format/html/edition_id/201/displaystory.html, last accessed 20 August 2007.
40. Kreutz, Andrej, *Russia in the Middle East*, p. 27.
41. Simon, Steven and Jonathan Stevenson, 'The road to Damascus', *Foreign Affairs*, 83, 3, May/Jun 2004. Database: Academic Search Premier.
42. Shumilin, A., 'The US vs. rogue states of the Middle East', *International Affairs: A Russian Journal*, 5, 2003. http://www.ciaonet.org/olj/iarj/iarj_03_05/iarj_03_05a.html, last accessed 22 March 2006.
43. *Los Angeles Times*, 'Powell comes down on Syria and Iran', 31 March 2003. http://articles.latimes.com/2003/mar/31/news/war-powell31, last accessed 17 November 2008.
44. Timmerman, Kenneth R., 'Ex-official: Russia moved Saddam's WMD', *Newsmax.com*, 19 February 2006. http://archive.newsmax.com/archives/articles/2006/2/18/233023.shtml?s=lh, last accessed 17 November 2008.
45. Timmerman, Kenneth R., 'Ex-official: Russia moved Saddam's WMD'.
46. *The White House*, 'Fact sheet: implementing the Syria Accountability and Lebanese Sovereignty Restoration Act of 2003', 11 May 2004. http://www.white-

house.gov/news/releases/2004/05/20040511–7.html, last accessed 18 November 2008.

47. Rumer, Eugene, *Dangerous Drift: Russia's Middle East Policy*, Washington Institute for Near East Policy, Policy Paper No. 54, 2002, p. 2.
48. Katz, Mark N., 'Putin's foreign policy towards Syria', *The Middle East Review of International Affairs*, 10, 1, March 2006, p. 53.
49. Lantratov, Konstantin and Grigory Asmolov, 'MiGs will defend Syria and Iran', *Kommersant Online*, 19 June 2007. http://www.kommersant.com/p775460/r_1/arms_trade_/, last accessed 28 November 2008.
50. Katz, Mark N., 'Putin's foreign policy towards Syria', p. 56.
51. McCleod, Huge, 'From Syrian fishing port to naval power base: Russia moves into the Mediterranean military foothold part of closer ties with Damascus', *The Guardian*, 8 October 2008, p. 22.
52. *Al-Mustaqbal*, 'Syria allows Russian fleets usage of bases in Tartous and Latakia in return for dropping debts'.
53. *Al-Mustaqbal*, 'Syria allows Russian fleets usage of bases in Tartous and Latakia in return for dropping debts' [souriya samahhat al-ustoul al-russi fi lathkia wa tartous mukkabel iskkat al-duyun], 7 August 2007. http://www.almustaqbal.com/stories.aspx?StoryID=245561, last accessed 7 August 2008.
54. Baker III, James A. and Lee H. Hamilton, *The Iraq Study Group Report*, The United States Institute of Peace. http://www.usip.org/isg/iraq_study_group_report/report/1206/iraq_study_group_report.pdf, last accessed 20 December 2008.
55. Baker III, James A. and Lee H. Hamilton, *The Iraq Study Group Report.*
56. *The White House*, 'Fact sheet'.
57. Matthews, Owen (with Anna Nemtsova in Moscow), 'Past as prologue'.
58. *LBC website*, 'Russia has in interest in ensuring Lebanese stability', 28 January 2008.
59. Primakov, Evgenii, 'Lebanon: a step toward settlement', *Moscow News*, 3, 24 January 2008. http://www.mnweekly.ru/comment/20071206/55294972.html, last accessed 30 January 2008.
60. *The Moscow Times*, 'Primakov delivers message in Damascus', 3780, 8 November 2007, p. 2.
61. *Associated Press*, 'Report: Russia starts delivery of fighter jets to Syria', *International Herald Tribune*, 19 June 2007. http://www.iht.com/articles/ap/2007/06/19/europe/EU-GEN-Russia-Syria-Jets.php, last accessed 20 August 2007.
62. *Associated Press*, 'Report: Russia starts delivery of fighter jets to Syria'.
63. *Radio Free Europe/Radio Liberty Newsline*, 'Russian foreign minister sends mixed signals on US'. 5 February 2007. http://www.rferl.org/content/article/1143805.html, last accessed 23 January 2009.
64. Schenker, David, 'Syria: between negotiations with Israel and the Iranian Axis',

Jerusalem Center for Public Policy, 8, 2, 27 May 2008. http://www.jcpa.org/JCPA/Templates/ShowPage.asp?DRIT=1&DBID=1&LNGID=1&TMID=111&FID=283&PID=0&IID=2116&TTL=Syria:_Between_Negotiations_with_Israel_and_the_Iranian_Axis, last accessed 30 May 2008.

65. N. Ghadry, Farid, 'Syrian reform: what lies beneath', *Middle East Quarterly*, 12, 1, Winter 2005. http://www.meforum.org/article/683, last accessed on 25 Feb. 2005.
66. Murtazin, Andrei, 'Bashar Al-Asad rushes to hug Washington', *RIA Novosti*, 30 April 2008. http://en.rian.ru/analysis/20080430/106262366.html, last accessed 17 November 2008.
67. Murtazin, Andrei, 'Bashar Al-Asad rushes to hug Washington'.
68. Blanford, Nicholas, 'Syria eyes an edge amid Russia-US rift', *Christian Science Monitor*, 28 August 2008. http://www.csmonitor.com/2008/0828/p06s02-wome.html, last accessed 8 September 2008.
69. Petrov, Nilita, 'Russia pushing weapons sales in the Middle East and beyond', *Middle East Times*, 27 August 2008. http://www.metimes.com/International/2008/08/27/russia_pushing_weapons_sales_in_middle_east_and_beyond/3200/, last accessed 8 September 2008.
70. *BBC News Online*, 'Russia's Lavrov says Beirut flights not Syria evacuation', 23 January 2013. http://www.bbc.co.uk/news/world-middle-east-21160289, last accessed 24 January 2013.
71. *RIA Novosti*, 'Russia closes Aleppo Consulate', 15 January 2013. http://en.rian.ru/world/20130115/178794483.html, last accessed 27 January 2013.
72. *Naharnet*, 'Putin meets Suleiman, promises international conference on Syrian refugees', 23 January 2013. http://www.naharnet.com/stories/en/69439-putin-meets-suleiman-promises-international-conference-on-syrian-refugees, last accessed 24 January 2013.

8. THE ISRAEL PARADOX AND THE PALESTINIAN PROBLEM

1. Yevtushenkov, Vladimir, 'After the lull: Russia and the Arab world at a new stage', *Russia in Global Affairs*, 3, July–September 2005. http://eng.globalaffairs.ru/numbers/12/950.html, last accessed 30 November 2007.
2. Slezkine, Yuri, *The Jewish Century*, Princeton: Princeton University Press, 2004, p. 105.
3. Freedman, Robert O., 'Russian policy toward the Middle East under Yeltsin and Putin', *Jerusalem Viewpoints*, 461, 2 September 2001. http://www.jcpa.org/JCPA/Templates/ShowPage.asp?DRIT=2&DBID=1&LNGID=1&TMID=111&FID=443&PID=0&IID=1125&TTL=Russian_Policy_Toward_the_Middle_East_Under_Yeltsin_and_Putin, last accessed 11 April 2007.
4. Epstein, Alek D., 'Russia and Israel: a romance aborted?', *Russia in Global Affairs*,

4, October–December 2007. http://eng.globalaffairs.ru/numbers/21/1161.html, last accessed 18 November 2007.
5. *RFL/RL*, 197, 17 October 1994, p. 2.
6. Kreutz, Andrej, *Russia in the Middle East: Friend or Foe*, Westport, Connecticut, London: Praeger Security International, 2007, p. 60.
7. Karny, Yo'av, *Highlanders: A Journey to the Caucasus in Quest of Memory*, New York: Farrar, Strauss and Giroux, 2000, p. 271.
8. Rumer, Eugene, *Dangerous Drift: Russia's Middle East Policy*, Washington DC: Washington Institute for Near East Policy, Policy Paper 54, 2002, p. 145.
9. Slezkine, Yuri, *The Jewish Century*, p. 69.
10. Shevtsova, Lilia, *Putin's Russia*, Washington DC: Carnegie Endowment for International Peace, Washington DC, 2003, p. 162.
11. Katz, Mark N., 'Putin's pro-Israel policy', *Middle East Quarterly*, Winter 2005. http://www.meforum.org/article/690, last accessed 29 September 2005.
12. Katz, Mark N., 'Putin's pro-Israel policy'.
13. Kreutz, Andrej, *Russia in the Middle East*, p. 72.
14. Brown, Archie, 'Vladimir Putin's leadership in comparative perspective', in Ross, Cameron (ed.), *Russian Politics under Putin*, Manchester: Manchester University Press, 2004, p. 8.
15. Cohen, Ariel, 'Calling up the past', *Russia in Global Affairs*, 1 December 2003. http://eng.globalaffairs.ru/numbers/5/503.html, last accessed 9 January 2009.
16. Freedman, Robert O.,'Russian policy toward the Middle East under Yeltsin and Putin'.
17. Kreutz, Andrej, *Russia in the Middle East*, p. 72.
18. Khripunov, Igor, 'Russia's weapon's trade: domestic competition and foreign markets', *Problems of Post-Communism*, 46, 2, March–April 1999, p. 44.
19. Satanovsky, Evgenii, 'A new Middle East', *Russia in Global Affairs*, 3, July–September 2005. http://eng.globalaffairs.ru/numbers/12/951.html, last accessed 9 January 2008.
20. Freedman, Robert O., 'Negative scenarios', *Bitterlemons-international.org*, 5, 43, 22 November 2007. http://www.bitterlemons-international.org/previous.php?opt=1&id=204#835, last accessed 12 August 2008.
21. Sadr, Ihsaneh I., 'The impact of Iran's nuclearisation on Israel', *Middle East Policy*, 12, 2, Summer 2005, p. 67.
22. Primakov, Evgenii, 'Is Israel's call for peace with Syria yet another diversion', *Moscow News*, 29, 26 July 2007. http://www.mnweekly.ru/columnists/20070726/55263936.html, last accessed 30 January 2008.
23. Bourtman, Ilya, 'Putin and Russia's Middle Eastern policy', *Middle East Review of International Affairs*, 10, 2, June 2006, p. 2.
24. Weir, Fred, 'Israel and Russia: trade and restive Arab world outweigh differences on Iran', *Christian Science Monitor*, 25 June 2013. http://www.csmonitor.com/World/Europe/2012/0625/

Israel-and-Russia-Trade-and-restive-Arab-world-outweigh-differences-on-Iran, last accessed 27 January 2013.

25. Bourtman, Ilya, 'Putin and Russia's Middle Eastern Policy', p. 5.
26. *Stratfor Intelligence*, 'Olmert's cancelled trip to Moscow: the broader picture', 9 September 2008. http://www.stratfor.com/geopolitical_diary/geopolitical_diary_olmert_s_cancelled_trip_moscow_broader_picture, last accessed 12 September 2008.
27. Saivetz, Carol R., 'Gorbachev's Middle East policy: the Arab dimension', in Goldberg, David H. and Paul Marantz (eds), *The Decline of the Soviet Union and the Transformation of the Middle East*, San Francisco and Oxford 1994, p. 11.
28. Beliaev, Igor and John Marks, *Common Ground on Terrorism*, London: Norton, 1991, p. 58.
29. Kreutz, Andrej, *Russia in the Middle East*, p. 54.
30. Kreutz, Andrej, *Russia in the Middle East*, p. 64.
31. Kreutz, Andrej, *Russia in the Middle East*, p. 67.
32. Freedman, Robert O., 'Russian policy toward the Middle East under Yeltsin and Putin'.
33. *BBC News*, 'Russia backs Palestinian state', 11 August 2000. http://news.bbc.co.uk/1/hi/world/middle_east/876352.stm, last accessed 22 December 2008.
34. Epstein, Alek D., 'Russia and Israel: a romance aborted?'.
35. Kreutz, Andrej, *Russia in the Middle East*, p. 76.
36. Wilson, Scott, 'Hamas sweeps Palestinian elections, complicating peace efforts in Mideast', *Washington Post*, 27 January 2006, p. 1.
37. *Pravda.ru*, 'USA cuts funds to Palestine, Russia prepares to deliver arms to Hamas', 17 February 2006. http://english.pravda.ru/russia/politics/17–02–2006/76118-Hamas-0, last accessed 17 February 2006.
38. Primakov, Evgenii, 'New opportunity for the Middle East?' *Moscow News*, 5 July 2007. http://mnweekly.rian.ru/columnists/20070705/55260820.html, last accessed 7 August 2007.
39. Primakov, Evgenii, 'New opportunity for the Middle East?'.
40. Primakov, Evgenii, 'New opportunity for the Middle East?'.
41. *Radio Free Europe/Radio Liberty Newsline*, 'Putin hails Palestinian President', 1 August 2007. http://www.rferl.org/content/article/1143923.html, last accessed 2 February 2008.

9. SAUDI ARABIA AND JORDAN: ROYAL OPPORTUNITIES

1. Sadi, Waleed, 'With Russia the US faces Middle East frustration', *Zawya Online*, 4 December 2007. http://www.zawya.com/printstory.cfm?storyid=DS041207_dsart40&l=064520071204, last accessed 4 December 2007.
2. Parkhomenko, Sergei, 'Poteria tempa' (Losing Tempo), *Nezavisimaia gazeta*, 22 October 1992, p. 4.

3. Sokirko, Viktor, 'Iordantsy bol'she ne prinimaiut ranenykh Chechentsev' (Jordan no longer taking part in Chechen crisis), *Komsomol'skaia pravda*, 16 March 1996, p. 1. Djokhar Dudaev was then president of the breakaway Chechen republic.
4. Berman, Ilan, 'Russia and the Mideast vacuum', *IASPS Papers in Strategy*, Institute for Advanced Strategic and Political Studies, Washington DC, 12, June 2001, p. 9.
5. *NUPI Center for Russian Studies*, 'Primakov tours Middle East', 30 October 1997. http://www2.nupi.no/cgi-win//Russland/krono.exe?1314, last accessed 20 December 2008.
6. *Jordan Times*, 'Regent congratulates Primakov', 12 September 1998. http://www.jordanembassyus.org/091298001.htm, last accessed 20 November 2007.
7. *The Russia Journal*, 'Putin meets King of Jordan', 28 August 2001. http://www.russiajournal.com/node/7461, last accessed 26 December 2008.
8. *The Russia Journal*, 'Putin meets King of Jordan'.
9. J. F. O. and Paul Quinn-Judge, 'Defenseless targets', *Time Europe*, 5 September 2004. http://www.time.com/time/europe/html/040913/story.html, last accessed 19 November 2007.
10. Hahn, Gordon M., *Russia's Islamic Threat*, New Haven and London: Yale University Press, 2007, p. 64.
11. Hahn, Gordon M., *Russia's Islamic Threat*, p. 64.
12. *APS Diplomat Recorder*, 'Jordan's King Abdullah meets with Putin', 20 August 2005. http://findarticles.com/p/articles/mi_hb6507/is_/ai_n29204904, last accessed 22 November 2008.
13. *RIA Novosti*, 'Russia, Jordan oppose resolving conflicts by force', 13 February 2007. http://en.rian.ru/world/20070213/60685998.html, last accessed 22 December 2007.
14. Kedrov, Vladimir, 'Russia-Jordan an important visit', *Zawya*, 9 February 2007. https://zawya.com/story.cfm/sidZAWYA20070209071511/Russia-Jordan%20-%20an%20important%20visit
15. *APS Diplomat Recorder*, 'Jordan's King Abdullah meets with Putin'.
16. Sadi, Waleed, 'With Russia the US faces Middle East frustration'.
17. Yodfat, A., *The Soviet Union and the Arabian Peninsula*, London: Croom Helm, 1983, p. 97.
18. Iusin, Maksim, 'Our visit is a drive for markets, including arms markets', *Izvestiia*, in *Current Digest of the Post-Soviet Press*, XLIV, 18, 3 June 1992, p. 15.
19. Staalesen, Atle, Chapter 11, 'Orthodoxy and Islam in post-Soviet Russia: opposing confessional cultures or unifying force?', in Kolstø, Pål and Helge Blackkisrod (ed.),*Nation-Building and Common Values in Russia*, Lanham, Boulder, Oxford: Rowan and Littlefield Publishers Inc., 2004, p. 306.
20. Staalesen, Atle, Chapter 11, 'Orthodoxy and Islam in post-Soviet Russia, p. 306.

21. Katz, Mark N., 'Saudi-Russian relations since 9/11', *Problems of Post-Communism*, 51, 2, November/December 2002, p. 4.
22. Katz, Mark N., 'Saudi-Russian relations since 9/11', p. 5.
23. Doran, Michael Scott, 'The Saudi paradox', *Foreign Affairs*, 83, 1, January/February 2004.
24. *Reuters UK*, 'Iran says may hit Western warships if attacked', 19 January 2010. http://uk.reuters.com/article/idUKTRE60I1MS20100119, last accessed 21 January 2010. This was a threat made by Iranian Defence Minister Ahmad Vahidi in early 2010 following a pattern of similar threats in the previous decade.
25. Sergei Lavrov interviewed by Sami Amarah in Moscow, *Asharq Alawsat* (Saudi Arab Daily—English edition), 25 October 2006. http://aawsat.com/english/news.asp?section=3&id=6818, last accessed 8 January 2008.
26. Arbatov, Alexei, 'Russia and the Iranian nuclear crisis', *Carnegie Endowment For International Peace*, 23 May 2006. http://www.carnegieendowment.org/publications/index.cfm?fa=view&id=18363&prog=zgp&proj=znpp, last accessed 26 December 2007.
27. Arbatov, Alexei, 'Russia and the Iranian nuclear crisis'.
28. Black, Ian, 'Lebanese ally of Bashar al-Assad held in Beirut over "sensitive" security issue', *The Guardian*, 9 August 2012. http://www.guardian.co.uk/world/2012/aug/09/lebanese-assad-ally-held-beirut, last accessed 16 February 2013.
29. Mattair, Thomas R., 'Mutual threat perceptions in the Arab/Persian Gulf: GCC perceptions', *Middle East Policy*, 14, 2, Summer 2007, p. 138.
30. Abdul Ghafur, P.K., 'Putin visit will boost ties', *Arab News*, 12 February 2007. http://www.arabnews.com/services/print/print.asp?artid=92060&d=12&m=2&y=2007&hl='Putin%20Visit%20Will%20Boost%20Ties', last accessed 25 July 2008.
31. *Al-Jazeera TV*, Doha, 17 February 2007. Interview in Arabic.
32. Freedman, Robert O., 'Russian policy toward the Middle East under Putin: the impact of 9/11 and the war in Iraq', *Alternatives* (Turkish Journal of International Relations), 2, 2, Summer 2003. http://www.alternativesjournal.net/volume2/number2/putin.htm, last accessed 9 January 2008.
33. Yevtushenkov, Vladimir, 'After the lull: Russia and the Arab world at a new stage', *Russia in Global Affairs*, 3, July–September 2005. http://eng.globalaffairs.ru/numbers/12/950.html, last accessed 30 Nov, 2007.
34. Yevtushenkov, Vladimir, 'After the lull'.
35. Osborn, Andrew, 'Russia becomes largest arms seller to the Third World'.
36. Cohen, Ariel, 'Putin's Middle East visit: Russia is back', *The Heritage Foundation*, Web Memo 1382, 5 March 2007. http://www.heritage.org/research/russiaandeurasia/wm1382.cfm
37. Sfakianakis, John, 'Saudi-Russian trade deepen', *Arab News*, 21 November 2007. http://arabnews.com/node/305906, last accessed 5 July 2010.

38. Daly, John C.K., 'Saudi-Russian military cooperation', *Eurasia Daily Monitor*, 5, 137, 18 July 2008. http://www.jamestown.org/edm/article.php?article_id=2373238, last accessed 10 September 2008.
39. Nocetti, Julien, 'From Moscow to Mecca: Russia's Saudi Arabian diplomacy', *IFRI* Russia/NIS Center, June 2010, p. 7. http://www.ifri.org, last accessed 15 February 2013.
40. Pilko, Alexei, 'Russia-Saudi Arabia relations and the Arab Spring', *Russia and India Report*, 25 September 2012. http://indrus.in/articles/2012/09/25/russia_saudi_arabia_relations_and_the_arab_spring_17873.html, last accessed 16 February 2013.
41. *RIANovosti*, 'Saudi Arabia condemns Russian statements on Syria', 11 March 2012. http://www.en.rian.ru/world/20120311/172099331.html, last accessed 14 February 2013.
42. Smith, Mark A., 'Russia and the Persian Gulf: the deepening of Moscow's Middle East policies', *Conflict Studies Research Centre*, Defence Academy of the United Kingdom, August 2007.

10. IRAN, TURKEY AND THE FRAGILE SOUTH

1. Staalesen, Atle, Chapter 11 'Orthodoxy and Islam in post-Soviet Russia: opposing confessional cultures or unifying force?', *Nation-building and common values in Russia*, Lanham, Boulder, Oxford: Rowan and Littlefield Publishers Inc., 2004, p. 314.
2. Reddaway, Peter and Dmitri Glinski, *The Tragedy of Russia's Reforms: Market Bolshevism against Democracy*, Washington DC: United States Institute of Peace Press, 2001, p. 70.
3. CIA World Fact Book, July 2009 figures. www.CIA.gov, last accessed 29 April 2010.
4. Bukkvoll, Tor, 'Arming the Ayatollahs: economic lobbies in Russia's Iran policy', *Problems of Post-Communism*, 49, 6, November/December 2002, p. 33.
5. Adeli, Mohammad Hoseyn, *E'temad* Iranian website, provided and translated by *BBC Worldwide Monitoring*, 1 November 2007. http://acturca.wordpress.com/2007/11/09/iran-commentator-analyzes-iran-russia-ties-in-last-two-centuries/, last accessed 22 August 2008.
6. Rumer, Eugene, *Dangerous Drift: Russia's Middle East Policy*, Washington Institute for Near East Policy, Policy Paper No. 54, 2002, p. 17.
7. Berman, Ilan, 'Russia and the Mideast vacuum', *IASPS Papers in Strategy*, Institute for Advanced Strategic and Political Studies, Washington DC, No. 12, June 2001, p. 20.
8. Moisi, Dominique, 'Russia's transformation from people power to Putin power', *Daily Star*, 2 November 2006. http://www.dailystar.com.lb/article.asp?edition_id=1&categ_id=5&article_id=76589.

9. Bukkvoll, Tor, 'Arming the Ayatollahs', p. 29.
10. Mizin, Victor, 'The Russia-Iran nuclear connection and US policy options', *Middle East Review of International Affairs*, 8, 1, March 2004, p. 76.
11. Bukkvoll, Tor, 'Arming the Ayatollahs', p. 32.
12. Nasr, Vali, 'When the Shiites rise', *Foreign Affairs*, 85, 4, July/August 2006. Database: Academic Search Premier.
13. Bowker, Mike, *Russia, America and the Islamic World*, Aldershot: Ashgate, 2007, p. 104.
14. Bowker, Mike, *Russia, America and the Islamic World*, p. 95.
15. Dannreuther, Roland, Chapter 2 'Russia and the Middle East', in Carter, Hannah and Anoushiravan Ehteshami (eds.), *The Middle East's Relations with Asia and Russia*, London and New York: Routledge Curzon, 2004, p. 26.
16. Freedman, Robert O., 'Putin, Iran, and the nuclear weapons issue', *Problems of Post-Communism*, 53, 2, March/April 2006, p. 39.
17. Bukkvoll, Tor, 'Arming the Ayatollahs', p. 30.
18. Interview with Evgenii Primakov on *Rossiya Al-Yaum* (Russia Today) TV, broadcast on 1 January 2008 in a review of the Middle East in 2007.
19. Katz, Mark N., 'Putin, Ahmadinejad and the Iranian nuclear crisis', *Middle East Policy*, 13, 4, Winter 2006, p. 125.
20. Mizin, Victor, 'The Russia-Iran nuclear connection and US policy options', p. 74.
21. Paton Walsh, Nick in Moscow and Julian Borger in Washington, 'Putin defends Iran and eyes up nuclear fuel deal', *The Guardian*, 19 February 2005. http://www.guardian.co.uk/world/2005/feb/19/syria.iran, last accessed 8 October 2008.
22. Arbatov, Alexei, 'Russia and the Iranian nuclear crisis', *Carnegie Endowment for International Peace*, 23 May 2006. http://www.carnegieendowment.org/publications/index.cfm?fa=view&id=18363&prog=zgp&proj=znpp, last accessed 26 December 2007.
23. Freedman, Robert O., 'Putin, Iran, and the nuclear weapons issue', p. 46.
24. Simonov, Pavel, 'Russia won the elections in Iran?', *Axis Information and Analysis*, 27 June 2005. http://www.axisglobe.com/article.asp?article=195
25. *Tehrantimes.com*, 'Russia, France issue statement on Iran's nuclear issue', 15 February 2006. http://www.tehrantimes.com
26. Freedman, Robert O., 'Putin, Iran, and the nuclear weapons issue', p. 44.
27. *Radio Free Europe/Radio Liberty Newsline*, 'Iranian legislators accuse Russia of bad faith', 12 March 2007. http://www.rferl.org/content/article/1143829.html, last accessed 28 January 2009.
28. Khripunov, Igor, 'Russia's weapon's trade: domestic competition and foreign markets', *Problems of Post-Communism*, 46, 2, March/April 1999, p. 48.
29. Bowker, Mike, *Russia, America and the Islamic World*, p. 118.

30. Tymoshenko, Yulia, 'Moscow's Mideast myopia', *Haaretz.com*, 16 January 2007. http://www.haaretz.com/hasen/spages/813794.html, last accessed 16 January 2007.
31. *Radio Free Europe/Radio Liberty Newsline*, 'Iran president envisages collapse of "arrogant" powers', 3 January 2007. http://www.rferl.org/content/article/1143784.html, last accessed 20 January 2009.
32. Fathi, Nazila, 'In Iran, Putin warns against military action', *New York Times*, 17 October 2007. http://www.nytimes.com/2007/10/17/world/middleeast/17iran.html?_r=1&ref=middleeast, last accessed 30 March 2007.
33. *Radio Free Europe/Radio Liberty Newsline*, 'Foreign minister stresses need for caution on Iran', 1 November 2007. http://www.rferl.org/content/article/1143985.html, last accessed 2 February 2009. The report quoted the Russian *Kommersant* newspaper, 31 October edition.
34. Bowker, Mike, *Russia, America and the Islamic World*, p. 115.
35. Bukkvoll, Tor, 'Arming the Ayatollahs', p. 38.
36. Matthews, Owen (with Anna Nemtsova in Moscow), 'Past as prologue: Moscow presents itself as the new "middleman" in the Middle East. But its role may actually be that of spoiler', *Newsweek International*, 27 February 2006. http://www.msnbc.msn.com/id/11436739/site/newsweek/
37. Cohen, Ariel, 'The Russia-Iran S-300 Air Defence Systems deal: beware of Russians bearing gifts', *The Heritage Foundation*, 20 March 2009. http://www.heritage.org/Research/RussiaandEurasia/wm2350.cfm, last accessed 7 May 2009.
38. *Haaretz.com*, 'US warns Russia against sales of advanced missiles to Iran', 22 December 2008. http://www.haaretz.com/hasen/spages/1048960.html, last accessed 26 January 2009.
39. Arkhipov, Ilya, 'Russia may sell S-300s to Iran if Syrian government falls', *Bloomberg*, 3 July 2012. http://www.businessweek.com/news/2012–07–03/russia-may-sell-s-300s-to-iran-if-syrian-government-falls, last accessed 23 February 2013.
40. Arkhipov, Ilya, 'Russia may sell S-300s to Iran if Syrian government falls', *Bloomberg*, 3 July 2012. http://www.businessweek.com/news/2012–07–03/russia-may-sell-s-300s-to-iran-if-syrian-government-falls, last accessed 23 February 2013.
41. Simonov, Pavel, 'The future of Russian-Iranian relations', *Axis Information and Analysis*, 13 July 2005. http://www.axisglobe.com/article.asp?article=232
42. *Axis Information and Analysis*, 8 December 2005. http://www.axisglobe.com/news.asp?news=5030
43. Mamedova, N., 'Russia and Iran have interests, not love', *Daily Star*, 29 January 2010, p. 6.
44. Bender, Corey, 'Why Russia won't budge on Iran', *US News*, 30 October 2012. http://www.usnews.com/opinion/blogs/world-report/2012/10/30/russia-united-states-divided-on-iran

45. Bukkvoll, Tor, 'Arming the Ayatollahs', p. 31.
46. Sanaie, Mehdi, 'Problems and prospects of Iranian-Russian relations', *Russia in Global Affairs*, 2, July to September 2007. http://eng.globalaffairs.ru/numbers/20/1137.html, last accessed 30 November 2007.
47. *Radio Free Europe/Radio Liberty Newsline*, 'Putin "plays foil to US" in Libya', 17 April 2008. http://www.rferl.org/content/article/1144094.html, last accessed 14 June 2009.
48. Aras, Bulent, 'Turkish-Russia relations: implications for Eurasia's geopolitics', *Power and Interest News Report*, 9 February 2005. http://pinr.com/report.php?ac=view_report&report_id=265&language_id=1, last accessed 30 July 2007.
49. Kiniklioglu, Suat, 'The aNATOmy of Turkish-Russian relations', *The Brookings Institute*, 23 May 2006, p. 2. http://www.brookings.edu/comm/events/20060523 sabanci_3a.pdf, last accessed 25 June 2007.
50. Martin, Lionel, 'Putin in Turkey: the unending quest for multipolarity', *Eurasia Daily Monitor*, 1, 146, 13 December 2004. http://www.jamestown.org/programs/edm/single/?tx_ttnews%5Btt_news%5D=27287&tx_ttnews%5BbackPid%5D=175&no_cache=1, last accessed 5 January 2008.
51. Freedman, Robert O., 'Russian policy toward the Middle East under Putin: the impact of 9/11 and the war in Iraq', *Alternatives* (Turkish Journal of International Relations), 2, 2, Summer 2003. http://www.alternativesjournal.net/volume2/number2/putin.htm, last accessed 9 January 2008.
52. Cagaptay Soner, and Nazli Gencsoy, 'Improving Turkish-Russian relations: Turkey's new foreign policy and its implications for the United States', *The Washington Institute for Near East Policy*, Policy Watch No. 942, 12 January 2005. http://www.ciaonet.org/pbei/winep/policy_2005/2005_942/index.html, last accessed 8 December 2008.
53. Akturk, Sener, 'Turkish-Russian relations after the Cold War', *Turkish Studies*, 7, 3, September 2006, p. 344.
54. Singh, K. Gajendra, 'Putin's visit to Ankara: Russian-Turkish relations in perspective', *South Asia Analysis Group*, No. 1101, 27 August 2004. http://www.saag.org/common/uploaded_files/paper1101.html, last accessed 30 July 2007.
55. Arsu, Sebnem and Brian Knowlton, 'Turks warn US on resolution on Armenian genocide', *International Herald Tribune*, 30 March 2007. http://www.iht.com/articles/2007/03/30/news/turkey.php, last accessed 10 February 2009.
56. Maksimenko, Vladimir I., Chapter 10, 'Russia's assets and liabilities in southwest Asia', in Chufrin, Gennady, (ed.), *Russia and Asia: the Emerging Security Agenda*, New York: Oxford University Press, 1999, p. 160.
57. Freedman, Robert O., 'Russian policy toward the Middle East under Putin'.
58. Zubarevich, Natalia V. and Yuri E. Fedorov, 'Russian-southern tier economic interaction', in Menon, Rajan, Yuri E. Fedorov and Ghia Nodia (eds), *Russia, the Caucasus and Central Asia*, New York: East West Institute, 1999, p. 120.

59. Cagaptay, Soner and Nazli Gencsoy, 'Improving Turkish-Russian relations'.
60. Kiniklioglu, Suat, 'The aNATOmy of Turkish-Russian relations', p. 6.
61. *The Economist*, 'Russia and Turkey: cool pragmatism', 8 December 2012. http://www.economist.com/news/europe/21567974-they-may-disagree-about-syria-russia-and-turkey-keep-close-business-relations-cool-pragmatism, last accessed 22 February 2013.
62. Tekin, M. Ali and Iva Walterova, 'Turkey's geopolitical role: the energy angle', *Middle East Policy*, 14, 1, Spring 2007, p. 85.
63. Warhola, James W. and William A., Mitchell, 'Warming of Russian-Turkish relations', *Demokratizatsia*, Winter 2006. http://findarticles.com/p/articles/mi_qa3996/is_200601/ai_n16537297, last accessed 3 December 2008.
64. Tekin, M Ali and Iva Walterova, 'Turkey's geopolitical role', p. 89.
65. Kiniklioglu, Suat, 'The aNATOmy of Turkish-Russian relations', p. 6.
66. Warhola, James W., and William A., Mitchell, 'Warming of Russian-Turkish relations'.
67. Maksimenko, Vladimir I., Chapter 10, 'Russia's assets and liabilities in South-West Asia', p. 163.
68. Akturk, Sener, 'Turkish-Russian relations after the Cold War', p. 345.
69. Zagorski, Andrei V., 'Traditional Russian security interests in the Caucasus and Central Asia; perceptions and realities', in Menon, Rajan, Yuri E. Fedorov and Ghia Nodia (eds), *Russia, the Caucasus and Central Asia*, New York: East West Institute, 1999, p. 66.
70. Khripunov, Igor, 'Russia's weapon's trade: domestic competition and foreign markets', p. 44.
71. Torbakov, Igor, 'In search of trilateral power, Putin goes East', *Eurasia Daily Monitor*, 1, 141, 6 December 2004. http://www.jamestown.org/programs/edm/single/?tx_ttnews%5Btt_news%5D=27251&tx_ttnews%5BbackPid%5D=175&no_cache=1, last accessed 5 January 2008.
72. Korepin, Serge, 'Turkey and Russia: a new friendship', *Center for Strategic and International Studies*, 18 August 2011. http://csis.org/blog/turkey-and-russia-new-friendship, last accessed 10 November 2011.
73. Rumer, Eugene, *Dangerous Drift*, p. 8.
74. Allison, Roy, Chapter 1, 'The military and political security landscape in Russia and the South', in Menon, Rajan, Yuri E. Fedorov and Ghia Nodia (eds), *Russia, the Caucasus and Central Asia*, New York: East West Institute, 1999, p. 35.
75. Zagorski, Andrei V., 'Traditional Russian security interests in the Caucasus and Central Asia', p. 63.
76. Blank, Stephen, 'The future of Caspian security', *Problems of Post-Communism*, 50, 1, January/February 2003, p. 10.
77. Billington, James H., *Russia in Search of Itself*, Washington DC: Woodrow Wilson Center Press, 2004, p. 69.

78. Akerman, Ella and Graeme P. Herd, Chapter 15, 'Russian foreign policy: the CIS and the Baltic States', in Ross, Cameron (ed.), *Russian Politics under Putin*, Manchester: Manchester University Press, 2004, p. 280.
79. Akerman, Ella and Graeme P. Herd, 'Russian Foreign Policy', p. 283.
80. Zagorski, Andrei V., 'Traditional Russian security interests in the Caucasus and Central Asia', p. 62.
81. Rumer, Eugene, *Dangerous Drift*, p. 6.
82. Rumer, Eugene, *Dangerous Drift*, p. 58.
83. Spruyt, Hendrik and Laurent Ruseckas, 'Economics and energy in the South', in Menon, Rajan, Yuri E. Fedorov and Ghia Nodia (eds), *Russia, the Caucasus and Central Asia*, New York: East West Institute, 1999, p. 105.
84. Spruyt, Hendrik and Laurent Ruseckas, 'Economics and energy in the South', p. 105.
85. Haghayeghi, Mehrdad, 'The coming of conflict to the Caspian Sea', *Problems of Post-Communism*, 50, 3, May/June 2003, p. 34.
86. Lee, Yusin, 'Toward a new international regime for the Caspian Sea', *Problems of Post-Communism*, 52, 3, May/June 2005, p. 42.
87. Haghayeghi, Mehrdad, 'The coming of conflict to the Caspian Sea', p. 32.
88. Freedman, Robert O., 'Putin, Iran, and the nuclear weapons issue', p. 42.
89. Haghayeghi, Mehrdad, 'The coming of conflict to the Caspian Sea', p. 34.
90. Haghayeghi, Mehrdad, 'The coming of conflict to the Caspian Sea', p. 39.
91. Spruyt, Hendrik and Laurent Ruseckas, 'Economics and energy in the South', p. 104.
92. Podberezsky, Igor V., Chapter 3, 'Between Europe and Asia: the search for Russia's civilisational Identity', in Chufrin, Gennady (ed.), *Russia and Asia: the Emerging Security Agenda*, New York: Oxford University Press, 1999, p. 1.
93. Allison, Roy, 'The military and political security landscape in Russia and the south', p. 55.
94. Haghayeghi, Mehrdad, 'The coming of conflict to the Caspian Sea', p. 36.

11. CONCLUSION: REVOLUTIONS, TYRANTS AND PUTIN

1. Osborn, Andrew, 'Russia becomes largest arms seller to Third World', *The Independent*, 31 October 2006. http://news.independent.co.uk/europe/article1943298.ece, last accessed 1 April 2009.
2. *Reuters*, 'Witnesses report rioting in Tunisian town', 19 December 2010. http://af.reuters.com/article/topNews/idAFJOE6BI06U20101219, last accessed 31 March 2012.
3. Tisdall, Simon, 'The lure of Putinism', *The Guardian*, 19 February 2009. http://www.guardian.co.uk, last accessed 20 February 2009.
4. Latest UN figures in March 2013.

5. *RTR 24*, Russian TV News, 5 April 2012.
6. Smith, Lee, 'Obama's about face on Syria', *Now Lebanon*, 28 March 2012. http://www.nowlebanon.com//NewsArticleDetails.aspx?ID=381021#ixzz1rHJHYyCu, last accessed 4 Apr. 2012.
7. Tisdall, Simon, 'The lure of Putinism', *The Guardian*.

BIBLIOGRAPHY

Aron, Leon and Jensen, Kenneth M. (eds), *The Emergence of Russian Foreign Policy*, Washington DC: United States Institute of Peace Press,1995.

Baranovsky, Vladimir (ed.), *Russia and Europe: The Emerging Security Agenda*, Oxford: Oxford University Press, 1997.

Beliaev Igor, and Marks, John, *Common Ground on Terrorism*, London: Norton, 1991.

Billington, James, *Russia in Search of Itself*, Washington DC: Woodrow Wilson Center Press, 2004.

Bowker, Mike, *Russia and the Islamic World*, Aldershot: Ashgate, 2007.

Breslauer, George (ed.), *Soviet Strategy in the Middle East*, Boston, Ma.: Unwin and Hyman, 1990.

Carter, Hannah, and Ehteshami, Anoushiravan (eds), *The Middle East's Relations with Asia and Russia*, London and New York: Routledge Curzon, 2004.

Chufrin, Gennady (ed.), *Russia and Asia: The Emerging Security Agenda*, New York: Oxford University Press, 1999.

Cobban, Helena, *The Superpowers and the Syrian-Israeli Conflict*, New York: Praeger, 1991.

Colton, Timothy J. and McFaul, Michael, *Popular Choice and Managed Democracy: The Russian Elections of 1999 and 2000*, Washington DC: Brookings Institute Press, 2003.

Dagan, Avigdor, *Moscow and Jerusalem*, London: Abelard-Schuman, 1970.

Farid, Abdel Magid, *Nasser: The Final Years*, Reading: Ithaca Press, 1994.

Golan, Galia, *Soviet Policies in the Middle East from WWII to Gorbachev*, Cambridge: Cambridge University Press, 1990.

Goldberg, David H., and Marantz, Paul (eds), *The Decline of the Soviet Union and the Transformation of the Middle East*, San Francisco and Oxford: Westview Press, 1994.

Goldgeier, James M., *Power and Purpose: US Policy Toward Russia After the Cold War*, Washington DC: Brookings Institute Press, 2003.

Gorodetsky, Gabriel (ed.), *Soviet Foreign Policy 1917–1991: A Retrospective*, London: Frank Cass, 1994.

Gow, James (ed.), *Iraq, the Gulf Conflict and the World Community*, London: Brassey's (UK), 1993.

Hahn, Gordon M., *Russia's Islamic Threat*, New Haven and London: Yale University Press, 2007.

Hamzeh, Ahmad Nizar, *In the Path of Hezbollah*, New York: Syracuse University Press, 2004.

Heller, Mark A., *The Dynamics of Soviet Policy in the Middle East: Between Old Thinking and New*, Tel Aviv; Tel Aviv University, 1991.

Hollis, Rosemary (ed), *The Soviets, their Successors and the Middle East*, London: Macmillan, 1993.

Ivanov, Igor, *New Russian Diplomacy: Ten Years of Moscow's Foreign Policy*, Washington DC: Brookings Institution Press, 2002.

Karny, Yo'av, *Highlanders: A Journey to the Caucasus in Quest of Memory*, New York: Farrar, Strauss and Giroux, 2000.

Keylor, William R., *The Twentieth Century World: An International History*, New York: Oxford University Press, 1992.

Kolstø, Pål and Blackkisrod, Helge (eds), *Nation-building and Common Values in Russia*, Lanham, Boulder, Oxford: Rowan and Littlefield Publishers Inc., 2004.

Kreutz, Andrej, *Russia in the Middle East: Friend or Foe*, Westport, Connecticut, London: Praeger Security International, 2007.

Lawson, Patrick (ed.), *Iran's Strategic Intentions and Capabilities*, Washington DC: NDU Press, 1994.

Light, Margot (ed.), *Troubled Friendships; Moscow's Third World Ventures*, London: British Academic Press and Royal Institute of International Affairs, 1993.

Lo, Bobo, *Russian Foreign Policy in the Post-Soviet Era: Reality, Illusion and Mythmaking*, Gordonsville VA: Palgrave Macmillan, 2002.

Menon, Rajan, Fedorov Yuri E. and Nodia, Ghia (eds), *Russia, the Caucasus and Central Asia*, New York: East West Institute, 1999.

Mooney, Peter, *The Soviet Superpower: the Soviet Union 1945–1980*, London: Heinemann Educational, 1982.

Moser, Robert G., *Unexpected Outcomes: Electoral Systems, Political Parties and Representation in Russia*, Pittsburg: University of Pittsburg Press, 2001.

Petro, Nicolai and Rubinstein, Alvin Z., *Russian Foreign Policy: From Empire to Nation State*, New York: Longman, 1997.

Pravda, Alex, Light, Margot, Malcolm, Neil and Allison, Roy (eds), *Internal Factors in Russian Foreign Policy*, Oxford: Oxford University Press, 1996.

Reddaway, Peter and Glinski, Dmitri, *The Tragedy of Russia's Reforms: Market*

Bolshevism Against Democracy, Washington DC: United States Institute of Peace Press, 2001.
Ross, Cameron (ed.), *Russian Politics under Putin*, Manchester: Manchester University Press, 2004.
Rumer, Eugene, *Dangerous Drift: Russia's Middle East Policy*, Washington DC: Washington Institute for Near East Policy, Policy Paper 54, 2002.
Sestanovich, Stephen (ed.), *Rethinking Russia's National Interests*, Washington: Center for Strategic and International Studies, 1994.
Shearman, Peter, *Russian Foreign Policy Since 1990*, Oxford: Westview, 1995.
Shevtsova, Lilia, *Putin's Russia*, Washington DC: Carnegie Endowment for International Peace, 2003.
Shiraev, Eric and Zubok, Vladislav, *Anti-Americanism in Russia from Stalin to Putin*, New York: Palgrave, 2000.
Slezkine, Yuri, *The Jewish Century*, Princeton: Princeton University Press, 2004.
Tsygankov, Andrei P., *Russia's Foreign Policy: Change and Continuity in National Identity*, New York, Oxford: Rowan and Littlefield Publishers Inc, 2006.
Vassiliev, Alexei, *Russian Policy in the Middle East: From Messianism to Pragmatism*, Reading: Ithaca Press, 1993.
Yodfat, A., *The Soviet Union and the Arabian Peninsula*, London: Croom Helm, 1983.

Selected Periodicals and Journals

Al-Mustaqbal
Alternatives (Turkish Journal of International Relations)
Arab News
Asharq Alawsat
Christian Science Monitor
Communist and Post-Communist Studies
Demokratizatsia
Eurasia Daily Monitor
Europe-Asia Studies
Financial Times
Foreign Affairs
Foreign Policy in Focus
Global Affairs
International Affairs
International Herald Tribune
Izvestiia
Jewish Telegraphic Agency
Jordan Times
Komsomol'skaia pravda

Los Angeles Times
Mezhdunarodnyi Istoricheskii Zhournal (International Historical Journal)
Middle East Journal
Mideast Monitor
Middle East Policy
Middle East Quarterlyv
Middle East Review of International Affairs
Moscow News
New Arabia
Newsweek International
New York Times
Nezavisimaia gazeta
Political Science Quarterly
Problems of Post-Communism
Russia in Global Affairs
Soviet Foreign Policy
Soviet Studies
The Daily Star (Beirut)
The Guardian
The Independent
The Sunday Express
Time Magazine
Turkish Studies
Washington Post

Selected Articles

Akerman, Ella and P. Herd, Graeme P., 'Russian foreign policy: the CIS and the Baltic States', in Ross, Cameron (ed.), *Russian Politics under Putin*, Manchester: Manchester University Press, 2004.

Akturk, Sener, 'Turkish-Russian relations after the Cold War', *Turkish Studies*, 7, 3, September 2006.

Arbatov, Alexei, 'The vicissitudes of Russian politics', in Baranovsky, Vladimir (ed.), *Russia and Europe: the Emerging Security Agenda*, Oxford: Oxford University Press, 1997.

Arbatov, Alexei, 'Is a new Cold War imminent?', *Russia in Global Affairs*, 2, July–September 2007.

Berman, Ilan, 'Russia and the Mideast vacuum', *IASPS Papers in Strategy*, Washington DC: Institute for Advanced Strategic and Political Studies, 12, June 2001.

Blank, Stephen, 'The post-Soviet states and the post-Saddam Middle East', *Middle East Review of International Affairs*, 7, 2, June 2003.

BIBLIOGRAPHY

Blank, Stephen, 'The future of Caspian security', *Problems of Post-Communism*, 50, 1, January/February 2003.

Bourtman, Ilya, 'Putin and Russia's Middle Eastern policy', *Middle East Review of International Affairs*, 10, 2, June 2006.

Brown, Archie, 'Vladimir Putin's leadership in comparative perspective', in Ross, Cameron (ed.), *Russian Politics under Putin*, Manchester: Manchester University Press, 2004.

Bukkvoll, Tor, 'Arming the Ayatollahs: economic lobbies in Russia's Iran policy', *Problems of Post-Communism*, 49, 6, November/December 2002.

Byman, Daniel, 'Hezbollah's dilemma', *Foreign Affairs*, 13 April 2005.

Cagaptay, Soner and Gencsoy, Nazli, 'Improving Turkish-Russian relations: Turkey's new foreign policy and its implications for the United States', *The Washington Institute for Near East Policy*, Policy Watch No. 942, 12 January 2005.

Cohen, Ariel, 'Calling up the past', *Russia in Global Affairs*, 1 December 2003.

Daniels, Robert V. 'Evgenii Primakov: contender by chance', *Problems of Post-Communism*, 46, 5, September/October 1999.

Dannreuther, Roland, 'Russia and the Middle East', in Carter, Hannah and Anoushiravan Ehteshami (eds), *The Middle East's Relations with Asia and Russia*, London and New York: Routledge Curzon, 2004.

Doran, Michael Scott, 'The Saudi paradox', *Foreign Affairs*, 83, 1, January/February 2004.

Dunlop, John B., 'Russia: confronting a loss of empire 1987–1991', *Political Science Quarterly*, Winter 1993–4.

Epstein, Alek D., 'Russia and Israel: a romance aborted?', *Russia in Global Affairs*, 4, October–December 2007.

Evans Jr., Alfred B., 'Putin's legacy and Russia's identity', *Europe-Asia Studies*, 60, 6, August 2008.

Freedman, Robert O., 'Russian policy toward the Middle East under Yeltsin and Putin', *Jerusalem Viewpoints*, 461, 2 September 2001.

Freedman, Robert O., 'Russian policy toward the Middle East under Putin: the impact of 9/11 and the war in Iraq', *Alternatives* (Turkish Journal of International Relations), 2, 2, Summer 2003.

Freedman, Robert O., 'Putin, Iran, and the nuclear weapons issue', *Problems of Post-Communism*, 53, 2, March/April 2006.

Ghadry, Farid N., 'Syrian reform: what lies beneath', *Middle East Quarterly*, 12, 1, Winter 2005.

Golan, Galia 'The Soviet Union and the Israeli action in Lebanon', *International Affairs* (Royal Institute of International Affairs), 59, 1, Winter 1982–1983.

Haghayeghi, Mehrdad, 'The coming of conflict to the Caspian Sea', *Problems of Post-Communism*, 50, 3, May/June 2003.

Hashim, Ahmad, 'Saddam Husayn and civil-military relations in Iraq: the quest for legitimacy and power', *Middle East Journal*, 57, 1, Winter 2003.

Katz, Mark N., 'Saudi-Russian relations since 9/11', *Problems of Post-Communism*, 51, 2, November/December 2002.

Katz, Mark N., 'Putin's pro-Israel policy', *Middle East Quarterly*, Winter 2005.

Katz, Mark N., 'Putin, Ahmadinejad and the Iranian nuclear crisis', *Middle East Policy*, 13, 4, Winter 2006.

Katz, Mark N., 'Putin's foreign policy towards Syria', *The Middle East Review of International Affairs*, 10, 1, March 2006.

Karsh, Efraim, 'Soviet-Syrian relations: the troubled partnership', in Light, Margot (ed.), *Troubled Friendships; Moscow's Third World Ventures*, London: British Academic Press and Royal Institute of International Affairs, 1993.

Kuvaldin, Viktor (Gorbachev policy adviser 1989–91), 'From Cold War to new World Order' in Gabriel Gorodetsky (ed.), *Soviet Foreign Policy 1917–1991: a Retrospective*, London: Frank Cass, 1994.

Kramer, Mark, 'The role of the CPSU International Department in Soviet foreign relations and national security policy', *Soviet Studies*, 42, 3, July 1990.

Khasanova, Gulnara, 'Nation-building and values in Russian textbooks', in Kolstø, Pål and Helge Blackkisrod (eds), *Nation-building and Common Values in Russia*, Lanham, Boulder, Oxford: Rowan and Littlefield Publishers Inc., 2004.

Khripunov, Igor, 'Russia's weapon's trade: domestic competition and foreign markets', *Problems of Post-Communism*, 46, 2, March/April 1999.

Lee, Yusin, 'Toward a new international regime for the Caspian Sea', *Problems of Post-Communism*, 52, 3, May/June 2005.

Legvold, Robert, 'Russia's unformed foreign policy', *Foreign Affairs*, 80, 5, September/October 2001.

Lynch, Dov, '"The enemy is at the gate": Russia after Beslan', *International Affairs*, 85, 1, 2005.

Malashenko, Alexey, 'Into the labyrinth of Russia's intensifying Islamism', *The Daily Star* (Beirut), 21 April 2006.

Malcolm, Neil, 'Russian foreign policy decision-making' in Shearman, Peter: *Russian Foreign Policy Since 1990*, Oxford: Westview, 1995.

Mattair, Thomas R., 'Mutual threat perceptions in the Arab/Persian Gulf: GCC perceptions', *Middle East Policy*, 14, 2, Summer 2007.

Mendelson, Sarah E., 'The Putin path', *Problems of Post-Communism*, 47, 5, September/October 2000.

Mirsky, Georgy, 'The Baghdad puzzle', *Russia in Global Affairs*, 2, July–September 2007.

Mizin, Victor, 'The Russia-Iran nuclear connection and US policy options', *Middle East Review of International Affairs*, 8, 1, March 2004.

Moshes, Arkady, 'Reaffirming the benefits of Russia's European choice', *Russia in Global Affairs*, 3, July–September 2005.

Nasr, Vali, 'When the Shiites rise', *Foreign Affairs*, 85, 4, July/August 2006.

Payne, Laura, 'U.S.-Russia security relations', *Foreign Policy in Focus*, 3. 26, September 1998.

Podberezsky, Igor, 'Between Europe and Asia: the search for Russia's civilizational identity', in Chufrin, Gennady (ed.), *Russia and Asia: The Emerging Security Agenda*, New York, Oxford University Press, 1999.

Qimao, Chen, 'Sino-Russian relations after the break-up of the Soviet Union,' in Chufrin, Gennady (ed.), *Russia and Asia: The Emerging Security Agenda*, New York, Oxford University Press, 1999.

Rahr, Alexander, 'Why Schroder loves Russia', *Russia in Global Affairs*, 4, October–December 2004.

Sadr, Ihsaneh I., 'The impact of Iran's nuclearisation on Israel', *Middle East Policy*, 12, 2, Summer 2005.

Saivetz, Carol R., 'Gorbachev's Middle East policy: the Arab dimension', in Goldberg, David H. and Paul Marantz (eds), *The Decline of the Soviet Union and the Transformation of the Middle East*, San Francisco and Oxford: Westview Press, 1994.

Sakwa, Richard, 'Putin's leadership: character and consequences', *Europe-Asia Studies*, 60, 6, August 2008.

Sanaie, Mehdi, 'Problems and prospects of Iranian-Russian relations', *Russia in Global Affairs*, 2, July–September 2007.

Sánchez-Andrés, Antonio, 'Arms exports and restructuring in the Russian defense industry', *Europe-Asia Studies*, 56, 5, July 2004.

Satanovsky, Evgenii, 'A new Middle East', *Russia in Global Affairs*, 3, July–September 2005.

Shanahan, Rodger, 'Hezbollah's dilemmas', *Mideast Monitor*, 1, 1, February 2006.

Schenker, David, 'Syria: between negotiations with Israel and the Iranian Axis', *Jerusalem Center for Public Policy*, 8, 2, 27 May 2008.

Shumilin, A., 'The US vs. rogue states of the Middle East', *International Affairs: A Russian Journal*, 5, 2003.

Simon, Steven and Stevenson, Jonathan, 'The road to Damascus', *Foreign Affairs*, 83, 3, May/Jun 2004.

Spruyt, Hendrik and Ruseckas, Laurent, 'Economics and energy in the South', in Menon, Rajan, Fedorov, Yuri E. and Ghia Nodia (eds) *Russia, the Caucasus and Central Asia*, New York: East West Institute, 1999.

Staalesen, Atle, 'Orthodoxy and Islam in post-Soviet Russia: opposing confessional cultures or unifying force?', in Kolstø, Pål and Blackkisrod, Helge (eds), *Nation-building and Common Values in Russia*, Lanham, Boulder, Oxford: Rowan and Littlefield Publishers Inc., 2004.

Talbott, Strobe, Lyne, Roderic and Watanabe, Koji, 'A trilateral view of a changing relationship with Russia', *Russia in Global Affairs*, 4, October–December 2006.

Tekin, M Ali, and Walterova, Iva, 'Turkey's geopolitical role: the energy angle', *Middle East Policy*, 14, 1, Spring 2007, p. 85.

Trenin, Dmitri 'Russia leaves the West', *Foreign Affairs*, 85, 4, July/August 2006.

Tsygankov, Andrei P., 'Russia's international assertiveness: what does it mean?', *Problems of Post-Communism*, 55, 2, March/April 2008.

Ulunian, R.A., 'Soviet Cold War perceptions of Turkey and Greece', *Mezhdunarodnyi Istoricheskii Zhournal* (International Historical Journal), 20, 2002.

Warhola, James W and Mitchell, William A., 'Warming of Russian-Turkish relations', *Demokratizatsia*, Winter 2006.

Yavlinsky, Grigory, and Kogan-Yasny, Viktor 'Passive isolationism endangers Russia but also the West', *Daily Star* (Beirut), 4 July 2007.

Yevtushenkov, Vladimir, 'After the lull: Russia and the Arab world at a new stage', *Russia in Global Affairs*, 3, July–September 2005.

Zagorski, Andrei V., 'Traditional Russian security interests in the Caucasus and Central Asia; perceptions and realities', in Rajan, Menon, Yuri E. Fedorov and Ghia Nodia (eds), *Russia, the Caucasus and Central Asia*, New York East West Institute: New York, 1999.

Frequently visited websites

CWIHP.org, Cold War International History Project

http://www.rferl.org, *Radio Free Europe/Radio Liberty Newsline*

http://www.osce.org/documents/, OSCE

http://www.30giorni.it, *30 Days*, Catholic Church monthly

http://www.naharnet.com, *Naharnet*

http://news.bbc.co.uk, *BBC Online*

http://en.rian.ru, *RIA Novosti*

http://www.un.org, United Nations

http://www.whitehouse.gov, *The White House*

http://web.israelinsider.com, *Israel Insider*

http://www.kommersant.com, Kommersant Online

http://www.usip.org, The United States Institute of Peace

http://www.metimes.com, *Middle East Times*

http://www.zawya.com, *Zawya Online*

http://www.russiajournal.com, *The Russia Journal*

http://yale.edu

CNN.com

Indiainfo.com

Ha'aretz.com
Pravda.ru
Reuters UK
Tehrantimes.com

INDEX